Charles O. Ermatinger

Canadian Franchise and Election Laws

A Manual for the use of revising officers, municipal officers, candidates, agents and electors

Charles O. Ermatinger

Canadian Franchise and Election Laws
A Manual for the use of revising officers, municipal officers, candidates, agents and electors

ISBN/EAN: 9783337189525

Printed in Europe, USA, Canada, Australia, Japan

Cover: Foto ©Suzi / pixelio.de

More available books at **www.hansebooks.com**

CANADIAN

FRANCHISE

—AND—

ELECTION LAWS.

A MANUAL FOR THE USE OF REVISING OFFICERS, MUNICIPAL OFFICERS, CANDIDATES, AGENTS, AND ELECTORS.

C. O. ERMATINGER,

ONE OF HER MAJESTY'S COUNSEL, AND MEMBER FOR EAST ELGIN IN THE LEGISLATURE OF ONTARIO.

TORONTO:

CARSWELL & CO., PUBLISHERS.

1886.

THE thanks of the author of this work are due to W. R. Meredith, Q.C., M.P.P., Dalton McCarthy, Q.C., M.P., Hon. L. O. Taillon, Attorney-General of Quebec, Mr. J. B. Abbott of Montreal, Mr. A. R. Creelman of Toronto, and to Judges Hughes, Sinclair, and Macdougall, for valuable hints and assistance received from them in the course of preparation of the work; also to the Attornies-General of the other provinces, for copies of their respective franchise and election acts.

CONTENTS.

LIST OF AUTHORITIES CITED.

INTRODUCTION.

Object of work.

In compiling the present work the author has had chiefly in view the preparation of a book which may prove to be of use to Revising and Municipal officers, Candidates and their agents, and those members of the legal profession who may feel the want of a manual of the laws relating to the franchise and election of members to the popular legislative chambers of the Dominion of Canada and its Provinces, rather than the compilation of an exhaustive treatise upon the subjects dealt with.

Dominion Franchise.

By the British North America Act (section 44) the Imperial Parliament enacted that, until the Parliament of Canada should otherwise provide, all laws in force in the several Provinces at the Union relative to the Qualification and Disqualification of members of the Legislative Assembly in the several Provinces, the voters at elections of such members, the proceedings at elections, and the trial of Controverted Elections were, with other laws incidental thereto, to apply to Elections of members to serve in the House of Commons of Canada for the same several Provinces—with a proviso, conferring the franchise upon every male subject of the age of twenty-one, who was a householder in the District of Algoma. Under this enactment and also under section 40 of The Dominion Elections Act, 1874, the several Provincial franchise laws have continued to apply to voters for elections of members of the House of Commons up to the present time. In 1870, in 1882, in 1883, and again in 1884, bills were submitted to Parliament to provide for a uniform franchise for the Dominion, but none passed into law until the session of 1885, when the Act embraced in this volume was passed.

Uniformity of Franchise.

Uniformity of franchise throughout the Dominion, which was one of the chief features and objects of the bill, was somewhat departed from in the cases of Prince Edward Island and British Columbia. It was urged that, inasmuch as manhood suffrage prevailed in the latter Province and a somewhat similar law in the former, a considerable number of persons would, in those Provinces, be disfranchised, should the bill as first introduced become law. Amendments were therefore adopted by which the right to vote at Dominion elections was continued to all those, in the two Provinces named, who possessed such right at the date of the passage of the Act (20th July, 1885). Thus vested rights of franchise in those provinces have been respected, while at the same time gradual assimilation of the law into a state of uniformity throughout the Dominion is provided for. The note (*wb*) to section 9 of the Act (p. 40 *post*) must be read in the light of this statement of the effect of that section, while the closing sentence of note (*f*) to section 2 (p. 9), should be passed over as being possibly misleading. In connection with the subject of the Prince Edward Island franchise, attention is drawn to the provision of the provincial law requiring a residence for 12 months prior to the date of the Writ of Election. If this restriction holds good in regard to Dominion elections and the registration of voters therefor, it is obvious that those for whose benefit the amendment above referred to was adopted may still be disfranchised, unless the revising officers, whose lists will not be revised contemporaneously with the date of the Writs of Election, accept residence up to the date of registration as sufficient evidence or guarantee of a continued residence

P. E. Island and Brit. Columbia.

Existing rights of franchise continued.

Gradual assimilation in those Provinces.

Errata.

Resid'nce under P. E. I. Act.

up to the date of the writs. Residence up to the date of the last provincial writs cannot well be accepted, as subsequent to that date the residence may have been broken, in which case the voter would no longer "continue to be qualified" under the existing provincial law, and thus would not be qualified, by virtue of the provincial law, to be registered and to vote under section 9 of the Dominion Act. The qualifying year under the Dominion Act is the year next before the 1st of January preceding the making up of the lists. Any person entitled to vote under the Dominion Act, who has not the provincial qualification, or who acquires the provincial qualification subsequent to 20th July, 1885, will nevertheless be entitled to be registered under the Dominion law if he can qualify under that law, in both Prince Edward Island and British Columbia. For instance, non-resident owners will be entitled to be registered and to vote under the Dominion Act, in the latter province, though not qualified under the Provincial law; while persons possessing the Provincial qualification who come of age after 20th July, 1885, cannot qualify under the Provincial laws, but if they possess the Dominion qualification they can be registered and vote under the Dominion Act in either Province.

Persons qualified by Dom. Act but not by Prov. Act.

The enfranchisement of the Indians in the older Provinces is another prominent feature of the Dominion Act. The laws relating to the Indians are dealt with in notes to those sections of the Act referring to the subject (see pages 15 and 44). Indians in Manitoba, British Columbia, Keewatin and the North-West Territories, and any Indian or any reserve elsewhere in Canada who is not in possession and occupation of a separate and distinct tract of land in such reserve and whose improvements on such separate tract are not of the value of at least one hundred and fifty dollars, and who is not otherwise possessed of the qualifications entitling him to be

Indian Franchise.

registered on the list of voters under the Act, are excluded from the franchise.

Fishermen's Franchise.

A special Fisherman's franchise is also created in favour of fishermen owning real property and fishing appliances worth $150 altogether.

Government officials.

The right of voting at Dominion Elections is also intended to be conferred upon all those government officials hitherto by law disqualified, with the exception of the Judges and Election officers.

No lodger franchise *eo nomine*.

No lodger franchise has been in terms created in this country, as it has been in England. If the English decisions be followed here, a lodger cannot qualify as a tenant, (*a*). Whether he may qualify as "an occupant" of real property—which by section 2 of the Dominion Act (p. 21, *post*) includes any portion of the house, etc.—remains to be decided here, as the "inhabitant occupier," who is in England distinguished from a lodger, is one who holds "as owner or tenant" (*b*), while an occupant, under our Act, is one who holds "otherwise than as owner, tenant or usufructuary." If a lodger may qualify as an occupant, he will still require the qualification in value, which is in cities $300, in towns $200, and in counties $150 (*c*). By the Ontario Fran. and Rep. Act, 1885, lodgers are expressly excluded from the household suffrage.

The following are entitled to be registered under the Dominion Act, if of age, British subjects, and not disqualified:

In Cities and Towns.

Dominion qualifications.

Owners of real property of the actual value in cities $300, towns $200.

(*a*) *Bradley* v. *Baylis*, L. R. 8, Q. B. D. 218; see *post*, p. 93.

(*b*) See Rep. People Act, 1867, s. 3.

(*c*) See *post* pp. 29 and 34; Ontario Act, cities and towns $200; in villages and townships $100, *post*, p. 100; Quebec Act, cities $300, other municipalities $200, or $20 annual value, *post*, p. 172.

Tenants of real property at $2 per month, $6 per quarter, $12 per half year, or $20 per year, or where amount of rent is not stated in assessment roll an assessed value in cities $300, in towns $200.

Occupants of real property of the actual value of, in cities $300, in towns $200.

Residents of cities or towns deriving $300 income from some trade, office, calling, etc., or from some investment in Canada.

Sons of owners resident with the father upon the property for the qualifying year, if the real property is of sufficient value to give both father and sons votes. If insufficient to give all votes, then the father and sons in the order of seniority may be registered. If father be dead, all sons resident with the mother (being owner) if the property be of sufficient value to give all votes. If insufficient to give all votes, then the sons in order of seniority may be registered. "Father," includes grandfather, stepfather and father-in-law, "mother," includes stepmother and mother-in-law; and "son," includes a grandson, stepson and son-in-law, not otherwise qualified. Occasional absence for not more than six months, in all, does not disqualify the son.

In Counties.

Owners of real property of the actual value of $150.

Tenants of real property at $2 per month, $6 per quarter, $12 per half year, or $20 per year in money or kind (except when the real property is situated in an incorporated village, in which case the rental must be payable in money only), or where amount of rent is not stated in assessment roll, an assessed value of $150.

Occupants of real property of the actual value of $150.

Residents of counties deriving $300 income from some trade, office, calling, etc., or from some investment in Canada.

Farmer's sons resident with the father upon the farm (not less than 20 acres) during the qualifying year, if the father is the owner of the farm, and it is of sufficient value to give both father and sons a vote. If insufficient to give votes to all, then the father and sons in order of seniority may be registered. If the father be dead then all sons resident on the farm of the mother with her, if it be sufficient in value to qualify all. If insufficient in value, then the right to be registered belongs to the sons in the order of the seniority—"father" "mother" and "son," having the same meaning as given above, as to cities and towns, and the same proviso as to occasional absence governing.

Sons, grandsons, stepsons, and sons-in-law, of owners of real property other than farms, on like conditions as in cities and towns, except as to the qualifying values.

Fishermen owning real property, and boats, nets, fishing gear and tackle, of the actual value altogether of $150.

The time spent by sons in prosecution of their occupations as mariners or fishermen, or at institutions of learning, creates no disqualification in any case.

Ontario Provincial qualificat'ns

The following (being of full age, of male sex and British subjects) are entitled to vote under the Ontario Provincial Law, residence within the electoral district being in all cases essential:

Owners, tenants and occupants of real property of the the actual value of, in cities and towns $200, in incorporated villages and townships $100.

Residents who derive an annual income from some trade, occupation, calling, office or profession of $250 and are assessed therefor.

Wage-earners or persons deriving, during the qualifying year, wages or income of $250, in which in townships the fair value of any board and lodging received in lieu of wages may be included.

Householders, not including lodgers or boarders.

Sons, stepsons, grandsons or sons-in-law of, and resident with, a "land-holder" *i.e.*, an owner of and resident upon real property of at least 20 acres in extent, or $400 actual value in cities and towns, or $200 actual value in townships; or a resident tenant of a dwelling house, where such dwelling house and the land, if any, held therewith, is of at least an actual value of $400 in cities and towns and $200 in townships and incorporated villages—with a similar proviso as to occasional absence to that contained in the Dominion Act as above.

Indians "enfranchised" under the Indian Act, and Indians and persons with part Indian blood, who do not reside among Indians, though participating in the annuities of their band. Where there are no voters' lists, those unenfranchised Indians receiving annuity moneys are however disqualified, though living apart. In all cases the Indian's qualification must be same as that of a white person.

Resident owners of real estate which has been granted or patented by the Crown, of the value of $200 and householders resident six months next preceding the election, are entitled to vote in the unorganized districts.

The following are qualified under the Quebec Provincial Law, providing they be of the male sex, of full age, and British subjects: Quebec Provincial qualificat'ns

Owners or occupants of real estate, in a city entitled to return one or more members, valued by the revised valuation roll at $300 in real value. In any other municipality $200 in real value, or $20 annual value.

Tenants paying an annual rent of $30 on real estate, estimated according to such valuation roll in real value at least $300 in such a city; and tenants paying an annual rent of $20 on real estate, estimated according to such valuation roll in real value at least $200, in any other municipality.

In New Brunswick the following persons, if they fulfil the usual requisites as to age, allegiance, sex and legal capacity, are qualified to vote at Provincial elections: New Brunswick Provincial qualifications.

Persons assessed for real estate to the amount of $100.

Persons assessed for personal property, or personal and real together, amounting to $400.

Persons assessed for $400 annual income.

The Nova Scotia Provincial qualifications.

The Nova Scotia Franchise Act of 1885, confers the Provincial Franchise upon the following persons if of age, subjects of Her Majesty, and not disqualified :

Every male person assessed for $150 real property, or $300 personal or real and personal together.

Every male person in possession of such property at the time of last assessment, and specially exempted from taxation.

Every male yearly tenant of real property of $150 value, where assessment levied upon the owner, or the assessed value of whose personal property combined with the real property so occupied amount together to $300.

The son of every person qualified as above, if property sufficient to qualify more than one voter, where such son resides with the father, or upon property owned by the father in the district during the qualifying year.

The son of every widow possessing such qualification, with like conditions as to residence with the mother or upon her property.

Every person possessing the above qualifications at the time of assessment, but whose name is omitted from the assessors' returns, is entitled to be registered.

Occasional and temporary absence of sons for not more than four months, and the time spent by fishermen or mariners, and students at their occupations, or at institutions of learning respectively, work no disqualification.

Manitoba Provincial qualifications.

In Manitoba the provincial qualification is vested in those persons who are British subjects, males, and of age, who are,

Owners of real estate valued at $100 at least.

Tenants of real property of the value of $200, under an annual rent of $20.

Occupants and householders on land of an annual value of $20, who must have been resident in the electoral district for three months. Indians receiving annuities are excluded.

In British Columbia, British subjects of full age resident in the Province for twelve months, and in the electoral district for two months preceding the election, vote at provincial elections. Chinamen and Indians are however excluded. British Columbia Provincial qualifications.

In Prince Edward Island the Provincial Franchise is conferred upon The P. E. Island Provincial qualifications.

Residents in the polling division for twelve months before the date of the writ, who have performed or paid for statute labour,

Residents in Charlottetown and Summerside who have paid provincial or civic poll tax for the qualifying year,

Owners or occupants of real estate of the clear annual value of 40 shillings, who have paid the taxes on such property for the qualifying year, of whom residence is not required, the holder of property being moreover at liberty to vote in every district where he possesses the property qualification.

British allegiance and full age are necessary to all the qualifications.

In the North-West Territories the *bona fide* male residents and householders of adult age, not being aliens, or unenfranchised Indians, within the electoral district, who have resided in the electoral district for at least 12 months immediately preceding the issue of the writ—constitute the voters at elections of members of the North-West Council. The N. W. Territories qualifications.

Chinamen are excluded from the Dominion as well as the British Columbia Provincial Franchise. To become voters in any of the other provinces, they must of course become naturalized subjects. Chinamen.

For further particulars as to the different franchise systems of the Dominion, and the qualifications and disqualifications thereunder, as well as the systems of registration prevailing, the reader is referred to the text of the various Acts as given in the following pages. The introductory reference here given is intended to serve merely as an outline of the several laws.

Change in Ontario laws.

Recent important changes in the Ontario Provincial Franchise Laws—involving in fact the adoption of a new franchise by the province altogether—the larger number interested as compared with other provinces, the approach of a general provincial election, and the impracticability of treating similarly, within a reasonable compass, the whole of the franchise laws of the Dominion—have made it necessary to devote a larger space and more attention in the following pages to the Ontario laws than to those of the other provinces.

The Election laws.

The chapters on the election laws, for similar reasons, have been prepared with special reference to the laws of the Province of Ontario, as well as those of the Dominion. The differences in the Ontario laws are pointed out throughout the various chapters.

Having in view the object already announced as the aim of the present work, the author has confined himself to a short treatise upon the laws affecting the election of members up to the close of the election, and a chapter upon the disqualifications as regards members. The controverted election laws do not come within the province of this work and are not dealt with.

Frequent changes in the law must always gradually impair the usefulness of a work such as the present Especially must this be the case where, as in this case, the different laws dealt with are subject to repeal and alteration by so many different legislative bodies. Though the laws as here given may be soon superseded by others, the work for the sake of reference and comparison will still, it is hoped, be of some value, while certain features and defects may be the more readily brought to the attention of those in whose hands lies the power to remedy them.

It may here be mentioned that new forms of voters' oaths must of necessity be provided before Dominion Elections are held under the new Dominion Franchise. Dominion voters' oaths.

The unsettled condition of the law as to the payment of expenses of canvassers and speakers in Dominion Elections is elsewhere pointed out. Canvassers and orators.

PART I.

THE FRANCHISE LAWS.

THE

DOMINION FRANCHISE.

AN ACT RESPECTING THE ELECTORAL FRANCHISE.

(48 Vic., cap. 40.)

[Assented to 20th July, 1885.]

HER Majesty, by and with the advice and consent of the Senate and House of Commons of Canada, enacts as follows:— Preamble.

1. This Act may be cited as "*The Electoral Franchise Act.*" Short title.

INTERPRETATION.

2. In this Act, unless it is otherwise expressly provided, or unless there is in the context something inconsistent with or repugnant to such construction, the following words and expressions have the meanings hereinafter assigned to them, respectively:— Interpretation.

"Owner" *(a)*, when it relates to the ownership of real Owner; in Quebec.

(a) "*Owner.*"—Ownership is the right of enjoying and disposing of things in the most absolute manner, provided that no use be made of them which is prohibited by law or by regulations (Civil Code of Lower Canada, 406), and the person enjoying this right is termed the "proprietor" *(le propriétaire)*. Usufruct is the right of enjoying things of which another has the ownership, as the proprietor himself, but subject to the obligation of preserving the substance thereof (Civil Code, 443), and the person enjoying this right is termed the "usufructuary" *(l'usufruitier)*. In construing the Act, both proprietor and usufructuary are to be deemed to come

property situated in the Province of Quebec, means "pro-

---

within the term "owner" or "*propriétaire*." Usufruct may be established by law or by the will of man *(Ib* , 444). It may be established purely or conditionally, and may commence at once or from a certain day *(Ib.*, 445). It ends by the natural or civil death of the usufructuary, if for life;—By the expiration of the time for which it was granted;—By the confusion or reunion in one person of the two qualities of usufructuary and of proprietor;—By non-user of the right during thirty years, and by prescription acquired by third persons;—and by the total loss of the thing on which the usufruct is established *(Ib.*, 479). Usufruct may also cease by reason of the abuse the usufructuary makes of the enjoyment, either by committing waste on the property or by allowing it to depreciate for want of care. The creditors of the usufructuary may intervene in contestations, for the preservation of their rights; they may offer to repair the injury done and give security for the future. The courts may, according to the gravity of the circumstances, either pronounce the absolute extinction of the usufruct, or only permit the entry of the proprietor into possession of the object charged with it, subject to the obligation of annually paying to the usufructuary or his representatives a fixed sum, until the time when the usufruct shall cease *(Ib.*, 480). It is to be presumed that in the latter case the usufructuary will no longer be deemed an "owner" within the meaning of the Act.

The question suggested in the House of Commons, as to whether a tenant by emphyteutic lease (*bail emphytéotique*), or the person who has the original right of property (*domaine direct*), or both, are covered by the definition of "owner," as given in this clause, was the subject of debate, and of some difference of opinion among lawyers of high standing at the bar of the Province of Quebec, during the passage of the measure through the House (*Hansard*, vol. 17, 1499-1509). Emphyteusis or emphyteutic lease is a contract by which the proprietor of an immoveable conveys it for a time to another, the lessee subjecting himself to make improvements, to pay the lessor an annual rent, and to such other charges as may be agreed upon (Civil Code, 567). The duration of the emphyteusis cannot exceed ninety-nine, and must be for more than nine years (*Ib.* 568). A salient feature of this contract is that it carries with it alienation; and so long as it lasts, the lessee enjoys all the rights attached to the quality of the proprietor (*Ib.* 569) and he may alienate, transfer and hypothecate the immoveable so leased (*Ib.* 570); and it may be seized and sold as real property under execution against the lessee (*Ib.* 571). The lessee may moreover bring a possessory action against all who may disturb his possession, and even against the lessor (*Ib.* 572). It is to be observed that these incidents are substantially the same as those which belong to the estate of an ordinary tenant for years, whatever the length of term, in the other provinces, under the English law, unless they be restricted by covenants contained in the lease; which estate will not entitle the tenant to be classed as an "owner" under the next clause of this Act. The emphyteutic contract, however, according to the French writers, operates a dismemberment of the property, and divides it into two parts, called the *domaine direct* and the *domaine utile*. The lessee acquires the latter, which consists in the right to enjoy the property leased *à titre de propriétaire*, as owner or proprietor, and to hypothecate or alienate it in any way, subject to the rights of creditors and purchasers at the expir-

prietor" or "usufructuary" *(usufruitier)* either in his own

ation of the lease; the lessor retaining the *domaine direct*, that is to say, the original right of property, subject to the right which he has transferred to the lessee. The annual rental which is paid is looked upon rather as being paid in recognition of this *domaine direct* (*in recognitionem directi dominii*) retained by the lessor in the property, than as actually representing the fruits and revenues thereof. It is a real charge due by the property and is immoveable, although the lessee may be the personal debtor in respect of it. The French authors agree as to the quality of the lessee as an absolute proprietor or owner of the property, during the term of the lease; and this view seems to have been adopted in Quebec by judicial authority in the case of *ex-parte, The Grand Trunk Railway Company* L. C. Rep. vol. 6, p. 54, where it was held that the capital of an indemnity paid by the company for expropriating certain lands, subject to an emphyteutic lease, should be paid to the lessee, as he was the proprietor. It is conceived that, as by the clause now under review a separate definition of the term "owner" is given for the Province of Quebec, the law of that Province will be the medium of interpretation of that clause; notwithstanding that one of the general objects of the measure is the assimilation of the franchise, so far as practicable, into a state of uniformity throughout all the provinces. The definition of the term "owner" in the Quebec Provincial Act (38 Vic. c. 7, s. 2, ss. 3), which will be found in a subsequent part of this volume, is somewhat similar to that given in this clause, and it is usual under that Act to class the emphyteutic tenant as an owner. The *usager*, or holder by a right of use or habitation, has been similarly classed, though it may be doubted whether such classification in the case either of the *usager* or of the holder by right of superficies is strictly proper, notwithstanding that the former is classed with usufructuaries in the Code (487 *et seq.*), while the latter may be also termed, in a sense, a proprietor *(Ib.* 521). They would seem more naturally to fall under the head of "occupants." It may be further remarked in connection with this subject of interpretation in Quebec that by Con. Stats. of Canada, cap. 6, s. 5, ss. 4 and 5 (based upon 12 Vic. c. 27, and 22 Vic. c. 82) it was provided "The word 'owner' shall signify proprietor, either in his own right or in right of his wife, or as usufructuary (*usufruitier*) of a real estate in *fief*, in *censive*, in *franc alleu*, or in free and common soccage. So that in Lower Canada whenever any person has the mere right of property, and some other person has the usufructuary enjoyment (*la jouissance et l'usufruit*) of the same for his own use and benefit, the person who has the mere right of property therein shall not have the right of voting as the owner of such real property, at any such election; but in such case such usufructuary (*usufruitier*) shall alone be entitled to vote at such election upon such lands or tenements." The definition in the clause under review so closely follows this, in its phraseology, as to fully justify the conclusion that whether the interpretation of the term "owner" as given in the present Quebec Provincial Act be a safe guide, or not, the law as interpreted under the Act previously in force there, as above quoted, will be applicable.

Usufructuary. right, or in the right of his wife *(b)*, of real property in "franc alleu" *(c)*, or in free and common soccage *(d)*: and when one person has the mere right of property or legal estate in any real property in the said Province and some other person has the usufructuary enjoyment *(la jouissance et l'usufruit)* of the same property for his own use as aforesaid, the person who has the mere right of property or legal estate therein shall not have the right of being registered as a voter or of voting under this Act in respect of such property, but in such case the person having the usufructuary enjoyment *(usufruit)* shall alone have the right of being registered as a voter and of voting in respect of such property under this Act;

(b) "*In the right of his wife.*"—The definition in this respect is the same as that contained in the Ontario Act (see *post*), which has not been altered in this particular by the Act of 1885. The Quebec Provincial Act defines an "owner" as anyone "who possesses real estate *or whose wife possesses real estate*," etc. In the Manitoba Act the word "owner" signifies proprietor in his own right only. The question is naturally suggested, whether the words of this clause and of the Ontario Act are *in effect* the same as those contained in the Quebec Act, under which the husband of a woman who possesses real estate, whether such property be in the community or not, or whether the husband and wife be living apart or not, is entitled to vote upon the qualification of such property. It was assumed in the debate in the House upon a proposed amendment to strike out the above words, that they would be, so far as the Provinces other than Quebec are concerned. Though this can form no ground for judicial interpretation, it may be considered that such view was well founded, since it has been the practice under similar wording heretofore to allow the husband to vote upon the qualification of the wife's property, notwithstanding that modern legislation and decisions have tended towards the establishment of a complete control by the wife over her own property. In this connection, however, the following words of Richards, C. J., in the *Prescott case*, 1 H. E. C. 1 (June 1871), where the *status* of a petitioner was attacked on the ground that his only qualification as a voter and as a petitioner was in respect of his wife's property, may be quoted. He says: "I think that the Election Act of 1868, by the term 'owner,' means to give the right to vote to the husband whose wife has an estate for life, or a greater estate in the land; and that *when in possession of such an estate* he is *proprietor in right of his wife*." (See note *f*, *post*). In Quebec the property of the wife may or may not be held in community. In the absence of agreement to the contrary, community of property exists from moment of marriage (Civil Code 1260). It may be excluded by the contract of marriage, or altered or modified at pleasure by the same contract, and is called in

"Owner" when it relates to the ownership of real property situate elsewhere in Canada than in the Province of Quebec, means the proprietor either in his own right

Owner; in other Provinces.

---

such case conventional community (Ib. 1262), but after marriage, the marriage covenants cannot be altered (*Ib.* 1265). Legal community may be dissolved—1. By natural death; 2. By civil death; 3. By separation from bed and board; 4. By separation of property; 5. By the absence of one of the consorts in certain cases and within certain restrictions (Ib. 1310). The wife, when separated either from bed and board or as to property only, regains the uncontrolled administration of her property: but she cannot alienate her immovables without the consent of her husband or, upon his refusal, without being judicially authorized (Ib. 1318). The wife, who has obtained a separation of property, must contribute in proportion to her means and to those of her husband, to the expenses of the household, as well as to those of the education of their common children. She must bear these expenses alone if nothing remain to the husband (Ib. 1317). With respect to conventional community, the consorts may stipulate that there shall be no community, or that they shall be separate as to property (1415). In the former case the wife has not the right to administer her property, nor receive the fruits thereof (1416); the husband, with regard to such property, has all the rights and is subject to all the obligations of a usufructuary (1419). When the consorts have stipulated by their contract of marriage that they shall be separate as to property, the wife retains the entire administration of her property, moveable and immoveable, and the free enjoyment of her revenues (1422). Each of the consorts contributes to the expenses of marriage according to the covenants contained in their contract (1423). The wife cannot, in any case, nor by virtue of any stipulation, alienate her immoveables without the special consent of her husband, or, on his refusal, without being judicially authorized (1424). The distinction between the clause under review and the corresponding clause of the present Quebec Provincial Franchise Law has been already pointed out. Whatever doubts may exist as to the effect of the clauses being the same, there can be no doubt as to the applicability of the interpretation placed upon the correspond ing clause of the Act formerly in force in that Province, which declares that "owner" shall signify proprietor, *either in his own right or in the right of his wife*, or as usufructuary of a real estate," etc., 22 Vic., cap. 82, s. 23; Con. Stats. of Can. cap. 6, s. 5, subs. 4, and the construction formerly placed upon those words was the same as that which the present Provincial law provides, under which all husbands whose wives own real estate are entitled to vote.

(c) "*Franc allen*"—*Franc alleu* (or *aleu*) *Roturier*—Merlin Repertoire v. Franc alleu "un héritage *exempt de droits seigneuriaux.*" Merlin cites le Grand Coutumier, Bk. 1, cap. 10. "C'est héritage non féodal, sur lequel aucun n' a droit de prendre aucune pension pour *fonds de terre.*" These latter words are synonymous with "*cens*" ("La redevance censuelle due au seigneur," Merlin v. Fond de terre). Also *Continue d'Orleans Art. 255*, "héritage tellement franc, qu'il ne doit fonds de terre, et n'est tenu d'aucun seigneur foncier, et *ne doit saisine*, désaisine, *ni autre servitude quelleque ce soit.*" There is now little practical difference between *franc alleu* and free and common soccage.

or for his own benefit *(e)*, or if such proprietor be a married man it means the proprietor in his own right, or in the right of his wife *(f)*, of freehold estate *(g)*, legal or equitable *(h)*, in lands and tenements held in free and common soccage *(i)* of which such person is in actual possession *(j)*, or is in receipt of the rents and profits;

(*d*) "*Free and common soccage.*"—See note (*i*), *post.*

(*e*) "*Either in his own right or for his own benefit*"—These words would seem to exclude a trustee who has no beneficial interest. *South Grenville* (Ont.) 1 H. E. C. 163; *Holden's* vote, *Ib.* 171; *Jones'* vote, *Ib.* 176. A mortgagee or trustee cannot vote unless he be in actual possession or in receipt of the rents and profits, under 7 and 8 Will. 3, c. 25, s. 6. This provision was expressly repealed in England by the Statute Law Revision Act, 1867. In Prince Edward Island every mortgagor or *cestui que trust* in actual possession by himself or his tenant, of real estate of the yearly value of forty shillings, is entitled to vote. See 42 Vic. cap. 2, s. 329, Prince Edward Island. See also sec. 9, *post.*

(*f*) "*In right of his wife.*"—It is not improbable that these words will be construed—having regard to the usual presumption in favor of the franchise and to the fact that the property may otherwise be unrepresented, and to former practice—as conferring the qualification of voters in respect of their wives' property upon husbands whose wives have separate property, either under settlement or under the Married Woman's Acts (see note *b*, *ante*); but the right of the husband in any case would seem to be qualified by the closing words of the clause, requiring "such person"—apparently the husband in the case of a married man—to be "in actual possession or in receipt of the rents and profits" (see note *g*). It is scarcely possible to construe the word "person" as referring to the wife, according to the language of the clause; though it may be argued that if the husband be construed an "owner" in right of his wife, where he has no interest in the wife's property, he may with equal propriety be held to be the "person" in actual possession or in receipt of the rents and profits, in right of the wife, even where he is *not* in actual possession or she alone is in receipt of the rents and profits. The Ont. Assessment Act (Rev. Stat. Ont. c. 180, s. 20, subs. 7) provides that "'owner' shall signify proprietor in his own right or in the right of his wife, of an estate for life, or any greater estate, either legal or equitable, except where the proprietor is a widow, and in such latter case the word 'owner' shall signify proprietor in her own right of any such estate." By s. 14 of the same Act land *occupied by the owner* shall be assessed in his name; such assessment being the basis of the franchise under the Ontario provincial Acts. The words of Richards, C. J., in the Prescott case, 1 H. E. C. 1, as quoted in note *b*, *ante*, are referable to the provisions of the Assessment Acts, though it may be remarked that in the Election Act of 1868 (provincial), to which the Chief Justice referred, the definition of "owner" does not contain the provision as to actual possession or receipt of the rents and profits, which appear in the clause under review. Under the Ontario Married Women's Property Act, 1884, women married after 1st

July, 1884, or acquiring property after that date, hold their property as *femmes sole*, with complete powers of disposition, apart from their husbands (as to non-retrospective character of this Act, see *Baynton* v. *Collins*, L. R. 27 Chy. D. 604 ; re. *Thompson* v. *Curzon*, L. R. 29 Chy. D. 177 ; *Turnbull* v. *Forman*, L. R. 15 Q. B. D. 234 ; *Conolan* v. *Leyland*, L. R. 27 Chy. D. 632 ; recognized in a recent case by the Ont. Court of Appeal); under the former Acts of 1859 and 1872, by decisions of the Courts, the control of the wife was not so complete (though under the Act of 1872, the wife was held by one learned judge to be capable of conveying apart from her husband, *Boustead* v. *Whitmore*, 22 Grant, 222 ; see also *Furniss* v. *Mitchell*, 3 Ont. Ap. R. 510). If the degree of interest or control of the husband in the wife's property or the question of the survival of tenancy by the curtesy are to be the guides in determining whether he is "owner in right of his wife," many enquiries and distinctions of some nicety will be necessary to be made by the Revising officers, in reference to the date of marriage, date of acquiring property, nature of the settlement, where there is a settlement, etc., too numerous and abstruse for discussion within the limits of a foot note. Decisions under the several Acts will be found noted in Robinson & Joseph's Digests, under the heads of *Husband and Wife*, *Estate by the Curtesy*, etc. It may be stated generally, that the husband has no control over the wife's separate property. "The right of possession of the property to which she is entitled to her separate use, is an exclusive right against her husband," *per* Lindley, L.J., in *Weldon* v. *De Bathe*, L.R. 14, Q. B. 346. Under certain circumstances an injunction will be granted to prevent him entering or interfering with the property, *Donnelly* v *Donnelly*, 9 Ont. R. 673 ; *Symonds* v. *Hallett*, L. R. 24 Chy. D. 346. Similar laws prevail in New Brunswick and Nova Scotia. In Prince Edw. Island and British Columbia the Provincial Franchise Acts will govern.

(g) "*Freehold Estate*" i.e., either an estate of inheritance or a life estate. A tenant either for his own life or for the life of another is a freeholder. In the latter case he has what is called an estate *pur autre vie*. All estates which may last for life, though they may be sooner determined are freeholds, *Co. Littleton 42*. Examples of life estates—a grant to a person by name without further words of limitation ; a grant to a man and woman during coverture, or to a widew during widowhood : or so long as the grantee dwells in a certain house, or pays a certain sum, *Ib.* 354. The reversion expectant on a life estate does not give the right to vote to the reversioner, though it is otherwise if the lease be merely for years. See Chambers *Dictionary of Elections* 599 ; Heywood on Elections 60 ; *Gloucestershire Election*, Heywood 64 : *Bedfordshire Election* (*Conquest's case*) 2 Luders, 422.

(h) "*Legal or Equitable.*"—A mere equitable right is not sufficient to give a vote. For instance, where a father, the owner of a lot, told his son that he might have the lot and advised him to get a deed drawn, and the lot had been assessed to his son for 3 or 4 years, and was rented to a tenant by the father with the assent of the son who paid to the father his wages, but the father collected the rent, *Held*, that there being nothing but a voluntary gift from the father to the son, without possession, the son's vote was bad : *Lundy's vote*, *S. Grenville*, 1 H. E. C. 163. So where a father had made a will of a lot to his son who was assessed for it, and the son took the crops except what was used by the father, who resided on the lot with his wife, the

son residing and working on another farm, it was held that the son had not such a beneficial interest in the lot as would entitle him to vote, *Mullin's vote, Ibid.* As also where a contract to purchase had been made, but the conveyance had, at the request of the purchaser, being delayed, and the vendor was still in actual possession, *Anelay* v. *Lewis*, 17 C. B. 316; 25 L. J. C. P. 121. So where a voter has sold his estate to a person who at the sale executed a bond to permit him to receive the rents and profits for life, it was held that the vote was bad. *Gloucestershire Election*, 1 Stephens Law of Elections, 456. So also, the receipt of the rents and profits of an estate by a stranger to the estate will give him no right to vote, nor will it deprive the real owner of his vote, *Gloucester Elections*, 1 Stephens Law of Elections, 457; *Bedfordshire* (*Trotman's case*) 2 Luders, 431. Likewise a person assessed for Crown lands, to which he has no title, though receiving rent for it from a tenant, is not qualified to vote. *Clark's vote, Lincoln* (2) 1 H. E. C. 500. So where a father had made a will in his son's favour, and told the son if he would work the place and support the family he would give it to him; and the entire management remained in the son's hands from that time, the property being assessed in both names, the profits to be applied to pay the debts due on the place. *Held*, that as the understanding was that the son worked the place for the support of the family, and beyond that for the benefit of the estate, which he expected to possess under his father's will, he did not hold immediately to his own use and benefit, and was not entitled to vote. *Weort's case*, Stormont (1) 1 H. E. C. 34. So where the owner of mortgaged property died intestate, leaving a widow and sons and daughters, and the property was sold under the mortgage, and the deed made to the widow, but three of the sons furnished some of the purchase money and all remained in possession, and the eldest son was assessed as occupant, *Held*, that as the eldest son did not shew that the property was purchased for him, and the presumption from the evidence being that it was bought for the mother, such eldest son had no right to vote. *Morrow's vote*, South Grenville, 1 H. E.C. 163. (In the two latter cases however the sons might now be entitled to vote as "farmer's sons," or "son of an owner of real property," if the property were of sufficient value). Where the voter only received the deed of the property after he was assessed and after the revision of the assessment roll, though he had previously been assessed for and paid taxes on the place for several years, *Held*, not entitled to vote. *Cahay's case*, Stormont, 1 H. E. C. 21. But if a person have such an equitable title as the courts will recognize, he is entitled to the vote. As where there has been an agreement for sale and the vendee has taken possession under the agreement, or has become otherwise entitled to a specific performance of the contract, *Seton* v. *Slade*, 7 Ves. 274; *Gallaway* v. *Ward*, 1 Ves. 318; *Rawlings* v. *Burgess*, 2 V. and B. 387; *Holden's vote, S. Grenville*, 1 H. E. C. 171. The question in the cases affecting the right of vendor and vendee to vote has been thus stated—who is to have the rents and profits of the estate, by virtue of the agreement until the legal conveyance is made; or who must bear any loss which may happen, or be entitled to any benefit which may accrue to the estate, between the time of the agreement and conveyance? *Rogers on Elections*, 33; Heywood on Elections 111. If there be any doubt as to what a Court of Equity would do, the vendee should be treated as having an inchoate right merely, but not an equitable estate. *Rex* v. *Ged-*

dington, 2 B. and C. 129. Or no estate but merely an equitable right *Rex* v. *Llantillio Grosseny*, 5 B. and C. 462. Conditions may be introduced which will have the effect of preventing a vendee from acquiring an equitable estate. *Levy* v. *Lindo*, 3 Mer. 84 ; *King* v. *King*, 2 My. and K. 442; *Wall* v. *Bright*, 1 J. and W. 494 ; *Ackland* v. *Gainsford*, 2 Mad. 28. Where a verbal agreement was made between the voter and his father in Jan. 1870, and on this agreement the voter from that time had exercised control and took the proceeds to his own use although the deed was not executed until September following, the vote was held good. *Gollinger's vote*, Stormont, 1 H. E. C. 39. Where the deed was taken in the father's name, the son furnishing the money, the father in occupation with the assent of the son, and the proceeds not divided. *Held*, that being the equitable owner, notwithstanding the deed to the father the son had the right to vote. *Blair's vote, Stormont*, 1 H. E. C. 21. Where an estate was devised to trustees to sell, for the payment of debts, and the surplus to be divided between the voter and two others, and the estate had not been sold, the vote was held good. *Rice's case, Middlesex Election*, 2 Peck. 106. Where an estate was devised to one T in trust to pay legacies to the younger children, and T refused to take the land subject to the trust. but the younger children, with his consent, took possession of the land in satisfaction of their legacies, *Held*, that they were entitled to vote. *(Ibid) Smith's case*, 2 Peck. 424. Where the devisee of an estate charged with an annuity put the annuitant in possession in satisfaction of the annuity, *Held*, that the annuitant had a right to vote. *Bonfield's case, Bedfordshire Election*, 2 Luders, 440. Where a person conveyed an estate to trustees for the payment of debts out of rents and profits, to be re-conveyed when the debts were all paid, but at the time of the election the debts were not paid, *Held*, that he had no vote. *Yorkshire Election—Heywood on Elections*, 108.

(i) "*Free and Common Soccage.*"—The prevailing tenure outside the Province of Quebec. "Soccage, in its most general and extensive signification, seems to denote a tenure by any certain and determinate service. And in this sense it is by our ancient writers constantly put in opposition to chivalry or knight service, where the render was precarious and uncertain. Littleton also defines it to be, where the tenant holds his tenement of the lord by any *certain* service, in lieu of all other services ; so that they be not services of chivalry, or knight service. And, therefore, afterwards he tells us that whatsoever is not tenure in chivalry is tenure in soccage ; in like manner as it is defined by Finch, a tenure to be done out of war. The service must, therefore, be certain in order to denominate it soccage ; as to hold by fealty and 20s. rent ; or by homage, fealty and 20s. rent ; or by homage and fealty without rent ; or, by fealty and certain corporal service, as ploughing the lord's land for three days ; or, by fealty only without any other service ; for all these are tenures in soccage." Black. Com. Book II. cap. 6.—*Free* soccage, where the services are not only certain, but honorable, is contra-distinguished from *villein* soccage, where the services, though certain, are of a baser nature. By 31 Geo. III., c. 31, 1791, Con. Stat. Can., by which it was provided that all lands to be granted in Upper Canada should be in free and common soccage, it was also provided, that, if the grantees desired it, grants should be on the same tenure in Lower Canada. Leith's Black. 18.

(j) "*In actual possession, etc.*"—Do these words mean the same as "in actual

Tenant.

"Tenant" *(k)* means as well a person who is bound to render to his landlord some portion of the produce or of the revenues or profits of the property leased, in lieu of rent, as a person who pays rent in money therefor ;

occupation" in the subsection defining "occupant"? If so, the owner of vacant unproductive property would be excluded from the franchise. It is to be remembered, however, that the statutes are to be construed favorably to the right of franchise. Slight acts of ownership will at all events constitute actual possession, even if the term be construed to exclude constructive possession, see *Elliott* v. *Brown*, 9 Ont. Ap. R. 228.

(k) "*Tenant.*"—A tenant as here defined, evidently means the possessor of an estate less than a freehold—see definition of "owner," *ante*. Of estates that are less than freehold there are three sorts. 1. Estates for years. 2. Estates at will. 3. Estates at sufferance. Bl. Com. (12th Ed.) book 2, cap. 9, p. 140. An estate for years is a contract for the possession of lands or tenements, for some definite period. *Ib.* An estate at will is where lands and tenements are let by one man to another, to have and to hold at the will of the lessor.—*Ib.* p. 145. An estate at sufferance, is where one comes inte possession of land by lawful title, but keeps it afterwards without any title at all.—*Ib.* p. 149. But, if the landlord afterwards receives rent, or does any act by which he proves his assent to the continuance of the tenant, this turns the estate at sufferance into a tenancy from year to year.—*Ib.* 151. As under this act (secs. 3 subs. (4) and 4 subs. (4) the tenant must pay rent, in money or kind, to entitle him to be registered as a tenant, a tenant at sufferance can hardly be termed a tenant within the meaning of the Act. This remark does not, however, apply to a tenant at sufferance in Quebec, who is bound to pay the annual value of the property and whose holding is as an annual lease.—See Civil Code 1608. Where a former tenant of a house died intestate, leaving a widow and infant children in possession, and no letters of administration were taken out, but, the widow having married again, her husband went into possession and paid all rent and taxes, and maintained the children, he was held entitled to vote. *McLoughlin's case*—Alcock's Reg. cases 249.—Tenants on shares are entitled to vote ; but, where an owner agreed with two tenants that he would furnish a team of horses, the farming implements, and seed for a certain lot, they agreeing to do the work as he should direct, harvest the grain, pay for their share of thrashing, keep up fences, etc., and receive for the first year one third, and for the second year one half, the crops, it was held not to be a letting of the land on shares, giving to the tenants a term of possession, but a contract for remuneration for their care and labor in growing the crops as the owner should direct. *Park* v. *Humphrey*, 14 U. C. C. P. 209.—A. owned a farm and agreed to pay B. to work it on shares, each supplying the seed and labor, and to have one half of the profits, B. to pay $60 for implements and $160 a year, but he was not placed in posession of any distinct portion of the farm, owing to the shape of the farm, the parties being equally in possession of the whole : *Held*, that B. was an occupant with A., and not his tenant. *Oberlin* v. *McGregor*, 26 U. C. C. P. 460.

The word "tenant" has been held to exclude persons holding, as officials or servants, if required to occupy for the purpose of the office or service, but not otherwise, *Hughes v. Chatham Overseers*, 5 M. & G. 54; *Fox v. Dalby*, L. R. 10 C. P. 285; *Clark v. Bury St. Edmund's Overseers*, 26 L. J. C. P. 12; *Dobson v. Jones*, 5 M. & Gr. 112. "There is no inconsistency in the relation of master and servant and that of landlord and tenant. A master may pay his servant by conferring on him an interest in real estate. either in fee, for years, at will, or for any other estate or interest, and if he do so the servant then becomes entitled to the legal incidents of the estate as much as if it were purchased for any other consideration. But it may be that a servant may occupy a tenement of his master's, not by way of payment of his services, but, for the purpose of performing them, *required* to occupy in the performance of his contract to serve his master"—*Per* Tindal, C. J., in *Hughes v. Chatham Overseers*, 5 M. & G. 54. A man occupying a house as toll collector has been, in Ontario, held not qualified to vote, *McArthur's vote, Brockville*, 1 H. E. C. 129. In England the distinction has been abolished by sec. 3 of the Rep. of the People Act, 1884, by which a man inhabiting a dwelling house by virtue of any office, service or employment, such house not being inhabited by any person under whom he serves, is declared a tenant.

The party must be lessee of a corporeal hereditament, or the assignee of a lease of such an hereditament; a chattel rent charge, or a rent charge issuing out of a leasehold estate, does not qualify under the English Acts; *Warburton v. Denton* L. R. 6 C. P. 267; 40 L. J. C. P. 49; 23 L. T. 129; 19 W. R. 210; 1 H. & C. 432; nor, it is conceived, under this Act, does a rent charge of any description, except it form the income, or part of the income, of an income voter, but see *Dodds v. Thompson*, L. R. 1 C. P. 133; 35 L. J. C. P, 97; *Dawson v Robbins*, 2 C. P. D. 38; 46 L. J. C. P. 62.

As "real property" by a subsequent clause of this section is defined to include "any portion" of a house, store, office or building, it would seem that what was known as "structural severance" in England is not necessary in order to qualify the holder to vote under this Act, any more than it is under the present English Acts. Lely & Foulkes Parliamentary El. Acts, p. 18—note "*House, Warehouse, etc.*," also note on p. 55 Ibid. But there must be an exclusive possession by the tenant of the "portion" rented. In *Selby v. Greaves*, L. R. 3 C. P. 594, where it was held that a portion of a room in a factory was demised, the Court proceeds upon the express ground that the owner of the factory had parted with the exclusive possession of the part in respect of which the question arose. Willes, J., says at p. 602: "The conclusion I arrive at is, that the letting was not a mere letting of an onstand for the lace machines, but a letting of a *defined* portion of the room, separated from the remaining portion, with exclusive possession by the person taking it, and *that possession* was taken under that demise." Montague Smith, J., "Upon the construction of the agreement, I think the *half room* was let in such a manner as to grant to the tenant the exclusive occupation of that part." See also *Smith v. Egginton*, L. R. 3 C. P, 594; but see *Hancock v. Austin* 14 C. B. (N. S.) 634. Where rooms in a factory, in which each tenant had his own spinning machine, worked by a steam engine belonging to and worked by the landlord, but each tenant had the exclusive use of his own room, and kept the key of the door which he approached by a com-

Occupant. "Occupant"*(l)* means a person in actual occupation *(m)*

mon staircase; *Held*, that each tenant was entitled to vote. *Wright* v. *Town Clerk of Stockport*, 5 M. & Gr. 33; see also *Regina ex. rel. Forward* v. *Bartels* (Long's case), 7 C. P. 539; *Cirencester Election*, 2 Fraser 451; *Great Marlow Election*, (Crosby's case), B. & Aust. 100; *Score* v. *Huggatt*, 7 M. & Gr. 95; *Rex.* v. *Nusworth*, 5 A. & E. 201; *Toms* v. *Luckett*. 5 C. B. 23; *Wansey* v. *Perkins*, 7 M. & Gr. 145; *Evans and Fynche's Case*, Cro. Car. 473; *Middlesex Election (Anstey's Case)*, 2 Peck, 109; *Stamper v. Overseers of Sutherland*, L. R. 3 C P. 403; *Barnes* v. *Peters*, L. R. 4 C. P. 539; *Boon* v. *Howard*, L. R. 9 C. P. 277; *Bradley* v. *Baylis*, L. R. 8 Q. B. D. 195. As to difference between tenant and a lodger, see Ont. Franchise Act, 1885, s. 3, sub. s. 8, and notes, *post*.

A lessee or tenant for years, who is not restrained by his lease from subletting or assigning, may demise for any less term than he himself has, or may assign his lease, *Woodfall's* Landlord and Tenant (12 Ed.), s. 11.—Civil Code of Lower Canada, 1638, though only the tenant in possession for the year next before the 1st January preceding the revision, can be registered under s 3, subs. 3 and s. 4, subs. 4, *post*. In fact every tenant, except a tenant at will or at sufferance, has a right, in the absence of a contract to the contrary, to make a subtenancy, as incident to his tenancy—Woodfall, p. 12 (But see *Brockville Case*, *Dunham's vote*, 1 H. E. C. 136). But whether the tenant assigns his whole term, or sublets, which latter he may do by reserving a reversion of even one day only, he loses the right to vote, it is considered, by parting with the possession of the whole of the property leased. See sub. s. (4) of secs. 3 and 4. He who cultivates land on condition of sharing the produce with the lessor, can neither sublet nor assign his lease, in Quebec, unless the right to do so has been expressly stipulated—Civil Code, 1646.

(l) "*Occupant.*"—Occupancy is the taking possession of those things which before belonged to nobody.—Black. Com. 12th Ed., book 2, cap. 16. This right was confined by the common law of England to a single instance, viz: where a person who held an estate *pur autre vie*, or for the life of another, died during the life of the *cestui que vie*, or him by whose life it was held: in this case, he that could first enter on the land might lawfully retain the possession so long as *cestui que vie* lived, by right of occupancy, *Ib.* The term "occupant," however, as used in this and similar acts, has a more extended meaning and includes all those actual occupiers of property who cannot be classed as either owners or tenants, and yet are entitled to vote by virtue of such property. For instance, a squatter upon Crown Lands is considered to have a sufficient title to give him a vote.—Brough's *Law of Elections*, 12. Persons occupying jointly with the owner are usually assessed as occupants. Thus, before the farmer's son franchise was created in Ontario, many sons were assessed as occupants of their father's farms, where the fathers had given up the management and control of the farms to them, and though living on and supported from the farms.--*See Stormont (Provincial) case*, 1 H. E. C. 21, *Brockville*, *Ib.*, 129, *3 Grenville*, *Ib.* 163. In a milling business, where the agreement between the father and son was, that if the son would take charge of the mill and manage the business, he should have a share of the profits, and the son, in fact, solely managed the business, keeping possession of the mill, and applying a portion of the proceeds to his own use, it was held that the son had

of real property otherwise than as "owner," "tenant," or "usufructuary," in his own right, or in the case of a married man, in his own right or in the right of his wife, and who receives to his own use and benefit the revenues and profits thereof;

"Person" means a male person, including an Indian *(n)*, Person.

such an interest in the business, and, while the business lasted, such an interest in the land as entitled him to be on the roll.—*Stormont Election, (Bullock's vote.)* 1 H. E. C. 27; 7 C. L. J. (N. S.) 213. See also *Owen Baker's vote*, 1 H. E. C. 31; *S. Grenville (Thomas Fitzgerald's vote), Ib.* 165.

(m) The occupant must be in *actual possession*, as distinguished from possession in law. See *Murray* v. *Thornibey*, 2 C. B. 217; *Heyden* v. *Overseers of Tiverton*, 4 C. B., 1; *Carroll* v. *Barry*, 15 Ir., C. L. R., 373; *Webster* v. *Ashton-under-Lyne Overseers*, L. R., 8 C. P. 281; 42 L. J. C. P. 38.—See the words "actual occupation" in the text.

(n) "*Including an Indian.*"—Indians in Canada were not hitherto entitled to all the privileges of British subjects unless they were enfranchised under 43 Vic., cap. 25, (Can.) or some of the previous statutes of which that Act is a consolidation, *(Howell on Naturalization* 10). By sec. 2, sub-sec. 5, of that act, the term *enfranchised Indian* means any Indian, his wife, or minor, unmarried children, who has received letters patent, granting him in fee simple any portion of the reserve which may have been allotted to him, his wife, and minor children, by the band to which he belongs, or any unmarried Indian who may have received letters patent for any allotment of the reserve. Sections 99-101 specify the mode of obtaining the letters patent. Before the issue of the letters patent, the Indian must declare to the Superintendent-General of Indian Affairs, the name or surname by which he or she wishes to be enfranchised, and thereafter known; and, on his or her receiving such letters patent, in such name or surname, he or she shall be held to be also enfranchised, and be known by such name, and if a married man, his wife and minor unmarried children, also, are held to be enfranchised, and from the date of such letters patent, any act or law making any distinction between the legal rights, privileges, disabilities and liabilities of Indians, and those of Her Majesty's other subjects, shall cease to apply to such Indian, or to the wife or minor unmarried children of such Indian, so declared to be enfranchised. "Any Indian admitted to the degree of doctor of medicine, or to any other degree by any University of Learning, or who may be admitted in any part of the Dominion to practice law, either as an advocate, or as a barrister, or counsellor, or solicitor, or attorney, or to be a notary public, or who may enter holy orders, or may be licensed by any denomination of Christians as a minister of the Gospel, may, upon petition to the Superintendent-General, *ipso facto*, become enfranchised under the Act," and the Superintendent may give him a suitable allotment of land from the lands belonging to the band of which he is a member.—Sec. 99, sub-sec. 1, *Ibid.* By the Ontario Election Act, all Indians enfranchised as above, and all Indians or persons with part Indian blood, who do not reside among Indians, though they partici-

pate in the annuities, interest moneys and rents of a tribe, band, or body of Indians, are, subject to the same qualifications in other respects, and to the same provisions and restrictions as other persons in the electoral district, given the right to vote. But, the Indians, or persons with part Indian blood, who are entitled to vote where there is no voters' list, shall be the following, namely :—"All Indians or persons with part Indian blood who have been duly enfranchised, and all unenfranchised Indians or persons with part Indian blood who *do not* participate in the annuities, interest, moneys, or rents of a tribe, band, or body of Indians, *and do not reside* among Indians, subject to the same qualifications in other respects, and to the same provisions and restrictions as other persons in the electoral district."—(See Franchise and Rep. Act, 1885, Ont., S. 3, "*Sixthly.*") It will be seen that under the Ontario laws, only Indians who have received their patents and thereby became enfranchised, or who, while receiving their Indian annuities, live apart from other Indians, and possess the qualification of ordinary white voters, can vote in organized districts or municipalities: and in the unorganized municipalities they cannot vote, even when they live apart and possess the ordinary qualification of white voters, unless they give up their annuities. Under the Act under review, Indians in Manitoba, British Columbia, Keewatin and the North-West Territories, and any Indian on any reserve elsewhere in Canada, who is not in possession and occupation of a separate and distinct tract of land in such reserve, and whose improvements on such separate tract are not of the value of at least one hundred and fifty dollars, and who is not otherwise possessed of the qualifications entitling him to be registered on the list of voters under this Act, are excluded.—See sec. 11, (c). All Indians, therefore, outside the Provinces and territories mentioned, who occupy separate allotments, though in the reserves, and while in receipt of their annuities, are given the franchise in Dominion elections.

Indians are subjects (*Reg. ex rel. Gibb* v. *White*, 5 Pr. R. U. C. 315). An Indian, who is a British subject, and otherwise qualified (as by holding real estate in fee simple to a sufficient amount), was in Upper Canada held to have an equal right with any other British subject to hold the position of reeve of a municipality, even though not "enfranchised," and though receiving, as an Indian, a portion of the annual payments from the common property of his tribe.—*Ibid.* A person entered into an agreement to farm the land of an Indian woman on shares for five years and took possession. He was found guilty of a misdemeanor under 13 and 14 Vic. cap. 74. (*Regina* v. *Hagar*, 7 U. C. C. P. 380). Such arrangement therefore could not confer a right to vote upon a white person. The prohibition against the sale, leasing, etc., of lands by Indians, applies only to lands reserved for their occupation, and not to lands to which any individual Indian has acquired a title.—*Totten* v. *Watson*, 15 U. C. Q. B. 392. It may be of interest to mention that in a recent Ontario case (*Bryce et al* v. *Salt*, before the Master in Chambers, Oct. 2nd, 1885), it has been held that there is nothing to prevent an Indian, though living on the reserve, as one of a band, from suing or being sued, and judgment may be ordered against him, though such judgment will not bind any property of the Indian, except property subject to taxation under sec. 75 of the Act of 1880.

Parliament in 1884 enacted a law entitled "The Indian Advancement Act, 1884," which after reciting that "it is expedient to provide means by which Indians on

and excluding a person of Mongolian or Chinese race *(o)*:

reserves in divers parts of the Dominion, may be trained for the future exercise of municipal privileges and powers," provides that whenever any band or bands shall be declared by order in Council to be considered fit to have the Act applied to them, it shall so apply from the time appointed in such Order, which shall not bear date earlier that 1st January, 1885 (Sec. 3); that any reserve to which the Act is to apply shall be divided into sections (Sec. 4): for the election of Councillors for each section by the electors thereof, being the male residents of the full age of 21 years (Sec. 5); for a first meeting of the Councillors, and the election of one of them as Chief Councillor (Sec. 6); for annual elections thereafter (Sec. 7); for the making of By-laws, etc., subject to the approval and confirmation of the Superintendent-General, to have the force of law on the reserve, upon the following subjects. 1. The religious denomination of teachers of schools; 2. Public Health: 3. Decorum at elections and generally; 4. The repression of intemperance and profligacy; 5. Sub-division of the lands among the members of the band; 6. Trespass by animals; 7. The construction and repair of school-houses and other buildings; and 8. Roads and bridges, and the appointment of road-masters and fence viewers; 9. Watercourses, ditches, fences, etc., and the preservation of wood: 10. Punishment of trespassers; 11. Raising money by assessment and taxation on the lands of Indians unfranchised or in possession of lands by location ticket in the reserve; 12. Appropriation of moneys of the band to carry out by-laws, etc; 13. Imposition of penalties and enforcement thereof; 14. Amendment, repeal or re-enactment of by-laws. This Act provides the machinery whereby the Indians may enjoy self-government in municipal matters. The Franchise Act will give many of them a voice in the affairs of the nation at large.

See, as to penalty on Indian agent seeking to induce or compel an Indian to be registered as a voter, or to vote or refrain from voting, sec. 64, *post*.

(o) "*Mongolian or Chinese race.*"—The Mongols were a race originally inhabiting what is known as Mongolia. Their empire, under the great conqueror Jenghiz Khan, who died in 1227, extended from the China Sea to the banks of the Dnieper. They had conquered the Cathayans or Chinese and had over-run, to a great extent, the Russian territory. The conquests of Jenghiz and his successors spread not only over China and the adjoining East, but westward over Northern Asia, Persia, Armenia, part of Asia Minor and Russia, threatening to deluge Christendom. Though the Mongol wave retired, as it seemed almost by an act of Providence, when Europe lay at its feet, it had levelled or covered all political barriers from the frontier of Poland to the Yellow Sea. China and Russia ultimately absorbed the native and acquired territories of the Mongols. With the absorption of the Khanate of Bokhara and the capture of Khiva by the Russians, the individual history of the Mongol tribes came to an end, and their name has left its imprint only on the dreary stretch of Chinese owned country from Manchuria to the Altai Mountains, and to the equally unattractive country in the neighborhood of the Koko-nor. For the purposes of the Act the Mongolians or Chinese are classed as one race—as probably they were in fact—though they are by no means to be found only within the limits of the Chinese Empire. (See Encycl. Brit. 9th Ed. under *Mongols, China, Asia, etc.*)

Farm. "Farm" means land actually occupied by the owner thereof and not less in quantity than twenty acres; and "farmer" means such owner thereof;

City. "City" means a place incorporated as a city or recognized as such, by or under any Act of the Parliament of Canada or of the Legislature of the Province in which it is situate; except the cities of Hull and St. Hyacinthe, in the Province of Quebec, which, for the purposes of this Act, shall be held to be towns;

Exceptions.

Town. "Town" means a place incorporated as a town or recognized as such, by or under any Act of the Parliament of Canada or of the Legislature of the Province in which it is situate;

Incorporated village. "Incorporated village" means a place incorporated as a village or recognized as such, by or under any Act of the Parliament of Canada or of the Legislature of the Province in which it is situate;

Parish. "Parish" means any tract of land which is generally reputed to form a parish, whether such tract has or has not been wholly or in part originally erected into a parish by the civil or ecclesiastical authorities, and which now exists as a territorial division;

Father, mother. "Father" includes grandfather, stepfather and father-in-law, and "mother" includes stepmother and mother-in-law;

Farmer's son. "Farmer's son" means any male person not otherwise qualified to vote and being the son of an owner and actual occupant of a farm, and includes a grandson, stepson or son-in-law;

Son of owner of real property. "Son of an owner of real property" in cities and towns means any male person not otherwise qualified to vote and being the son of an owner and occupant of real property, and includes a grandson, stepson or son-in-law;

and in counties means any male person not otherwise qualified to vote and being the son of an owner and occupant of real property other than a farm, and includes a grandson, step-son or son-in-law;

"Electoral district" means any place (consisting of or comprising any city, town, county, township, parish, district or municipality, or portion thereof,) in Canada, entitled to return a member to the House of Commons of Canada; Electoral District.

"Election" means an election of a member to serve in the House of Commons of Canada; Election.

"Voting" and "to vote" mean voting and to vote at the election of a member to serve in the House of Commons of Canada; Voting; to vote

"List of voters" means the list of registered voters, to be prepared and revised under the provisions of this Act in each year, for each sub-division or polling district of an electoral district, when finally revised, except when the first general list or an unrevised list is especially mentioned or referred to; List of voters.

"Actual value" (*p*) or "value" means the then present market value of any real property, if sold upon the ordi- Actual value; value.

(*p*) "*Market value.*"—The value of property is a matter as to which opinions usually differ widely, according as the valuator may be of a sanguine or of a gloomy temperament, and according to whether he be a property owner and fixes the present value upon the basis of future increase, being able to wait for his price, or whether he is not a property owner or has property for which he cannot find a purchaser. A man who is impressed with a consideration of how much a thing is worth will entertain a widely different opinion from him who simply looks at it as a thing to be purchased in expectation of profit, whether by the employment of it or selling it again; Draper, C. J., in *McQuaig v. The Unity Fire Insurance Co.*, 9 U. C. C. P. 88; See Harrison's Mun. Manual, 4th Ed., pp. 632 and 767. The Ontario Assessment Act provides that "real and personal property shall be estimated at their actual cash value, as they would be appraised in payment of a just debt from a solvent debtor." (Rev. Stat. Ont., cap. 180, s. 23.) This clause fixes a somewhat different standard of valuation when it defines value to mean "the then present market value of any real property, if sold upon the ordinary terms of sale." The

nary terms of sale, in respect of which any person claims to be qualified, whether as owner, tenant, occupant or farmer's or other owner's son, as determined by the revising officer, upon the best information in his possession at the time of such revision: Provided that the assessment rolls as finally revised (q) for municipal purposes, shall be *primâ facie* evidence of the value of such property;

Proviso.

" market value " depends upon the number of persons who at the moment are willing to purchase, coupled with the unwillingness of the owners to sell, and in a less degree by the amount of capital held for investment in land at the time. "The ordinary terms of sale" will differ according to locality. They will usually, however, be found to include terms of credit. These, too, differ in different localities. The instructions of the Canada Permanent Loan and Savings Co., the largest loan Co. in the Dominion, to its valuators are to value the property at what it would bring at a forced sale after due notice for cash, or what may be considered equivalent to cash—say, one-fourth down, and the balance in three or four annual instalments at 7 per cent. per annum. This is, perhaps, as safe a *general* guide as can be given. The amount at which property can be rented for a term of years, and the interest which such rental would yield a purchaser, are stated by the same instructions to be a corrective to an erroneous estimate, arising from temporary or exceptional circumstances, and generally a safe criterion of value.

The latter part of this clause makes the assessment rolls, as finally revised for Municipal purposes, *prima facie* evidence of the value of property. This basis was adopted after much discussion in the House of Commons. (*Hansard*, Vol. 17, No. 62; p. 1650 to 1662). Under the Quebec Provincial law the valuation roll was held conclusive as to value, and no one who was not on it could be on the Electoral list (*Electoral lists of Kamouraska*, 3 Q. L. R. 308, S. C. 1877), though the description on the roll did not necessarily prove the quality of the person (*Grattan v. Corporaton of Village of St. Scholastique*, 7 R. L. 356, Mag. Ct. 1875). In Ontario the revised assessment roll was considered by the *rota* Judges conclusive as to value, as regarded a scrutiny after the Election. (*Stormont*, 1 H. E. C., *Stewart's vote*, 25, *N. Victoria*, 1 H. E. C. 584). But it did not preclude the County Judge from considering the values on complaint filed on the revision of the Voter's List by him. (Rev. Stat. Ont, cap. 9, s. 9, Form 6, List 3.)

(q) "*Finally revised.*"—By the Ontario Voters' List Act (Rev. Stat. cap. 9, s. 2, sub-sec. 9) "An assessment roll shall be understood to be finally revised and corrected when it has been so revised and corrected by the Court of Revision for the Municipality, or by the Judge of the County Court, in case of an appeal, as provided in the '*Assessment Act*,' or when the time during which such appeal may be made has elapsed, and not before." The date of the final revision of the roll varies according to whether appeals are entered or not. (*a*) If there has been no appeal to

"Real property" *(r)* **means a lot or portion of a lot or other portion or sub-division of real property, or a house, store, office or building of any description whatsoever, or any portion thereof *(s)*, situate upon real property, and forming part thereof *(t)*;** Real property.

---

the Court of Revision, the roll is finally revised as soon as passed (after 26th May) by said Court and certified by the Clerk (Rev. Stat. cap. 180, s. 57). (*b*) Where there has been a complaint or appeal to the Court of Revision, but none to the County Judge, then when five days after date limited for closing the Court of Revision (1st July) have elapsed, *i.e.* 7th July (s. 59, sub-s. 2). (*c*) Where there has been an appeal to the County Judge, then on such day prior to 1st Aug., as the decision of the Judge is given (s. 60).

It has been held in Quebec that a secretary-treasurer was acting properly in making the voters' list out, pending an appeal. *Hickson et al.* v. *Abbott*, 25 L. C. J. 289.

(r) "*Real Property.*"—Things real are such as are permanent, fixed or immovable, which cannot be carried out of their place; as lands and tenements. Black, Com. 12 Ed. Book 2, cap. 2. As to "immovables" in Quebec, see Civil Code, Book 2, title 1.

(s) "*House, etc......or any portions thereof.*"—Prior to the Parliamentary and Municipal Reg. Act, 1878, in England, much difficulty had arisen in defining the words "house" and "building," but the result of the cases appears to have been that the occupation of part of a house only conferred the qualification in a case where such part was structurally severed from the rest. *Cook* v. *Humber*, 11 C. B. (N. S.) 733; 3 L. J. C. P. 73; *Ellis* v. *Burch*, L. R. 6 C. P. 327; 40 L. J. C. P. 169; *Boon* v. *Howard*, L.R. 9 C. P. 327. To meet this difficulty the above Act provided that the terms "house, warehouse, counting-house, shop or other building," shall include any part of a house where that part is separately occupied for the purpose of any trade, business or profession, and that the term "dwelling-house" shall include any part of a house where that part is separately occupied as a dwelling, and that part shall not be deemed to be occupied otherwise than separately by reason only that the occupier is entitled to the joint use of some other part (s. 5). It is clear that under this English Act, structural severance is no longer necessary to constitute either a "house" or a "dwelling-house," Lely and Foulkes' Parliamentary El. Acts, 55, and it is conceived that this provision of our Act will receive a similar interpretation. See note "*Tenant*" *ante*. "Building" includes a cowhouse, *Whitmore* v. *Winlock Town Clerk* 5 M. & G. 9; a quite separate room in a factory; *Wright* v. *Stockport Town Clerk*, 5 M. & G. 33; and a shed used for storing. *Powell* v. *Farmer*, 18 C. B. (N.S.) 168; the building must be of some permanence, *Norrish* v. *Harris*, L. R. 1 C. P. 155; 35 L. J. C. P. 101; a counting-house need not be structurally severed, *Piercy* v. *Maclean*, L. R. 5 C. P. 252; 39 L. J. C. P. 115; 21 L. T. 213; 18 W. R. 132; 1 H. & C. 321; see Ont. Franchise Act, 1885, s. 2, sub-sec. 7 and 8, *post* and notes.

(t) "*And forming part thereof.*"—A suspension bridge may form part of land and real property: *The Niagara Falls Suspension Bridge Co.* v. *Gardner*, 29 U. C. Q.

Section.

"Section" means a section of this Act;

The Province.

"The Province" means that Province of the Dominion in which the revising officer in the case or matter referred to, is appointed;

The revising officer.

"The revising officer" means any revising officer appointed for the place referred to in the context, and competent to do the thing required:

As to Sundays and holidays.

2. If the time limited by this Act for any proceeding or for the doing of any act under its provisions expires or falls upon a Sunday or day which is a public holiday or holiday under "*The Interpretation Act*," (u) the time so limited shall be extended to, and such act may be done upon, the day next following which is not a Sunday or such a holiday as aforesaid.

QUALIFICATION OF VOTERS IN CITIES AND TOWNS.

Who shall be registered as voters if qualified as to—

3. Every person shall, upon and after the first day of January in the year of Our Lord one thousand eight hundred and eighty-six, be entitled to be registered on the list of voters for any electoral district or portion thereof in Canada, being a city or town or part of a city

---

B. 194. A windmill stood in a common upon a plot of grass ground, large enough to clear the wings, enclosed by a fence put up by the voter. It was fixed on a post upon pattens in a foundation of brickwork. Nothing was shewn as to whether the plot of ground did or did not belong to the voter. Vote held good. *Bedfordshire Election (Marshall's Case)*, 2 Luders, 441.

(u) "*A public holiday or holiday under 'The Interpretation Act'*"—The holidays under the Interpretation Act (31 Vic. cap 1, s. 7, *Fifteenthly*) are Sundays, New Year's Day, the Epiphany, the Annunciation, Good Friday, the Ascension, *Corpus Christi*, St. Peter and St. Paul's Day, all Saint's Day, Conception Day, Easter Monday, Ash Wednesday, Christmas Day, the Birthday of the reigning Sovereign, and any day appointed by Proclamation for a general Fast or Thanksgiving. To these must be added the First day of July, or when that day falls on Sunday, the second day of July which is made a "holiday under 'The Interpretation Act'" by 42 Vic. cap. 47. It may be open to question whether the words "a public holiday" would include a holiday set apart or proclaimed by Provincial Acts or authority, or by Municipal authority. It is conceived they would not.

or town, or including any city or town or part of a city or town, and when so registered to vote at any election for such district, if such person—

(1.) Is of the full age of twenty-one years (*v*), and is not by this Act (*w*) or by any law of the Dominion of Canada (*x*), disqualified or prevented from Age.

(*v*) "*Full age of twenty-one years*"—The full age of 21 years is completed on the day preceding the twenty-first anniversary of a person's birth (*Anon*, 1 Salk. 44). A person born on the 16th Aug. 1725, who died on the 15th Aug. 1746, was held to have lived to attain the age of 21 years. (*Toder* v. *Sansam*, 1 Brown's P. C. 468).

(*w*) "*By this Act.*"—As to who are disqualified by this Act. See sec. 11, *post*.

(*x*) "*By any law of the Dominion of Canada.*"—Persons who have been found guilty of any corrupt practice are disqualified from voting for eight years. See chapter on "Penalties" under Dominion law, *post*. As to what are corrupt practices, see chapters on "Corrupt Practices," *post*, also, note to sec. 11, *post*. It is believed that this section and section 58, *post*, in effect repeal sec. 40 and the latter part of sec. 133 of the Dominion Elections Act, 1874, whereby "all persons qualified to vote at the election of representatives in the House of Assembly or Legislative Assembly of the several provinces, composing the Dominion of Canada, *and no others*," (sec. 40) were given the franchise for Dominion elections. Under the Provincial laws certain persons are expressly disqualified; for instance, under the Ontario Act (Rev. Stats. c. 10, s. 4), besides the judges, the following officials are disqualified, all officers of the Customs of the Dominion of Canada, all clerks of the Peace, County Attorneys, Registrars, Sheriffs, Deputy-Sheriffs, Deputy Clerks of the Crown, and agents for the sale of Crown lands, all postmasters in cities and towns, and all officers employed in the collection of duties payable to Her Majesty in the nature of duties of excise. These may be said to have been disqualified under a "*law of the Dominion of Canada*," as their disqualification was adopted by the sections of the Dominion Elections Act above referred to. But, as these sections are repealed as above mentioned, they can no longer, it is conceived, be termed a "law of the Dominion of Canada," and the persons disqualified by the Provincial laws will be no longer, *ipso facto*, disqualified from voting for members of the House of Commons, unless they come within section 11, *post*. Of the officials disqualified under the Ontario law, as above, the judges only are named in sec. 11, consequently all the others will, it is presumed, be entitled to vote, except when acting as returning officers, election clerks, etc. (See sec. 11, sub-s (b). It may be said that inasmuch as sec. 58, *post*, only provides that the previous "*qualification* of voters at such elections and the lists of voters" are to be superseded by those prescribed by this Act, without mentioning previous *disqualifications*, the repeal of the latter cannot be implied, unless they be held to be "inconsistent with this Act." Yet it is conceived that the effect of the sections referred to is as has been stated, and that a law repealed by a subsequent section of this Act cannot be held to be a *law of the Dominion of Canada* within subs. (1) of sec. 3.

Allegiance.

voting (*y*), and

(2.) Is a British subject by birth or naturalization (*z*), and

---

(*y*) "*Voting.*"—See Interpretation. *ante.*

(*z*) "*A British subject by birth or naturalization.*"—By the Common Law of England every person born within the dominions of the Crown, no matter whether of English or foreign parents, and in the latter case, whether the parents were settled or merely temporarily sojourning in the country, was an English subject, save only the children of foreign ambassadors (who were excepted because their fathers carried their own nationality with them), or a child born to a foreigner during the hostile occupation of any part of the territories of England (*Howell on Naturalization*, p. 8). This was modified and extended by the statutes 25 Edw. III., st. 2; 7 Anne, cap. 5; 4 Geo. III., cap. 21; 13 Geo. III., cap. 21. By these Acts the status of British subjects was conferred upon the children and grandchildren of British subjects born out of the dominions of the Crown; while the children of those subjects who, at the time of those children's births, were traitors, or felons, or engaged in war against the Crown, were excluded. It was further held that the child of an English merchant, born beyond the sea, by a foreign wife, was a natural born subject. *Collingwood* v. *Pace*, 1 Ventris 427. The law as above briefly defined became the law of the Provinces of New Brunswick, Nova Scotia (See *Salter* v. *Hughes*, Oldright's Rep. 409), Prince Edward Island, British Columbia and Ontario, the first four being acquired by settlement which carried with it the laws of the mother country, while these laws were introduced into Ontario by the change from French to English law in 1792. A like result in Quebec flowed from the cession of Canada by the French to the English (see 36th Article of Capitulation of Canada between Major-General Amherst and the Marquis de Vaudreuil and Treaty of Paris, 1763) *Chapman* v. *Hall*, Cowper's Reports, 204), and the Civil Code of 1865, which latter provides that, "a person born in any part of the British Empire, even if an alien, is a British subject by right of birth, as also he whose father or grandfather, by the father's side, is a British subject, although he be himself born in a foreign country; saving the exceptions resulting from special laws of the Empire." The Imperial Statute conferring the status of British subjects on grandchildren born abroad was repealed by the Imperial Act of 1870, and the effect of that repeal is said to be that such grandchildren born after 1870 would be aliens in all the Provinces other than Ontario and Quebec, where the law as introduced in 1792 and 1865 respectively would remain unaltered by the English repealing statute (*Canada Law Times*, vol. 1, p. 17).

The old maxim "Once a British subject, always a British subject," involving sometimes the anomaly of double allegiance, was affirmed in Canada by Robinson, C. J., in *Doe d. Hay* v. *Hunt*, (11 U. C. R. 381), and its subsequent relaxation was noticed by Draper, C. J., in *Reg.* v. *McMahon*, 26 U. C. R. 195, though he referred to the rule of indelible allegiance as still prevailing in the Province, while in the case of *Regina* v. *Lynch* (26 U. C. R. 208) the maxim was recognized as being the law of the Province. The Imperial Statute of 1870 made the law consistent with modern views, by providing for change of allegiance both by British subjects and aliens, and this statute may be regarded as the parent of the Dominion Statute of 1881 (44 Vic. cap 13) which recognizes the following: 1. British subjects by birth. 2. By naturalization (sec. 17). 3. By "declaration of British nationality," made within two years after coming into force of the Act by persons naturalized in foreign state before the Act, but desirous of remaining British subjects (sec. 9, sub-s. 1). 4. By special certificate, where nationality as a British subject is doubtful (sec. 18). 5. By certificate under the Act obtained by persons who were naturalized previously to the Act, (sec. 19). 6. By resumption of British nationality, *i e.*, where a "statutory alien" obtains a "certificate of re-admission to British nationality" (sec. 20).* 7. By naturalization, where the foreign state of which he was a subject, having by a convention, or by its laws recognized the right of expatriation, by such convention or laws, requires a residence or service in Canada of more than three years as a condition precedent to its subjects divesting themselves of their status as such subjects, and an oath has been taken and certificate granted, shewing residence or service for such period (sec. 24). 8. By naturalization, where an alien, who, whether under this Act or otherwise, has become entitled to the privileges of British birth in Canada, and desiring to divest himself of his status as a subject of a foreign state, takes the oath of residence or service for the period of time required by such convention or laws of foreign state (sec. 25). 9. By re-admission within Canada of a widow, who being a natural born British subject, is deemed to be a statutory alien in consequence of her marriage, (sec. 27). 10. Children of parents naturalized within Canada, becoming resident during infancy. 11. Children of parents who have been re-admitted to British nationality. (*Howell on Naturalization*, pp. 9 and 10). Section 10 and following secs. to sec. 15 inclusive, of the Act of 1881, provide for the ordinary proceedings for naturalization of aliens to be now followed, and the period of residence fixed by order in Council as mentioned in sec. 10, is five years immediately preceding the taking of the oaths. A much simpler and speedier mode for those aliens who resided in the older provinces on or before 1st July 1867, or in Rupert's Land or the N. W. Territories on or before 15th July, 1870, or in British Columbia on or before 20th July 1871, or in Prince Edward Island on or before 1st July, 1873, to be become naturalized, is prescribed by sec. 42.

It is presumed that resident and assessed inhabitants of the Province are British subjects till something is shewn to the contrary, from which it can be determined that they are aliens, *Queen ex. rel. Carrol* v. *Beckwith*, 1 U. C. P. R. 284. But proof of foreign birth raises a presumption of alienage which must be rebutted by proof of naturalization of the alien, and that presumption cannot be rebutted by proof that the person assumed to vote as a naturalized subject and even took the oath at a previous election. Our statutes for the naturalization of aliens provide means of preserving and furnishing to the alien the proof of his naturalization, and for the reception of that proof whenever the fact has to be established by evidence, *Schenck's vote, Lincoln* (2), 1 H. E. C. 500. Where a voter in support of his own vote swore that he was born in the U. S., but that his parents were British subjects, and that he derived the knowledge of both facts from his parents—*Held*, that his whole statement must be taken together and vote good—*Mulrennan's vote.*—*Ib.* The evidence of a voter that he understood from his parents that he was born in the

Ownership.

(3.) Is the owner (*a*) of real property (*b*) within any such city or part of a city, of the actual value of three hundred dollars, or within any such town or part of a town, of the actual value of two hundred dollars;—or

Tenancy.

(4.) Is the tenant (*c*) of any real property within any such city or town (*d*) or part of a city or town, under a lease (*e*) at a monthly rental of at least two dollars, or at a quarterly rental of at least six dollars, or at a half-yearly rental of at least twelve dollars, or at an annual rental of at least twenty dollars, and has been in possession thereof (*f*) as such tenant for at least one year next before the first day of January, in the year of Our Lord one thousand eight hundred and eighty-six or in any

U. S., but that his father was born in Canada, and that he (the voter) had lived in Canada from infancy, received, and vote held good, *Wright's vote, Brockville*, 1 H. E. C. 138; see also *Place's vote, Stormont*, 1 H. E. C. 21; *Reg. ex. rel. McVean* v. *Graham*, 7 U. C. L. J. 125; *Doe dem. Hay* v. *Hunt*, 11 U. C. Q. B. 367. A person born in the U. S. before the Revolution who continued to reside there was held to be an alien, *Doe d. Patterson* v. *Davis*, 5 O. S. 494; *Doe dem. Thomas* v. *Acklan*, 2 B. & C. 779; see also *Doe d. Robinson* v. *Clarke*, 1 U. C. Q. B. 37; but see *Stewart* v. *Roome*, 6 Dict. of decisions 4649. An alien who came to Canada in 1850, and had taken the oath of allegiance in 1861, but had taken no proceedings to obtain a certificate of naturalization, was held not entitled to vote—*Bacon's vote, Brockville*, 1 H. E. C. 129. A voter born in the U. S. whose father (an alien) had taken the oath of allegiance on obtaining the patent for his land under 9 Geo. IV. cap. 21—*Held*, not qualified to vote, *Healey's vote.—Ib.* A Justice of the Peace appointed under a commission for the town only, and not for the county, has authority to administer the oaths required by the Act of 1871 outside the town, but within the county—*Johnson's vote, Lincoln* (2), 1 H. E. C. 572.

(*a*) "*Owner.*"—See Interpretation, *ante*, and notes.

(*b*) "*Real property.*"—See Interpretation, *ante*.

(*c*) "*Tenant.*"—See Interpretation, *ante* and notes.

(*d*) "*City or Town.*"—See Interpretation, *ante*.

(*e*) "*Lease.*"—i. e. either a verbal or written letting. Under the Ontario Act the franchise is given to owners, tenants and occupants of property worth, in cities and towns, $200; and in incorporated villages and townships, $100; and the amount of rental does not govern, except in so far as it is an evidence of value.

(*f*) "*In possession thereof.*"—See note to sec. 2, "*tenant*," *ante*.

subsequent year, and has really and *bonâ fide* (*g*) paid one year's rent for such real property at not less than the rate aforesaid: Provided, that the year's rent so required to be paid to entitle such tenant to vote shall be the year's rent up to the last yearly, half-yearly, quarterly or monthly day of payment, as the case may be, which shall have occurred next before the date of the certificate of the final revision of the list of voters made by the revising officer as hereinafter mentioned; except where the rental is an annual one and for a larger sum than twenty dollars, in which case at least twenty dollars of the last year's rent which shall have accrued next before the date of the said certificate must have been paid; and provided also, that a change of tenancy (*h*) during the year

Proviso; as to rent.

Proviso; as to change of tenancy.

(*g*) "*Bona fide.*"—Where the voter had been originally, before 1865 or 1866, put upon the assessment roll merely to give a man a vote, but by a subsequent arrangement, the occupancy became a *bona fide* one; *Held*, that if he had been put on originally merely for the purpose of giving a vote, and that was the vote questioned, it would have been bad, but having been continued several years after he really became the occupant for his own benefit, he was entitled to vote.—*Stormont* (*Gore's vote*), 1 H. E. C. 21. See note to sec. 27 of Ontario Voters' Lists Act, *post.*

(*h*) "*Change of tenancy.*"—The English Redistribution of Seats Act, 1885, s. 10, contains a provision that "the occupation in immediate succession of different pre- "mises situate within a Parliamentary borough shall, for the purposes of qualifying "a person for voting in any division of such borough, in respect of occupation "(otherwise than as a lodger), have the same effect as if all such premises were "situate in that division of the borough in which the premises occupied by such "person at the end of the period of qualification are situate." A question has been mooted, whether having regard to the provisions of the English Act, the occupation of premises in immediate succession in different divisions of a county (as to which there is no similar provision to the above regarding tenants in boroughs), instead of in the same division or constituency, will, after the first registration, qualify. See Hunt's Fran. and Reg. Law, p. 2. It may be remarked that the Reform Act of 1832 and the Rep. of People Act of 1867 contained provisions permitting registration of persons who occupied different premises in immediate succession, the former as to boroughs, the latter as to counties. By the Act of 1878 (41 and 42 V., c. 26, s. 6, subs. 2), a *lodger's* "successive occupation" must be of lodgings *in the*

shall not deprive the tenant of the right to vote if such change is without any intermission of time, and the several tenancies are such as would entitle the tenant to vote had such tenant been in possession under either of them, as such tenant, for the year next before the date of the said certificate; and provided further that where on any revised or final assessment roll the amount of the tenant's rent is not stated, the fact that the real property in respect of which he is entered on such roll as the tenant thereof is assessed in cities at three hundred dollars or more, or in towns at two hundred dollars or more, shall be *primâ facie* evidence of his right to be registered as a voter;—or

Proviso; as to valuation of property on assessment roll.

Occupancy.

(5.) Is the *bona fide* occupant (*i*) of real property within any such city or part of a city, of the actual value of three hundred dollars, or within any such town or part of a town of the actual value of two hundred dollars, whether such occupation is under a license of occupation or agreement to purchase from the Crown or from any other person or corporation, or exists in any other manner except as owner or tenant: Provided in any case, that such person has been in possession (*j*) of such real property as such occupant for one year next before the first day of January, in the year of Our Lord one thousand eight hundred and eighty-six or in any

Proviso.

---

same house. It may be argued that the "several tenancies" referred to in the sub-section now under review, must be of premises all of which are within the "city or town or part of a city or town" which forms the electoral district, or which is included therein, in the absence of a provision similar to that contained in the English Act of 1885 regarding the borough franchise, above quoted. See sec. 4, subs. (4) *post*.

(*i*) "*Occupant*."—See Interpretation and note, *ante*.

(*j*) "*Possession*."—See Interpretation, note "*occupant*," *ante*.

subsequent year, and is and has been for such time in the enjoyment of the revenues and profits thereof, for the use of such occupant, or in the case of a married man, for his own use or for the use of his wife ; or— In case of married man.

(6.) Is a resident (*k*) within such city or town, or part Residence.

(*k*) "*Is a resident.*"—"To constitute a residence, a party must possess at least a sleeping apartment, but an uninterrupted abiding is not requisite, and absence, no matter how long, if there be the liberty of returning at any time, and no abandonment of the intention to return whenever it may suit the party's pleasure or convenience so to do, will not prevent a constructive legal residence." This is the definition of "residence" in the 27th sec. of the English Act of 1832, adopted by Erle, C. J., from Elliott on Registration, 2nd ed., p. 204, in *Powell* v. *Guest*, 34 L. J., C. P. 69. Sleeping elsewhere for the purpose of business, if the lodgings have been occupied by the family of the lodger, and if he be not deprived of the power of returning, is no break of residence, *Taylor* v. *Kensington Overseers*, L. R. 6, C. P. 309 ; 40 L. J., C. P. 45 ; 23 L. T. 493 ; 19 W. R. 100 ; 1 H. & C. 421 ; see also *Bond* v. *St. George, Hanover Square Overseers*, L. R. 6, C. P. 312 ; 40 L. J., C. P. 47 ; 23 L. T. 494 ; 19 W. R. 101 ; 1 H. & C. 427. The residence need not be continuous, nor need it be by the party himself ; but if it be quitted, or if his family or servants only be resident for part of the time, there must be a *bona fide* intention on his part to return *Whitehom* v. *Thomas*, 7 M. and G. 1. A clergyman who exchanges duties and residences with another clergyman breaks his residence. *Ford* v. *Pye*, L. R. 9, C. P. 269 ; 43 L. J., C. P. 21 ; 29 L. T., 584 ; 22 W. R. 159 ; 2 H. & C. 157 ; and so does a rector who remains abroad under a license of non-residence. *Durant* v. *Carter*, L. R. 9, C. P. 261 ; 43 L. J., C. P. 17 ; 2 H & C. 142. And a man detained in a gaol more than seven miles from a borough under a sentence of imprisonment without the option of a fine, *Powell* v. *Guest*, 18, C. B. (N.S.) 72 ; 33 L. J., C. P. 69. An articled clerk, articled to a London Solicitor, who had had a bedroom kept for his exclusive use at his father's house in Exeter, and who was absent under his articles during part of the six months mentioned in sec. 31 of 2 Will. IV, c. 45, was held to have broken his residence because his articles were deemed to prevent him from being at liberty to return when he pleased. *Ford* v. *Drew*, 5 C. P. D. 59 ; 49 L. J., C. P. 172 ; 41 L. T, 478 ; 28 W. R. 137. An officer in the army, serving with his regiment, who when he obtained leave of absence, lived in his mother's house in apartments reserved for his use, and had no other home, was held to be subject to the will and pleasure of the Crown as to residence, and therefore not capable of acquiring a constructive residence. *Ford* v. *Hart*, L. R. 9, C. P. 273 ; 43 L. J., C. P. 24 ; 29 L. T. 685 ; 22 W. R. 159 ; 2 H. and C. 167. See also *Beal* v *Ford*, 3 C. P. D. 73 ; 47 L J., C. P. 56 ; 37 L. T. 408 ; 2 H & C. 374. *Regina* v. *Norwood*, L. R. 2, Q. B. 457. *Oldham Election*, (*Baxter's case*) 1 O'M. & H. 158.

of a city or town, and derives an income (*l*) from his earnings, or from some trade, calling, office or profession, or from some investment in Canada, of not less than three hundred dollars annually, and has so derived such income and has been such resident for one year next before the said first day of January, in the year of Our Lord one thousand eight hundred and eighty-six, or in any subsequent year; or—

As son of owner.

(7.) Is the son of any owner of real property (*m*) and not otherwise qualified to vote, and

If father is living.

(*a*.) If his father (*n*) is living, is and has been resident upon such property continuously with his father, being such owner, in such city or town or part of a city or town for one year next before the first of January, in the year of Our Lord one thousand eight hundred and eighty-six, or in any subsequent year, if the real property on which his father resides and in respect of which such father is qualified to vote under this Act as owner, is of sufficient value if equally divided amongst them as co-owners, to qualify them as voters under this Act, in which case both the father and such one or more sons as may desire may be so registered as voters; and if the said real property is not of sufficient value to give the father and each of several sons the right to vote in respect of such value when equally divided, then the right to be regis-

If value not sufficient to qualify all sons

(*l*) "*Income.*"—This word in its natural and commonly accepted sense means the balance of gain over loss, *Lawless* v. *Sullivan*, L. R. 6 App. Cases 373, reversing judgments of Supreme Courts of Canada and New Brunswick in regard to the interpretation of that term in the Assessment Acts of the latter Province.

(*m*) "*Son of an owner of real property.*"—See Interpretation, *ante*.

(*n*) "*Father.*"—See Interpretation, *ante*.

tered as a voter and to vote in respect of such real property shall belong only to the father or to the father and the eldest or such of the elder sons, being so resident as aforesaid, as the value of the real property when equally divided will qualify; —or

(b.) If his father is dead, is and has been resident upon such property continuously with his father, or his mother (o) after the death of his father (being such owner) (p) in such city or town or part of a city or town, for one year next before the first day of January in the year of our Lord, one thousand eight hundred and eighty-six, or in any subsequent year, if the real property on which his father (or his mother after the death of his father) resided or resides, and in respect of which such father would be qualified to vote under this Act as owner if living, is of sufficient value if equally divided among all of his sons as co-owners, to qualify them as voters under this Act, in which case such one or more sons as may desire may be so registered as voters; and if the said real property is not of sufficient value to give each of several sons the right to vote in respect of such value when equally divided, then the right to be registered as a voter and to vote in respect of such real property shall belong only to the eldest or such of the elder sons, being so resident as aforesaid, as the value of the real property when equally divided will qualify:—

If father is dead.

Mother being owner.

If value not sufficient to qualify all sons

(o) "*Mother.*"—See Interpretation, *ante.*

(p) ("*Being such owner.*")—These words evidently refer to "mother," see the expression "or his mother after the death of his father," further on, also s. 4, sub-s. 7, (b) *post.*

Proviso; as to residence, and as to absence.

Provided, that in either case, in order to entitle him to vote, each such son must at the time of the election for the electoral district in which he tenders his vote, be so resident with his father (or mother after the death of his father); but occasional absence of a son from the residence of the father or mother, for not more in all than six months in the year, shall not disqualify such son as a voter under this Act.

IN COUNTIES.

Who shall be registered as voters, if qualified as to—

4. Every person shall, upon and after the first day of January in the year of Our Lord one thousand eight hundred and eighty-six, be entitled to be registered on the list of voters for any electoral district or portion thereof in Canada, other than a city or town or portion of a city or town, and when so registered to vote at any election for such electoral district, if such person—

Age.

(1.) Is of the age of twenty-one years and is not by this Act or by any law of the Dominion of Canada disqualified or prevented from voting; and

Allegiance.

(2.) Is a British subject by birth or naturalization; and

Ownership.

(3.) Is the owner of real property within any such electoral district of the actual value of one hundred and fifty dollars;—or

Tenancy.

(4.) Is the tenant of any real property (*q*) within any such electoral district, under a lease, at a monthly rental of at least two dollars, or at a quarterly rental of at least six dollars, or at a half-yearly rental of at least twelve dollars, or at an annual

(*q*) "*Tenant of any real property.*"—See *ante*.

rental of at least twenty dollars, in money, in kind or in money's worth (r) of like value (except when the real property is situated in an incorporated village, in which case the rental must be payable in money only), and has been in possession thereof as such tenant for at least one year next before the first day of January in the year of Our Lord one thousand eight hundred and eighty-six or in any subsequent year, and has really and *bona fide* paid one year's rent for such real property at not less than the rate aforesaid: Provided, that the year's rent so required to be paid to entitle such tenant to vote shall be the year's rent up to the last yearly, half-yearly, quarterly or monthly day of payment, as the case may be, which shall have occurred next before the date of the certificate of the final revision of the list of voters made by the revising officer as hereinafter mentioned; except where the rental is an annual one and for a larger sum than twenty dollars, in which case at least twenty dollars of the last year's rent which shall have accrued next before the date of the said certificate must have been paid; and provided also, that a change of tenancy *(s)* during the year shall not deprive the tenant of the right to vote, if such change is without any intermission of time, and the several tenancies are such as would entitle the tenant to vote had such tenant been in possession under either of them, as such tenant, for the year next before the date of the said certificate: Provided further, that where on any revised or final assessment roll

Proviso; as to rent.

Exception.

Proviso; as to change of tenancy.

Proviso; if rent is not stated.

(r) "*In money, in kind or in money's worth.*" See Interpretation, "Tenant," *ante.*

(s) "*Change of tenancy.*"—See note to same words in sec. 3, sub-s. 4, *ante.*

the amount of a tenant's rent is not stated, the fact that the real property in respect of which he is entered on such roll as tenant thereof is assessed at one hundred and fifty dollars, or over that sum, shall be held to be *prima facie* evidence of his right to be registered as a voter; or—

Occupancy.

(5) Is the *bona fide* occupant of real property within such electoral district of the actual value of one hundred and fifty dollars, whether such occupation be under a license of occupation or agreement to purchase from the Crown or from any other person or corporation, or exists in any other manner except as owner or tenant: Provided in any case, that such person has been in possession of such real property as such occupant, for one year next before the first day of January in the year of Our Lord one thousand eight hundred and eighty-six, or in any subsequent year, and is and has been for the said time in the enjoyment of the revenues and profits thereof for the use of such occupant, or in the case of a married man for his own use or for the use of his wife; or—

Proviso; as to length of possession.

Residence and income.

(6.) Is a resident within such electoral district, and derives an income from his earnings in money or money's worth, or from some trade, office, calling, or profession or from some investment in Canada, of not less than three hundred dollars annually, and has so derived such income and has been such resident for one year next before the said first day of January in the year of Our Lord one thousand eight hundred and eighty-six or in any subsequent year; or—

(7.) Is a farmer's son (*t*) not otherwise qualified to vote; and— **As a farmer's son.**

(*a.*) If his father is living, is and has been resident continuously on the farm of his father, in such electoral district, for one year next before the first day of January in the year of our Lord one thousand eight hundred and eighty-six or in any subsequent year, if the said farm is of sufficient value, if equally divided amongst them as co-owners, to qualify them as voters under this Act, in which case the father, and such one or more sons as may desire may be registered on the list of voters; and if there be more than one son resident as aforesaid on the farm, and claiming to be registered as voters in respect thereof, and the farm is not of sufficient value to give the father and each of such sons the right to vote in respect of such value when equally divided, then the right to be registered as a voter and to vote in respect of the farm shall belong only to the father or to the father and the eldest or such of the elder of the sons, being so resident as aforesaid, as the value of the farm when equally divided will qualify; or— **If father is living.** **Case of several sons; and value of property not sufficient to qualify all.**

(*t*) "*Farmer's son.*"—The enfranchisement of this class was introduced in Ontario by 40 Vic. c. 9 of the Statutes of that Province. It was considered that the sons of farmers residing at home with their parents had practically an interest in the farm, which in many cases had been promised and in others willed to them, though the parent continued to be the legal owner. In such cases the sons were held entitled to vote as tenants, but in the majority of cases the relation of landlord and tenant could not be made out, and the son could not consequently qualify for the franchise, though an arrangement often existed by which the son was to become in time the owner of the farm. As the farmers' sons were as a rule intelligent, industrious and permanent residents of the Province, the franchise was extended to them by the above Act; but no similar franchise was conferred upon the sons of any other class of property owners. By this Act and the Ontario Fran. and Rep. Act of 1885. the right to vote is extended on like conditions to the sons of other landowners in cities, towns or elsewhere, thus doing away with the objection which formerly existed—that one class was enfranchised while another under similar circumstances was not. The young men of the cities and towns had formerly also to pay a tax by 31 Dec. preceding the election in order to entitle them to vote on income. This provision of the Ontario Act is now also repealed, while no such provision exists in this Act.

If father is dead

(*b*.)* If his father is dead,—is and has been resident continuously on the farm of his father (or mother after the death of his father) in such electoral district, for one year next before the first day of January, in the year of our Lord eighteen hundred and eighty-six, or in any subsequent year, if the said farm is of sufficient value, if equally divided among all of the sons of such father as co-owners, to qualify them as voters under this Act, in which case such one or more sons as may desire may be registered on the list of voters;—and if there be more than one son resident as aforesaid on the farm and claiming to be registered as voters in respect thereof, and the farm is not of sufficient value to give each of such sons the right to vote in respect of such value when equally divided, then the right to be registered as a voter and to vote in respect of the farm, shall belong only to the eldest or such of the elder of the sons, being so resident as aforesaid, as the value of the farm when so equally divided will qualify:

Case of more than one son; and value of property not sufficient to qualify all.

Proviso; as to residence and absence.

Provided that, in either case, in order to entitle him to vote, the son must at the time of the election for the electoral district in which he tenders his vote, be so resident with his father (or mother after the death of his father); but occasional absence of a son from the farm for not more in all than six months in the year shall not disqualify such son under this Act as a voter;—or

A son of owner, not a farmer.

(8.) Is the son of any owner of real property in such electoral district, other than a farm (and not otherwise qualified to vote) and—

If father is living.

(*a*.) If his father is living,—is and has been resident

upon such property continuously with his father, being such owner, for one year next before the first day of January in the year of our Lord one thousand eight hundred and eighty-six, or in any subsequent year, if the real property on which his father resides and in respect of which such father is qualified to vote under this Act as owner, is of sufficient value if equally divided amongst them as co-owners, to qualify them as voters under this Act, in which case both the father and such one or more sons as may desire may be registered as voters; and if the said property be not of sufficient value to give the father and each of such sons the right to vote in respect of such value when equally divided, then the right to be registered as a voter and to vote in respect of such real property shall belong only to the father, or to the father and the eldest or such of the elder of the sons, being so resident as aforesaid, as the value of the real property when equally divided will qualify; or—

If value not sufficient to qualify all sons.

(*b.*) If his father is dead,—is and has been resident upon such property continuously with his father (or his mother after the death of his father) being such owner, for one year next before the first day of January in the year of our Lord one thousand eight hundred and eighty-six, or in any subsequent year, if the real property on which his father (or his mother after the death of his father) resided or resides, and in respect of which such father would be qualified to vote under this Act as owner if living, is of sufficient value, if equally divided amongst all his sons as co-owners, to

If father is dead

qualify them as voters under this Act, in which case such one or more sons as may desire may be registered as voters;—and if the said property be not of sufficient value to give each of such sons the right to vote in respect of such value when equally divided, then the right to be registered as a voter and to vote in respect of such real property shall belong only to the eldest or such of the elder of the sons, being so resident as aforesaid, as the value of the real property when equally divided will qualify:

If value of property insufficient to qualify all sons.

Provided that, in either case, in order to enable him to vote, such son must, at the time of the election for the electoral district in which he tenders his vote, be so resident with his father (or mother after the death of his father); but occasional absence of the son from the residence of the father or mother for not more in all than six months in the year, shall not disqualify such son as a voter under this Act; or—

Proviso; as to residence and as to absence.

(9.) Is a fisherman, (*u*) and is the owner of real property and boats, nets, fishing gear and tackle within any such electoral district, which together are of the actual value of one hundred and fifty dollars.

Fishermen.

APPLICABLE TO ALL ELECTORAL DISTRICTS.

5. The qualifications required of voters under section three, shall apply to voters in a city or town or the part of a city or town attached to a county or riding of a county in any electoral district, for electoral purposes

In a city or town attached to a county or riding.

(*u*) "*Fisherman*."—This provision is intended to enfranchise a class of voters, chiefly in the maritime provinces, whose vocation is such that they do not acquire much property in the shape of real estate.

under this Act, and the qualifications required of voters under section four, shall apply to voters in such municipalities or places not being cities or towns or portions of cities or towns, as are attached to or included for electoral purposes in cities or towns or portions of cities or towns.

Joint tenancy, in common, or other co-tenancy

6. Whenever two or more persons are, either as business partners, joint tenants, tenants in common, or by any other kind of joint interest, (*v*) the owners, tenants or occupants of any lot or portion of a lot or parcel of real property in any electoral district, each of such persons whose share therein is sufficient (*w*) in value, or in the case of tenants, in amount of rent, according to the provisions of this Act, to qualify such person as a voter in respect of real property, shall be entitled to be registered on the list of voters, and to vote in respect of such share as if it were held in such person's individual name, and not jointly with one or more.

Place of registry

7. Persons qualified under this Act as voters in res-

(*v*) "*Any other kind of joint interest.*"—This, it is conceived, will not entitle members of joint stock incorporated companies to vote on the companies' property, even where the property is sufficient in value, if divided among all the shareholders to give each one the necessary qualification; see Nova Scotia Fran. Act, 1885, s. 5; Quebec El. Act, 38 Vic., c. 7, s. 10; Manitoba Act, Res. Leg. Assembly (Consol'd.) s. 63, *post.*

(*w*) "*Whose share therein is sufficient.*"—If A and B possessed together property of the value of $300, A for a third, and B for two-thirds, B could vote, but not A, and the same as to rent; *Electoral Lists of Kamouraska*, 3 Q. L. R. 308, S. C. 1877. B's qualification would not however in the above case be sufficient in value to give a vote in a city, under this Act. The provision under this sec. is similar to that under the Quebec Act, 38 Vic., c. 7, s. 9; Manitoba Act, s. 62. Under the Nova Scotia Act of 1885, the property is apportioned according "to the best of the assessors' judgment," (s. 5), while under the new Ontario Act all or none of the partners must have votes. See Ont. Fran. and Representation Act, 1885, s. 3, subs. "Firstly" (3) *post.* See also Prince Edward Island Act, 34 Vic. c. 34, s. 14. Where two or more partners were in business and one of them owned the freehold, where the business was carried on, both partners could under the former Ontario law vote, if the assessment were sufficient, *South Grenville Election, Fitzgerald's vote*, 1 H. E. C. 165.

for voters. pect of income shall only be registered as voters and vote in the polling district where they reside at the time of registration; and persons qualified otherwise than on income shall only be registered as voters and vote in the polling district where the real property in respect of which they are qualified is situate; but when the property is partly within one polling district and partly within another, although all within one electoral district, the person qualified in respect thereof shall be entitled to be registered and to vote in either of such polling districts for which he may desire to be registered as a voter.

Property extending into more than one polling district.

As to time spent by sons as mariners, fishermen or students.

8. In the case of the sons of farmers, or of owners other than farmers, the time spent by such sons as mariners or fishermen in the prosecution of their several occupations, or as students in any institution of learning within the Dominion of Canada, shall be considered as spent at home *(wa)*.

Special provisions as to B. C. and P. E. I.

9. In the Provinces of British Columbia and Prince Edward Island *(wb)*, besides the persons entitled to be registered as voters and to vote under the foregoing provisions of this Act, every person who at the time of the passing of the same :—

Age.

(1.) Is of the age of twenty-one years and is not by this Act or by any law of the Dominion of Canada disqualified or prevented from voting, and

British subject.

(2.) Is a British subject by birth or naturalization and resident in the Province, and is entitled to

---

(wa) See Nova Scotia Fran. Act (1885), s. 3.

(wb) British Columbia and Prince Edward Island are the only provinces which have been allowed to retain their Provincial Franchise laws in respect to Dominion Elections. The provisions of their respective franchise Acts will be found in subsequent chapters. The system of registration provided by this Act will, however, prevail hereafter, for Dominion purposes, in these, as in the other provinces.

vote in the said Provinces respectively by the laws now severally existing in the same,

Shall have a right to be registered as a voter and to vote so long as he shall continue to be qualified to vote under the provisions of the said last mentioned laws and no longer. Registration as voters.

10. Except the persons duly qualified and registered as voters under this Act, no person shall be entitled to vote at any election for the House of Commons of Canada after the time when the duplicates of the first list of voters, finally revised and certified as hereinafter provided, for the electoral district for which the election is to be held, shall have been forwarded to the Clerk of the Crown in Chancery at Ottawa, as also hereinafter provided:—but at any election held before the time aforesaid, the voters shall be those entitled to vote thereat under the laws now in force, (*x*) which shall continue to apply to such election and all proceedings thereat or relating thereto. No voters for H. C. but those qualified under this Act after a certain time. Provision until such time.

WHO SHALL NOT VOTE AT ELECTIONS.

11. The following persons shall be disqualified and incompetent to vote (*y*) at any election to which this Act Persons disqualified as voters.

(*x*) "*Laws now in force.*"—The several provincial laws. See sec. 40 of The Elections Act, 1874.

(*y*) *Disqualified and incompetent to vote.*"—See as to further disqualifications, s. 3, subs. (1) and notes thereunder, *ante*, also chapter on "Penalties," *post*. By sections 31 and 39 the lists as finally revised "shall be binding on any judge or other tribunal appointed for the trial of any petition complaining of an undue return of a member to serve in the House of Commons." This is apparently intended to abolish all right to a scrutiny of the votes. If, therefore, the revising officer should insert the name of a disqualified person upon the list of voters and his name remains thereon after the final revision and such person votes, it would seem that his vote cannot be struck off, though he would be subject to the penalties prescribed by the election law and the revising officer would be subject to the penalty prescribed by section 63, *post*. It may well be doubted, however, whether the effect of the sections (31 and 39) with section 58 is to nullify the provisions of the Elections Act, which direct

applies, except that the persons or officers named in paragraph "b" of this section shall only be disqualified and incompetent to vote at elections for the electoral districts for which they hold such offices or positions respectively:

Judges.

(a) The Chief Justice and Judges of the Supreme Court of Canada, the Chief Justices and Judges of the Superior Courts in the Provinces of Canada, and the judges of all other courts in the said Provinces of Canada, and the judges of all other courts in the said Provinces, whether such courts are now in existence or are hereafter erected;

Election officers and agents, etc., of candidates.

(b.) Revising officers, returning officers, and election clerks, and any person who at any time either

---

that on proof of certain corrupt acts, a vote shall be struck off the votes polled for the candidate (who has by himself or his agents been proved guilty of corruption) for every person proved on the trial of an election petition to have been corrupted, (see 37 Vic. cap. 9, secs. 73, 94 and 96). It is true the Acts as to Elections, Controverted Elections and corrupt practices are "to apply to elections and proceedings thereat to which this Act is to apply" only "in so far as they are not inconsistent with this Act, and except always as to the qualfication of voters, which shall be those prescribed by this Act, and to which all the provisions of the said Acts which depend on such qualification shall be construed as referring"; while "all the provisions of the said Acts inconsistent with this Act" are "repealed," (see sec. 58, *post*); yet how can it be said that the provisions referred to are inconsistent with this Act where they provide for the subsequent disqualification of persons, properly qualified and registered under this Act, for deeds committed by such persons *after* such registration takes place? If they are, then it will be futile to claim the seat for any defeated candidate, on the ground that a sufficient number of such votes have been corrupted to change, if struck off, the result of the election in his favor. It may be that the lists will be held to be "binding" (under secs. 31 or 39) on the Election Courts, so far as the right, at the time of registration, of any voter—even one disqualified by virtue of his office or otherwise—to vote is concerned; *Stowe* v. *Joliffe*, L. R. 9 C. P. 734; 43 L. J. Rep. C. P. 265; *Hayward* v. *Scott*, 5 C. P. D. 231; *Ryder* v. *Hamilton*, L. R. 4 C. P. 559; 38 L. J. C. P. 260; 17 W. R. 795; but the question as to whether votes of persons at that time qualified, but whose subsequent corrupt acts disqualify them, can be struck off on the trial of a Petition, when the seat is claimed for the unsuccessful candidate, is one which will still remain for the Election Courts to decide. The Ontario Voters' List Finality Act, 41 Vic. c. 21, sec. 3, preserves the right of scrutiny in regard to this class of votes, and as to the votes of all disqualified persons. See also notes to sec. 31, *post*.

during the election or before the election is or has been employed (z) at the same election or in reference thereto by any candidate or by any person whomsoever, as counsel, agent, attorney or clerk at any polling place at any such election, or in any other capacity whatever, and who has received or expects to receive either before, during or after the said election from any candidate or from any person whomsoever for acting in any such capacity as aforesaid, any sum of money, fee, office, place or employment, or any promise, pledge or security whatever for any sum of money, fee, office, place or employment; except only that the returning officer may vote in the case of equality of votes between candidates, where the addition of a

Exception in cases of ties.

(z) "*Is or has been employed, etc.*"—Under similar English Acts (7 & 8 Geo. IV. c. 37; and 30 & 31 Vic., c. 102, s. 11) a solicitor who was a paid agent was held disqualified; *New Windsor* (*Barton's Case*), K. & Omb. 180. As was also an elector employed as a special messenger during the election, even where such was shown to be his ordinary calling, *Evesham Election, George's Case*, Fal. & Fitz. 527; and a check clerk employed and paid by one candidate, whose vote was even struck off another candidate who had not employed him; *Bedford, Wilcox's Case*, P. & K. 136, s. c. C. & R. 94. A town clerk who read the proclamation and sat in the polling-booth with the mayor during the election, and received payment therefor, was also held disqualified; *New Windsor, Secker's Case*, 185; but a constable who was a regular constable of the borough, and for whose services a sum of money was included in the town clerk's account to be paid to him, was not disqualified; *Ib. Lovegrove's Case*, K. & Omb. 183; nor the town sergeants of the corporation, paid out of the rates for their services at the election, *Ipswich* (*Cook's Case*), K. & Omb, 384, though two of them who acted as doorkeepers of a candidate's committee room were disqualified, *Ib.*; an elector who was employed to erect hustings and whose bill was afterwards paid was not disqualified, *Ib. Page's Case*, K. & Omb. 387, nor the paid leader of a band, *Monmouth, Partridge's Case, Ib.*, 421, nor a cabman, *Southampton*, 1 O'M. & H. 223; nor Printers also acting as messengers—*Northallerton*, 1 O'M. & H. 170. Employment of voters to keep order at the doors of the polling stations, however, disqualifies them—*Gloucester*, 2 O'M. & H. 62. See also *Charlevoix Case*, 5 Sup. Ct. 133. The employment of sons of voters as messengers, their wages being paid to their fathers, held to invalidate the fathers' votes—*Southampton*, 1 O'M. & H. 223. See also *Worcester*, K. & O. 246. See sec. 73 of the Dom. El. Act, 1874, also Imperial Ballot Act. 1872, s. 25.

vote would entitle any such candidate to be declared elected;

Certain Indians not qualified.

(c.) Indians in Manitoba, British Columbia, Keewatin and the North-West Territories, and any Indian on any reserve elsewhere in Canada who is not in possession and occupation of a separate and distinct tract (a) of land in such reserve, and whose improvements on such separate tract are not of the value of at least one hundred and fifty dollars, and who is not otherwise possessed of the qualifications entitling him to be registered on the list of voters under this Act.

WHEN REVISING OFFICER MAY NOT BE A CANDIDATE.

Revising officer may not be candidate.

12. No revising officer for any electoral district while he is a revising officer, or for two years thereafter, shall be qualified to be a candidate in any electoral district for which, or for any part of which, he has been such revising officer.

(a) "*Separate and distinct tract.*"—By the Indian Act, 1880, s. 17, no Indian shall be deemed to be lawfully possessed of any land in a reserve, unless he or she has been or shall be, located for the same by the band or council of the band, with the approval of the Superintendent-General: Provided, that no Indian shall be dispossessed of any land on which he or she has improvements, without receiving compensation therefor (at a valuation to be approved by the Supt.-Genl.), from the Indian, who obtains the land, or from the funds of the band, as may be determined by the Superintendent-General. Sec. 18,—On the Superintendent-General approving of any location aforesaid, he shall issue in triplicate a ticket granting a location to such Indian, one triplicate of which he shall retain in a book to be kept for the purpose; the other two he shall forward to the local agent—one to be delivered to the Indian in whose favor it was issued, the other to be filed by the agent, who shall also cause the same to be copied into a register of the band, to be provided for the purpose. S. 19.—The conferring of any such location title, as aforesaid, shall not have the effect of rendering the land covered thereby subject to seizure under legal process, and such title shall be transferrable only to an Indian of the same band, and then only with the consent and approval of the Supt.-General, which shall be given only by the issue of a ticket in the manner prescribed in the next preceding section. See resolution of meeting of Revising Officers for Ontario, *post*.

REGISTRATION OF VOTERS.

13. The Governor General in Council may, within three months after the coming into force of this Act, and from time to time thereafter, when the office is vacant, appoint a proper person to be called "the revising officer" (*b*), for each or any of the electoral districts of Canada, who shall hold office during good behaviour, but who shall be removable on address by the House of Commons (*c*), and whose duties shall be to prepare, revise and complete, in the manner hereinafter provided, the lists of persons entitled to vote under the provisions of this Act in such electoral district, and every such officer shall, before entering upon his duties, take an oath of office before any Judge of a Superior Court or Court of Record of the Province in which he is to act, in the form A contained in the Schedule to this Act, which he shall forthwith thereafter cause to be filed with the Clerk of the Crown in Chancery at Ottawa; and in the event of the death, resignation, removal, inability or refusal to act of any such revising offier, another may, in the same way, be appointed in his stead, who shall hold office under the same tenure, and with the same duties and powers.

Appointment of revising officers. Tenure of office. Their duties. Oath of office. Case of death or resignation, etc.

14. A revising officer to be appointed under this Act shall, in every Province except Quebec and British Columbia, be either a judge or a junior judge of some county or district court in the Province in which he is to act, or

Who may be appointed as such.

(*b*) "*The Revising Officer.*"—In England the Revising Barrister is a temporary official only. He is appointed by the Judges on Circuit. Here he is intended to be a permanent official like a Judge. At a recent meeting of the Revising Officers appointed for Ontario, attention was drawn to the fact of the absence of any provision for the working of the Act in the event of the temporary absence or illness of the Revising Officer.

(*c*) "*Address by the House of Commons.*"—The Judges of the Superior Courts are removable on address of the Senate and House of Commons (B. N. A. Act, s. 99.) The Revising Officer is to be amenable to the popular branch alone.

a barrister of at least five years' standing at the bar of such Province; in the Province of Quebec he shall be either a judge of the Superior Court for Lower Canada, or an advocate, or notary of that Province of at least five years' standing, and in the Province of British Columbia he shall be either a judge of a superior court or of a county or district court, or a barrister of at least five years' standing, or a stipendiary magistrate: Provided always, that the same revising officer may be appointed for, and be required to discharge the said duties in respect of more than one electoral district, and may be appointed for a portion of any electoral district.

Proviso; May be appointed for more or less than one district.

Duties of revising officer as to first list of voters.

15. The revising officer who prepares the first list of voters for any electoral district, or any portion thereof, under this Act, shall (*d*), as soon as possible after taking the oath of office, obtain a certified copy or certified copies, as the case may be, of the last revised or final assessment roll or rolls, if any there be, in the electoral district, or part of a district, for which he is appointed, and also a certified copy or certified copies of the last revised list or lists of voters in such electoral district or part of a district, prepared and revised under the Statutes of the Province (*e*) relating to assessments and voters' lists respectively, for elections to the Provincial Legislature, and, where there are no such lists (*f*), a certified copy or

To procure certain lists, etc.

(*d*) "*Shall.*"—See notes to sec. 2, sub-secs. 1 and 7 of Ont. Voters List Act, *post*; note to s. 8 of the Voters' Lists Finality Act (Ont.) *post*; also *Re Lincoln Election*, 2 Ont. Ap. R. 351.

See Resolution of Ontario Revising Officers, *post*.

(*e*) "*Prepared and revised under the Statutes of the Province*"—Assessment Rolls and the Provincial Lists will be the basis used in making up the Dominion Lists for 1886. The latter lists will be used as a basis in the preparation of future lists, though the rolls, or where there are none the Provincial Lists, will be again consulted, see sec. 33 *post*.

(*f*) "*No such lists.*"—As in Prince Edward Island.

certified copies of the poll book or books at the last election in each electoral district; and he shall proceed, as speedily as possible, with the aid thereof and of such other information as he can obtain (*g*), to ascertain and prepare a separate list for each municipality within his appointment, and wherever there is not a municipality, or where the electoral district is a municipality, a separate list for each township, parish (*h*), polling district or other known division of the electoral district, of the persons who, according to the provisions of this Act, are entitled to be registered as voters, and to vote under this Act, at any election for such electoral district; which list shall contain the names of such persons in alphabetical order and shall be in the form B contained in the schedule to this Act, indicating in the proper column thereof whether such persons respectively are qualified in respect of real property, as owners, tenants, occupants, purchasers in occupation under the Crown (*i*), or otherwise, stating the number of the lots, portions of lots, and concessions, streets or other most available description of the real property in respect of which they are so qualified, and their post office addresses as nearly as can be ascertained by the said officer, or as farmers' sons or the sons of owners of real property other than farmers, stating the numbers of the lots, portions of lots, concessions,

To prepare list of voters under this Act.

Form and contents of lists.

Qualification, etc., of voters.

As to farmers' sons and voters on income.

(*g*) "*Such other information as he can obtain.*"—See resolutions of meeting of Revising Officers for Ontario, *post.*

(*h*) "*Parish.*"—See Interpretation, *ante.*

(*i*) "*Purchasers in occupation under the Crown.*"—This class will not include mere squatters, who however may be entitled to be placed on the list as "occupants," if they are in actual occupation. If however they place another person in possession—even if they receive rent from such person—they will not be entitled to be on the list, either as owners, for they have acquired no title, tenants, for they pay no rent, or occupants, for they are not in actual occupation and in receipt of the revenues and profits. See *Lincoln* (2); *Clark's vote*, 1 H. E. C. 515. See Interpretation, *ante.*

or streets, or other available description of the real property of their fathers or mothers, in respect of which they are qualified as farmers' or other owners' sons, as hereinbefore provided, or whether they are qualified in respect of income; and as to sons of farmers or of other owners as aforesaid, and voters on income, stating also in the said list, in the proper columns thereof, the residences and post office addresses of such persons, as nearly as can be ascertained by him; and after having so prepared the said list, the revising officer shall sign the same as such: Provided, that such assessment rolls as aforesaid shall be taken by the revising officer as *primâ facie* evidence of value (*j*), and such voters' lists or poll books as aforesaid, as the case may be, as *primâ facie* evidence of qualification (*k*) to vote.

Signing lists.

Assessment rolls, etc., to be *primâ facie* evidence.

Publication of lists.

16. The revising officer shall then forthwith cause to be printed a sufficient number of copies of the said lists, being not less than two hundred, and, after certifying them in the form C contained in the schedule hereto, shall, on or before the first day of March, one thousand eight hundred and eighty-six, publish the said lists, by causing one copy of each list to be posted up in the office of the clerk or other corresponding officer of each municipal, parochial or other known territorial division in the electoral district, for which the said list is prepared and to which it relates, and by mailing to the member or members of the House of Commons and to the unsuccessful candidate at the then last election for such electoral district, to the sheriff, warden, mayor, aldermen or coun-

Mailing copies to certain officials.

(*j*) *Prima facie evidence of value.*"—But not conclusive. See Interpretation. "actual value," and note thereon, *ante*,

(*k*) "*Prima facie evidence of qualification.*"—This proviso gives to the work of the Revising Officer more the character of a work of revision than it would necessarily possess were there no basis to start upon.

cillors, clerk of the peace and treasurer, clerk, or officers corresponding thereto, under whatever official name they are known, of any county, city, town or part of a city, included in such electoral district, and to the reeve, councillors, mayor, clerk, parish court commissioner and treasurer, or officers corresponding thereto as aforesaid, of each township, parish or village municipality in such electoral district, two copies each, addressed to the post office addresses of such persons respectively; and the copy of every such list so posted up shall be open to inspection by any person, free of charge, in the office where it is deposited, during the business hours of such office, until the day fixed, as hereinafter provided, for the preliminary revision of the said list; and copies of the list may be procured by any person on application to the revising officer, as soon as he can furnish them, on paying therefor a price proportionately (*l*) sufficient to cover the price paid for printing the same, but not to exceed fifty cents for a copy of the list of voters for any electoral district. In the event of their being no municipal divisions in the electoral district, a copy or copies of the said list, certified as aforesaid, shall be posted up in one or more of what the revising officer considers the most public place or places in each township, parish, polling district or other known division of the electoral district; and two copies each shall be mailed to officers or persons in such electoral district corresponding, as nearly as may be, to those particularly mentioned in this section with respect to municipalities.

Copy to be posted up and open to inspection free.

And copies to be furnished on payment of price.

If there are no municipal divisions in the electoral district

Mailing copies.

17. Two copies of that part of the list relating to such municipality, or parochial or other known division as aforesaid, certified as aforesaid, shall also be mailed at the

Copies to be mailed to postmasters and others to be posted up.

(*l*) "*Proportionately*," i.e., in proportion to the whole number printed.

time of the publication thereof as aforesaid, to each of the postmasters in the said known division; and each of the said postmasters, and every sheriff, warden, clerk of the peace and treasurer, parish court commissioner or other officer to whom two copies each of the said lists are to be mailed under this Act, shall forthwith after receiving them post up one of them in a conspicuous place in his office, where the said list shall remain until the day fixed, as hereinafter provided, for the preliminary revision thereof, and shall be open to inspection by any one during the office hours of the office; and to each of the copies of the lists so made or published under this and the next preceding section, shall be appended a notice in the form D in the schedule to this Act.

With notice of time of sitting for preliminary revision.

Notice of such sitting, how given.

18. Notice that the said list and the time of holding the sitting mentioned in the notice appended thereto have been published in manner aforesaid, shall also be given by the revising officer forthwith after such publication, by at least one insertion thereof, in the form D in the schedule to this Act, in one or more newspapers, if any, published within the electoral district; and in case no newspaper is published therein (*m*), then in one or more newspapers published in a neighboring electoral district or districts.

Sitting for pre-

19. The revising officer shall hold a sitting (*n*), as men-

(*m*) "*In case no newspaper is published therein.*"—It is worthy of note that in this case the notice of the preliminary revision is to be published in one or more newspapers published in a neighbouring electoral district or districts; but not so, with regard to the notice of the final revision, under sec. 25.

(*n*) "*A sitting.*"—The Revising officer is to hold only one sitting for the preliminary revision at the place he deems most convenient. Afterwards he prepares separate lists for each polling district and proceeds to hold a separate sitting in each municipality, etc., under sec. 26, where the list for each district is finally revised. At the preliminary revision no names are witheld from insertion or struck from the list by reason of their being objected to. Those objected to are so marked, and are left for

tioned in the said notice, for the preliminary revision of the lists at such place in the electoral district, or in such portion as may be within his commission, as he shall deem most convenient for that purpose, on a day not less than four weeks after the publication of the list as aforesaid; and any person desiring to add any names to the said list, or desiring otherwise to amend the same, shall, at least one week before (*o*) the day fixed for such preliminary revision (and in the case of a person desiring to object to any name, at any time before the day so fixed) deposit with or mail to the revising officer, by registered letter,

liminary revision.

Amendments and objections to be notified to revising officer.

---

consideration at the final revision. This arrangement saves the trouble and expense to contestants and voters whose votes are objected to of attending with their witnesses at the place fixed for the preliminary revision, which may be at a long distance. They may await the coming of the Revising officer to hold court in their own municipality or parish As to the preliminary revision of future lists (after 1886), see sec. 33, *post;* see also resolution of meeting of revising officers for Ontario, *post.*

(*o*) "*At least one week before.*—i. e., seven clear days. When a statute says a thing shall be done so many days, or so many days at least, before a given event, the day of the thing done and that of the event must both be excluded—*The Queen* v. *Shropshire*, 8 A. & E. 173; *Mitchell* v. *Foster*, 9 Dowl. 527; *In Re Sams* v. *Toronto*, 9 U. C. Q. B. 181; *Norton* v. *Salsbury*, 4 C. B. 37; *Adey* v. *Hill*, *Ib.* 40; *Clarke* v. *Beaton*, 5 C B. 87; *Howes* v. *Peirce*, L. R. 1 C. P. Div. 670; *Dempsey* v. *Dougherty*, 7 U. C. Q. B. 313; *Lely and Foulkes El. Acts* 106; but if the last day for giving the notice falls on Sunday or a holiday, then under sec. 2, sub-s. 2, *ante*, the notice may be given on the following day. As to what is a holiday see note to sec. 2, sub-s. 2. It has been held under the English Act that the overseers may, if they choose, waive the irregularity of a notice sent after the date fixed by the Act by one claiming to be put on the register, and the revising barrister cannot expunge his name—*Leonard* v. *Allways*, 48 L. J. C. P. 81, 40 L. T. 197; *Davies* v *Hopkins*, 27 L. J. C. P. 6; *Lely and Foulkes El Acts*, 76. But it is doubted whether they can waive such irregularity in the case of a notice of objection to the vote of another. See *Godsell* v. *Innons* 17 C. B. 295. It is thought that they cannot, on the ground that a party objected to is entitled as of right to take advantage of every irregularity of the party objecting. See *Lely and Foulkes El. Acts*, 78; *Freeman* v. *Newman*, 12 Q. B. D. 373; 53 L. J. Q. B. 108; 51 L. T. 396; 32 W. R. 246; 1 Colt. 342. The notice is not a matter of so great importance as regards the preliminary revision, as a fresh notice may be given for the final revision under sec. 26, *post*. The above remarks, however, equally apply to the latter notice.

Notice to person, the insertion of whose name is objected to.

at his office or place of address, a notice in the form E (*p*) in the schedule to this Act; and in the event of any such objection being that a name already on the list should be struck off, the person so objecting shall give notice in writing to the person whose name is objected to within the same time and in the like form as to the revising officer, by delivering such notice to such person, or by mailing the same by registered letter to his last known post office address.

Preliminary revision.

20. On the day and at the time and place appointed, the revising officer shall publicly proceed to the preliminary revision of the lists, basing such revision on the evidence and information before him *(pa)* in support of any claims for addition to the list of voters, or of any proposed amendments or corrections, but not including any objection to the insertion of any name, which he shall merely note on the list opposite the name objected to; and he shall then and there correct the lists, on the said basis, to the best of his judgment and ability, upon such evidence and information, and shall note every objection on the

How to be conducted and recorded.

(*p*) "*A notice in the form* E."—Where forms are prescribed slight deviations therefrom, not affecting the substance, or calculated to mislead, shall not vitiate them. Interpretation Act, 31 Vic, cap. 1, sec. 7, *Thirty-firstly.*—Under the English Act the objector himself must sign the notice, as the Act so directs—*Lely* v. *Foulkes El. Act* 78; *Toms* v. *Cumming*, 7 M. & G. 88. Our Act merely directs that the objector "shall give notice in writing," while the form E has a space for "*name of complainant*" and his P. O. address. The objector, a solicitor of Horsham (where he had always lived), who was a clerk to the magistrates and coroner, omitted to state his place of abode. The revising barrister finding as a fact that no person could have been misled by the omission, it was held that this was a mistake which he might and ought to have corrected under s. 28, subs. 2, of the English Act of 1878, which expressly gives him power to do so.—*Adams* v. *Bostock*, 8 Q. B. D. 259; 51 L. J. Q. B. 175; 45 L. T. 443; 30 W. R. 460; 1 Colt. 275. As to other mistakes in the notices and lists, and the correction thereof, under powers given in the English Acts, see *Lely and Foulkes El. Acts*, 153-4-5-6-7-8, and 226-7-8, and cases therein cited.

(*pa*) See resolution of Ontario Revising Officers, *post*.

said lists as aforesaid; he shall also attest with his initials any addition or change therein; and he shall also append to such lists the names of claimants whose claims he has not admitted, and shall sign such appended lists.

Certifying revised lists.

21. The revising officer, having completed the said preliminary revision of the said first lists for the electoral district, or such portion thereof as is within his commission, shall sign the same as such revising officer and certify each of the said lists, and shall, on or before the first day of May, one thousand eight hundred and eighty-six, by an order under his hand, in the form F in the Schedule to this Act, divide (*pb*) every city, town, ward, parish, township or other municipal or corresponding division in the electoral district (or in default of such municipal or other corresponding division, every tract of land therein) having, according to the list relating to it, more than three hundred voters therein, by well defined boundaries, such as streets, highways, side lines, concession lines, or the like, into polling districts, in such manner that the number of voters in the several polling districts in the electoral district shall be as nearly equal as may be, and shall not in any one case exceed two hundred: Provided always, that where the electoral district does not contain three hundred voters, or where the voters are scattered over a large extent of country, the said revising officer may,

Division of electoral district into polling districts.

Proviso; in cases of voters much scattered.

(*pb*) The Returning Officer had power under sec. 11 of the Elections Act, 1874, to sub-divide into districts similar to those provided for under this section. This power is not in express terms repealed, though it may be argued that this section, coupled with sections 46 and 58 *post*, has that effect; especially as section 41 provides for an annual re-division by the Revising Officer, where a change of population makes such re-division necessary, or the Revising Officer deems that the convenience of voters would be thereby promoted. Even if the power of the Returning Officer in this respect is not taken away, it will scarcely be found necessary for him to exercise it hereafter, and his so doing will always create more or less confusion as the arrangement of voters in the published lists would then be departed from.

See resolution of meeting of Revising Officers for Ontario, *post*.

nevertheless, sub-divide the electoral district into as many polling districts as he thinks advisable for the convenience of the voters, even though the number in each be less than two hundred.

Numbering polling districts

22. The polling districts in each municipality or other corresponding division as in the next preceding section mentioned shall be numbered, with a local designation attached to such number (*q*), in and by the order of the revising officer by which they are established, and such order shall be, forthwith after the making thereof, filed and kept by the revising officer for the purposes of this Act: Provided always, that in Prince Edward Island polling divisions may comprise parts of several townships.

Proviso; as to P. E. Island.

Separate list for each polling district.

23. Immediately after the sub-division of the municipality into polling districts as in section twenty-one provided, the revising officer shall prepare from the first lists of voters as preliminarily revised by him as aforesaid, a separate list of voters for each polling district, containing in alphabetical order the names of all voters qualified to vote in such polling district, (noting the names objected to) and in the same form as nearly as may be, as the form referred to in section fifteen, and shall sign the same as such officer, and shall append thereto the names of claimants whose claims have not been admitted.

Unadmitted claims to be appended.

(*q*) "*With a local designation attached to such number.*"—e. g., "Township Digby, No. 1," etc. This is to enable electors to ascertain their individual polling district and polling place with as little trouble as possible. The order of the revising officer will describe the limits of the polling district, and such description will be published along with the separate list for that district, under sec. 24, *post.*

The provision as to Prince Edward Island was inserted in deference to established divisions there, and to prevent confusion which might result from their alteration.

FINAL REVISION OF THE FIRST LISTS OF VOTERS.

Publication of such list, with description of each polling district.

24. After the completion of the preliminary revision of the lists of voters and the preparation of lists for polling districts, and after the signature of the latter by the revising officer, he shall, for the purpose of making the final revision thereof, cause a sufficient number of copies of each such list, with the description of the polling district to which it relates, to be printed, and shall certify the same as such officer, and on or before the first day of June, one thousand eight hundred and eighty-six, shall publish the same by causing copies to be posted up in three conspicuous public places in the polling district to which it relates, and by delivering copies thereof to any persons applying for the same, upon being paid according to the rates mentioned in section sixteen, but not to exceed ten cents for a copy of the list for each polling division, to each of which copies shall be appended a notice in the form G in the schedule to this Act, fixing a time and place for the final revision of each of the said lists; and the said revising officer shall also deliver or transmit, by registered letter, copies of such lists as follows: to each member of the Council of every city, town, township or village in any electoral district, and to the clerk and treasurer thereof, and to each postmaster in every such municipality or polling division, one copy of every list relating to such municipality or polling division; to the sheriff, warden, clerk of the peace and county judge of the judicial county or district, one copy of each of the several lists relating to such electoral district, or part of electoral district which may be within such judicial county or district; and ten copies of each of the several lists relating to such electoral district to the member or members of the House of Commons for the said electoral

Copies to be procurable at fixed rates

Copies to be sent to certain officials.

And to members of H. of C. and unsuccessful

candidates. district or part of an electoral district, and to the unsuccessful candidate or candidates at the last election for the same.

Notice of final revision. 25. The revising officer shall also at the same time publish the said notice appointing the time and place for the said final revision, in a newspaper, if any there be, published in the municipality or other division of the electoral district to which the polling district affected by such list belongs, by one insertion thereof in such newspaper.

As to time and place for final revision. 26. The day to be fixed as aforesaid for such final revision shall not be less than five weeks after (*r*) the publication by posting up of the said lists as aforesaid, and the place shall be in the city, town, township, parish, incorporated village or other known territorial division (and in the Province of Prince Edward Island, the existing provincial electoral district) which includes the polling district, and in the electoral districts of the Province of Nova Scotia, in such places comprising not less than three polling districts as the revising officers may think most convenient; and any person desiring to object or to add to, or in any way amend or correct such list on the final revision, shall have the right to do so, if he shall have previously given the proper notice (*s*) for that pur-

Notice of objections & amendments.

(*r*) "*Not less than five weeks after.*"—To avoid all question as to computation of time, the day fixed should be after the expiration of five weeks from and exclusive of the day of publication. See *Isaacs et al* v. *The Royal Ins. Co.*, L. R. 5, Ex. 296, Kelly C. B.

(*s*) "*Proper notice.*"—The notice given for the preliminary holds good for the final revision without further notice and notice of further claims and objections may be given under this section for the final revision.

Where a lodger's claim omitted to state (according to the form in the English Act, 48 Vic. cap. 15) the amount of his rent, and the address of his landlord, and these particulars were supplied at the revision, but the revising barrister declined to insert them, the Court approved of and affirmed his decision. *Pickard* v. *Baylis*, 5 C. P. D. 235; 49 L. J. C. P. 182; 21 W. R. 256. 1 Colt. 98. But this case, it is said, though

pose at the preliminary revision, or upon giving the same notice and following the same procedure as is provided for in section nineteen as to objections or amendments on the preliminary revision; and the notice of such objections or claims from any person shall be given in the manner specified in the said section nineteen, not less than two weeks before (*t*) the day named for the final revision.

Time limited for such notice.

27. At the time and place named in the notice of the revising officer, he shall hold open court for the said final revision, and shall hear and dispose (*u*) of any objection or complaint and any application to add to, amend or correct the list, as in the next preceding section mentioned, of which notice shall have been given as aforesaid, hearing the parties (*v*) making the same, if they appear, and any evidence (*w*) that may be adduced before him

Proceedings at final revision.

Correction of lists.

a strong authority to guide the exercise of the discretion, is no express authority binding a similar exercise of it in every case. *Lely & Foulkes*, El. Acts 157. An omission to state the place of residence of an objector describing himself only as on the list of parliamentary voters, and being in fact well-known, was held curable in *Adams* v. *Bostock*, 8 Q. B. D. 259; 51 L. J. Q. B. 175; 45 L. T. 443; 30 W. R. 460; 1 Colt. 275; and so was an omission of the word "parliamentary" before "voters" in *James* v. *Howarth*, 5 C. P. D. 225; 49 L. J. C. P. 169. It is to be observed in regard to these cases that under the English Acts 41 and 42 Vic., c. 26, s. 28 subs. 2, the revising barrister is given express power to correct mistakes in any claim or notice of objection. See also notes to sec. 19, *ante*.

(*t*) "*Not less than two weeks before.*"—*i.e.*, two clear weeks. See note to sec. 19, *ante*.

(*u*) "*Shall hear and dispose.*"—Under the Ontario Voters' Lists Act, a mandamus has been granted to compel a County Judge to hear and dispose of a complaint, where such Judge had refused to do so on the ground that the notice of complaint was insufficient, but which notice the Court held to be sufficient. *Re McCullough and the County Judge of Leeds and Grenville*, 35 U. C. Q. B. 449.

(*v*) "*Hearing the parties.*"—Under the English Act, 6 Vic, c. 18, s. 41, it is expressly provided that no person may appear or be attended by Counsel at the revising barristers court.

(*w*) "*Evidence.*"—The word Evidence, considered in relation to law, includes all the legal means, exclusive of mere argument, which tend to prove or disprove any matter of fact, the truth of which is submitted to judicial investigation. Taylor on

in support of or in opposition thereto, and shall either affirm or amend the list accordingly, as to him seems right and proper, attesting with his initials, any changes, additions, or erasures in the list.

Powers of revising officer for such revisions.

28. The revising officer shall, for the purposes of the said preliminary revision of the first lists of voters and of the final revision of the first lists of voters for polling districts, as well as for the revision of any subsequent lists of voters in polling districts under this Act, have all the powers of any court of record in the Province, as to compelling the attendance and the examination of witnesses, the production of books and documents, and the taking of evidence under oath before him, at any court or sittings held by him for any such preliminary or final revision, and shall have, generally, all the powers of a court of record (*x*).

Witnesses and evidence, etc.

Evidence, 8th ed 1. Evidence is either parol or documentary. Two of the main securities which the law provides for the truth of testimony in judicial proceedings are that it be delivered, first, under the religious and moral sanction of an oath, affirmation or declaration; and next, at the risk of a prosecution for perjury, *Ib.* 1378, p. 1172. It has been the established principle until recently, of English law, that no witnesses are to be believed, unless they deliver their evidence on oath. The only exceptions to this rule were statutory and were granted reluctantly by the Legislature to satisfy the conscientious scruples of Quakers, Moravians and Separatists; and members of these sects were accordingly allowed to give evidence on affirmation instead of oath Powell on Evidence, 3rd ed., 28. Under the English Act, 6 Vic., cap. 18, sec. 39, any person whose name shall be on any list of voters for any county, city or borough may oppose the claim of another to have his name inserted, "by evidence or otherwise." It is presumed that the word "evidence" in this section will be construed to mean only "legal evidence," and that witnesses will be sworn, as that is contemplated and provided for by the succeeding section. Considerable discussion took place in the House upon the meaning of the word evidence in this clause. *Hansard*, Vol. 17, 2396 to 2404. See also secs. 43 and 50, *post.*

(*x*) "*Powers of a Court of Record.*"—Every Court of Record has attached to its jurisdiction, the power to punish for contempt; but if the Court is one of inferior jurisdiction, the Superior Court may intervene and prevent any usurpation of jurisdiction by it; though the Superior Court will not act as a Court of Appeal in such cases. —*Ex parte Pater*, 5 B. & S. 299; *Ex parte Lees and the Judge of the Co'y of Carleton*, 24 U. C. C. P. 214.

29. After the lists for the several polling districts in an electoral district have been so completed, revised and corrected, they shall be certified in the form C contained in the Schedule to this Act by the revising officer, and kept by him for the purposes of this Act, and a duplicate of each, certified as aforesaid, shall be transmitted forthwith by him to the Clerk of the Crown in Chancery at Ottawa, who, on receipt of all the said lists for any electoral district, shall, in the then next issue of the *Canada Gazette*, insert a notice in the form H contained in the schedule to this Act, on and after the publication of which notice in the *Canada Gazette*, the persons whose names are entered on the said lists as voters, shall be held to be duly registered voters (*y*) in and for such electoral district, subject to correction or amendment by the judgment on appeal as hereinafter mentioned: Provided however, that in the event of any such appeal, such lists after the publication of the last mentioned notice in the *Canada Gazette*, shall apply to every election for such electoral district, taking place before such appeal has been disposed of (*z*), or the result thereof communicated to the revis-

Copies of lists certified to be sent to Clerk of the Crown.

Notice in Gazette and its effect, except in case of appeal.

Proviso: in case of such appeal, as to ballots of persons whose names are subjects of an undecided appeal.

(*y*) "*Shall be held to be duly registered voters.*"—See secs. 11, 31 and 39, and notes thereto.

(*z*) "*Taking place before such appeal has been disposed of.*"—Under the English Act, 6 Vic. cap. 18, s. 69, the right of voting is not affected by any appeal pending: and the subsequent decision of any appeal, pending at the time of the issuing of the writ "shall not in any way whatsoever alter or affect the poll taken at such election, nor the return made thereat by the returning officer." And this is still the law in England.

By the English Ballot Act, 1872, s. 7, it is enacted that, "at any election for a "county or borough, a person shall not be entitled to vote unless his name is on the "Register of voters for the time being in force for such county or borough, and every "person whose name is on such register shall be entitled to demand and receive a "ballot paper and to vote: Provided that nothing in this section shall entitle any "person to vote who is prohibited from voting by any statute, or by the common law "of Parliament, or relieve such person from any penalties to which he may be liable "for voting." The following comment upon this section appears in Lely and Foulkes'

ing officer; but the ballot of any person whose name has been included in the certified list of voters, and is the subject of an undecided appeal, shall be numbered by the deputy returning officer, and a corresponding number shall be placed opposite his name, on the poll book; and upon the counting of the ballots, the ballots so numbered shall be by the deputy returning officer separated from the ordinary ballots and returned to the proper officer, sealed up at the same time as other ballots, to await the decision of such appeal;—and if under such decision the name of any such person shall be struck from the list of

Effect of the decision of such appeal.

Parliamentary Election Acts, p. 436. "This section must be read with s. 79 of the "Registration Act, 1843, which provides that 'the register of voters shall be deemed "'and taken to be conclusive evidence, that the persons therein named continue to "'have the qualifications which are annexed to their names respectively in the "'register in force in such election,' the provisoes limiting that enactment being re-"pealed by this Act, and the effect of the section being extended by this section, s. "79 clearly applies only to the effect of the register at the election, and there is "nothing in this section to extend its effect to the trial of an election petition. The "first words of the section 'at any election' limit its application to the election, and "the second of the two cases dealt with is the title 'to receive a ballot paper and "vote,' showing that voting *de facto* and not *de jure* is intended. The contrary, "however has been decided in *Stowe* v. *Joliffe*, L. R. 9 C. P. 734: 43 L. J. Rep. C. "P. 265, in which case it was held by Coleridge, C. J., Keating and Grove, J. J., "that the register was conclusive on the election judge, except as enacted in the "proviso. At the time of the decision (1874) there was no appeal against it, but it "might now be overruled by the Court of Appeal, though it probably would not, "having been acted on for more than ten years and approved in some degree in "*Hayward* v. *Scott*, 5 C. P. D. 231." Whether the vote of an alien can be struck off on a scrutiny under the English Act was considered in *Ryder* v. *Hamilton*, L. R. 4 C. P. 559; 98 L. J. C. P. 260; 17 W. R. 795.

Our Act, it will be observed, contains no such proviso as the English Ballot Act, and goes farther than the English Act of 1843, as it provides that "the said lists shall be binding on any judge or other tribunal appointed for the trial of any petition," etc. See further as to the effect of this section, note to sec. 11, *ante*. Future lists are provided for by sec. 39, *post*.

The Ontario Voters Lists Finality Act, 41 Vic. c. 21, s. 3, provides that the certified lists shall be final and conclusive, *upon any scrutiny*, except as to disqualified persons and some others who are specified.

See as to *mandamus* and *certiorari* proceedings, note to s. 3 of the Ontario Voters' Lists Finality Act, *post*.

voters, the vote given by such person shall be ascertained from his ballot, and shall be struck from the poll upon a recount; and if any person whose name has been excluded from such certified list of voters, and whose exclusion is the subject of an undecided appeal, shall desire to vote, the deputy returning officer shall receive his ballot and shall number the same and the name of the voter in the poll book, and keep separate such ballots, as hereinbefore provided; and if upon such appeal, the decision of the revising officer shall be maintained, the vote of such person may be ascertained and struck from the poll upon a recount;—and if an appeal respecting the vote of any person placed on the poll book under the provisions hereof, be not decided within the delay fixed by the existing election law for a recount, such delay shall be extended until six days after the decision of the appeal.

Extension of time for recount in certain cases.

30. The revising officer and the clerk of the Crown in Chancery shall supply copies of such lists to any person or persons applying for the same and paying therefor at the same rate as is to be payable for copies of lists furnished under section sixteen.

Copies of lists.

31. After the lists of voters have been so finally revised, or amended and corrected on appeal and certified and brought into force as hereinbefore prescribed, and until other lists are, in a future year, under this Act as hereinafter provided, made, revised, amended and corrected on appeal, and certified, and brought into force in their stead, those persons only whose names are entered upon such lists as so revised, amended and corrected shall be entitled to vote at any election of a member of the House of Commons, in the polling sub-divisions and electoral districts for which such lists were respectively

Lists finally corrected to be valid until corrected on appeal or superseded by others made; and the said lists shall be binding on any judge or other tribunal appointed for the trial of any petition complaining of an undue election or return of a member to serve in the House of Commons.

Certified copies to returning officers.

32. The revising officer shall also furnish to the returning officer for his electoral district, or such portion thereof as is within his appointment, within forty-eight hours after demand of the returning officer therefor, one copy of the list of voters then in force for each polling district in such electoral district, with a description of such polling district as contained in the order of the revising officer constituting the same, which list and copy of description shall be duly certified by the revising officer.

FUTURE LISTS AND REVISION THEREOF.

Renewal of lists after 1886 and proceedings therefor.

33. On or as soon as possible after the first day of January in each year after the year of Our Lord one thousand eight hundred and eighty-six, the revising officer, being duly sworn as hereinbefore provided, shall obtain a certified copy, or certified copies, as the case may be, of the last revised or final assessment roll or rolls (*a*), if any there be, in the electoral district or part of an electoral district for which he is appointed, and where there are no assessment rolls, a certified copy or certified copies of the last revised list or lists of voters in such electoral district; and with such copies and such other information as he can obtain, he shall proceed to revise the lists of voters then in force under this Act for such

Revising and

(*a*) "*Assessment roll or rolls.*"—The proceedings under this section are somewhat different from those under secs. 15 to 23 inclusive, *ante*, owing to the existence of the separate lists for the different polling districts for the year previous, which the various officers will have together with the last revised assessment rolls, as guides. The provision that certified copies of the rolls are to be obtained will involve a considerable expense without any apparent advantage as both the Dominion list for the previous year, as well as the Provincial lists will be available.

electoral district, entering thereupon the names of all persons not already in such lists, and who, according to the provisions of this Act, are entitled to have their names so entered, indicating in the proper columns thereof whether they are qualified in respect of real property, as owners, tenants, occupants, purchasers in occupation under the Crown or otherwise, and stating the numbers of the lots, portions of lots and concessions, streets, or other available description of real property in respect of which they are qualified, and their post office addresses as nearly as can be ascertained by the said officer,—or as farmers' sons or other owners' sons as aforesaid, stating the number of the lots, portions of lots, concessions or streets or other available descriptions of the real property of their fathers or mothers in respect of which they are qualified as farmers' or other owners' sons as hereinbefore provided, or whether they are qualified in respect of income; and as to the sons of farmers, or other owners' sons as aforesaid, and voters on income, stating also in such lists in the proper column thereof the residence and post office addresses of such persons as nearly as can be ascertained by him, and noting on the said lists the names of any persons who are dead or who are not, according to the provisions of this Act, entitled to be registered as voters, stating the reason of such note, and making any other verbal or clerical corrections which seem necessary; and he shall attest all such additions, erasures or corrections, with his initials, and sign such lists as such revising officer: Provided, that such assessment rolls as aforesaid shall be *primâ facie* evidence of value (*b*).

correcting former lists.

Contents of revised lists: as to qualification, etc., of voters.

Initialing corrections and signing corrected lists.

Rolls *primâ facie* evidence of value

(*b*) "*Primâ facie evidence of value.*"—See "Interpretation," "actual value," and note thereon, *ante*.

Publication of corrected lists.

34. After the said lists of voters have been so preliminarily revised, the said revising officer shall publish and distribute them, and notice of the time and place fixed by him for the final revision thereof respectively, as nearly as may be, in the manner and form provided for in sections twenty-four and twenty-five, in respect of the final revision of the first lists of voters in polling districts under this Act (*ba*).

Objections how made and dealt with.

35. The practice and requirements provided for in sections twenty-six and twenty-seven, as to persons desiring to object to any name on the said first lists, or to add any name thereto, or otherwise to amend the same, shall apply to similar applications in reference to the lists to be prepared under the two sections next preceding.

Holding court for final revision of lists and proceedings thereat.

36. At the time and place named in the notice required under section thirty-four, the revising officer shall hold open court for the final revision of the list for each polling district, and shall proceed, with the same powers as are assigned to the revising officer by section twenty-eight, as to the enforcing of the attendance of witnesses, the taking of evidence under oath, the enforcing of the production of books and papers, the adjournment of the court, and otherwise, to hear the complaints, objections, and applications made as hereinbefore provided, and the evidence in reference thereto, and to decide thereupon, adding to, striking off, or otherwise amending or correcting the lists accordingly, and attesting every addition, correction, or erasure, or other amendment in the lists, with his initials, in the manner provided in section twenty-seven in respect of the final revision of the first lists of voters in polling districts.

(*ba*) This section and the succeeding sections down to sec. 40 are but repetitions, *mutatis mutandis*, of secs. 24 to 32 inclusive, as to which see *ante*, and notes thereto.

37. After the lists for the several polling districts in an electoral district have been so completed, revised and corrected, they shall be certified in the form C contained in the schedule to this Act by the revising officer, and kept by him for the purposes of this Act, and a duplicate of each, certified as aforesaid, shall be transmitted forthwith by him to the Clerk of the Crown in Chancery at Ottawa, who, on receipt of all the said lists for any electoral district, shall, in the then next issue of the *Canada Gazette*, insert a notice in the form H contained in the schedule to this Act,—on and after the publication of which notice in the *Canada Gazette*, the persons whose names are entered on the said lists as voters, shall be held to be duly registered voters in and for such electoral district, subject to correction or amendment by the judgment on appeal as hereinafter mentioned: Provided, however, that in the event of any such appeal, such lists after the publication of the last mentioned notice in the *Canada Gazette*, shall apply to every election for such electoral district, taking place before such appeal has been disposed of, or the result thereof communicated to the revising officer; but the ballot of any person whose name has been included in the certified list of voters and is the subject of an undecided appeal, shall be numbered by the deputy-returning officer, and a corresponding number shall be placed opposite his name on the poll book; and upon the counting of the ballots, the ballots so numbered shall be by the deputy returning officer separated from the ordinary ballots and returned to the proper officer sealed up, at the same time as other ballots, to await the decision of such appeal;—and if under such decision the name of any such person shall be struck from the list of voters, the vote given by such person shall be ascertained from his

Certifying completed lists and transmission of duplicates to Clerk of Crown

Notice in *Gazette* and its effects.

Proviso: in case of appeal, as to ballots of persons whose names are subjects of undecided appeals.

ballot and shall be struck from the poll upon a recount; and if any person whose name has been excluded from such certified list of voters, and whose exclusion is the subject of an undecided appeal, shall desire to vote, the deputy returning officer shall receive his ballot, and shall number the same and the name of the voter in the poll book, and keep separate such ballots as hereinbefore provided; and if upon such appeal the decision of the revising officer shall be maintained, the vote of such person may be ascertained and struck from the poll upon a recount; and if an appeal respecting the vote of any person placed on the poll book under the provisions hereof be not decided within the delay fixed by the existing election law for a recount, such delay shall be extended until six days after the decision of the appeal.

Extension of time for recount

Copies of lists how obtainable.

38. The revising officer and the Clerk of the Crown in Chancery shall supply copies of the said lists to any person or persons applying for the same and paying therefor at the rate payable for copies of lists furnished under section sixteen.

Effect of revised lists unless altered on appeal or superseded by others.

39. After the lists of voters have been so finally revised, or amended and corrected on appeal, and certified and brought into force as hereinbefore prescribed and until other lists are, in a future year, as herein provided, made, revised, amended, and corrected on appeal and certified, and brought into force in their stead, those persons only whose names are entered upon such lists as so revised, amended and corrected, shall be entitled to vote at any election of a member of the House of Commons, in the polling districts and electoral districts for which such lists were respectively made; and the said lists shall be binding on any judge or other tribunal appointed for the trial of any petition complaining of an undue election or return of a member to serve in the House of Commons.

40. The revising officer shall also furnish to the returning officer for his electoral district, within forty-eight hours after demand of the returning officer therefor, one copy of the list of voters then in force for each polling district in the electoral district, with a description of the said polling district as contained in the order of the revising officer constituting the same, and then in force, which list and copy of description shall be duly certified by the revising officer; and a copy of the said list of voters for each polling district shall be furnished by the returning officer to the deputy returning officer for such polling district; and such list shall be kept by the poll clerk, who shall use the same for the purposes of "*The Dominion Elections Act*, 1874." **Certified copies to returning officers.**

41. Whenever the number of voters in any polling district, as constituted under section twenty-one, shall increase so as to exceed two hundred, or whenever the revising officer then in office considers that the convenience of the voters would be promoted by a new and different sub-division, he shall, before proceeding to make the new lists of voters then next required under this Act, again sub-divide any city, town, ward, parish, township or townships, or other municipal or corresponding division (or any tract of land where there is no municipal division), in which such polling district is situate, into polling districts, in like manner as hereinbefore provided, so as to conform to the intent and meaning of this Act, and so again from time to time as like occasion shall require, using on all occasions after the first division thereof, the then last revised and corrected lists of voters for that purpose; and the revising officer, after making such subdivision by an order in the form prescribed in section twenty-one, shall publish such order by posting up in **Alteration of polling districts in case of change of population.**

some public place in each polling district, a copy thereof certified by him; and the revising officer shall use such amended polling districts in preparing the new lists of voters, which shall be revised and corrected as provided with respect to the polling districts first constituted by him *(bb)*.

Use of new polling districts

GENERAL PROVISIONS.

Power of revising officer to summon witnesses and obtain necessary information.

42. The revising officer shall, on the application of any person supporting or opposing any objection, claim or proposed amendment to a list of voters at any of the courts or sittings for preliminary or final revision under this Act, issue a summons in the form J in the schedule to this Act contained, to any person to attend at such court or sitting, and, if required, to produce any books or papers in the possession or power of such person, and to give evidence thereat relating to any matter connected with any such revision; and in the event of such person not attending after being served with such summons, the revising officer may punish such person as for a contempt of a court of record: Provided, however, that no such person shall be compelled to attend under any such summons unless the witness' fees allowed in the Province of Quebec in the Superior Court, in the Province of Ontario in the Division Court, and in the other Provinces of the Dominion in the County or Division Court, shall have first been paid or tendered to such person.

Proviso: fee to be tendered.

Power of amendment or adjournment and of summary proceeding.

43. The judge or revising officer shall have power at any court or sitting held under this Act by him, to amend or give leave to amend, when he sees fit, any of the proceedings taken in reference to any list of voters, to direct notice to be given to other persons, and to adjourn any

(bb) This power was previously only conferred upon the Returning officers, (The Dom. Elections Act, 1874, sec. 11).

See resolution of meeting of Revising Officers for Ontario, *post*.

court or sittings, on the hearing of any claim or objection or proposed amendment, to a future day; and he shall not be bound by strict rules of evidence (c) or forms of procedure, but shall hear and determine all matters coming before him as such judge or revising officer in a summary manner, and so as in his judgment to do justice to all parties *(bc)*.

Applicants for corrections may appear by counsel.

44. The parties to any application before any judge or revising officer may appear by agent, solicitor or counsel *(ca)*; and any elector may appear, in person or by agent, at any sitting of the revising officer in the electoral district in which he is such elector in support of or in opposition to any claim, objection or application arising before such revising officer; and the revising officer may award costs to or against any party in the case, which costs shall only be for witnesses' fees and the expenses of summoning such witnesses; and the said costs may be levied by order of the revising officer *(d)*, by distress *(e)*, as under warrant on a conviction under the "*Act respecting the duties of Justices of the Peace, out of Sessions, in relation to Summary Convictions and Orders.*"

Costs.

32-33 Vic., c. 31.

(c) "*Evidence.*"—See sec. 27, and note, *ante*.

(bc) Somewhat similar powers of amendment are given to the revising barrister by the English Parliamentary and Municipal Registration Act, 1878, s. 28.

(ca) By the English Parliamentary Registration Act, 1843, s. 41, "no party or other person shall appear or be attended by Counsel" at the Revision Court.

(d) "*By order of the Revising Officer.*"—The costs may be levied directly by the order of the revising officer. Under the English Act (6 Vic., cap. 18, secs. 46 and 71) the revising barrister makes an order for costs, which is handed to the person in whose favour it is given, and on proof of service of such order, demand of payment, and refusal or neglect to pay, a Justice of the Peace is required to issue a warrant for distress; and by section 13 of the Act of 1865, every order for costs by a revising barrister in the case of any objection must be made before his proceeding to hear any objection stated in any other notice of objection.

(e) "*By distress.*"—It would seem not to be intended to confer the power of imprisoning in default of distress found, which power is conferred upon Justices under the Act referred to in the text.

See note to sec. 52, *post*.

Provision in default of lists for any year.

45. If from any cause the list of voters for any polling district is not made, revised and corrected at the time when it ought, under section forty, to be sent to the returning officer at any election to be held after the first list of voters for the electoral district in which it lies has been made, revised and corrected, then the last list of voters, revised and corrected for such polling district, shall be sent to the returning officer, and used at such election.

Returning officer to fix polling stations before election.

46. Notwithstanding anything contained in any statute of Canada heretofore enacted, the returning officer for each electoral district for which lists of voters made under this Act are to be used, shall, forthwith on the receipt of the writ of election, obtain from the revising officer for the electoral district or part of a district for which he is returning officer, at least one copy of the list of voters as finally revised and certified by the revising officer and then in force, for each of the polling districts in such electoral district, and a copy of the order dividing the electoral district into polling districts, and shall forthwith fix a polling station in and for each of such polling districts in a central and convenient place therein.

As to lists certified while an appeal is pending.

47. If at any time when the revising officer is required to furnish or certify any list of voters, whether to a returning officer, deputy returning officer, or to any other officer or person, there is any appeal pending, or in which the decision, if given, has not been notified to the revising officer with respect to such list, the revising officer shall furnish such list as then last revised and corrected by him, noting thereon the names of all persons who have been retained on the list of voters, notwithstanding objection, the names of all persons who have been struck off the list of voters, and of all persons who have applied

to be placed on the list of voters and whose applications have been refused, and who have respectively appealed from his decision; and the list shall serve and avail, according to the provisions of this Act, for the election with reference to which it is furnished; but whenever any appeal is decided so as to require the correction of the list, and the formal order or judgment has been served upon him, he shall correct the list accordingly, and forthwith notify the Clerk of the Crown in Chancery that he may correct the duplicate lists in his hands accordingly, and the said clerk of the Crown in Chancery shall correct the same accordingly: Provided, that if the decision in appeal, requiring the correction of any list of voters, is notified to the revising officer by service of the formal order or otherwise, before the day of polling, an amended copy of the list of voters shall be furnished by the revising officer to the returning officer or deputy returning officer before the said day, and shall contain the correction in question, certified as hereinbefore provided, in which case the election shall take place upon such amended list if received in time by the deputy returning officer *(ea)*.

Correction when appeal is decided, and notice thereof.

Provision if decision is notified before day of polling.

48. For the revision of the first or any subsequent list of voters under this Act, in polling districts of cities, towns or villages, the revising officer, instead of holding a court in each polling district, may appoint some central place in such city, town, or village at which to hold his court of revision for the several polling districts therein,

One place may be appointed for court of revision in cities, etc

(ea) As to the proceedings at the election in regard to votes which are subjects of appeal, see secs. 29 and 37, *ante*.

In England the notice of the judgment in appeal is given direct by the Court to the Sheriff or returning officer who corrects the lists accordingly (6 Vic., cap. 18, sec. 67).

appointing, if he thinks proper, a separate day and holding a separate court for each polling district *(eb)*.

APPEAL.

Appeal from decision of revising officer.

49. In any case where the revising officer is not also a judge *(f)* of any court, any person or persons who, under the foregoing sections, shall have made any complaint, objection or application, in respect of the list of voters in any polling district, whether such list be the first or any subsequent list of voters, prepared under this Act for such polling district, or any person or persons with reference to whom such complaint, objection or application shall have been made, who shall be disatisfied with the decision of the revising officer in respect thereof, may give to the said revising officer or his clerk, on the day of such decision or within seven days thereafter *(g)*, notice in writing of his intention to appeal from such decision, stating shortly in such notice the decision complained of, and at least one reason for appealing against it, and shall, within the same time, cause a copy of such notice to be served upon the party in whose favor such decision was given, either personally or by leaving it at his residence or place of business, or by mailing the same in a registered letter addressed to his last known post office address; and the revising officer shall forthwith transmit such notice, together with a copy of his own decision, to the judge to be appealed to

Notice thereof.

Transmission of notice and copy of decision to judge.

(*eb*) See Ont. Voters' Lists Act (Rev. Stats. Ont., c. 9) ss. 18 and 19, and notes, *post*.

(*f*) "*Not also a judge.*"—Where the Revising officer is a judge there is no appeal.

(*g*) "*Within seven days thereafter.*"—i.e., within the seven days next succeeding the day of such decision. *Ex parte. Fallon*, 5 T. R. 283; *Williams* v. *Burgess*, 9 Dowl. 544; *Lester* v. *Garland*, 15 Vesey, 248; *Barnes* v. *Boomer*, 10 Grant (U.C.) 532; *Clark* v. *Gamble*, 28, U. C. C. P. 75; *Scott* v. *Dickson*, 1 Pr. R. (U. C.) 366; *Montgomery* v. *Brown*, 2 L. J. N. S. 72; *Vrooman* v, *Shuert*, 2 Pr. R. (U. C.) 122, and cases *Ibid* 126, 144; 145, 233, 259; *Edgar* v. *Magee*, 1 Ont. R. 287; *Hans* v. *Johnson*, 3 Ont. R. 100. If the last of such seven days falls on Sunday, or a "holiday" notice may be given on the following day. See sec. 2., subs. 2, *ante*.

as hereinafter provided, and shall sign (*h*) the same as revising officer, and shall deliver to such appellant or his counsel or agent, and to the respondent or his counsel or agent, if required, a certified copy of such decision.

Appellant to have a copy of decision.

50. The judge appealed to shall thereupon appoint a convenient time and place for the hearing of the appeal, which place shall be within the municipality, parish or other local territorial division within which the polling district in which the appeal arises is situate, of which time and place due notice shall be given to the revising

Judge to appoint time and place for hearing appeal.

Notice to parties.

(*h*) "*Shall forthwith transmit....shall sign.*"—In England, under the Act of 1843, sec. 42, the notice of appeal must be given, on the day of decision, to the revising barrister in Court, who thereupon, if he thinks it reasonable and proper that such appeal should be entertained, shall state a case in the form of a special case for the opinion of the Court above, and shall then and there read the statement to the appellant in open Court, and *shall then and there sign the same* ; at the end of the statement the appellant, or some one on his behalf, writes a declaration to the effect, "I appeal from this decision," and the said barrister *shall then indorse* upon the statement the name of the county, and polling district, etc., and the name and place of abode of the appellant and respondent, and shall sign and date such indorsement ; and deliver the statement, with the indorsement, to the appellant, to be by him transmitted to the Court above. Under sec. 62, the appellant shall, within the first four days of the next Michaelmas Term, transmit to the masters of the Court above the statement so signed by the revising barrister, and shall therewith also give or send a notice in writing, signed by him, stating his intention to prosecute the appeal, and a similar notice to the respondent ; whereupon the masters shall forthwith enter the appeal.

Doubts have arisen in England whether the words italicized above, in the English Act are imperative or merely directory, so that an irregularity in the matter of signature may be waived by consent. The Court heard an appeal on an unsigned case in *Burton* v. *Brooks*, 21 L. J. C. P. 7, the respondent waiving his right to object, and consenting to have the signature inserted, though Jervis, C. J., appears to have thought that s. 62 rendered the words imperative. In *Scott* v. *Durant*, 34 L. J. C P. 81, the point was raised but not decided. In *Wanklyn* v. *Woollet*, 4 C. B. 86, a case not having a signed indorsement was held insufficient. The Court refused to hear an appeal, where the revising barrister had died without signing, in *Nettleton* v. *Burrell*, 14 L. J. C. P. 37; The Irish Court of Appeal, in *Topham* v. *Kelleher*, 6 L. R. Ir. 285, C. A., held similar provisions in the Irish Registration Act, both as to signing and indorsement to be directory only, and not imperative. In *Shermyn* v. *Whyman*, L. R. 6, C. P., Brett, J., said, at p. 247, both on principle and on the

officer and to the parties interested, in such manner as as the judge shall order. And if, at the time and place

If appellant does not appear, etc.

so appointed, the appellant does not appear in person or by agent, or, appearing, withdraws his appeal, the appeal shall be dismissed; but if the appellant appears, and neither the revising officer nor any other party does so,

If appeal is unopposed.

or, so appearing, does not oppose the appeal, the judge, on sufficient proof or admission of service of the notice in manner above mentioned, shall maintain the same, except in the case of an appeal by a person struck off the list of voters or whose name the revising officer has refused to place thereon, in which case the judge shall require satisfactory evidence of the right of the appellant to be placed on the list of voters before he shall main-

Summary hearing and decision if the case is contested.

tain the appeal. But if the appeal be opposed by the revising officer or other party, if any, then appearing, or if the respondent makes default in so appearing, the judge, on being satisfied of the service of such notice in

---

authority of *Wanklyn* v. *Woollet*, that s. 42 was directory if taken by itself, but was made imperative by sec. 62. It is urged also that the words are imperative on the ground that the enactment, being for the public benefit, cannot be waived, Lely and Foulkes, El. Acts, p. 95. In *Pring* v. *Estcourt*, 4 C. B. 71, the Court allowed an appeal to be entered without the *indorsement* having been signed, although the *case* had been. This appeal was afterwards dismissed upon another ground; and in *Wanklyn* v. *Woollet*, 4 C. B. 86, the same Court appears to have directly, though not expressly overruled it and held, in a considered judgment, that where an indorsement was not signed until the fifth day of term, the appellant could not be heard. By the English Act of 1878, s. 37, any person feeling aggrieved by a revising barrister neglecting or refusing to state any case, may apply to the High Court for a rule to compel him to do so and to have the appeal heard. It is worthy of remark that it is said that in no case since the passing of the Act, and up to 1885, has it been necessary to bring the provisions of this section into operation. (See also *Re Simpson* v. *County Judge of Lanark*, 9 Ont. Pr. R. 358).

It is conceived that, inasmuch as the Canadian Act leaves no discretion with the revising officer as to stating a case, where the notice of appeal is given, a person, who has given such notice, could by *mandamus*, or analagous proceeding, in any of the Provinces, compel him to transmit the notice and his decision duly signed to the appellate Judge, according to the provisions of s. 49.

manner above mentioned, shall, either immediately or at such time as he shall then fix for the purpose, and at the same place, proceed to hear and decide upon the said appeal summarily, hearing the parties and receiving such legal evidence (*i*) as shall be adduced before him respecting the facts in dispute, but without being bound by any technical rules of procedure; and such decision shall be subject to no further appeal; and if any judgment be rendered in appeal which shall require an alteration in the certified list, such judgment shall be forthwith notified, in such manner as the judge shall order, to the revising officer: Provided always, that any elector may appear in person or by agent at any sitting of the judge in appeal in the electoral district in which he is such elector, in support of or in opposition to any claim, objection or application arising before such judge *(ha)*.

No further appeal.

Any elector may appear in person or by agent.

51. For the purposes of any such appeal and in respect thereof the judge shall have all the powers conferred upon the revising officer by section forty-two of this Act, with regard to summoning witnesses, obtaining evidence, and punishing the persons summoned before him.

Powers of judge as to witnesses, etc.

52. The judge in appeal may award costs (*j*) to or

Costs; how levied.

(*i*) "*Legal evidence.*"—See note to sec. 27, *ante.*

(*ha*) Parliament adopted in this section the plan of requiring the appellate judge to hear the whole case, including the evidence, anew, in preference to providing for the appeal being disposed of on evidence transmitted, or a case stated, as under the English Act, by the Revising Officer.

(*j*) "*May award costs.*"—The following rulings in the Imperial Courts as to costs of appeal may be cited: Where the decision of the Revising Barrister is affirmed without hearing the respondent, the appeal will be dismissed with costs, *Passingham* v. *Petty*, 17 C. B. 299; *Faulkner* v. *Overseers of Upper Boddington*, 3 C. B. N. S. 421. Where only one side is heard the successful party is entitled to costs, *Allen* v. *House*, 7 M. & G. 157; 1 Lutw. 255; but this is not a general rule, *Walker* v. *Payne*, Lutw. 324, as for instance where a doubtful question of law is involved, *Croucher* v. *Browne*, 2 C. B. 97; 1 Lutw. 388; even though the Court decide against the appeal, *Cooke* v. *Humber*, 11 C. B. N. S. 49. In a case held to be a reasonable one for argument costs are not given, *Sherlock* v. *Steward*, 7 C. B. N. S.

against any party in the case, which costs shall only be for witnesses' fees and the expenses of summoning such witnesses; and the said costs may be levied by order of the judge, by distress (*k*), as under a warrant on a conviction under the "*Act respecting the duties of Justices of the Peace out of Sessions, in relation to Summary Convictions and Orders.*" 32-33 Vic., c. 31.

Courts for appeal.

53. The appeal shall be—

In Ontario.

(*a*.) In the Province of Ontario, to the judge of the County Court in whose county the polling district where the appeal arises is situate;

In Quebec.

(*b*.) In the Province of Quebec, to the judge of the Superior Court resident in or having judicial charge of the judicial district containing the polling district in which the appeal arises;

28; 29 L. J. C. P. 87; K. & G. 286; *Collier* v. *King*, 11 C. B. N. S. 478; *Topper* v. *Nicholls* 18 C. B. N. S. 141; H. & P. 202. Where the decision is against the franchise, costs will be given or withheld according as the Court considers there was reasonable ground for the appeal; but where the decision against the appellant supports the franchise, costs will be given as of course, *Clark* v. *Overseers of Bury St. Edmund's*, 1 C. B. N. S. 23; K. & G. 90; *DeBoinville* v. *Arnold*, 1 C. B. N. S. 22; K. & G. 72. The general rule, even when the Court decides against the appellant's claim for the franchise, is to give the respondent his costs, unless the Court is of opinion there was reasonable ground for the appeal upon the construction of the Statutes; *Harris* v. *O'Connor*, I. R., 1 Reg. & Nott, 64; *Barclay* v. *Penott*, 1 C. B. N. S. 52; K. & G. 59; *Heclis* v. *Blain*, 18 C. B. N. S. 110. The Court will not give costs against the appellant, if there has been a miscarriage in the case, *Carmichael's Case*, 15 Jr. C. L. R. 371. Where the respondent alone appears, the decision of the Revising Barrister will be affirmed, and the appeal dismissed with costs, unless it appears that a similar point is involved in another case for argument, *Bage* v. *Perkins*, 7 M. & G. 156; 1 B. & A. 414; 1 Lutw. 255; and where it was suggested that there was a similar point for argument, the Court reserved judgment pending the argument, *Crocker* v. *St. Marys, Lambeth*, 7 M. & G. 156; 1 Lutw. 255. Where the point depended on a question of fact which the Revising Barrister did not decide, the Court remitted the case to be re-stated, and the appeal having been abandoned, the respondent was refused costs, *Lawe* v. *Maillard*, L. R. 4 C. P. 547; Hunt's Fran. & Regn. Law 126-7.

(*k*) "*By distress.*"—See note to S. 44, *ante*.

(c) In the Provinces of Nova Scotia, New Brunswick, Manitoba and Prince Edward Island, to the judge of the County Court; In N. S., N. B., Man. and P. E. I.

(d.) In the Province of British Columbia, to the County Court Judge; but in any electoral district which is not included within the jurisdiction of any county judge, to the Supreme Court, which court shall assign the duty of trying any appeal to some judge of the said court. In British Columbia.

OFFICERS AND THEIR DUTIES.

54. The revising officer shall appoint as his clerk a person residing in the electoral district competent to perform the duties required of him under this Act, and such as shall be by the revising officer assigned to him as clerk of the said courts of revision, or otherwise, during the preparation of and revision of the lists of voters; and such clerk shall be subject to removal by the revising officer. Clerk of revising officer.

55. The revising officer may also appoint for the purpose of serving papers, posting up notices and attending and keeping order at courts of revision, and doing such other duties as may be assigned to him by the revising officer, a competent person as a bailiff and constable, who shall be subject to the orders of the revising officer, and to be removed by him at pleasure. Bailiff or constable.

56. The revising officer shall keep at his office in the electoral district a list of the notices of objections, claims and proposed amendments sent in to him under sections nineteen, twenty-six and thirty-five, which list, as well as the said notices and notices of appeal, shall be open to inspection by any one desiring to inspect the same before the said objections, claims or proposed amendments are disposed of by the revising officer. Revising officer to keep lists of objections, etc.

Time for completing first and subsequent lists of voters.

57. The first lists of voters for polling districts to be prepared and brought into force under this Act shall be completed, finally revised and certified and duplicates thereof forwarded to the Clerk of the Crown in Chancery at Ottawa, on or before the first day of August, one thousand eight hundred and eighty-six, and the lists in future years to be revised under this Act shall be so finally revised, certified and duplicates thereof forwarded to the said Clerk of the Crown in Chancery as aforesaid, on or before the first day of August in each year after the year one thousand eight hundred and eighty-six.

APPLICATION OF EXISTING ACTS—OFFENCES.

Application of existing Acts.

58. The Acts of the Parliament of Canada in force respecting elections of members to serve in the House of Commons, or controverted election of such members, or corrupt practices at elections, shall apply to elections and proceedings thereat to which this Act is to apply, in so far as they are not inconsistent with this Act, and except always as to the qualification of voters at such elections and the lists of voters, which shall be those prescribed by this Act, and to which all the provisions of the said Acts which depend on such qualification shall be construed as referring; and all provisions of the said Acts inconsistent with this Act are hereby repealed *(ka)*.

Exception.

Repeal of inconsistent provisions.

Lists to be used before final revision.

59. At any election that may be held in any electoral district before the lists of voters under this Act shall have been finally revised and certified under this Act, the lists of voters for the previous year shall be used: Provided, that in the case of any election before the final revision and publication of the certificate of the first list provided for by this Act, the lists of voters that

(ka) See notes to sec. 3, subs. (1), and to sec. 11, *ante*.

would have been used if this Act had not been passed shall be used at such election *(kb)*. Proviso: as to first lists.

60. Section fifty-three of "*The Dominion Elections Act*, 1874," shall apply to the case of an elector in whose name another person has voted, provided the elector personated takes the oath in the schedule P to the said Act, *mutatis mutandis (kc)*. Personation clause of 37 V., c. 9, to apply.

61. Every person who in any oath or affirmation taken or made under this Act, wilfully swears or affirms falsely shall be deemed guilty of wilful and corrupt perjury. Perjury clause.

62. Every officer or person who is by law the custodian of any assessment roll, or list of voters, or of any other list or document, which, under the foregoing provisions of this Act, the revising officer is required to obtain and use for the purpose of preparing any list of voters, or of any duplicate or duly certified copy thereof, shall furnish the same, or a certified copy or copies thereof to the revising officer, as by him required; and any such officer or person refusing or omitting to furnish the same to the revising officer within a reasonable time, upon being paid or tendered the cost of preparing the same according to the law in force in the Province, shall, for each such refusal or omission, be held to be guilty of a misdemeanor and shall be punishable accordingly *(kd)*. Copies of certain lists to be furnished to revising officer. Penalty for default.

63. Every person appointed to any office or position under this Act, or required by this Act to do any matter or thing, shall, for every wilful misfeasance or wilful act of commission or omission contrary to this Act, forfeit to any person aggrieved the penal sum of five hundred dol- Penalty for malfeasance under this Act.

(*kb*) See sec. 10, *ante*.

(*kc*) This a virtual re-enactment of the section referred to, which might otherwise be held to be repealed by sec. 58, *ante*.

(*kd*) As to the power of the Dominion Parliament to impose duties on Provincial officers, see *Valin* v. *Langlois*, 5 App. Cases, L. R. 115; 3 Sup. Ct. 1.

lars, or such less sum as the jury, or judge, when the case by the law of the Province is triable without a jury, before whom any action to be brought for the recovery of the before mentioned sum may be tried, shall consider just to be paid to such party; and the same shall be recoverable by such party with full costs of suit, by action for debt in any court of competent jurisdiction: Provided always, that nothing herein contained shall be construed to interfere with any other remedy, civil or criminal, against such person.

Proviso: as to other remedies.

Punishment of persons being agents within 43 V., c. 28, influencing Indians to be, or not to be registered as voters.

64. Every person who is an agent within the meaning of "*The Indian Act*, 1880," and who, either directly or indirectly, seeks to induce or compel any person who is an Indian or of part Indian blood and qualified to vote only in respect of property forming part of a reserve, as defined by the said Act, to cause his name to be registered as a voter or to vote or refrain from voting at any election of a member of the House of Commons, shall be held to be guilty of a misdemeanor, and, if found guilty thereof, shall be punishable by a fine not exceeding two hundred dollars, or by imprisonment for any term not exceeding six months, or by both, and shall not be entitled to hold any office or place of emolument in the appointment of the Governor *(l)*, or of the Superintendent General of Indian Affairs, for a period of two years from the date of his conviction.

Punishment of offences not otherwise provided for.

65. Any wilful offence against this Act, for which no other punishment is provided, shall be a misdemeanor, and punishable as such.

(*l*) "*The Governor*."—i. e. Governor-General of Canada. See Interpretation Act, 31 Vic., cap. 1, sec. 7, "Secondly."

Such agent if guilty of inducing or compelling an Indian to vote, would be also liable to any further penalties imposed for the offence of "undue influence" under the Election Acts.

See chapters on "Corrupt Practices" and "Penalties," *post*.

SCHEDULE OF FORMS.

A.

(See S. 13.)

Oath of Office of a Revising Officer.

I, of the of , in the County of and Province of , the revising officer appointed under "*The Electoral Franchise Act,*" in and for the electoral district (*or* part of the electoral district) of in the Province of do hereby solemnly swear (*or* affirm) that I will well and faithfully discharge the duties assigned to me by the said Act without favor or partiality; that I will place no name on the list of voters for the said electoral district (*or* part of said electoral district) or any of the polling districts thereof, and will strike no name off the same, unless I shall be satisfied that the same should by law be placed on or struck off the same; and that I will in all respects conform to the said Act and the law to the best of my judgment and ability. So help me GOD.

Sworn before me, a judge of the Court of , in and for the Province of , being a Court of Record, at the of in the *County* of and Province aforesaid this day of A. D., 188	A.B. *Revising officer for the electoral district (or part of the electoral district) of*

C.D.
A Judge, &c.

B.

(See S. 15.)

LIST of Voters for the Year commencing 1st January, 18 , in the (Electoral District *or* part of the Electoral District of *or* Polling District No. *of the Electoral District of .)

No.	Name in full. (Surname first.)	Residence.	P.O. Address.	Nature of Qualification.	Municipality or Place where Qualification is situate, if Real Estate.	Concession, Street and No. of Lot or other particular description of qualifying Property.	Nature of Title to Qualifying Property.	Name of Parent, if the Voter is Qualified as a Son of a Farmer or other Owner of Real Property; also nature of Parent's Title to the Real Property.	Remarks.

Dated 188

A. B.,
Revising Officer for the electoral district (or part of the electoral district) of

*There should be a "local designation attached to such number," e.g., "Township of Digby, No. 1," or "No. 1, Township of Digby."—See *ante* ss. 22 and 24.

C.

(See Ss. 16, 29 and 37.)

Revising Officer's Certificate of List of Voters.

I, , the undersigned revising officer for the electoral district (*or* part of the electoral district) of in the Province of , do hereby certify that the foregoing list consisting of pages, is a true copy of the list of voters for the local municipality *or* for the electoral district *or* part of the electoral district of as originally prepared (*or* preliminarily revised, *as the case may be*), *or* polling district number in the said Electoral district before (*or* after) the final revision thereof, *as the case may be*, for the year , under "*The Electoral Franchise Act.*"

Dated 188

A. B.

Revising Officer for the electoral district (or *part of the electoral district*) *of*

D.

(See Ss. 17 and 18.)

Notice by Revising Officer of preliminary revision of First List of Voters.

The Revising Officer for the Electoral District (*or* part of the electoral district) of in the Province of , appointed under "*The Electoral Franchise Act*," hereby gives notice that he has completed and published in the manner directed by the said Act, the first general list of voters for the said electoral district (*or* part of the said electoral district), and that he will hold a sitting pursuant to the said Act for the preliminary revision of such list at in the of *County* of , in the said

Province, at o'clock in the on the day of 188 . Any person objecting to any name on the said list may at any time before the said day, and any person desiring to add any name thereto, or desiring otherwise to amend the same, may, on or before the day of 188 , deliver to the said revising officer or mail to him by registered letter at his office or place of address, a notice in writing in the form for that purpose contained in the schedule to the said Act, as nearly as may be, setting forth the name or names objected to, and the grounds of objection, or the name or names proposed to be added to the list, with the grounds therefor, and particulars of the qualification and residence of the persons whose names are proposed to be added, or the particulars of any other proposed amendment, and the grounds therefor: and every such notice must be signed by the person so giving notice, and must set forth his residence, occupation and post-office address. In the event of the person so giving notice objecting to the name of any person already on the list, the person so objecting must also deliver to or mail to the last known address of the person whose name is objected to, by registered letter, and at the same time as the notice is given to the revising officer, a copy of the notice given.

Dated , 188

A. B.

Revising Officer for the electoral district (or *part of the electoral district) of*

E.

(See S. 19.)

Notice of Complaint or Application.

I , of the of , in the County of , in the electoral district of , Province of , under "*The Electoral Franchise Act*," hereby give notice that I will apply to have the first general list for the electoral district (*or* part of the electoral district) of (*or* the list for the municipality *or* polling district No. of the said electoral district) (*or* the lists for the year as preliminarily revised), *as the case may be,* amended *or* added to, *as the case may be ; (then state the name or names objected to with the grounds therefor, or the name or names desired to be added, with full particulars of their residences, addresses, occupations, qualifications, and if real property, where situated, and the grounds for applying to have them added, or the nature of any other proposed amendments to the list and the grounds therefor)*, at the sitting to be held by the revising officer for the said electoral district (*or* part of the said electoral district), at o'clock in the noon, on the day of , 188 , at in the said electoral district.

Dated , 188 .

To the Revising officer for the said electoral district (*or* part of the said electoral district), (*or to the person whose name is objected to.*)

(*Name of complainant.*)

P. O. Address.

F.

(*See S. 21.*)

Order of Revising Officer dividing Electoral District into Polling Districts.

I, , the revising officer for the electoral district (*or* part of the electoral district) of , Province of under "*The Electoral Franchise Act,*" do hereby order and direct that the said electoral district (*or* part of the said electoral district), be and the same is hereby sub-divided into polling districts, described as follows :

Number one

Bounded on (*here fill in as particular a description, by concession, street or other dividing lines, as possible, of the bounds of each polling district.*)

(*And so on as to others*).

Dated , 188 .

A. B.,

Revising Officer for the electoral district (or *part of the electoral district of*

G.

(*See S. 24.*)

Notice by Revising Officer of Final Revision of Lists of Voters for each Polling District.

The revising officer for the electoral district (*or* part of the electoral district) of in the Province of , under "*The Electoral Franchise Act*," hereby gives notice that he will hold a sitting on the day of , 188 , at o'clock in the ; at in the of , in the said electoral district, for the final revision of the list of voters for polling district No. , of the said electoral district.

All objections and claims for additions to or amendment of the said list, with the grounds therefor, and the name, addition and post office address of the person objecting to any name on the list, or claiming to add to or amend the list in any other respect, unless the same have already been sent or delivered at the preliminary revision of the said list, must be delivered to the said revising officer at , or sent to him by registered letter, addressed to him at , before the day of 188 , in the same form, as nearly as may be, as of notice of complaint, in the schedule to "*The Electoral Franchise Act.*"

If the objection be to the name of any person already on the list, the person so objecting must, at the same time, deliver or mail by registered letter to the person so objected to, at his last known address, a copy of the notice of objection.

Dated 188 . A. B.,

Revising Officer for the electoral district (or *part of the electoral district*) *of*

H.

(See Ss. 29 and 37.)

Notice to be published in the Canada Gazette by the Clerk of the Crown in Chancery.

Notice is hereby given that I have received the lists of voters, finally revised, for all the polling districts of the electoral district of for the year , under "*The Electoral Franchise Act.*"

Dated , 188

C. D.,
Clerk of the Crown in Chancery at Ottawa.

J.

(See S. 42.)

Summons to Witness.

To

You are hereby required and summoned personally to attend before me, the undersigned revising officer, on , the day of , 188 , at o'clock in the at in the County of , and Province of , and then and there to testify what you may know concerning the then to be investigated by me as such revising officer, and so on from day to day, and you shall bring with you the papers herein particularly described, that is to say :

And herein fail not at your peril.

Given under my hand at aforesaid, this day of , 188 , under "*The Electoral Franchise Act.*"

A. B.,
Revising Officer for the electoral district (or *part of the electoral district*) *of*

RESOLUTIONS OF ONTARIO REVISING OFFICERS.

At a meeting of Ontario Revising Officers, appointed under The Dominion Franchise Act, held at Toronto on Monday, November 9th, 1885, the following were present:—Judges Hughes, Elgin; Elliott, Middlesex; Macpherson, Grey; Miller, Halton; Bell, Kent; Dennistoun, Peterboro'; Barrett, Bruce; Boys, Simcoe; Finkle, Oxford; Carmen, Stormont and Glengarry; Senkler, Lincoln; Baxter, Welland; Woods, Kent; Burnham, Ontario; Dartnell, Ontario; McCarthy, Dufferin; Sinclair, Wentworth; Dean, Victoria; Doyle, Huron; Drew, Wellington; Lane, Grey; Lacourse, Waterloo; Benson, Northumberland and Durham; McDougall, and Morgan, York; Scott, Peel; Upper, Haldimand; and Messrs. J. Grayden Smith, North Perth; Bell, Hamilton; Mahaffy, Muskoka; and Boyd, Toronto.

Judge Jones, of Brant, was moved into the chair and Judge McDougall appointed Secretary.

A debate took place upon Section 15 of the Franchise Act, when the following resolutions were adopted to regulate the action of the Revising-officers in their practice thereunder:—

Resolved,—"That in the organized districts no name shall be added to the preliminary list which does not appear in the last revised assessment roll or last revised list of voters, unless an application is made in writing by the person desiring to be added or by some one on his behalf, disclosing grounds which would *primâ facie* entitle him to be put on the preliminary voters' list, and the said application be filed with the Revising-officer.

Resolved,—"That the Revising-officer, in receiving the application mentioned in the next preceding resolution, shall only act upon the same when it is supported by a statutory declaration, or such other evidence as may reasonably satisfy the mind of such Revising-officer.

Resolved,—"That in Indian Reserves the Revising-officer describe the voter's property on which he votes as the part of the Indian Reserve named, occupied, and possessed by the said voter, or such better description as he can give."

A discussion upon the practice that should prevail under Sections 19 and 20 of the Franchise Act as to the revision of the preliminary list took place, resulting in the following resolution:—

"Under sections 19 and 20 it would appear that evidence cannot be heard to support objections to strike names off the preliminary list of voters, but to settle all doubts on the question, it is *Resolved*,—That as a matter of practice it is advisable that in making the preliminary revision of the voters' lists under the Franchise Act, the Revising-officer should not take any evidence in support of applications to strike the names off the list. But that all such investigation be deferred to the final revision, such a practice being calculated to save time and expense to the parties interested."

The next section considered was No. 24, and an interesting debate followed as to its proper interpretation.

The following resolution was finally adopted:—

"That in the case of a ward in a city or town containing less than 300 voters, although more than 200, such ward should not be subdivided into polling districts."

It was the unanimous opinion of those present that at the final revision of the list, a court need only be held in each municipality to consider objections, and that it was not necessary to hold such court in each polling district. (See secs. 26, 34 and 48, *ante*.)

THE

ONTARIO PROVINCIAL FRANCHISE.

AN ACT TO AMEND THE LAWS RELATING TO THE FRANCHISE AND THE REPRESENTATION OF THE PEOPLE.

HER Majesty, by and with the advice and consent of the Legislative Assembly of the Province of Ontario, enacts as follows:—

1. This Act may be cited and known as *The Franchise and Representation Act, 1885* (a). Short title

2. Section 2 of *The Election Act*, and its sub-sections, are hereby repealed, and the following is substituted instead thereof: R. S. O. c. 10, s. 2, repealed.

2. Unless otherwise declared or indicated by the context, where any of the following words or expressions occur in this Act, they shall have the meanings hereinafter expressed, that is to say:— Interpretation.

(a) Only that portion of the Act which relates to the Franchise is here given, together with those sections of the Election Act still unrepealed, and which relate to the same subject, the balance of these Acts being devoted chiefly to the description of the different electoral divisions, the procedure at elections, corrupt practices, etc.

Owner. (1) The word "owner" shall signify and mean proprietor either in his own right (*b*) or in the right of his wife (*c*), of an estate for life, or any greater estate (*d*) either legal or equitable (*e*).

Occupant. (2) The word "occupant" (*ee*) shall signify and mean a person *bonâ fide* occupying (*f*) property otherwise than as owner or tenant, either in his own right or in the right of his wife, but being in possession of such property and enjoying the revenues and profits arising therefrom to his own use.

Tenant. (3) The word "tenant" shall include any person who instead of paying rent in money is bound to render to the owner any portion of the produce of such property (*ff*).

(*b*) "*Proprietor in his own right.*"—The form of oath to be administered to an owner is "you were actually, truly and in good faith possessed to your own use and benefit, as either owner, etc., in your own right or in right of your wife." A trustee cannot vote *per* Mowat, V. C., in *South Grenville, Jones' vote*, 1 H. E. C. 175; and where an owner has sold to a tenant in possession, though the land is not fully paid for nor deed executed, he is a trustee for the purchaser, *Ib.* 170. A mortgagee not in possession, is in the same position. See also notes to Dominion Franchise Act, s. 2, under "in his own right, etc," and "legal or equitable," *ante*.

(*c*) "*In the right of his wife.*"—See note to Dominion Franchise Act, s. 2, under same heading, *ante*.

(*d*) "*An estate for life, or any greater estate.*"—The term *estate for life* includes an estate for the life of another, usually called an estate *pur autre vie*, or for more lives than one, Black. Com. Book 2, c. 8. The words quoted embrace all freehold estates. See note to Dom. Franchise Act, s. 2, "freehold estate," *ante*.

(*e*) "*Legal or equitable.*"—See note to Dom. Franchise Act, s. 2, under same words, *ante*.

(*ee*) See note to Dom. Franchise Act, s. 2, "occupant," *ante*.

(*f*) "*Bonâ fide occupying,*"—These words are, it is conceived, tantamount to the words "in actual occupation" used in the Dominion Act, and mean actual possession as distinguished from possession in law, especially when read in connection with the subsequent words "in possession of such property and enjoying the revenues and profits, etc." See note to Dom. Act. The latter words would seem to exclude the husband of a woman who occupies property separately from him from the right to vote in respect of such property.

(*ff*) See note to Dom. Franchise Act, s. 2, "tenant."

(4) The expression "landholder" (*fx*) shall mean and include: Landholder.

(*a*) Any person who being the owner of and residing and domiciled upon real property of at least twenty acres in extent, or of at least an actual value (*g*) in cities and towns of four hundred dollars, and in townships and incorporated villages of two hundred dollars, is, in the last revised assessment roll (*h*) of the municipality where such property is situate, entered and assessed as owner of said property of at least the number of acres or the assessed value aforesaid, and

(*b*) Any person actually residing and domiciled in any dwelling house as tenant thereof, where such dwelling house and the land, if any, held therewith by such person as such tenant is of at least an actual value in cities and towns of four hundred dollars, and in townships and incorporated villages of two hundred dollars, and is at not less than such value entered and assessed in the name of such person in the last revised assessment roll of the municipality wherein the same is situate.

(5) The expression "landholder's son" shall mean and include a son, step-son, grandson, or son-in-law, as the case may be, of any landowner. Landholder's son.

(6) The expression "wage-earner" (*hh*) shall mean any Wage-earner.

(*fx*) This is a new term, not found in the former Acts, nor in the Dom. Act. It is introduced in order to define the class whose sons shall, as such, be now entitled to the franchise conferred only upon farmers' sons by the previous Act. It includes either a male or female.

(*g*) "*Actual value.*"—See Dom. Franchise Act, s. 2, *actual value*, and note thereunder, *ante* p. 19.

(*h*) "*Last revised assessment roll.*"—See *post*.

(*hh*) This is another new term, not found in the former Acts.

person entered in the last revised assessment roll of a city, town, incorporated village or township, as one having or deriving an annual income or wages of not less than two hundred and fifty dollars, but who is not entered or assessed in said roll for a taxable income of at least two hundred and fifty dollars.

Dwelling house (7) The expression "dwelling house" (*x*) shall mean and include any part of a house when that part is separately occupied or resided in as a dwelling, and also any land where such land is separately occupied or resided upon as and is a part of the premises belonging to and used with such dwelling.

For requirements as to residence, etc., see *post*, s. 3 (7 of amended El. Act) "*Thirdly.*"

By *The Assessment Amendment Act 1885*, "the expression 'wage earner' shall mean any male person of the full age of twenty-one years, and a subject of Her Majesty by birth or naturalization, who is actually resident and domiciled in any municipality, and who is not otherwise entered or assessed in the assessment roll of said municipality in respect either of property or taxable income so as to entitle him to vote at an election for a member of the Legislative Assembly of this Province."

(*x*) See Imperial Parliamentary and Mun'l. Reg'n. Act, 1878, s. 5, by which the term "dwelling house" is made to "include any part of a house where that part is separately occupied as a dwelling," and whereby also joint occupancy of some other part does not affect the qualification as to the part so separately occupied. In *Thompson* v. *Ward* and *Ellis* v. *Burch*, L. R. 6, C. P. 327, and *Boon* v. *Howard*, L. R. 9, C. P. 277, the Court had been equally divided on the question whether certain rooms in a house, not structurally severed from the rest, but separately occupied and rated, were dwelling houses within the meaning of s. 3 of the Act of 1867; and the above amendment was made in 1878 to meet the difficulty and obviate the necessity for a structural severance, which it is conceived, will be unnecessary, under the Ontario Act also, notwithstanding that the latter Act does not contain the declaration contained in the English Act of 1867, as to a joint occupancy of part not preventing separate occupation of the other part constituting the latter a "dwelling house." It may be mentioned that the earlier English Act (1867) defined a dwelling house as including "any part of a house occupied as a *separate dwelling*," while the Act of 1878 altered the definition so as to include any part "*separately occupied* as a dwelling," and the latter form of phraseology is adopted in the Ontario Act. See judg't. of Bagallay, L. J. in *Bradley* v. *Baylis*, L. R. 8 Q. B. at p. 228; see further Dom. Franchise Act, s. 2 "real property," and note to words "house, etc." thereunder, *ante*.

(8) The expression "householder" shall mean any person entered in the revised assessment roll of a city, town, township or incorporated village as sole tenant and occupant of and actually resident in a dwelling-house situate therein, but shall not mean nor include, **Householder.**

(*a*) Any person who is so entered or who is actually a joint tenant or occupant (*i*) of such dwelling-house with any other person; nor

(*b*). Any person who is a mere lodger or boarder (*j*) in a house.

(*i*) "*Joint tenant or occupant.*"—A person otherwise qualified does not become a joint occupier and so lose his qualification by letting to a lodger the exclusive use of a bedroom and the joint use of a sitting-room, *Brewer* v. *McGowan*, L. R. 5 C. P. 239; 39 L. J. C. P. 30. The English Act of 1867 contained a similar proviso to the above, but the Act of 1878 which defines the term "dwelling house," as in note to subs. (7) above, further declares that "where an occupier is entitled to the sole and exclusive use of any part of a house, that part shall not be deemed to be occupied otherwise than separately by reason that the occupier is entitled to the joint use of some other part."

(*j*) "*Lodger or boarder.*"—The question as to whether a man is a householder or a lodger is often one involving much difficulty. "There is, probably, no question on which there has been a greater variety of judicial opinion than this," per Jessel M. R. in *Bradley* v. *Baylis*, L. R. 8, Q. B. D. 218. In England there is a lodger franchise, as well as a householder franchise. This section is intended to provide only for the latter and to exclude the former. The question referred to came before the English Court of Appeal in three cases, *Bradley* v. *Baylis*, *Morfee* v. *Novis*, and *Kirby* v. *Biffin*, L. R. 8 Q. B. D. 195 to 246. In one of these cases, the tenant of two rooms which he took unfurnished at a weekly rent, had the exclusive use of such rooms and a key of the outer door of the house. His landlord had also the key of the outer door, and resided in all of the rest of the house, but supplied no attendance or service to such tenant. *Held*, that such tenant occupied the house as a lodger, and consequently that in respect of such occupation he could not acquire the dwelling house franchise under the Rep. of the People Act, 1867. One of the other cases was similar in character. In the third case, the tenant of two rooms which he took unfurnished at a weekly rent, had in common with the other tenants of the house, which was wholly let out on similar tenancies, the use of the passage, stair case, street door, and usual conveniencies of the house. The landlord and not the tenant was rated, and the landlord did all repairs, inside and out, but he did not reside in the house, nor did he, save as aforesaid, retain the control and dominion over the house, or render any services to any of the tenants: *Held*, that such tenant did not occupy the rooms as a lodger, but as an occupying tenant under the Rep. Peop. Act, 1867, and that he could therefore acquire the dwelling house franchise in respect of such occupation. And it has been since held that a householder qualified as such by occupying one of a set of rooms in a house not resided in by the landlord, does not become a lodger by reason of another room becoming vacant and consequently reverting to the landlord, *Ancketill* v. *Baylis*, 10 Q. B. D. 577, C. A., a decision which disposed of a *dictum* of Brett, L. J., in the former cases. Rooms in a college were said not to be lodgings in *Barnes* v. *Peters*, L. R. 4 C. P. 539; see also *Ford* v. *Hart*, L. R 9 C. P. 273. In *Bradley* v. *Baylis*, and associated cases, the judges of the Court of Appeal all expressed their inability to frame an exhaustive definition of a *lodger*, as contradistinguished from a *tenant*. Jessel, M. R., gives two examples or rules: *First*, as to unfurnished lodgings (the only class of cases, he considers, as to which questions are likely to arise) where the owner of the house does not let the whole of it, but retains a part for his own residence and resides there, and where he does not let out the passages, staircase and outerdoor, but gives to the inmates merely a right of ingress and egress, and retains to himself the general control with right of interfering, to turn out trespassers, etc., he considers the owner the occupying tenant and the inmate a *lodger*: *Secondly*, where the landlord lets out the whole of the house into separate apartments, and lets out each floor separately, so as to demise the passages, reserving simply to each inmate of the upper floors the right of ingress and egress over the lower passages, but parts entirely with the whole legal ownership, for the term demised, and retains no control over the house, there the inmates are occupying *tenants*. There are, he says, an immense number of intermediate cases, in some of which the inmates are *lodgers*, notwithstanding that they may have latch-keys to outer and inner doors, that the landlord may not reside there personally, but has servants occupying on his behalf part of the house, and whether he does repairs or not; while, on the other hand, though the landlord do not demise the whole house, but everything in it that can be demised, except the staircases, and passages, etc., as to which he gives the inmates the right of ingress and egress, but exercising no control and not residing in the house—in such case the inmates would be occupying *tenants*. Baggallay, L. J., adopts these rules. Brett, L. J., refers to the distinctions drawn in three cases in 7 Manning and Grainger, turning in each case upon the ownership of the key of the outer door, and summarized as follows: 1. The owner of the house had the key of the outer door and he resided in the house—*Held*, that a person who occupied the rooms in that house was a lodger with him; (2) The owner had let part of the house, reserving no control over it, and did not keep for himself the key of the outer door—*Held*, that the person occupying the part of the house occupied it as a householder and not a lodger: (3) The owner held the key of the outer door, but the person who occupied part of the house had a key also—*Held*, that such person was a lodger. "If you substitute," says his lordship, "in those cases the consideration of the owner of the house preserving a control over it, then the distinctions drawn in those cases will remain as very good guides." Cotton, L. J., says: "Now what is a *lodger*? I do not intend to try to give that which will be an exhaustive definition of a lodger. I have had to consider it several times in this Court, and, in my opinion, there is involved in the term 'lodger,' that the man must lodge in the house of another man and lodge with him. With respect to lodging in the house of

(9) The expression "local municipality" shall mean and include a city, town, incorporated village or township, as the case may be. Local Municipality.

(10) The word "election" shall mean an election of a member to serve in the Legislative Assembly. Election.

(11) The expression "to vote" shall mean to vote at the election of a member of the Legislative Assembly. To vote.

(12) The expression "electoral distrtct" shall mean any county or other place or portion of this Province, entitled to return a member to the Legislative Assembly. Electoral district.

---

another man; there is no difficulty about that. What constitutes his lodging with the landlord is the difficulty. In my opinion, it is not necessary that the person with whom he lodges, that is his immediate landlord, should live in the house to make him a lodger. Nor is it necessary that the immediate landlord should have the exclusive control over the key of the outer door; but, in my opinion, some control over the house must be exercised by the person in whose house a man lives to make him a lodger." Lindley, L. J., says: "The distinction, then, between tenants who are not lodgers and tenants who are lodgers, must be discovered from other sources than the statutes, and it is extremely difficult to draw the line between them. At the same time the word 'lodger' involves the idea of lodging with some one else from whom he hires his lodging; whilst the word tenant does not involve, though it does not exclude this idea; and this difference gives the clue to the distinction which the statutes have made. Taking this difference as a guide, it appears to me that where a house is wholly let out in unfurnished apartments, separately occupied by tenants, and their landlord does not reside in the house, and has no servant in the house to look after it for him, the tenants are rateable and are not lodgers; whilst on the other hand where a house is let out in unfurnished apartments to tenants, and their landlord resides in the house, or has a servant in it, to look after it for him, then it appears to me that such tenants are not rateable and are lodgers." See also *Pitts* v. *Smedley*, 7 M. & G. 33; 14 L. J. C, P. 73; *Wansey* v. *Perkins*, *Ib.* 151 and 75; *Score* v. *Huggett*, *Ib.* 95 and 74; *Stamper* v. *Overseers of Sunderland*, L. R. 3 C. P. 388.

Under the Municipal Act (Consolidated Municipal Act, 1883, s. 87) "every occupant of a separate portion of a house, such portion having a distinct communication with a public road or street by an outer door, shall be deemed a householder within this Act." This definition should be altered to that given in Franchise and Assessment Amendment Acts, 1885, otherwise great difficulty will be created in distinguishing from the roll those entitled to the Legislative and those entitled to the Municipal Franchise as householders.

Voters' list. (13) The expression "voters' list" shall mean the copy of the voters' list furnished in accordance with section 56 of this Act (*jj*).

Last revised assessment roll. (14) The expression "last revised assessment roll" shall mean the last revised assessment roll of a city, town, incorporated village or township (*jx*).

Corrupt practice. (15) The expression "corrupt practices" or "corrupt practice" shall mean bribery, treating and undue influence, or any of such offences as defined by this or any Act of the Legislature, or recognized by the Common

---

(*jj*) Section 56 provides for a copy of the first and third parts of the Voters' List for each subdivision being provided to the Deputy Returning Officers. A practical difficulty has in some cases presented itself, where the Returning Officer, on the eve of the election, subdivided the municipal subdivisions, and the municipal clerk was unable to separate the names as they appeared in the existing list for the municipal subdivision, owing to the property not being described with reference to the new subdivision or to voters possessing a qualification from property in both parts of such subdivision—the result being that the whole list for the municipal division was in some cases supplied for each new subdivision, the process of swearing the voters being the only safeguard against duplicate votes being polled. This difficulty now only arises where the Council has failed to subdivide polling divisions containing more than 300 voters, and the Returning Officer subdivides pursuant to subs. 6 of sec. 11 of the Elections Act as amended by the election Amendment Act, 1883.

(*jx*) The expression, it is presumed, means the roll as finally revised and corrected. See section 7 of the Election Act and its sub-sections as amended by sec. 3 of this Act, in which, it is presumed, the expressions "assessment roll" and "revised assessment roll," will have the same meaning. By the Voters' List Act (Rev. Stats. cap. 9, as amended by 48 Vic., c. 2, s. 2, subs. 11), "an assessment roll shall be understood to be finally revised and corrected, when it has been so revised and corrected by the Court of Revision for the municipality, or by the Judge of the County Court, in case of an appeal, as provided in the '*Assessment Act*,' or when the time during which such appeal may be made has elapsed and not before." The date of the final revision, therefore, varies according to whether appeals are entered or not. (*a*) If there has been no appeal to the Court of Revision, the roll is finally revised as soon as passed (after 26th May) by said Court and certified by the Clerk, Rev. Stats. cap. 180, s. 57; (*b*) where there has been a complaint or appeal to the Court of Revision, but none to the County Judge, then, when five days after the date limited for closing the Court of Revision (1 July) have elapsed, *i.e.*, 7th July, s. 59, subs 2; (*c*) where there has been an appeal to the County Judge, then on such day prior to 1st Aug. as the decision of the Judge is given, s. 60.

Law of the Parliament of England; also any violation of sections 151, 154, or 156 of this Act, and any violation of section 157 of this Act during the hours appointed for polling (*jy*).

QUALIFICATION OF MEMBERS.

[3. No qualification in real estate shall be required of any candidate for any seat in the Legislative Assembly (*jz*). No property qualification for members.

QUALIFICATION OF VOTERS.

Who shall not Vote.

4. The Chief Justice and the Justices of the Court of Appeal, the Chancellor and Vice-Chancellors of Ontario, the Chief Justices and the Judges of the Court of Queen's Bench and Common Pleas in Ontario, all County Judges, all Officers of the Customs of the Dominion of Canada, all Clerks of the Peace, County Attorneys, Registrars, Sheriffs, Deputy-Sheriffs, Deputy Clerks of the Crown, and agents for the sale of Crown Lands, all Postmasters in Cities and towns, all Stipendiary Magistrates, and all Officers employed in the collection of any duties payable to Her Majesty in the nature of duties of excise, shall be disqualified and incompetent to vote at any election, and if any public officer or person mentioned in this section votes at any such election, he shall thereby forfeit the sum of two thousand dollars, and his vote at such election shall be null and void. 46 V. c. 2, s. 10 (*ja*). Persons disqualified from voting. Penalty.

(*jy*) See chapter on "Corrupt Practices" *post*.

(*jz*) This section and the three following sections as to disqualifications taken from the Elections Act, as amended by the Act of 1883, are here inserted in their proper order.

(*ja*) All the persons mentioned in this section except the Judges, are, it is believed, qualified to vote under the Dominion Franchise Act for members of the House of Commons. See Dom. Franchise Act s. 3, subs. (1) note "*by any law of the Dominion of Canada;*" also note to s. 11 "*disqualified and incompetent to vote;*" ante.

Certain officers and persons not to vote.

5. No Returning Officer or Election Clerk, and no person who, at any time, either during the election or before the election, is or has been employed at the said election or in reference thereto, or for the purpose of forwarding the same by any candidate or by any person whomsoever, as counsel, agent, attorney or clerk, at any polling place at any such election, or in any other capacity whatever, and who has received or expects to receive, either before, during or after the said election, from any candidate or from any person whomsoever, for acting in any such capacity as aforesaid, any sum of money, fee, office, place of employment, or any promise, pledge or security whatever therefor, shall be entitled to vote at any election (*jb*).

2. The preceding provisions shall not apply to Deputy-Returning Officers and Poll Clerks appointed under this Act and receiving as such the fees to which such officers are entitled under this Act (*jc*).

No woman to vote.

6. No woman shall be entitled to vote at any election (*jd*).]

Who may Vote.

R.S.O., c. 10, s. 7, repealed.

3. Section 7 of *The Election Act*, and its sub-sections, are hereby repealed, and the following are substituted therefor:

(*jb*) See Dominion Franchise Act s. 11, subs. (b) and note thereunder, *ante*.

(*jc*) Such deputy returning officers and poll clerks, as well as two agents of each candidate may vote at a polling place other than the one at which they are entitled to vote, if they be appointed to act and are actually engaged at such polling place, on obtaining a certificate from the returning officer (but not in a municipality or territory for which there are no voters' lists or supplementary voters' lists) and only after having taken one or other of the oaths of qualification prescribed for voters. See s. 87 of the Elections Act as amended by 46 Vic., c. 2, s. 4.

(*jd*) Widows and unmarried women may vote at municipal elections, 47 Vic., c. 32, s. 3. Women may also vote on municipal money by-laws, at school elections, and vestry meetings, 23 Grant 49.

7. The following persons, and no others, being males and of the full age (*k*) of twenty-one years, and subjects of Her Majesty (*l*) by birth or naturalization, and not being disqualified under the preceding sections, or otherwise by law prevented from voting (*m*), shall if duly entered on the list of voters proper to be used at the election then pending, according to the provisions of *The Voters' Lists Act*, or of this Act, be entitled to vote at elections of members to serve in the Legislative Assembly of this Province, that is to say: **Who may vote at elections.**

Firstly.—Every male person entered on the revised assessment roll, upon which the voters' list to be used at the election is based for any city, town, incorporated village or township, for real property of the value hereinafter mentioned, and being at the time of the final revision and correction (*n*) of said assessment roll, and also at the time of the election, a resident of and domiciled within (*o*) the Electoral District for which he claims to vote. **Real property qualification.**

(2.) Such person must (subject to the provisions hereinafter contained) have been rated on such assessment roll as the owner, tenant or occupant of real property of the actual value of not less than the following (*oo*): **Value of real property necessary.**

(*k*) "*Full Age.*"—See sec. 3, subs. (1) of Dom. Franchise Act and note "*full age of 21 years,*" *ante.*

(*l*) "*Subjects of Her Majesty.*"—See sec. 3, subs. (2) of Dom. Franchise Act and note, *ante.*

(*m*) "*Otherwise by Law prevented from Voting.*"—A person found guilty of a corrupt practice is disqualified for eight years. Rev. Stats. cap. 10, secs. 161 and 164. As to what are corrupt practices see chapter on "Corrupt Practices"; also chapter on "Penalties," *post.* See, also, Dom. Fr. Act, sec. 3, subs. (1) and sec. 11, *ante.*

(*n*) "*Time of the final revision and correction.*"—See *ante*, note to sec. 2, subs. (14).

(*o*) "*A resident of and domiciled within.*"—See Dom. Fr. Act, s. 3, subs. (6) and note. Non-residents cannot vote under any of the provisions of this Act.

(*oo*) See notes to sec. 2 of Dom. Fr. Act under respective titles "owner," "tenant," "occupant," and "actual value," *ante.*

In cities and towns, two hundred dollars;

In incorporated villages and townships, one hundred dollars;

Joint owners. (3.) Where any real property is owned or occupied jointly by two or more persons, and is rated at an amount sufficient, if equally divided between them, to give a qualification to each, then each of them shall be deemed rated within this Act, otherwise none of them shall be deemed so rated (*op*).

Income franchise. *Secondly.*—Every male person who is residing at the time of the election in the local municipality in which he tenders his vote and has resided therein continuously (*p*) since the completion of the last revised assessment roll (*q*) of the municipality, and derives an income (*r*) from some

---

(*op*) See sec. 6 of Dom. Fr. Act and note thereunder, *ante*. Prince Edward Island Act, 24 Vic., c. 34, s. 14; Nova Scotia Fr. Act, 1885, s. 5; Quebec Election Act, 38 Vic., c. 7, s. 9, etc., "*if equally divided between them.*" Under the Dominion Act the partners are qualified according to their respective shares and if the share of any one partner does not come up to the amount necessary to qualify, he cannot be registered, though the partners whose shares are sufficient may be. The same rule prevails under the Quebec Act, *electoral lists of Kamouraska*, 3 Q. L. R. 308, s. c., 1877. The same appears to be the rule under the Prince Edward Island Act above cited. Under this Act the rule laid down is that all, or none, may vote. Under the Nova Scotia Act the assessment is to be apportioned "to the best of the assessors' judgment."

(*p*) "*Has resided therein continuously.*"—The residence for the period named must be continuous. Absence on duty with the militia, which is a compulsory legal absence, but temporary, is not a disqualification within the statute which requires voters to be resident for six months prior to the election, *Rex* v. *Mitchell*, 8 East, 511. Where, as by this sub-section, no qualification by occupation as owner or tenant was expressly required, it has been held that any actual residence is sufficient, and that a man who had for two months lived with his wife and child in a room in a cottage allotted to the wife's mother by the trustees of a charity, the rules of which prohibited the inmates from taking in strangers, did not break his residence; *Beal* v. *Ford*, 3 C. P. D. 73. See note to sec. 3, subs. (6) of Dom. Fr. Act, *ante*.

(*q*) "*Completion of the last revised assessment roll.*"—See note to sec. 2, subs. (14) *ante*.

(*r*) "*Income.*"—Income means the balance of gain over loss, *Lawless* v. *Sullivan*, L. R. 6 App. Cases 373, which reversed judgments of the Supreme Courts of Canada and New Brunswick as to the interpretation of the term in the Assessment Act of the latter Province.

trade, occupation, calling, office or profession (*s*) of not less than two hundred and fifty dollars (*t*) annually, and has been assessed (*u*) for such income in and by the assessment roll of the municipality upon which the voters' list used at the election is based.

Thirdly.—Every male person entered on the last revised assessment roll (*v*) as a wage-earner (*w*) who is residing at the time of the election in the local municipality in which he tenders his vote, and has resided therein continuously (*x*) since the completion of the last revised assessment roll of the municipality, and who has during the twelve months next prior to being so entered, derived or earned wages or income (*y*) from some trade, occupation, calling, office, or profession of not less than two hundred and fifty dollars. Wages franchise.

(*s*) "*Trade, occupation, etc.*"—The words in the former Act were "trade, calling, office or profession." The word "occupation" has been added, though without, apparently, widening the scope of this franchise. Persons deriving their income from investments, but not being professional money lenders or brokers, would seem to be excluded. There is no provision for cases of joint or partnership income, as under the last sub-section as to joint property; therefore, the partner whose share of the income entitles him to vote will be entitled to be on the list, though the other partner's share may be insufficient to qualify him. Income voters should, however, be assessed individually on the roll, as it has been held that a person cannot, on appeal to the Voters' List Court, be put on the list for income unless his name be upon the assessment roll, *Lincoln—Borrowman's case*, 2 Ont. Ap. R. 316.

(*t*) "*Two hundred and fifty dollars.*"—The former income qualification was $400.

(*u*) "*Has been assessed.*"—The income voter may waive the exemption given him by subs. (22) of sec. 6 of Rev. Stats. cap. 180; and is not now required to have paid his income tax before 1st Jan. previous to voting. See sec. 7, subs. (2) of Election Act, repealed by this sec.

(*v*) "*Last revised assessment roll.*"—See s. 2, subs. (14) *ante* and note.

(*w*) "*Wage earner.*"—See sec. 2, subs. (6).

(*x*) "*Has resided therein continuously.*"—See note to same words in last subsection.

(*y*) "*Wages or income.*"—The words "wages" and "income" seem to be treated here as if they were synonymous and the same qualifying words "trade," "occupation," etc., are used in the last sub-section. By sec. 2, subs. (8) of the Assessment Act, income is declared to be "personal property," and such property is, by sec. 6

(2.) In estimating or ascertaining the amount of wages or income so earned or derived by any person so entered as a wage-earner in the assessment roll of a municipality, not being a city, town or village, the fair value of any board or lodging furnished or given to or received, or had by such person as or in lieu of wages or as part thereof shall be considered or included (*yy*).

Householder. *Fourthly.*—Every male person entered as a householder (*yx*) in the last revised assessment roll (*z*) of the

of that Act, made liable to taxation. By subs. (22) of second sec. 6, "the annual income of any person, provided the same does not exceed four hundred dollars," is rendered exempt; but by section 7 of the same Act such person may waive such exemption and require his name to be entered for such income, for the purpose of being entitled to vote, and such income shall in such case be liable to taxation. It does not clearly appear whether the wage earner is to be placed in the same position. If wages and income are synonymous terms, it may be argued in the absence of an express declaration to the contrary, that he will. The income of a farmer derived from his farm, and the income of merchants, mechanics and other persons *derived from capital liable to assessment*, are exempt (Assessment Act s. 6, subs. 15); but a wage earner will not come within these classes. The provisions in the "Assessment Amendment Act, 1885," with regard to this class of voters and their entry on the roll, such provisions being analagous to those relating to the "landholder's son" class, together with various expressions made use of throughout the Act in reference to the subject, would lead to the conclusion that it was not the intention of the Legislature to render the income of wage earners liable to be taxed. (See Assessment Amendment Act, 1885, s. 2, subs. 4, s. 4, s. 5 subs. 1, ss. 6, 8 and 10; see also, s. 22 of the Voters' Lists Act, and note, *post*; and sec. 8, subs. 5 of same Act and note *post*). And this is further rendered reasonably clear by a comparison of this sub-section, which provides merely that the person must be entered on the assessment roll *as a wage earner*, while the preceding sub-section provides that the income voter must be "assessed for such income."

(*yy*) A considerable part of the earnings of farm laborers is often paid in the shape of board and lodging. As a mere lodger or boarder cannot qualify as a householder. (see sec. 2, subs. 8 and note), the value of his board and lodging is to be taken into account in this way; but the value of the board or lodging supplied to a wage earner resident in a city, town, or incorporated village, who is in many cases also remunerated in part in this way, is to be excluded from the computation in his case. As to the meaning of the word "lodging," see note to s. 2, subs. 8, *ante*.

(*yx*) "*Householder.*"—For definition see *ante*, s. 2, subs. 7 and 8, and notes.

(*z*) "*Last revised assessment roll,*" "*has resided there continuously.*" See *ante*.

The value of the property is no criterion of the right to vote of this class of voters. All householders are entitled to vote under this section. They are to be entered on

local municipality in which he tenders his vote, who is residing at the time of the election in the said municipality, and has resided there continuously since the completion of said last revised assessment roll.

Fifthly.—Every landowner's son (*a*) who is resident (*b*) at the time of the election in the local municipality in which he tenders his vote, and has resided therein with and in the residence or dwelling of the landholder whose son he is, for twelve months next prior to the return by the assessors of the assessment roll (*c*) on which the voters' lists used at the election is based, and who has been duly entered and named in said assessment roll as such landholder's son. **Landholders' sons.**

(2.) Occasional or temporary absence from such residence or dwelling for a time or times not exceeding in the whole six months of the twelve hereinbefore mentioned, shall not operate to disentitle a landholder's son to vote under this Act.

Sixthly.—Where there is a voters' list, all Indians, or persons with part Indian blood, who have been duly en- **Indians.**

---

the roll under section eighteen of the Assessment Act, as amended by sec. 3 of the Assessment Amendment Act, 1885, the letter H being placed opposite their names. The value of the property is of importance in determining whether the son of a householder is entitled to a vote as a "landholder's son."

(*a*) "*Landholder's son.*"—See sec. 2, subs. 4 and 5, *ante*. To entitle the son to vote the father must own real property of at least twenty acres in extent, or of at least an actual assessed value in cities and towns of $400, and in townships and incorporated villages of $200 ; or must be resident in and tenant of a "dwelling house," (see s. 2, subs. 7), which with the land, if any, held therewith is of at least an actual assessed value, in cities and towns of $400 and in townships and incorporated villages of $200. See sec. 2, subs. 4, *ante*.

(*b*) "*Resident*"—See note to subs *Secondly*, and to sec. 3, subs. 6 of Dom. Fran. Act. *ante*.

(*c*) "*For twelve months next prior to the return of the assessment roll.*"—The period of residence is different from that prescribed by previous subsections, though residence in the municipality at the time of the election is requisite in all cases. As to when roll is returned see secs. 43, 44 and 46 of the Assessment Act.

franchised, (*d*) and all Indians or persons with part Indian blood who do not reside among Indians, though they participate in the annuities, interest, moneys and rents of a tribe, band or body of Indians, subject to the same qualifications in other respects, and to the same provisions and restrictions as other persons in the electoral district;

(2.) But the Indians or persons with part Indian blood who are entitled to vote where there is no voters' list shall be only the following, namely: "All Indians, or persons with part Indian blood, who have been duly enfranchised, and all un-enfranchised Indians or persons with part Indian blood who do not participate in the annuities, interest, moneys, or rents of a tribe, band or body of Indians, and do not reside among Indians, subject to the same qualifications in other respects, and to the same provisions and restrictions, as other persons in the electoral district."

(3.) Where there is no voters' list (*e*) any person alleged by a candidate, or the agent of a candidate, to be an Indian, or person with part Indian blood, shall, if required by such candidate or agent, or by the returning officer, take the following oath or affirmation in addition to any other oath required by a voter under the law:—

You swear that you do not participate in the annuities, interests, moneys or rents of any tribe, band or body of Indians, and do not reside among Indians.

(*d*) "*Duly enfranchised.*"—See Dom. Fran. Act, s. 2, "person," note "*including an Indian,*" *ante.* According to the Indian Act, 1880 (Dom.) s. 2, subs. 5, the term "enfranchised Indian," means, any Indian, his wife or minor unmarried child, who has received letters patent granting him in fee simple any portion of the reserve, which may have been allotted to him, his wife and minor children, by the band to which he belongs, or any unmarried Indian, who may have received letters patent for an allotment of the reserve.

(*e*) "*No voters list.*"—In those unorganized districts referred in the next subs. following. See notes to following subs.

Or, at his option, the following :—

You swear that you are not an Indian, nor a person with part Indian blood.

Seventhly.—In such of the municipalities, townships and places in the Electoral Districts of Algoma East, Algoma West, East Victoria, East Peterborough, North Hastings, North Renfrew, South Renfrew, Muskoka and Parry Sound as have no assessment roll, and subject to the provisions hereinafter contained, every male person of the full age of twenty-one years, being a subject of Her Majesty by birth or naturalization, and being not otherwise disqualified, who is at the time of the election a resident of and domiciled within the Electoral District for which he claims to vote, and is actually and *bona fide* owner of real estate in such electoral district of the value of two hundred dollars or upwards, or who is at the time of the election a resident householder of such place, and has been such owner or householder for the six months next preceding the election. etc.

(2.) A person is not an owner within the meaning of the said provision designated seventhly, where the land of which he claims to be owner has never been granted or patented by the Crown, and a person who is a mere lodger or boarder in a house is not a "resident householder" in respect of such house.

(3.) In any part of the Electoral District of Algoma West, Algoma East, Muskoka, or Parry Sound in which there is no assessment roll or voters' list, residence by an owner shall be necessary for the same period as residence by a householder, in order to qualify a voter.

Eighthly.—No person shall be entitled to vote in unorganized territory on property which is wholly or partly in an organized municipality (*ee*).

(*ee*) This latter provision is intended to abolish a practice which had arisen under the previous doubtful state of the law, which was the subject of judicial investigation in the *Muskoka case, 1883.*

In certain districts there are assessment rolls, but no voters' lists. To these sec. 78 of the Election Act as amended by sec. 22 of Act of 1884 and sec. 12, subs. (6) of this Act applies. It is as follows:

78. (1) In any municipality in the electoral districts of Algoma East, Algoma West, East Victoria, East Peterborough, North Hastings, North Renfrew, South Renfrew and Muskoka and Parry Sound, where there is an assessment roll, but for which no voters' lists containing the names of the voters in such municipality have been filed with the clerk of the peace, or certified by the county judge. the returning officer shall, upon receipt of the writ, procure from the clerk of the municipality an alphabetical list or lists of all persons entitled to vote in the municipality or in the polling sub-divisions thereof (if the municipality is divided into polling sub-divisions); and the Clerk shall forthwith, upon being requested so to do, furnish the Returning Officer with such list, or lists, having first certified to the correctness thereof before a justice of the peace;

(2) Every list of voters so prepared (or a similar list otherwise procured by the Returning Officer, at the expense of the clerk, in case of the failure of the clerk to furnish the same within a reasonable time), shall be the voters' list to be used at the election for such municipality or polling sub-division;

(3) In every municipality in the said districts in which there is an assessment roll, it shall be necessary that the name of the elector shall appear upon the list of voters prepared under this section, or under *The Voters' List Act;* and in such case the same provisions as to qualification of voters and other matters shall apply as in other electoral districts, and the oath or affirmation to be required of voters shall be the same, save as mentioned in the next sub-section;

(4) No person shall be entitled to vote in any such municipality as an owner in respect of ungranted land, that is of land not theretofore granted by the Crown; but in case a person who is a resident householder within the meaning of this Act is entered in the assessment roll or voters' list as an owner or a freeholder, he may, notwithstanding, vote as a resident householder, provided that, if required by any candidate or the agent of any candidate, or by the Deputy Returning Officer, such person takes the oath or affirmation set forth in the First Schedule to this Act. 47 Vic. c. 4, s. 22; 48 Vic. c. 2, s. 12, subs. 6.

Where there are no assessment rolls, sec. 92 as amended by sec. 23 of Act of 1884 and s. 12, subs. 6 of this Act applies. It is as follows:

92. (2) In such of the municipalities, townships and places in the electoral districts of Algoma East, Algoma West, East Victoria, East Peterborough, North Hastings, North Renfrew, South Renfrew, and Muskoka and Parry Sound as have no assessment rolls, the person claiming to be entitled to vote shall declare his name, place of residence and occupation or calling, and also the property in respect of which he claims to be entitled to vote; and whether he so claims as owner of such property, or as a householder; and the Deputy Returning Officer shall cause the said particulars to be entered upon a list in the same manner as is prescribed in section 102 of the said Act, with reference to the tendered voters' list; and the list shall be dealt with in the same manner as the tendered voters' list is directed to be dealt with by sections 109 and 110 of the said *Election Act.*

(3) In any such place, every person who offers to vote at any polling place shall, if

4. Sections 8, 9 and 10 of *The Election Act* and sub-section 3 of section 3 of *The Voters' Lists Finality Act*, and section 14 of the Act passed in the 42nd year of the reign of Her Majesty and chaptered four, and section 14 of *The Election Law Amendment Act, 1884*, are hereby repealed (*ef*). R.S.O., c. 10, ss. 8-10; 41 V., c. 21, s. 3, subs. 3; 42 V., c. 4, s. 14; and 47 V., c. 4, s. 14, repealed.

5. Section 5 of *The Election Amendment Act, 1883*, is hereby repealed and the following is substituted therefor: 46 V., c. 2, s. 5, repealed.

The following is substituted for sub-section 2 of section 91 of *The Election Act* as amended by the 17th section of the Act passed in the 42nd year of Her Majesty's reign, chaptered 4:

(2.) Any person whose name is entered upon said list of voters as owner, tenant or occupant of real estate, or as a landholder's son, or as a householder, and who is required to take such oath or affirmation as aforesaid shall be at liberty to select (*f*) for himself for that purpose either of the said forms numbered 18 and 20 in Schedule A., whatever may be the description either in the voters' list or assessment roll as to the qualification or character in respect of which he is entered upon the Voter may select form of oath in certain cases.

---

required by any candidate, or the agent of any candidate, or by the Deputy Returning Officer, take, in lieu of the oath prescribed by section 91 of the *Election Act*, an oath or affirmation according to one of the forms of oaths given in the second schedule to this Act; and the Deputy Returning Officer is hereby empowered to administer the said oath.

(4) The Deputy Returning Officer shall not deliver a ballot paper to any person claiming to vote, until after such person has declared the several particulars above mentioned, nor until after these have been entered in the said list, nor until after the prescribed oath has been taken if required. 47 Vic. c. 4, s. 23; 48 c. 2, s. 12, ss. 6.

(*ef*) The first three sections referred to lists of defaulters in payment of income tax, now rendered unnecessary by the repeal of the provision requiring income taxes to be paid by 31st Dec., preceding the election. The sub-section of the Voters' List Finality Act, and 42 Vic., c. 4, s. 14 referred to are also rendered unnecessary for the same reason. The section of the Act of 1884 related to the franchise in unorganized districts, now regulated by provisions of this Act already given.

(*f*) "*To select.*"—This allows an option to the voter of qualifying as a "landholder's son," if he cannot as an owner, tenant, occupant or householder, and *vice versa*. See Prescott Election (Dom.), 1 H. E. C. 780.

said list or roll; and where the person claims to be entitled to vote in respect of taxable income or as a wage-earner, the oath or affirmation to be taken shall be according to form 19 in said Schedule A, and where the person claims to be entitled to vote in respect of a supplementary voters' list in any of the cases mentioned in sections 75 and 77 (*g*) of this Act, the oath or affirmation to be taken shall be according to form 21 in said Schedule A.

Forms of oath.

6. The forms of oaths or affirmations to be taken by voters shall be the forms appended to this Act (*gg*), and numbered 18, 19, 20 and 21, which are respectively substituted for the forms numbered 18, 19, 20 and 21, in Schedule A to *The Election Act*, as amended

(1.) By the Act passed in the forty-second year of Her Majesty's reign, chaptered four, and

(2.) By *The Election Amendment Act, 1883*;

But nothing in this Act contained shall be deemed or construed as repealing, altering, or affecting any of the provisions of sections 22 and 23 of *The Election Law Amendment Act 1884* (*gx*), or any of the forms of oaths in the schedules to said last mentioned Act contained or set forth.

Commencement of Act.

21. The several sections and provisions of this Act shall come into force and have effect as follows:

(1.) Sections 2 to 6 both inclusive of this Act shall come into force and have effect on, from and after the

(*g*) "*Sections 75 and 77.*"—Section 75 provides for the cases of territory being added to a city, town or village in another electoral district, and of villages being formed of territory in different districts, etc., and an election taking place before new voters' lists are made out. Section 77 provides for the case of a voters' list covering portions of two or more electoral districts.

(*gg*) For forms referred to see schedules, *post*.

(*gx*) These sections are given in full (as secs. 78 and 92 of the Election Act) in note to last sub-section of section 3, *ante*. They relate to the municipalities and districts where there are no regular voters' lists.

first day of January next after the passing of this Act, except as to any assessment roll or assessment taken or made subsequent to the first day of July next after the passing thereof, under the special provisions of section 44 of *The Assessment Act* (*h*); and with respect to any such last-mentioned assessment roll or assessment, and any list of voters based thereon, the said sections of this Act shall for all purposes, and as regards all matters, liabilities, duties and proceedings therein provided for, be deemed to come into force, and shall have effect on, from and after said first day of July (*i*).

(*h*) "*Section 44 of the assessment act*"—Gives power to Councils of cities and towns, separate from the county, to pass by-laws changing the time for making assessment, return of the roll, Court of Revision, etc., to the last half of the year, instead of the earlier portion, as provided by the Act for municipalities generally.

(*i*) The remaining sections of this Act, relate to the electoral areas, controverted elections, etc., the provisions as to the former coming into force from and after the dissolution of the present Assembly, the latter from the passing of the Act. They are here omitted as not touching the subject of the Franchise.

The various forms of voters' oaths are here given, as they tend to throw further light upon the preceding provisions.

FORMS.

Form 18.

(Referred to in R. S. O. c. 10, Section 91.)

(See sec. 5 of Fran. and Rep. Act, 1885, *ante.*)

FORM OF OATH OF PERSON VOTING AS OWNER, TENANT OR OCCUPANT OF REAL ESTATE, OR AS A HOUSEHOLDER

You *swear* (1) that you are the person named or purporting to be named by the name of on the list of voters now shewn to you. (2) That on the (3) day of one thousand eight hundred and you were actually, truly and in good faith possessed to your own use and benefit, as either owner, tenant or occupant, in your own right or in the right of your wife, of the real estate in respect of which your name is as aforesaid entered on the said list of voters, and are as such entitled to vote at this election;

That you were at the time of the final revision and correction of the assessment roll on which said list of voters is based and are now actually and in good faith a resident of and domiciled within this electoral district;

That you are of the full age of twenty-one years ;

That you are a subject of Her Majesty either by birth or by naturalization ;

That you have not voted before at this election, either at this or any other polling place ;

That you have not received anything, nor has anything been promised you either directly or indirectly, either to induce you to vote at this election, or for loss of time, travelling expenses, hire of team, or any other service connected therewith ;

And that you have not directly, or indirectly, paid or promised anything to any person, either to induce him to vote, or to refrain from voting, at this election.

So help you God.

---

(1) If the voter is a person who may by law affirm, then for "*swear*" substitute "*solemnly affirm.*"
(2) The Deputy Returning Officer should hereupon shew the voters' list to the voter.
(3) The date to be here inserted in administering the oath is AT THE CHOICE OF THE VOTER to be EITHER the day certified by the Clerk of the Municipality to be the date of the RETURN by the Assessor of the assessment roll upon which the voters' list used at the election is based ; or the day so certified to be the date when by law the said roll was to be considered and taken as FINALLY REVISED.

NOTE.—In the oath administered to a Deputy Returning Officer, poll clerk or agent VOTING UPON A CERTIFICATE issued under Sec. 87, for "*on the list of voters now shewn to you,*" substitute "*on the list of voters for the Municipality of* ," naming the municipality mentioned in the certificate.

FORM 19.

(Referred to in R. S. O. c. 10, Section 91.)

(See Fran. and Rep. Act, 1885, sec. 5, *ante.*)

ORDINARY FORM OF OATH OF PERSON VOTING IN RESPECT OF INCOME, OR AS A WAGE-EARNER.

You *swear* (1) that you are the person named or purporting to be named by the name of on the list of voters now shewn to you ; (2)

That on the (3) day of one thousand eight hundred and you were, and thenceforward have been continuously and still are a resident of this municipality ;

That at the said date, and for twelve months previously, you were from your trade, occupation, office, calling or profession, in receipt of an income or wages amounting to a sum not less than two hundred and fifty dollars (4).

That you are of the full age of twenty-one years ;

That you are a subject of Her Majesty either by birth or by naturalization ;

That you have not voted before at this election, either at this or any other polling place ;

That you have not received anything, nor has anything been promised to you, either directly or indirectly, either to induce you to vote at this election, or for loss of time, travelling expenses, hire of team, or any other service connected therewith ;

And that you have not directly, or indirectly, paid or promised anything to any person, either to induce him to vote, or to refrain from voting at this election.

So help you God.

(1) If the voter is a person who may by law affirm, then for "*swear*" substitute "*solemnly affirm.*"

(2) The Deputy Returning Officer should hereupon shew the voters' list to the voter.

(3) The date to be here inserted in administering the oath, is the day certified by the clerk of the municipality to be the DATE OF THE FINAL REVISION and correction of the assessment roll upon which the voters' list used at the election is based for the municipality.

(4) If the municipality in which the voter is voting is a Township there must be added at the end of this clause of the oath the words following: "Estimating as part "of said income or wages the fair value of any board or lodging had, given to, or re- "ceived by me during the said twelve months as or in lieu of wages."

NOTE.—In the oath administered to a Deputy Returning Officer, poll clerk or agent VOTING UPON A CERTIFICATE issued under sec, 87, for "*on the list of voters now shewn to you*" substitute "*on the list of voters for the municipality of* ," naming the municipality mentioned in the certificate.

FORM 20.

(Referred to in R. S. O. c. 10, s. 91.)

(See Fran. and Rep. Act, 1885, sec. 5, *ante.*)

FORM OF OATH FOR A LANDHOLDER'S SON.

You *swear* (1) that you are the person named or purporting to be named by the name of on the list of voters now shewn to you; (2)

That on the (3) day of one thousand eight hundred and , A. B. (4) was, as you verily believe actually, truly, and in good faith possessed to *his* (5) own use as owner, tenant or occupant of the property in respect of which your name is so as aforesaid entered on the said voters' list, and was then actually and in good faith residing and domiciled upon said property;.

That you are a *son* (6) of the said A. B.; (4)

That you resided within this municipality with the said A. B., for, and during the whole of the twelve months next before the return by the Assessor of the assessment roll on which the voters' list used at this election is based, not having been absent during that period, except temporarily and not more than six months in all;

That you are still a resident of this Electoral District, and are entitled to vote at this election;

That you are of the full age of twenty-one years;

That you are a subject of Her Majesty either by birth or by naturalization;

That you have not voted before at this election, either at this or any other polling place;

That you have not received anything, nor has anything been promised you, either directly or indirectly, either to induce you to vote at this election, or for loss of time, travelling expenses, hire of team, or any other service connected therewith;

And that you have not directly, or indirectly, paid or promised anything to any person, either to induce him to vote, or to refrain from voting at this election.

So help you God.

---

(1) If the voter is a person who may by law affirm, then for "*swear*" substitute "*solemnly affirm.*"

(2) The Deputy Returning Officer should hereupon show the voters' list to the voter.

(3) The date to be here inserted in administering the oath is the day certified by the clerk of the municipality to be the date of the RETURN by the assessor of the assessment roll upon which the voters' list used at the election is based ;

(4) The name of the voter's father, or step-father, or mother, or step-mother should be inserted here.

(5) If the name of the voter's mother is inserted, then for "*his*" substitute "*her*."

(6) If the voter is voting as a "*stepson*," or "*grandson*," or "*son in-law*," then for the word "*son*," substitute the word "*stepson*," or "*grandson*," or "*son in-law*," as the case may be.

NOTE.—In the oath administered to a Deputy Returning Officer, poll-clerk, or agent VOTING UPON A CERTIFICATE issued under Sec. 87, for "*on the list of voters now shown to you*," substitute "*on the list of voters for the Municipality of* ," naming the municipality mentioned in the certificate.

FORM 21.

(Referred to in R. S. O., c. 10, Section 91.)

(See Fran. and Rep. Act, 1885, sec. 5, *ante.*)

FORM OF OATH TO BE TAKEN BY VOTER ON A SUPPLEMENTARY LIST OF VOTERS, MADE WHERE ADDITIONS HAVE BEEN MADE TO A CITY, TOWN OR VILLAGE, OR A NEW VILLAGE HAS BEEN FORMED COMPOSED OF TERRITORY SITUATED IN TWO OR MORE ELECTORAL DISTRICTS.

You *swear* (1) that you are the person named or purporting to be named by the name of on the supplementary list of voters now shown to you ; (2)

That on the (3) day of one thousand eight hundred and you were actually, truly and in good faith possessed to your own use and benefit as owner, tenant or occupant, in your own right or in the right of your wife, of the real estate in respect of which your name is entered on the said supplementary list of voters, and are as such entitled to vote at this election ;

That you are actually and in good faith a resident of and domiciled within this Electoral District ;

That you are of the full age of twenty-one years ;

That you are a subject of Her Majesty either by birth or by naturalization ;

That you have not voted before at this election, either at this or any other polling place ;

That you have not received anything, nor has anything been promised you, either directly or indirectly, either to induce you to vote at this election, or for loss of time, travelling expenses, hire of team, or any other service connected therewith ;

And that you have not, directly or indirectly, paid or promised anything to any person, either to induce him to vote, or to refrain from voting at this election.

So help you God.

(1) If the voter is a person who may by law affirm, then for "*swear*," substitute "*solemnly affirm.*"

(2) The Deputy Returning Officer should hereupon show the voters' list to the voter.

(3) The date to be here inserted in administering the oath is AT THE CHOICE OF THE VOTER to be EITHER the day certified by the Clerk of the Municipality to be the date of the RETURN by the Assessor of the assessment roll upon which the voters' list used at the election is based; or the day so certified to be the date when by law the said roll was to be considered and taken as FINALLY REVISED.

NOTE.—In the oath administered to a Deputy Returning Officer, poll clerk or agent, VOTING UPON A CERTIFICATE issued under Sec. 87, for "*on the list of voters now shown to you*" substitute "*on the list of voters for the Municipality of* ," naming the municipality mentioned in the certificate.

Form referred to as "First Schedule" *(a)* in sec. 78 of the Election Act as amended. See note to Fran. and Rep. Act, 1885, s. 3, subs. "*eighthly,*" *ante.*

FORM OF OATH TO BE TAKEN IN MUNICIPALITIES IN ALGOMA, MUSKOKA AND PARRY SOUND, WHERE THERE IS A VOTERS' LIST.

By persons who vote as resident householders, but are entered in the list as owners or freeholders.

You *swear* (1) that you are the person named, or purporting to be named by the name of on the list of voters now shown to you; (2)

That you are actually, truly and in good faith a resident householder of this electoral district, in respect of the property for which you are assessed in this municipality as owner *(or freeholder)*, and for which you are entered as such in the list of voters now shown to you;

That you are now, and have been continuously for the six months immediately preceding this date, actually, truly, and in good faith, a resident of this electoral district;

That you are of the full age of twenty-one years;

That you are a subject of Her Majesty, either by birth or by naturalization;

That you have not voted before at this election, either at this or any other polling-place;

That you have not received anything, nor has anything been promised you, either directly or indirectly, either to induce you to vote at this election, or for loss of time, travelling expenses, hire of team, or any other service connected therewith;

And that you have not, directly or indirectly, paid or promised anything to any person, either to induce him to vote, or to refrain from voting, at this election.

So help you God.

---

(1) If the voter is a person who may by law affirm, then for "*swear*" substitute "*solemnly affirm.*"

(2) The Deputy Returning Officer should hereupon show the voters' list to the voter.

(a) The Oath in this Schedule is also to be taken by certain voters in North Victoria, East Peterborough, North Hastings, North Renfrew and South Renfrew. See Sec. 78, of *The Election Act*, given in note to Fran. and Rep. Act, 1885, s. 3, subs. "eighthly," *ante.*

Form referred to as the "Second Schedule" *(b)*, in sec. 92 of the Election Act as amended. See note to Fran. and Rep. Act, 1885, s. 3, subs. "eighthly," *ante*.

FORMS OF THE OATH TO BE TAKEN BY VOTERS IN ALGOMA, MUSKOKA AND PARRY SOUND, WHERE THERE IS NO ASSESSMENT ROLL OR VOTERS' LIST.

Resident Owner's Oath.

You *swear* (1) that you are *A. B.* (2) ; and that you have not voted before at this election, either at this or any other polling place ;

That you are actually, truly, and in good faith, possessed to your own use, as owner, of the land in respect of which your name has now on your information been entered on the Deputy Returning Officer's list ; that you have been such owner of the said property for the six months next preceding this election ; that the said land has been patented, and is of the value of at least two hundred dollars ;

That you are now, and have been continuously for six months immediately preceding this date, actually, truly, and in good faith, a resident of this Electoral District ;

That you are entitled to vote at this election in respect of the said property ;

That this, to the best of your belief, is the polling place nearest to the said property ;

That you are of the full age of twenty-one years ;

That you are a subject of Her Majesty, either by birth or by naturalization ;

That you have not received anything, nor has anything been promised you either directly or indirectly, either to induce you to vote at this election, or for loss of time, travelling expenses, hire of team, or any other service connected therewith ;

And that you have not, directly or indirectly, paid or promised anything to any person, to induce him either to vote or refrain from voting at this election :

So help you, God.

---

(1) If the voter is a person who may by law affirm, then for "*swear*" substitute "*solemnly affirm.*"

(2) Insert here the name of the voter.

Resident Householder's Oath.

You *swear* (1) that you are *A. B.* (2) ; and that you have not voted before at this election, either at this or any other polling place ;

That you are actually, truly, and in good faith, a resident householder in the said district, in respect of the property which has now on your information been entered on the Deputy Returning Officer's list as the property on which you vote ;

That you are now, and have been continuously for the six months immediately preceding this date, actually, truly, and in good faith, a resident householder of this Electoral District.

That you are entitled to vote at this election in respect of the said property ;

That this, to the best of your belief, is the polling-place nearest to the said property ;

(b) The oath in this Schedule is also to be taken by certain voters in North Victoria, East Peterborough, North Hastings, North Renfrew and South Renfrew. See Sec. 92, of *The Election Act*, given in note to Fran. and Rep. Act, 1885, s. 3, subs. "eighthly," *ante*.

That you are of the full age of twenty-one years ;

That you are a subject of Her Majesty, either by birth or by naturalization ;

That you have not received anything, nor has anything been promised you, either directly or indirectly, either to induce you to vote at this election, or for loss of time, travelling expenses, hire of team, or any other service connected therewith ;

And that you have not directly or indirectly, paid or promised anything to any person to induce him either to vote or to refrain from voting at this election :

So help you God.

---

(1) If the voter is a person who may by law affirm, then for "*swear*," substitute "*solemnly affirm.*"

(2) Insert here the name of the voter.

Indian's Oath.

(See Fran. and Rep. Act, 1885, s. 3 (7 of Election Act) subs. "Sixthly," *ante* ; also El. Law Am. Act, 1884, s. 12.)

Where there is not an Assessment Roll, if a candidate or his agent alleges that the voter is an Indian, one or other of the following oaths is to be administered to such voter, the voter having the right to select which.

"You *swear* that you do not participate in the annuities, interests, moneys, or rents of any tribe, band or body of Indians, and do not reside among Indians,"

or,

"You *swear* you are not an Indian, nor a person with part Indian blood."

The oaths required of other Voters are to be taken as in other cases, if required

THE

ONTARIO PROVINCIAL FRANCHISE.

AN ACT RESPECTING VOTERS' LISTS.

Revised Statutes of Ontario, cap. 9, as amended.

HER Majesty, by and with the advice and consent of the Legislative Assembly of the Province of Ontario, enacts as follows :—

Short title. **1.** This Act may be cited as *The Voters' Lists Act*.

Clerk to make list of voters. **2.*** (1) The clerk of each municipality shall (*a*), immediately after the first revision and correction (*b*) of the

* This and the succeeding subsections of sec. 2 are given as in the amending Act (The Voters' Lists Amendment Act 1885).

(*a*) "*The clerk of each municipality shall.*"—The clerk in respect to this duty acts as an officer of the public, rather than as a servant of the Council. The *shall* is imperative so far as the clerk is concerned (Rev. Stat. cap. 1, s. 8, subs. 2, Interpretation Act, *Re Lincoln Election*, 2 Ont. Ap. R.—per Moss, C. J. A., at p. 341),—see also sec. 24, *post*, as to mode of compelling the performance of this duty. A writ of mandamus will also lie for neglect or default in the premises, *Rex* v. *Mayor of Gravesend*, 2 B. & C. 602; *Regina* v. *Mayor of Lichfield*, 1 Q. B. 453.

(*b*) "*First revision and correction.*"—The words in the original section were "*final* revision and correction, etc." This amendment means that the clerk is to prepare the list immediately after the Court of Revision has completed its duties, without waiting for the decision of the Judge upon appeals from that Court or for the time allowed for appealing to elapse—see subs. 11, *post*. This will enable the clerk to commence his work upon the lists earlier than formerly.

assessment roll in every year, make a correct alphabetical list in three parts (Form 1) (†) of all persons being of the full age of twenty-one years and subjects of Her Majesty by birth or naturalization, and appearing by the assessment roll to be entitled to vote (c) in the municipality, prefixing to the name of each person his number upon the roll.

(2) The first of the three parts shall contain the names, in alphabetical order, of all male persons of full age and subjects as aforesaid, appearing by the assessment roll to be assessed for the real property or income requisite to entitle him to vote in the municipality at both municipal elections and elections for members of the Legislative Assembly (*d*). First part.

(3.) The second part shall contain the names, in alphabetical order, of all other male persons of full age and subjects as aforesaid, and of all widows and unmarried Second part.

† See *post*, note (m).

(*c*) "*Full age*," "*subjects of Her Majesty*," "*entitled to vote*."—See provisions of Franchise and Representation Act 1855 and notes thereto under similar headings, *ante*. The Election Act provides that, subject to the provisions of the 102d section (which provides for 'tendered ballots') "no person shall be admitted to vote unless his name appears on such list; and no question of qualification shall be raised at any election except to ascertain whether the person tendering his vote, is the same person intended to be designated in the said list; and other questions of qualification shall be raised and decided on election petition only," Rev. Stat. c. 10, s. 73. The roll, though it should give information as to age of assessed persons, can give none as to whether they are subjects or aliens. Any person who will be of age within 60 days from the "final revision and correction of the assessment roll" may apply to the Judge to have his name put on the list—s. 8, subs. 4, *post*. The only question of qualification settled by the Court of Revision under the Assessment Act, is, the one of value—*Stormont*, 1 H. E. C. 21; 7 C. L. J. 213; and this may be reviewed by the Judge. Being rated as tenant instead of owner or occupant or *vice versa*, *Held*, not to affect the vote, *Ib*.

(*d*) *i. e.*, those possessing qualifications common to both franchises. Owners, tenants, householders, farmers' sons and income voters, rated to an amount sufficient to qualify them to vote at municipal elections, are qualified to vote for members of the Legislative Assembly, (but see as to what constitutes a "householder" under Municipal Act 46 Vic. c. 18, s. 87).

women of full age and subjects as aforesaid, and appearing on the assessment roll to be entitled to vote in the municipality at municipal elections only, and not at elections for members of the Legislative Assembly *(e)*.

Third part. (4.) The third part shall contain the names, in alphabetical order, of all other male persons of full age and subjects as aforesaid, appearing by the assessment roll to be entitled to vote in the municipality at elections for members of the Legislative Assembly only, and not at municipal elections *(f)*.

Name to be entered once only (5.) The name of the same person shall not be entered more than once in any such part.

Lists for polling subdivisions. (6.) Where a municipality is divided into polling subdivisions the list (to be made in three parts as aforesaid) shall be made for each of such sub-divisions *(g)*.

(e) *e. g.*, Judges, Customs Officers, Clerks of the Peace, County Attorneys, Registrars, Sheriffs, Deputy Sheriffs, Deputy Clerks of the Crown, Crown Land Agents, Postmasters in cities and towns, Stipendiary Magistrates and Excise Officers. See Elections Act (Rev. Stats. c. 10, s. 4), *ante*.

(f) *e. g.*, householders, the property occupied by whom is worth less than the amount required to qualify for the municipal franchise, wage-earners and income voters whose income is not less than $250, but does not come up to the $400 necessary for the municipal qualification; all "landholders' sons" (unless it so happens that they can qualify as "farmers' sons," *i. e.*, sons of the *owner* of a farm of at least 20 acres, living on the farm with the father, the farm being worth sufficient to give both father and son a municipal vote), owners, tenants and occupants in cities, towns and incorporated villages whose property is rated at a sum sufficient to give the legislative, but not the municipal vote; and Indians qualified to vote at legislative, but not at municipal, elections.

(g) Section 11 of the Elections Act, as amended, provides for the subdivision of the municipality or ward. It is as follows:—

11. Every City, Town, Ward, Township or incorporated Village, having more than two hundred qualified voters therein shall be divided by well-defined boundaries such as streets, side lines, concession lines or the like, in the most convenient manner into polling subdivisions by by-law of the Municipal Council having jurisdiction over the locality, and in such manner that the number of qualified voters in the several polling subdivisions shall be as nearly equal as may be, and shall not in any one exceed two hundred.

2. Where a municipality is divided into polling subdivisions, the same polling subdivisions shall be used both for the election of members of the Legislative Assembly and for municipal elections; and the polling subdivisions for elections to the Legis-

(7.) If the qualification of any such person is in respect of real property, the clerk shall *(h)* opposite the name of

Real property on which voter qualifies to be named.

lative Assembly and municipal elections, shall hereafter be made the same in all cases, except that the Municipal Council of every City, Town or incorporated Village, may by by-law unite, for the purposes of municipal elections, any two adjoining polling subdivisions.

3. Any alteration of existing polling subdivisions, or creation of new polling subdivisions, shall be made before the publication of the voters' lists.

4. For the purpose of enabling the council to make the required alterations, the clerk of the municipality, as soon as he finds that the number of qualified voters in any subdivision exceeds two hundred, shall call the attention of the council to the fact.

5. In case, through oversight or from any other cause such alterations have not been made prior to the publication of the lists, the alteration in the polling subdivisions shall be made forthwith thereafter, but shall not take effect until the next voters' lists are being made out, and shall not affect the voting on or with respect to any previous voters' lists.

6. It shall not be necessary for a Returning Officer to re-divide a polling subdivision, on account of the same containing more than two hundred voters, so long as it does not contain more than three hundred; but if it contain more than three hundred, he shall divide it into two subdivisions.

7. Nothing in this section contained shall be held to relieve the council of any municipality from the duty of making a new division of the voters into polling subdivisions, or re-dividing a subdivision as often as the number of qualified voters in any polling subdivision exceeds two hundred. 46 V. c. 2, s. 2.

Section 12 provides for a re-division of the subdivisions from time to time, as like occasion shall require—sec. 13, that the subdivision shall be based in each case upon the then last revised and corrected assessment roll—sec. 14, for an appeal from any such subdivision by any five electors to the County Judge—sec. 15 for the numbering of the subdivisions consecutively by the by-law and for a deposit of the copy thereof with the Clerk of the Peace—sec. 16 for a subdivision by the returning officer in case of failure of the Council to subdivide or in case the time for appeal has not expired before receipt of the Writ, and s. 17 for remuneration of the returning officer in case he subdivides.

Where a voter properly assessed, who was accidentally omitted from the Voter's List for polling division No. 1, where his property lay, and entered on the Voters' List for polling division No. 2, voted in No. 1, though not on the list, his vote was held good, *Brockville—Little's vote*, 1 H. E. C. 129. A voter was assessed in two wards of a town; he parted with his property qualification in one of the wards, but voted in such ward; *held*, that the vote might be supported on the qualification in the other ward, which, if the voter had voted on it, would have made it necessary for him to vote in another polling subdivision, *Lincoln*, (2 Ont.,) *Gibson's vote*, 1 H. E. C. 500.

(h) "*Shall*."—This word is imperative, so far as the Clerk is concerned, but mandatory only, so far as it affects the right of the person to vote; *Lincoln Election*, 2 Ont. Ap. R. 341, 352. "I am of opinion that the right of a voter whose name has been entered on the voters' list to exercise the franchise is not destroyed by the want of a sufficient description, or any description of the real property on which his quali-

the person, insert, in the proper column of the voters' list, the number of any lot or other proper description (*i*) of any parcel of real property in respect of which each person is so qualified; adding thereto, where the person is so qualified in respect of more than one such lot or parcel, the words "and other premises"; and in the case of the person being a landholder's son or a wage-earner within the meaning of *The Election Act* and any Act amending the same, the clerk shall also, in the proper column of the voters' list, state that fact and the place at which the voter resides (*j*) in the municipality.

Entry where voter assessed in several subdivisions of same ward.

(8.) Where a ward of any municipality is divided into polling subdivisions, and it appears by the assessment roll that any person is assessed in each of two or more such polling subdivisions in the ward for property sufficient to entitle him to vote, the clerk shall enter his name on the list of voters in one such subdivision only, and shall, as required by the preceding subsection, insert opposite his name the additional words "and other premises"; and where, within the knowledge of the clerk, such person resides in one of such polling subdivisions, his

---

fication depends,"—per Moss, C. J., A. *Ib.* p. 328. Nor is it destroyed by an erroneous statement of the capacity in which he is entitled to vote, *Prescott Election* (*Dom.*), 1 H. E. C. 780 and see subs. 2 of sec. 91 of the Elections Act (Ont.) as amended by the Fran. and Rep. Act 1885, *ante*. See also *Stormont*, 1 H. E. C. 21; 7 C. L. J. 213; *Brockville*, 1 H. E. C. 129.

(*i*) "*Proper Description.*"—*e. g.*, number of house, lot, name of street, lane, etc.; see *Lincoln Election*, 2 Ont. Ap Rep. 328; *Flanders* v. *Donner*, 2 C. B. 63; *Ebsworth* v. *Farrar*, 4 C. B. 9; *Rex* v. *Aire and Calder Nav. Co.*, 4 B. & C. 243; *Rex* v. *Bromyard*, 8 B. & C. 242; *Ekersley* v. *Barker*, 7 M. & G. 76; 8 Scott N. R. 899; *Wood* v. *Willesden*, 2 C. B. 15: *Gadsby* v. *Warburton*, 7 M. & G. 11; *Nunn* v. *Denton*, 7 M. & Gr 70; *Danieli* v. *Camplin*, 7 M. & G. 167; *Judson* v. *Luckett*, 2 C. B. 197; *Birks* v. *Allison*, (*Dixon's case*,) 13 C. B. N. S. 24; *Jones* v. *Jones*, L. R. 4 C. P, 422; *Brockville*, 1 H. E. C. 129.

(*j*) "*Resides.*"—See notes to sec. 3 subs. 6 of Dom. Fran. Act, and sec. 3 (s. 7 of El. Act) subs. "Secondly" of Ont. Fran. & Rep. Act, *ante*.

name shall be entered as aforesaid in the list of voters for that polling subdivision (*k*).

Provision when property partly in one subdivision and partly in another.

(9.) Wherever it appears by the assessment roll that any person is assessed for property within the municipality sufficient to entitle him to vote, but that it lies partly within the limits of one of such subdivisions and partly within another or others, the clerk shall enter his name on the list of voters in one of the subdivisions only in which such property is situate, with the following words added: "Partly qualified in subdivision No. ."

Income qualification.

(10.) If the qualification is in respect of taxable income (*l*), the clerk shall, in the proper column of the voters' list, state that fact and the place at which the voter resides in the municipality.

When assessment roll to be regarded as finally revised.

(11.) An assessment roll shall be understood to be finally revised and corrected, when it has been so revised and corrected by the Court of Revision for the municipality, or by the Judge of the County Court, in case of an appeal, as provided in *The Assessment Act*, or when the time during which such appeal may be made has elapsed, and not before (*m*).

Copies of list to

3. Immediately after the clerk has made the said

(*k*) See note to subs. 6 *ante*, and cases cited.

(*l*) "*Taxable income.*"—See *ante*, Fran. and Rep. Act 1885, s. 3 (El. Act, s. 7) subs. "Secondly" and note—*Lawless* v. *Sullivan*, L. R. 6 App. cases, 373.

(*m*) See *ante* note to Ont. Fran and Rep. Act 1885, s. 2, subs. 14.

By sec. 3 of the Voters' List Amendment Act 1885 the expression "Form 1" in the above section 2, subs. 1, shall mean the form of voters' list to be used and made as provided by sec. 9 of *The Voters' Lists Amendment Act 1879*. The new feature introduced by this section consists in numbers being placed opposite each name in the list in the proper column, referring to a separate schedule of Post Offices, and so indicating the Post Office address of each person on the list; as well as in placing the letter J upon the list opposite the name of every male person over 21 and under 60 years of age, qualified to serve as a juror, in the column which contains the number of the voter on the roll, or in a separate column provided for the purpose, pursuant to the provisions of "The Jurors Act of 1879." See Form, *post*.

be printed. alphabetical list, and within forty days (*n*) after the final revision and correction of the assessment roll, the clerk shall cause at least two hundred copies of said list to be printed (in pamphlet form where practicable), and forthwith shall cause one of such printed copies to be posted up, and to be kept posted up in some conspicuous place in his own office, and deliver or transmit by post, by registered letter, or by parcel or book post, registered, three of such copies to each Judge of the County Court of the county to which, for judicial purposes, the municipality belongs; and two copies to each of the following persons, that is to say:

Copies to be posted in clerk's office and copies to be sent to certain officials.

(*a*) Every member of the Municipal Council of the Municipality except the Reeve;

(*b*) The Treasurer thereof;

(*c*) The Sheriff of the County;

(*d*) The Clerk of the Peace;

(*e*) Every Postmaster in the Municipality;

(*f*) Every Headmaster or Mistress of a Public or Separate School in the Municipality. 39 Vic., c. 11, s. 2. 48 V., c. 3, s. 8.

Clerk of the municipality to transmit copies to certain persons.

4. The Clerk of the Municipality shall forthwith, also deliver or transmit by post, by registered letter, or by parcel or book post, registerd, ten of such copies to each of the following persons, that is to say:

The M.P.

(*a*) The member of the House of Commons for the Electoral District in which the municipality or any part thereof lies.

(*n*) 40 days were substituted for 30 by the Act of 1885. The times appointed are directory only (see sec. 23, *post*). Non-transmission of the lists after posting up will not authorize an extension of time for filing a complaint under sec. 3, *ante*, whether such non-transmission be through negligence or be wilful. *Voters' List of Village of L'Orignal*, 9 P. R. 425.

(*b*) The member of the Legislative Assembly for the Electoral District in which the municipality or any part thereof lies. The M.P.P.

(*c*) Every candidate for whom votes were given at the then last election for the House of Commons, or for the Legislative Assembly, respectively; and Candidates.

(*d*) The Reeve of the Municipality. 39 V., c. 11, s. 2. Reeve.

5. Upon each of the copies so sent to each person, shall be a printed or written certificate (Form 2) over the name of the Clerk, stating that such list is a correct list of all persons appearing by the last revised assessment roll of the Municipality, to be entitled to vote at elections for members of the Legislative Assembly, and at Municipal Elections in said municipality; and further calling upon all electors to examine the said list, and, if any omissions or other errors are perceived therein, to take immediate proceedings to have the said errors corrected according to law (*o*). 39 V., c. 11, s. 2; 40 V., c. 10, s. 3; 48 Vic., c. 3, s. 9.

On each copy the clerk to certify as to certain matters.

Form 2.

6. The Sheriff shall immediately upon the receipt of his copies cause one of them to be posted up in a conspicuous place in the Court House; the Clerk of the Peace, upon receipt of his copies, shall cause one of them to be posted in a conspicuous place in his office; every Public or Separate school Headmaster or Mistress, shall, in like

Sheriff, Clerk of the Peace, Teacher and Postmaster to post up a copy.

(*o*) Where the clerk had list, with his certificate printed, ready for mailing on the date mentioned in certificate, and died before that date arrived, and his successor posted up and transmitted copies, as he found them: *Held*, that the provisions of the Act respecting duties of the clerk were directory, and that the County Judge had jurisdiction to revise the lists, *Re Goderich Voters' Lists of 1874*, 6 Pr. R. 213. A list not signed by the clerk would not be held invalid, it is thought, the provision as to signature being directory, *Morgan* v. *Perry*, 17 C. B. 334. But a false certificate being signed by the clerk and list posted up, though copies are withheld from transmission, the time for making complaints begins to run, and when expired cannot be extended, *Voters' List of L'Orignal*, 9 P. R. 425.

manner, post up one of his or her copies on the door of the school house; and every Postmaster shall post up one of his copies in the post office. 39 V., c. 11, s. 2.

Clerk to publish notice of first posting up by him. 7. The Clerk shall also forthwith cause to be inserted in some newspaper published in the Municipality, or in case no newspaper is published in the Municipality, then in some newspaper published in the Municipality next thereto, or in the County Town, a notice (Form 3) signed by him, which shall state that he has delivered or transmitted the copies of said list as directed by this Act, and shall also mention the date of the first posting up of said list in his office. One insertion of such notice shall be sufficient. 39 V., c. 11, s. 3; 40 V., c. 10, s. 2.

Revision of list. 8. (1*) The said list of voters shall be subject to revision by the County Judge, at the instance of any voter or person entitled to be a voter (p) in the municipality for which the list is made, or in the electoral district in which the municipality is situate, on the ground of the names of voters being omitted (q) from the list, or being

* This and the following subsections of sec. 8 are given as amended by 48 Vic, c. 3, sec. 4.

(p) "*Any voter or person entitled to be a voter.*"—The County Judge has the right to examine and decide whether the person objecting to any votes in the list of voters is a voter or person entitled to be a voter, although such complainant may appear on the roll as duly qualified. The Judge having found as facts that one of two complainants did not give the notice of his complaint required by the Act, and that the other was not entitled to be a voter: *Held*, that his decision could not be reviewed; *re Voters' List of Goderich*, 36 U. C. Q. B. 88. As to notice of complaint see sec. 9, *post*; as to substitution of new complainant. see sec. 19, *post*.

(q) "*On the ground of the names of voters being omitted.*"—This ground will include all those, owners, tenants, or occupants, householders, landholder's sons, and wage-earners, who are entitled to be on the list, but have been omitted both from the assessment roll and voters' list for any reason, including too low a valuation of their property, or any other reason. Income voters, other than wage-earners, cannot however be added unless their names are on the assessment roll. *Lincoln Election, Borrowman's case*, 2 Ap. Rep. 316; though as to landholder's sons and wage-earners, see subs. 5, *post*. Those who have become qualified between the time of assessment and the date of the final revision of the roll will also be included. See as to latter date, sec. 2, subs. 14 of The Fran. and Rep'n. Act, 1885, and note thereunder, *ante*.

wrongly stated therein (*r*), or of names of persons being inserted on the list who are not entitled to vote (*s*); and upon such revision (*t*) the assessment roll shall not be

(*r*) "*Or being wrongly stated therein.*"—This is the second ground. It includes misnomers, misdescriptions of property, title or locality of property. It is not always essential that a misnomer shall be corrected in order to enable the voter to vote, as the oath at the poll begins " you are the person named *or purporting to be named* by the name of —— on the list of voters now shewn to you," and a person may often conscientiously take this oath and vote, though his name be not properly given in the list. Where the surnames were correct, though the Christian names were erroneous, e.g., *Wilson* Wilson, for William Wilson, *Simond* Faulkener for *Alexander* Faulkener, or the names given were *idem sonans* with the true name, e.g., Thomas Sanderson for Thomas Anderson, the votes were held good. *Regina ex rel. Chambers* v. *Allison*, 1 C. L. J. N. S. 244. The mistake of the number of the lot however does not come under the same rule as the mistake of a name, as the latter is provided for in the statute and the voter's oath, per Mowat, V. C., in *South Grenville*, 1 H. E. C. 163. See as to mistakes in statement of qualification and description of property, notes to sub-sections 6 and 7, *ante*; *Stormont*, 1 H. E. C. 21; 7 C. L. J. 213; *Brockville*, 1 H. E. C. 129; *Prescott (Dom.)*, 1 H. E. C. 780. But sec. 2 of The Voters' Lists Amendment Act, 1879, which is still in force provides as follows:

2. The County Judge at any Court held by him for the Revision of the Voters' Lists, under "The Voters' Lists Act," may without any previous notice of appeal or complaint in that behalf, or an application made by or on behalf of the person named in the lists, correct any mistake which shall be proved to him to have been made in compiling any Voters' List in respect of the name, or place of abode, or nature of the qualification, or the local or other description of the property, of any person entered on the said list, and against or with respect to whose right to be entered on said list any appeal or complaint is either pending before or being heard by the Judge; but in any such case evidence may be produced and given before said Judge that such person has no qualification or no sufficient qualification in law to entitle such person to vote, and if the Judge, on the evidence before him, be of opinion that such person has not such qualification, he shall expunge and strike the name of such person from said list of voters.

(*s*) "*Or of the names of persons being inserted on the list who are not entitled to vote.*"—This ground of appeal will include persons whose property is assessed too high, persons who have died, lost their qualification, are under age or aliens; landholder's sons, wage-earners and income voters, whom non-qualification on the part of their parents, non-residence for the prescribed period, or non-receipt of income for the year preceding the entry of the names on the roll, disqualify.

(*t*) "*Such revision.*"—The duty of the Judge in reviewing the voter's list, only extends to correcting and varying it in respect of the qualification of those who are before him on the revision. *Re Lincoln Election*, 2 Ont. Ap. Rep. 316. Upon a revision of the voters' list, the Judge, without making any order in accordance with sec. 11 of that Act, added certain names which were not on the assessment roll, and made no mention in the list of the property or income upon which they were rated; *Held*, that the added list was a nullity. *Ib.*

conclusive evidence in regard to any particular, whether the matter on which the right to vote depends had or had not been brought before the Court of Revision, or had or had not been determined by that court; and upon such revision any person who is a wage-earner within the meaning of the *Election Act*, or of any Act amending the same, shall not be disentitled to have his name entered on said list, either by reason of his having omitted to make, sign, or deliver, any statement required by the provisions of *The Assessment Act* to be so made, signed or delivered by him, or by reason of his name not having been entered on the assessment roll as such wage-earner; and the decision of the judge under this Act, in regard to the right of any person to vote, shall be final so far as regards such person.

Appeal in case of persons disqualified under R.S.O., c. 10.

(2.) A complaint or appeal (Form 4) may be made on the ground of any person whose name is entered on the list being one of those who are disqualified or incompetent to vote under *The Election Act* (*u*).

Applications by persons who have acquired property since assessment.

(3.) If, before the final revision and correction of the assessment roll, any person named as a voter in the said list of voters has died, or having parted with the property in respect of which his name was entered in the voters'

(*u*) This is a ground of complaint distinct from those referred to in the previous subsection. It will cover all persons disqualified expressly by the Elections Act, s. 4, *ante*, as well as persons "otherwise by law prevented from voting" within section 7 (sec. 3 of Fran. & Rep. Act 1885, *ante*), including those found guilty of corrupt practices. As to who comprise this class and how they must be found guilty, see chapters on "Corrupt Practices" and "Penalties" *post*. Those found guilty of corrupt practices at Dominion Elections cannot be struck off the Provincial lists. Women also under sec. 6 of the Elections Act, *ante*, are disqualified from voting at Elections for the Legislature and their names may therefore be struck out of that part of the list which comprises the list of voters at such Elections (1st and 3rd parts) though they will be retained in the municipal list (2nd part)—see sec. 2 subs. 2, 3, and 4, *ante*.

list (*v*), has, within the meaning of section 7 of *The Election Act of Ontario*, ceased to be a resident (*w*) of the electoral district, the person who, at the time of such final revision and correction, was in possession of the said property shall, if otherwise qualified to vote, be entitled to apply (*x*) to the judge to be entered on the said list in-

(*v*) Though the proprietor or tenant may have sold or given up possession of the property between the time when his name is placed upon the assessment roll and the time of the final revision and correction thereof, his name cannot be struck off the voters' list in respect of the said property, unless he has also during the same period ceased to be a resident of the Electoral district. See sec. 3 of the Fran. and Rep. Act 1885 (s. 7 of the Elections Act) subs. "*Firstly.*"—The subsection in the Act for which this subsection was in 1879 substituted, allowed the person to whom the property was transferred to apply to the Judge to be entered on the list instead of the person originally named therein, whether the latter had left the Electoral division ornot; and the subsection also contained a provision that the person who had parted with such property might apply to the Judge to be entered on the list in respect of any other property which he might have acquired in the Municipality, and for which he had not been assessed, or for income. It was held, by some, at all events, of the Judges, that under this last provision it was essential that the person desiring to avail himself of it should give notice of complaint within the time limited for such notices to be given, and where a notice had been given by the purchaser or the new tenant or other person to strike his name off at the last moment limited for filing complaints, the former owner or tenant could not have his name inserted for other property acquired unless he or some one else had previously filed a notice on his behalf for that purpose. To meet this difficulty, probably, sec. 3 of the Voters' Lists Amendment Act 1879 was passed, and it is still in force. It is as follows:

"If on any complaint or appeal to strike out of the list the name of any person entered therein as a voter, the Judge, from any evidence produced and given before him, shall be of opinion that such person is entitled to be entered on said list in any character, or because of property or qualification other than that in which such person is so already entered in said list, the said judge shall not strike the name of such person from said list, but shall make such corrections in the said list as the said evidence in his opinion may warrant with respect to the right, character and qualification of such person to vote."

(*w*) "*Ceased to be a resident.*"—See Dom. Fr. Act s. 3 subs. (6) and note and subs. "*Secondly*" of s. 7 of the Elections Act (s. 3 of Ont. Fran. and Rep. Act 1885) *ante* and note.

(*x*) "*Be entitled to apply.*"—A mandamus will be granted to compel a judge to hear the complaint, where proper notice has been given even though the judge has held the notice insufficient. *Re McCullough and the Judge of Leeds and Grenville*, 35 U. C. Q. B. 449. It is the practice to allow these changes to be made on complaint of any voter who gives a notice of complaint covering names of voters

stead of the person first named in this section; and the proceedings to be taken in any such case shall be the same as in cases of appeals under this Act.

Persons who will be of age within 60 days from revision.

(4.) Any person who is rated, or entered, or liable to be rated, or entered on the assessment roll, either for real property or income of the amount requisite to entitle him to vote, or as a landholder's son or a wage-earner, within the meaning of *The Assessment Act* or of *The Election Act*, or of any Act amending the same, and who will be of the age of twenty-one years *(y)* at any time within sixty days from (*z*) the final revision and correction of the assessment roll, shall be entitled to apply to the judge to have his name entered upon the voters' list, or upon the assessment roll and the voters' list, as the case may require.

Application by landholders' sons and wage-earners.

(5.) Any such landholder's son and any wage-earner entitled to be assessed or entered in the assessment roll of any municipality under *The Assessment Act*, or any Act amending the same, shall, in all respects and for all purposes, have the right to apply and complain to the judge on the revision of the voters' lists, and to have his name entered and inserted in the list (*a*).

"omitted" under sec. 8, providing it covers the names in question—see Hodgins on Voter's Lists p. 21—notwithstanding the provision for a personal application by the transferee of the property contained in this subsection.

(*y*) "*Of the age of twenty-one years.*"—See subs. (1) of sec. 3 of Dom. Fran. Act and note "full age of twenty-one years," *ante*.

(*z*) "*Within sixty days from.*"—The first day is exclusive and the last inclusive, *Ex parte Fallon et ux.* 5 T. R. 283; *Williams* v. *Burgess*, 9 Dowl. 544; *Scott* v. *Dickson*, 1 U. C. P. R. 366.

(*a*) Why a person entitled to be assessed and to vote as an income voter is not included in this subsection is not quite apparent. It may be argued that he may still qualify as a wage-earner and so get the benefit of this sub-sec., a wage-earner being declared by the Assessment Amendment Act 1885 to be "any male person of the full age of twenty-one years and a subject of Her Majesty by birth or naturalization who is actually resident and domiciled in any municipality and *who is not otherwise entered or assessed* in the assessment roll of said Municipality in respect either of property or taxable income so as to entitle him to vote at an election for a member of the Legislative Assembly of this Province."

The Voters' Lists Amendment Act 1885 contains the following additional provision.

9. Any voter or person entitled to be a voter (*b*), making any complaint of any error or omission in the said list shall, within thirty days after (*c*) the Clerk of the municipality has posted up the said list in his office, give to the Clerk, or leave for him at his residence or place of business, notice (*d*) (Form 6) in writing of his complaint and

Proceedings on person complaining of errors in the list.

Notice to be given.

6. Any landholder's son and any wage-earner entitled as such to be assessed or to have his name entered in the assessment roll of any municipality, shall be so assessed and shall have his name so entered without any request in that behalf, unless he informs or notifies the assessor to the contrary ; and any person entitled to be entered in such assessment roll or in the voters' list based thereon, or to vote or to be a voter in the electoral district in which the said municipality is situate, shall, in order to have the name of such landholder's son or wage-earner entered and inserted in such assessment roll, or list of voters, as the case may be, have for all purposes the same right to apply, complain or appeal to any court or to any judge in that behalf, as such landholder's son or wage-earner would or can have personally, unless it is made to appear to the court or judge that such landholder's son or wage-earner actually dissents therefrom.

See also s. 22 and note *post*, and sec. 3 of the Fran. and Rep. Act 1885 subs. "Thirdly" note "wages or income", *ante*, also s. 9 of the Voters' Lists Finality Act, *post*.

(*b*) "*Any voter or person entitled to be a voter.*"—See note to same words in sec. 8, *ante*.

(*c*) "*Within thirty days after.*"—The day of posting up is excluded. The general rule for computation of time fixed by statute is, to hold the first day excluded and the last included, unless there is something in the statute to the contrary—*Ex parte Fallon, et ux.*, 5 T. R 283 ; *Williams* v. *Burgess*, 9 Dowl. 544 ; *Scott* v. *Dickson*, 1 U. C. P. R. 366 ; *Lester* v. *Garland*, 15 Ves. 248 ; the complaint must be entered within the time limited, *Regina ex rel. Telfer* v. *Allen*, 1 Pr. R. 214 ; *Regina ex rel. White* v. *Roach*, 18 Q. B. 226. No exception is made for Sundays or Statutory holidays in the computation of time under this Act ; and the notice may be served on Sunday, it not being "process" of a judicial character under 29 Car. II. c. 7 ; *Rawlins* v. *Overseers of West Derby*, 2 C. B. 72, s. c. 15 L. J. C. P. 70 ; or on a holiday *Clarke* v. *Fuller*, 2 U. C. R. 99. The lateness of the hour of service on the proper day does not affect its validity. Service any time before midnight will do—*Points* v. *Attwood*, 6 C. B. 38 ; 18 L. J. C. P. 19. As soon as the list is posted up the time begins to run and where no complaint is made within the thirty days, the judge is bound to certify, and the certificate is final—*Re the Voters' Lists of L'Orignal*, 9 P. R. 425 ; the omission to transmit copies to the official persons mentioned in the Act, whether negligent or willful, will not authorize an extension of the time, *Ib.*

(*d*) "*Notice.*"—The notice must be signed by the voter giving the same or his agent. The name in the beginning is not a sufficient signature. *In re Simpson* v. *Co'y Judge of Lanark*, 9 P. R. 358. The question of the validity of the notice can be raised before the judge hearing the appeal, after it has been received and entered in the list of appeals, the clerk who receives and enters it having no judicial duty to perform, *Ib.* The notice need not be signed on the day it bears date, so long as it be signed within the thirty days, *Jones* v. *Jones*, 35 L. J. C. P. 94. See as to illegibi-

intention to apply to the judge in respect thereof; and if the office of clerk is vacant by reason of death, resignation, or from any other cause, such notice may be given in like manner to the head of the council of the municipality, and the proceedings thereafter by the Clerk, Judge and parties respectively, and the respective powers and duties of the Judge, Clerk and other persons, shall be the same, or as nearly as may be the same, as in the case of an appeal from the Court of Revision (*e*); but no deposit shall be required to be made before any such complaint is heard or disposed of.

---

lity of signature *Trotter* v. *Walker—Hallam's case*, 32 L. J. C. P. 60. See note to Dom. Fran. Act s. 49, "*Shall forthwith transmit—shall sign*," *ante*. See also sec. 18 and note, *post*.

(*e*) "*An appeal from the Court of Revision.*"—The proceedings, subsequent to the notice of appeal, in the case of an appeal from the Court of Revision, as applied to this Act, are; the judge notifies the clerk of the day he appoints for hearing appeals; the clerk gives notice at least six days, (*i. e.*, six clear days) before the sitting of the Court to all parties complained against by causing the notice to be left at the person's residence or place of business, or if the person is not known, then the notice to be left with some grown person resident at the assessed premises, or if the person is not resident in the municipality, then to be addressed to such person through the Post Office; but in the event of failure by the Clerk to have the required service made, or to have the same made in proper time, the Judge may direct service to be made for some subsequent day upon which he may sit; the Clerk shall cause a conspicuous notice to be posted up in his office, or the place where the Council of the Municipality hold their sittings, containing the names of all the complainants and parties complained against, with a brief statement of the ground or cause of appeal, together with the date at which the Court will be held to hear the appeals. The Clerk shall be Clerk of the Court. The Judge shall hear the complaints at the time appointed by him and may adjourn the hearing from ti e to time and defer judgment thereon at his pleasure, but so that all complaints shall be determined and the list finally revised, corrected and certified within two months of the last day for making such complaints—Rev. Stat. cap. 180, s. 59, subs. 3, 4, 5, 6 and 7—41 Vic. c. 21, s. 8. As to notice of holding Court by publication in a newspaper see next subsection. The appearance of parties by their counsel, for the purpose of objecting to the sufficiency of the notice, is no waiver of it, *The Queen* v. *The Court of Revision of Cornwall*, 25 U. C. Q. B. 286; to dispense with proof of service there must be an actual appearance on the day the case is called on, *Grover* v. *Boutemps*, 4 C. B. 58; 16 L. J. C. P. 70, and see *Rawkins* v. *Overseers of W. Derby*, 2 C. B. 72; 15 L. J. C. P. 70.

(2.) If the notice is given to or left for the head of the council, he shall perform or cause to be performed *(f)* such necessary acts as should be performed by the Clerk if there were one.

The case of notice left with the head of the Council.

(3.) No judge shall proceed with the holding of any court for hearing complaints as aforesaid, unless and until notice (Form 10) of the time and place of holding said court shall by the clerk have been published at least ten days before the sittings of such court, in some newspaper published in the municipality, or, if there be no such paper, then in some newspaper published in the nearest municipality in which one is published *(g)*.

Notice of holding Court for complaints.

10. (1.) Any party may obtain from the County Court a subpœna (Form 13), or from the County Judge an order requiring the attendance at the court for hearing complaints as aforesaid, at the time mentioned in such subpœna or order, of a witness residing or served with such subpœna or order, in any part of this province; and requiring any such witness to bring with him and produce at the court any papers or documents mentioned in the subpœna or order, and every witness served with such subpœna or order shall obey the same, provided the allowance for his expenses, according to the scale allowed in Division Court, is tendered to him at the time of service *(h)*.

Compelling attendance of witnesses on revision of list.

(2.) Any person complaining, or any person in respect of the insertion or omission of whose name a complaint is made, shall if resident within the municipality, the

Person whose right is in question to attend.

(f) "*Performed.*"—In case of death of the clerk after he has prepared the lists and signed certificate under sec. 5, his successor may continue the proceedings. *Re Goderich Voters' Lists*, 6 Pr. R. 213.

(g) This subsection has been added to sec. 9 by 48 Vic. c. 3, sec. 10.

(h) This and the following subsections are substituted for sec. 10 of the original Act by The Voters' Lists Amendment Act, 1885, s. 7.

list of which is the subject of complaint, or within the municipality in which the court is held, upon being served with a subpœna or order therein, obey the same without being tendered or paid any allowance for his expenses; and where any such complaint is by or in respect of a person whose name is entered in the list of voters as being, or who is alleged to be, a wage-earner or landholder's son within the meaning of *The Assessment Act* or of *The Election Act*, or of any Act amending either of said Acts, such subpœna or order shall be deemed to have been sufficiently served upon such person under the provisions of this section:

(*a*) If such subpœna or order is served upon him personally; or

(*b*) Where such person has a known residence or place of business within said municipality, if a copy of such subpœna or order is left for him with some grown person, at such residence or place of business; or

(*c*) Where such person has no known residence or place of business within the municipality, if a copy of such subpœna or order is mailed to him through the post-office, with the postage thereon pre-paid and addressed to him at the post-office address contained in any written affirmation made by him under *The Assessment Act*, or any Act amending the same; or

(*d*) Where such person is a landholder's son as aforesaid, if a copy of such order or subpœna is left for him with some grown person at the residence of the landholder whose son he is (*i*).

(*i*) A person complained against is bound to give evidence when called, *Peterson* v. *Balfour*, 10 Ir. C. L. 553.

(3.) If any person, whose right to be a voter is the subject of inquiry do not attend in obedience to such subpœna or order, the Judge, if he think fit, in the absence of satisfactory evidence as to the ground of such non-attendance, or as to the right of such person to be a voter, may, on the ground of the non-attendance of such person, strike his name off the list of voters, or refuse to place his name on the list of voters, as the case may require, or impose a reasonable fine on such person according to his discretion, or do both (*j*).

Penalty on non-attendance of the person whose right is in question.

(4.) Any number of names may be inserted in one subpœna or judge's order, in any case of complaint. 39 V., c. 11, s. 9.

Insertion of several names in subpœna or order.

11. In case no complaint respecting such list is received by the Clerk of the municipality (*k*) within thirty days after (*l*) the Clerk has posted up the said list in his office, the Clerk shall forthwith apply (Form 14) either in person or by letter, to the Judge to certify (Form 15) three copies of such list as being the revised list of voters for the

List confirmed if no complaint within 30 days after the Clerk has posted up the list.

(*j*) The name cannot be restored where objector is not ready with his proofs at second hearing, *Blain* v. *Overseers of Pilkington*, 34 L. J. C. P. 55; *Oldham El.* (*Harper's case*) 1 O. & M. 157.

(*k*) Where a clerk having posted up the list in his office, did not transmit copies to all the persons mentioned in the Act (secs. 3 and 4) and having received no notices of complaint, applied to the deputy judge, pursuant to this section, after having made the necessary certificate and report, to certify three copies of the list, which such deputy judge accordingly did; and the county Judge found that the certificate and report were false and untrue, and made with intent to deceive the deputy judge, and that the latter had in ignorance certified the list and ordered the clerk's certificate and the certificate of the Deputy Judge to be cancelled: *Held*, that the omission to transmit the copies, whether negligent or wilful, not being essential to the legal revision or authentication of the list, could not authorize an extension of time, and that the Deputy Judge's certificate was final and could not be set aside. *Re Voters' Lists of L'Orignal* 9 Pr. R. 425, Osler, J., affirmed by the full Court of Queen's Bench on appeal. The Act formerly provided for notice of complaint being given within 30 days from the time of delivering and transmitting the copies as well as of posting up the list, but this was altered; see 39 Vic., c. 11, sec. 5.

(*l*) "*Within thirty days after.*"—See note to same words, s. 9, *ante*.

municipality; and the Judge shall retain one of such certified copies of the list, and deliver or transmit by post, registered, one of such certified copies to the Clerk of the Peace for the County or union of Counties within which the municipality lies, and one of such certified copies to the Clerk of the municipality, to be kept by him among the records of his office.

After final revision Judge to make statement of alterations and certify copy of list.

12. In case complaints are made as aforesaid, immediately after the list has been finally revised and corrected by the Judge, the Judge shall make or cause to be made, and shall sign, a statement (Form 16) in triplicate, setting forth the changes, if any, which he has made in the list; and shall certify in triplicate (Form 17) a corrected copy of the list. And such statement in triplicate and such corrected copies of the said list shall, if the Judge so order, and under his directions and supervision, be prepared by the clerk of the municipality, and for that purpose the Judge shall forthwith after said list has been so finally revised and corrected, transmit or deliver to said Clerk all necessary papers and directions, which said papers and directions together with such statement in triplicate and such corrected copies shall within, at latest, the week next after the said list has been so finally revised and corrected as aforesaid, be re-transmitted and delivered by said Clerk to said Judge, who thereupon shall immediately sign the said statement and certify the said corrected copies as aforesaid, but should the said statement and corrected copies not be re-transmitted and delivered by said Clerk to the Judge within the time above mentioned, the Judge shall immediately thereafter make and sign the said statement and certify the said corrected copies of the said list (*m*).

Statements and corrected copies of lists to be prepared by Clerk if Judge so directs.

(*m*) The provision in the above section for the preparation of the statements and

(2.) The Judge shall retain one of such certified copies and one statement, and shall deliver or transmit by post, registered, one of such certified copies and one statement to the Clerk of the Peace for the county or union of counties within which the municipality lies, and one of such certified copies and one statement to the clerk of the municipality, to be kept by him among the records of his office. How the Judge shall dispose of the statements and copies.

13. It shall be the duty of the municipality within which a Court is holden, to provide some suitable and convenient place, properly furnished, heated and lighted for the holding of such Court, and in case such is not done the Judge may hold said Court at such other place in the County as he may deem proper; and if the same is held elsewhere than in the County Court house, the proprietor or proprietors of the building in which it is held may recover from the municipality which should Municipality to provide a Court room.

---

corrected copies by the clerk under direction of the Judge was an amendment of the original section by the Act of 1879. Under the English Act, 6 Vic., c. 18, s. 47, the procedure is the revising barrister, having signed the list as revised, transmits it to the Clerk of the Peace for the county, who keeps the same among the records of the sessions, and has the lists copied and printed in a book or books, etc. And the said Clerk of the Peace shall sign and deliver the said book or books on or before the last day of November (now December) in the then current year to the sheriff of the county, to be by him and his successors in the office of sheriff safely kept, for the purposes hereinafter and in the said recited Act mentioned. In *Brumfit* v. *Bremner*, 30, L. J. C. P. 33; 9 C. B. (N. S.) 1, the name of the appellant was inadvertently erased by the revising barrister and erroneously omitted from the first impression of the register. The appellant discovered the omission, and communicated with the Clerk of the Peace, who inserted the name, and delivered a book, containing the name so inserted, to the Clerk of the Peace on the 13th January. The appellant becoming an objector at the next revision, the revising barrister declined to hear him, on the ground that he was not upon the register, because he was not upon the first impression sold of it: but the Court unanimously held that the revising barrister was wrong. Under this provision of the Ontario Act, however, the Judge is the last person to certify, and no such question as the above can arise, as the Clerk of the Peace is under the next subsection a mere custodian of the lists, as is the sheriff under the section of the English Act just quoted.

have made such provision the sum of five dollars for each and every day during which such building is used for the purposes of such Court: Any Court held in the

Courts in County Towns.

County Town shall be held in the County Court-house or in such other place in said County Town as the Judge may deem proper.

Judge may punish for contempt of Court.

14. In all proceedings before the Judge under this Act, the Judge shall have with reference to the matters herein contained, all the powers which belong to or might be exercised by him in the County Court (*n*).

Appointment of Bailiff.

15. The Judge shall have power to appoint some proper person to attend at the sitting of the Court as a

Duties.

Constable or Bailiff; and the duties and powers of such person thereat shall be as nearly as may be the same as those of the Bailiff of a Division Court (*o*) at a sitting of a Division Court and in reference thereto: and the ex-

Expenses.

penses (*p*) of the person so appointed and attending shall be borne by the municipality the list for which is the subject of investigation, and shall include such allowance for loss of time, trouble and travelling fees as shall be certified by the Judge to be reasonable; and the amount certified by the Judge shall be paid to such person

(*n*) See note to sec. 28 Dom. Fran. Act "Powers of a Court of Record" *ante*, also sec. 3 of the Voters' Lists Finality Act and note *post*.

(*o*) "*Bailiff of a Division Court.*"—By the Div. Court Act (Rev. Stat. c. 47 s. 46.) "Every Bailiff shall exercise the authority of a constable during the actual holding of the Court of which he is a Bailiff, with full power to prevent breaches of the peace, riots or disturbances within the Court Room or building in which the Court is held, or in the public streets, squares or other places within the hearing of the Court, and may, with or without warrant arrest all parties offending against the meaning of this clause, and forthwith bring such offenders before the nearest Justice of the Peace, or any other judicial officer having power to investigate the matter or to adjudicate thereupon."

(*p*) "*The expenses.*"—See s. 16 of The Voters' Lists Finality Act. *post*, which fixes the Bailiff's fees and takes away all discretionary power from the Judge as to the amount thereof.

by the Treasurer of the municipality upon the production and deposit with him of the Judge's certificate.

16. The Clerk of every municipality shall be subject to the summary jurisdiction and control of the County Judge in respect to the performance of his duty under this Act, and in respect to every act required to be performed by such Clerk touching the voters' list, in the same manner as officers of the County Court are to the Court *(q)*. Clerk to be subject to the summary jurisdiction of the Judge.

17. If the Judge who holds a Court, believes, or has good reason to believe, that any person or persons have contravened the twenty-sixth or twenty-ninth sections of this Act, or that frauds in respect to the assessment or the voters' lists have prevailed extensively in the municipality it shall be his duty to report the same to the Provincial Secretary, with such particulars as to names and facts as he may think proper *(r)*. Report by Judge as to frauds etc.

18. The Judge shall have power to amend any notice or other proceeding upon such terms as he shall think proper *(s)*. Amendment.

(q) A clause at the end of this section, repealed by 42 Vic. c. 3, s. 7 formerly provided for "reasonable compensation" to the Clerk. The amount of that compensation is now regulated by sec. 15 of The Voters' Lists Finality Act, as amsnded by 42 Vic. c. 3, s, 6, *post*—see further as to Clerk's duties, *ante*, notes to s. 2 and to s. 9 "*an appeal from the Court of Revision.*"

(r) This is a similar provision to that contained in the Elections Acts, providing for reports by the Judge in Election cases, except that the latter are made to the Speaker of the House.

(s) Powers of amendment have been gradually widened by Parliament and the Courts. Amendments of a slip in pleading are now always allowable and a refusal to allow an amendment is a proper ground of appeal, *Laird* v. *Briggs*, L. R. 19 Chy. Div. 22; *Clarke* v. *Yorke*, 31 W. R. 62; *Smith* v. *Smith*, 5 Ont. R. 690. Large powers and duties as to amendments were conferred and imposed upon revising barristers in England by the Parliamentary and Mun. Reg. Act s. 28. With regard to the discretionary power of amendment given by that enactment, where a lodger's claim omitted to state the amount of his rent, and the address of his landlord; and these particulars were supplied at the revision, but the revising barrister declined to

Abandonment by appellant and intervention of some other.

19. If any appellant or complainant, entitled to appeal dies or abandons (*t*) his appeal or complaint, or having been on the alphabetical lists made and posted by the clerk as aforesaid is afterwards found not to be entitled to be an appellant (*u*) the Judge may if he think proper allow any other person who might have been an appellant or complainant to intervene and prosecute such appeal or complaint, upon such terms as the Judge shall think just.

---

insert them, the Court approved of and affirmed his decision, *Pickard* v. *Baylis*, 5 C. P. D. 235; 49 L. J. C. P. 182. But this case, it has been remarked, though a strong authority to guide the exercise of the discretion, is no express authority binding a similar exercise of it in every case. An omission to state the place of residence of an objector describing himself only as on the list of parliamentary voters, and being in fact well known, was held curable in *Adams* v. *Bostock*, 8 Q. B. D. 259; 51 L. J. Q. B. 175; and so was an omission of the word "Parliamentary" before "voters" in *James* v. *Howarth*, 5 C. P. D. 225; 49 L. J. C. P. 169. The inclination of the Courts is in every way to favor the franchise, *Regina ex. rel. Ford* v. *Cottingham*, 1 C. L. J. N. S. 214, *Regina ex rel. Chambers* v. *Allison*, *Ib.* 244. "The presumptions of law always in favor of the franchise, and Acts of Parliament should be worked out to confer the franchise on those who seem to be within the spirit of the law entitled to it, rather than be strained to deprive parties of a right to vote," *per* Richards, C. J., in *Re McCullough and the Judge of Leeds and Grenville*, 35 Q. B. U. C. 452. See also, *Lincoln Election*, (*Borrowman's case*,) 2 *App. R.*; *Oldham Election*, 20 L. T. N. S. 304; *Elliott* v. *Overseers of St. Mary's*, 4 C. B. 76, *Howitt* v. *Stephens*, 5 C. B. N. S., 30; *Cooper* v. *Ashfield*, *Ib.* 16. As to amendments of mistakes in names, place of abode, nature of qualification of voters or description of property, without previous notice of complaint, see sec. 2 of Voters' Lists Amendment Act 1879, quoted in note to sec. 8 *ante*; as to alteration of qualification of voter complained against, without notice, see sec. 3 of the same Act, given in note to subs. 3 of sec. 8, *ante*; also Dom. Fran. Act s. 49, *ante*, note. "*Shall forthwith transmit, etc.*" *Re Simpson* v. *The County Judge of Lanark*, 9 Pr. R. 358.

(*t*) "*Dies or abandons.*"—Prior to the Parliamentary and Mun. Reg. Act, 1878, in England, the death of the objector extinguished the objection, while objections were not allowed to be withdrawn, *Proudfoot* v. *Barnes*, L. R. 2 C. P. 88; 30 L. J. C. P. 68; 15 L. T. 439. But by sec. 27 of that Act an objection may be withdrawn on notice, or be revived, on the death of the objector, by any other qualified person by notice.

(*u*) "*Entitled to be an appellant.*"—The appellant must be "a voter or person entitled to be a voter," ss. 8 and 9, *ante*.

See *Montreal Centre Election*, 18 L. C. Jurist 323.

20. In case of errors (*v*) being found in the said voters' list on the said revision thereof, whether such errors are in the omission of names, the inaccurate entry of names, or the entry of names of persons not entitled to vote, if it appear to the Judge that the Assessor was blameable for any of the said errors, the Judge shall order (*w*) (Form 18) the Assessor, either alone or jointly with any other person to pay all costs occasioned by the same; and in case of errors for which the Clerk was to blame, the Clerk, either alone or jointly with any other person, shall be charged with the costs; and in case of errors of the Court of Revision, the municipality shall, either alone or jointly with any person, pay the costs, subject to any claim which the municipality may justly have against the guilty parties; or the Judge may order the Assessor, Clerk or Municipality, in any such case, to pay the costs, if any party fail to recover the same from any other party named and ordered to pay the same; and, in all cases not herein provided for, the costs shall be in the discretion of the Judge; 37 V., c. 4, s. 10.

Costs occasioned by errors may be ordered to be paid by guilty parties.

(2.) No costs shall be allowed on any proceeding under this Act, other or higher than would be allowed in the Division Court under the lowest scale of costs in actions therein;

Division Court costs only allowed.

(3.) The only costs to which an appellant shall be liable shall be the witness fees, unless in case of bad faith on his part (*x*).

Liability of appellant for costs.

21. The payment of any costs ordered to be paid by the Judge may be enforced by an execution (Form 19)

Costs, payment of, how enforced

(*v*) See also secs. 24, 25, 26, 28, 29 and 30 *post*.

(*w*) "*Shall order.*"—These words are imperative in form; but the Judge must first find the official "blameable," and it is not usual to do so unless the error is *wilful*, or the result of negligence practically amounting to wilfulness.

(*x*) See note to s. 52 of Dom. Fran. Act, *ante*.

against goods and chattels, to be issued from any County Court upon filing therein the order of the Judge, and an affidavit showing the amount at which such costs were taxed and the non-payment thereof.

Persons whose names omitted from roll and inserted on revision liable to pay taxes.

22. If a person not assessed, or not sufficiently assessed, shall be found entitled to vote, the municipality shall be entitled to recover taxes from him *(y)* and to enforce payment thereof by the same means and in the same manner as if he had been assessed on the roll for the amount found by the Judge; and the Judge shall make an order (Form 20), setting forth the names of the persons so liable, and the sum for which each person should have been assessed and the land or other property in respect of which the liability exists, and such order shall be transmitted to the Clerk of the Municipality, and shall have the same effect as if the said particulars had been inserted in the roll.

Judge's order.

Failure of Clerk to perform duties not to vitiate the list.

23. The times appointed for the performance by the Clerk of the Municipality, of the duties required of him by this Act, shall be directory only to the said clerk; and the performance by him of any of the said duties within the times appointed, shall not render null, void or inoperative, any of the lists in this Act mentioned *(z)*.

(y) "*Shall be entitled to recover taxes from him.*"—It is conceived that it was not the intention of the Legislature by the Acts of 1885, to subject the income of a "wage-earner" to assessment for purposes of taxation—unless, possibly, the excess over $400, the limit of exemption of income. See sec. 3 of The Fran. and Rep. Act, 1885 (s. 7 of Election Act) subs. "Thirdly," note, "*wages or income*," *ante*; also s. 8, subs. 5 of this Act and note thereunder, *ante*. Nor will a "landholder's son," be bound to pay taxes, where his name is placed upon the list for property already assessed to the parent. It was decided in *Re Lincoln Election*, (*Borrowman's case*), 2 App. R. 316, that the Judge could not add to the list the name of an income voter not already assessed, and therefore the question above suggested could not arise in his case. He is now given such power as regards wage-earners and landholder's sons expressly by subs. 5 of s. 8.

(z) See *Goderich Voters' Lists*, 6 Pr. R. 213. *Re Voters' Lists of L'Orignal*, 9 Pr. R. 425.

24. In case the Clerk of any Municipality fails to perform any of the duties aforesaid, the Clerk of the Peace shall forthwith apply (Form 21) summarily to the County Judge or the junior or acting judge of the County Court for the county within which such municipality is situate, to enforce the performance of the same. Provision in case Clerk of Municipality fails to perform duties.

(2.) The application may also be made by any person entitled to be named as an elector on the list in respect of which the application is made. Elector may apply

(3.) The Judge shall on such application, require (Form 22) the Clerk of the Municipality, and any other person he sees fit, to appear before him and produce the assessment roll, and any documents relating thereto, or to the list in respect to which the application is made, and to submit to such examination on oath as may be required of him or them, and the Judge shall thereupon make such orders and give such directions as he may deem necessary or proper for the purposes aforesaid. Judge may require Clerk or other person to appear and submit to cross-examination, etc.

(4.) The Clerk of the Municipality shall be personally liable for and shall pay the costs of the proceedings, unless on some special grounds the Judge shall see fit to order otherwise, and in such special case the costs shall be in the discretion of the Judge ; 32 V., c. 21, s. 7, (8.) Liability of Clerk for costs.

(5.) Such proceedings and such order of the Judge shall not in anywise exonerate or release the clerk from liability to the penalty hereinafter imposed. 32 V., c. 21, s. 7 (9). Judge's order not to release Clerk from penalty.

25. If any Clerk of a Municipality omits, neglects or refuses to complete the Voters' List, or to perform any of the duties hereinbefore required of him for his municipality, such clerk, for each such omission, neglect or refusal, shall incur a penalty of two hundred dollars *(a)*. Penalty on Clerk for neglect, etc.

(*a*) Under a somewhat similar provision in sec. 76 of the Reform Act, 1832, in England, for wilful breach of duty, it has been held that the motive if wilful need not be corrupt, *Fair* v. *McGashy*, 7 C. & P. 380; *King* v. *Burrell*, 12 A. & E. 460.

Clerks, etc., wilfully falsifying lists to incur a penalty.

26. If any Clerk of a Municipality, or Clerk of the Peace, or any other person wilfully makes any alteration, omission or insertion, or in any way wilfully falsifies any such certified list or copy, or permits the same to be done, every such person shall incur a penalty of two thousand dollars.

Colourable transfer of property in order to confer vote.

27. No person shall make, execute, accept or become a party to any lease, deed or other instrument or become a party to any verbal arrangement, whereby a colorable interest in any land, house or tenement is conferred, in order to qualify any person to vote at an election; and any person violating the provisions of this section, besides being liable to any other penalty prescribed in that behalf, shall incur a penalty of one hundred dollars, and any person who induces, or attempts to induce another to commit an offence under this section, shall incur a like penalty *(b)*. 37 V., c. 4, s. 14.

(*b*) The "splitting" of votes or creation of "faggot voters," and the offence of "occasionality," as it is sometimes called, are struck at by this section. The English Acts 7 and 8 Will. III., c. 25, 10 Anne, c. 23, and 53 Geo. III., c. 49, deal with the same subject. The first of these provides that all conveyances made to multiply voices or to split or divide the interest in any houses or lands among several persons to enable them to vote should be void. The statute of Anne provided that all such fraudulent conveyances should be deemed and taken as against those who executed as free and absolute, and discharged from all trusts, conditions, clauses of re-entry, powers of revocation, provisoes of redemption, or other defeazances, and all collateral bonds, etc., for redemption, etc., were to be void. And a £40 penalty for such practices was also provided by the same Act. The statute of Geo. III. brought devises by will within the same rules. It has been held under these Acts: that the conveyance is void only if the vendor be privy to the object, *Marshall* v. *Brown*, 7 M. & G. 188, and even the privity of the vendor's solicitor does not avoid it, if the vendor himself be not privy, *Hoyland* v. *Bremner*, 2 C. B. 84; 15 L. J. C. P. 133. Moreover conveyances for *bonâ fide* consideration, *Thorniley* v. *Aspland*, 2 C. B. 160, or for the consideration only of natural love and affection, *Newton* v. *Hargreaves*, 2 C. B. 163, are good, although the avowed object of both parties be to create votes, *Newton* v. *Crowley, Overseers*, 2 C. B. 207; *Riley* v. *Crossley*, 2 C. B. 146, 15 L. J. C. P. 144. It is only fraudulent or collusive conveyances reserving a trust for the grantors which are bad, (*Riley* v. *Crossley*) and the question whether there was fraud or not so as to avoid the vote is one of fact for the revising barrister, *Newton Over-*

28. The penalties mentioned in the three next preceding sections may be recovered with costs of suit by any person suing for the same in any court of competent jurisdiction. Recovery of penalties.

29. To prevent the creation of false votes, where any person claims to be assessed, or claims that any other person should be assessed, as owner or occupant of any parcel of land, or as possessing the income which may entitle him to vote in the municipality at an election, and the assessor has reason to suspect that the person so claiming, or for whom the claim is made, has not a just right to be so assessed, it shall be the duty of the assessor to make reasonable enquiries before assessing such person (*c*). 37 V., c. 4, s. 1. Assessor to make enquiries before assessing persons claiming to be assessed.

30. Any assessor who wilfully and improperly inserts any name in the assessment roll, or assesses any person at too high an amount, with intent in either case to give to any person not entitled thereto an apparent right of voting at any election, or who wilfully inserts any fictitious name in the assessment roll, or who wilfully and improperly omits any name from the assessment roll, or assesses any person at too low an amount, with intent in either case to deprive any person of his right to vote, shall, upon conviction thereof before a court of competent jurisdiction, be liable to a fine not exceeding two hundred dollars, and to imprisonment until the fine be paid, or to Penalty on assessor for wrongfully assessing or omitting.

---

seers v. *Mobberley*, 2 C. B. 203; 15 L. J. C. P. 154. The fraudulent conveyance is bad only to the extent of avoiding the vote, and operates to pass a legal interest from the grantor to the grantee, *Phillpotts* v. *Phillpotts*, 10 C. B. 85; 20 L. J. C. P. 11.

(*c*) But "when an assessor has reasonable notice, before he returns his roll, that a change in occupancy has been made, and he omits to make the necessary changes, it may properly be considered when the assessor fails to do this, that he has wrongfully refused to insert the proper name on the roll," per Richards, C. J., in *Re McCullough and the Judge of Leeds and Grenville*, 35 U. C. Q. B. 452: see also *Fair* v. *McGushey*, 7 C. & P. 380; and *King* v. *Burrell*, 12 A. & E. 460.

imprisonment in the common gaol of the county or city, for a period not exceeding six months, or to both such fine or imprisonment, in the discretion of the court *(d)*. 7 V., c. 4, s. 13.

Clerks of the Peace and of Municipalities to furnish copies of the last revised voters' list.

31. The Clerk of the Peace and the Clerk of any Municipality having the custody of the list of voters of any municipality or part of any municipality or place, shall furnish a certified copy of such list, then last revised and corrected, or of any of the parts thereof, to any person who may require such copy or part, on being paid for the same by such person at the rate of four cents for every ten voters whose names are on such list or part; the said officers may furnish printed copies for each of which they shall be entitled to receive six cents instead of the fee aforesaid; and the officers shall verify any alterations made therein, by writing their initials in close proximity thereto. If the alterations or interlineations exceed one hundred, it shall be the duty of the said officers to furnish written copies *(e)*.

Fees to Clerk of Peace for copy of voters' lists. See Rev. Stat., c. 10, s. 56, or c. 174, ss. 28, 129

(2.) For each copy of the voters' list or of any of the parts thereof furnished to the Returning Officer, according to Form 8 in Schedule A to "*The Election Act*" or according to Schedule C to "*The Municipal Act*," the Clerk of the Peace furnishing the same shall be entitled to receive the sum of six cents for every ten voters whose names are on such list or part as the case may be.

Board of County Judges may make rules.

32. The Board of County Judges may, if requested so to do by the Lieutenant-Governor, frame rules and forms of procedure for the purpose of better carrying this Act into effect; and such rules and forms shall, after being

(d) See note to last section—also *Regina* v. *Snider*, 23 U. C. C. P. 336, and Interpretation Act, Rev. Stats. c. 1, s. 8, subs. 29.

(e) See also 41 Vic. c. 21, s. 10, *post*.

approved of by the Lieutenant-Governor in Council, have the same effect and force as if they formed part of this Act *(f)*.

33. The words Householder *(g)*(H), Freeholder (F), and Tenant (T), appearing on the assessment roll pursuant to the Assessment Act, shall, for the purposes of this Act, be held to also mean, respectively, Occupant *(h)* (Oc.), Owner (O), or Tenant (T), and shall be so entered in the voters' list by the Clerk of the Municipality.

Words "Householder", etc., on roll, how to be entered on list.

34. In carrying into effect the provisions of this Act, the forms set forth in the schedule hereto may be used, and the same or forms to the like effect shall be deemed sufficient for the purposes mentioned in the said Schedule *(i)*.

Forms given in this Act may be used.

(f) No such Rules or Forms have been framed.

(g) "*Householder.*"—See s. 2, subs. 8 of the Fran. and Rep. Act 1885 and notes, *ante*. There is a difference between the householder as defined, in that subsection, and as defined in s. 87 of the Con. Mun. Act, 1883.

(h) "*Occupant.*"—See s. 2, subs. 2 of the Fran. and Rep. Act 1885, and note, *ante*.

(i) The forms in the schedule have been altered in accordance with the various amendments.

By sec. 11 of The Voters' Lists Amendment Act, 1885, certain temporary provisions are made, pending the coming into force of the rest of the Act, whose provisions are embodied in the Voters' Lists Act as here given, and come into force on 1st January, 1886 "except as to any assessment roll or assessment taken or made subsequent to the first day of July next after the passing thereof, under the special provisions of section 44 of *The Assessment Act;* and with respect to any such last mentioned assessment roll or assessment, and any list of voters based thereon, this Act shall for all purposes, and as regards all matters, liabilities, duties, and proceedings therein provided for, be deemed to come into force, and have effect on and after said first day of July."

FORMS UNDER VOTERS' LISTS ACT.

FORM 1.

(See sec. 2 of Voters' Lists Act and secs. 8 and 9 of 42 Vic., cap. 3, and sec. 3 of 48 Vic., cap. 3).

FORM OF VOTERS' LIST.

(The italics signify changes in the form as given in the Rev. Stats., to make it uniform with the Acts of 1885).

Voters' List, 18 , Municipality of

SCHEDULE OF POST OFFICES.

1. North Augusta,
2. Maitland,
3. Wright's Corners,
4. Prescott.

Polling subdivision No. 1, comprising, etc :—(giving the limits).

PART I.—Persons entitled to vote at BOTH Municipal Elections and Elections to the Legislative Assembly.

No. on Roll.	NAME.	Lot.	Con. or Street.		Post Office Address.
6	J Anderson, Henry..	N. W. ¼ 6 and other premises.	3	Owner	1
14	Andrews, John....	W. 14 acr 8	1	Tenant	4
1	Archer, James ...	2	6	Income	4
50	Brown, Simon	W. ½ 9	2	*Landholder's* Son........	3
71	J Burton, Samuel. .	E. ½ 17	4	*Owner—partly qualified in subdivision No. 2.*	2
		etc.	etc.	etc.	etc.

PART II.—Persons entitled to vote at Municipal Elections ONLY.

No. on Roll.	NAME.	Lot.	Con. or Street.		Post Office Address.
4	Archer, Henry....	4	3	*County Judge*	2
82	Burke, Mary......	W. ½ 17	4	*Widow*.................	4

PART III.—Persons entitled to vote at Elections for the LEGISLATIVE ASSEMBLY ONLY.

No. on Roll.	NAME.	Lot.	Con. or Street.		Post Office Address.
43	Ackroyd, James ..	N ½ 3	4	*Householder*	3
8	Amos, Joseph.....	3	7	*Wage-earner*............	3
49	*Beatty, John*......	*2*	*9*	*Income*.................	*4*
57	*Cameron, Alex'r* .	*5*	*8*	*Landholder's Son*........	*2*
		etc.	etc.	etc.	etc.

Polling subdivision, No. 2—comprising, etc. (giving the limits).
etc., etc., etc.

Note.—In above Form (which is a form of a township list), *Henry Anderson* is a person qualified in respect of more than one lot or parcel in the same subdivision or in different subdivisions (s. 2, subs. 7 and 8). His name should not appear again for any other subdivision (s 2, subs. 8). The "J" signifies that he is qualified to act as a juror (see note to s. 2, subs. 11, *ante*).

James Archer must be on the assessment roll for at least $400 income, to appear on this part of list.

Simon Brown must be a Farmer's son, *i.e.*, the son of an *owner* of a farm of at least 20 acres and worth at least $200 if his father be living, and he be the only son, $300 if there be another older son; $100 if father dead and mother a widow and owner and no older son, etc.

Samuel Burton's qualification lies partly within subdivision No. 1 and partly within subdivision No. 2.

James Ackroyd lives in a "dwelling house" worth less than $100.

Joseph Amos is entered on the roll as a "wage-earner", and earns not less than $250 annually, but is not assessed for income of $400 or more, and therefore is not qualified for municipal purposes.

John Beatty is assessed for income of less than $400, but not less than $250.

Alexander Cameron is the son of a tenant of a dwelling house, etc., of the actual value of $200 or more, or of an owner of a farm worth $200 but less than 20 acres.

Form 2.

(*Section 5.*)

CERTIFICATE TO BE ENDORSED ON VOTERS' LIST.

I, A. B., Clerk of the Municipality of , in the County of , do hereby certifiy that parts one and three of the within (or above) list constitute a correct list for the year 18 , of all persons appearing by the last revised Assessment Roll of the said Municipality to be entitled to vote at elections of members of the Legislative Assembly; and that parts one and two constitute a correct list for said year of all persons appearing by the said roll to be entitled to vote at Municipal Elections in said municipality; and I hereby call upon all electors to examine the said list, and if any omissions or other errors are perceived therein, to take immediate proceedings to have the said errors corrected according to Law.

Dated this day of A. B.,
Clerk of

Form 3.

(*Section 7.*)

CLERK'S NOTICE OF FIRST POSTING OF VOTERS' LIST.

Voters List, 18 , Municipality of the of County of

Notice is hereby given, that I have transmitted or delivered to the persons mentioned in the third and fourth sections of "*The Voters' Lists Act*," the copies required by said section to be so transmitted or delivered of the list, made pursuant to said Act, of all persons appearing by the last revised Assessment Roll of the said municipality to be entitled to vote in the said municipality at elections for members of the Legislative Assembly, and at municipal elections; and that said list was first posted up at my office at on the day of 18 , and remains there for inspection.

Electors are called upon to examine the said list, and if nay omissions or any other errors are found therein, to take immediate proceedings to have the said errors corrected according to Law.

Dated, etc.

A. B.,
Clerk of the Municipality.

FORM 4.

(*Section 8, subs. 2.*)

VOTER'S NOTICE OF COMPLAINT ON GROUND OF DISQUALIFICATION.

To the Clerk of the Municipality of the Town of

I, *Angus Bell*, a voter (*or* "a person entitled to be a voter") in the said Municipality (or "for the Electoral District in which the Municipality is situated"), complain that the name of *John Jack*, is wrongly* entered in the Voters' List for the Municipality, he being a person disqualified under the section of "*The Election Act*"; and take notice, that I intend to apply to the Judge in respect thereof, in pursuance of the Statute in that behalf.

Dated day of 18 .

ANGUS BELL,
Residence—Township of York.

* "Wrongly" should be "wrongfully", as these terms are respectively used in Form 6, *post*.

FORM 5.

(*Section 8, subs. 3.*)

NOTICE AND APPLICATION BY VOTER TO WHOM PERSON ASSESSED HAS TRANSFERRED PROPERTY.

To the Clerk of the Municipality of the Town of

I, *Luke Doran*, a person entitled to be a voter in the said Municipality, complain that the name of *Peter Short* is wrongly inserted in the Voters' List for the said Municipality, he, having before the final revision and correction of the Assessment Roll transferred to me the property in respect of which his name is entered on the said List* (*or* "parted with the property in respect to which his name is entered on the Voters' List,* and that I am in possession of the same")—and take notice, that I intend to apply to the Judge to have my name entered on the said List, instead of the said *Peter Short*, pursuant to the provisions of the Statute in that behalf.

Dated the day of 18 .

LUKE DORAN.

* The words "and having ceased to be a resident of the Electoral District" ought to be inserted here in accordance with the provisions of s. 8, subs. 3, as amended by the Voters' Lists Amendment Act, 1885.

FORM 6.

(*Section 9.*)

VOTER'S NOTICE OF COMPLAINT.

To the Clerk of the Municipality of the Town of

I, *James Smith*, a voter (*or* "person entitled to be a voter") for the Electoral District of , in which the said Municipality is situated, complain (*state the names of the persons in respect to whom complaint is made, and the ground of complaint touching each person respectively—or set forth in lists as follows, varying according to circumstances*), that the several persons whose names are set forth in the subjoined list No. 1 are entitled to be voters in the said Municipality, as shown in said list, but are wrongfully omitted from the Voters' List; That the several persons whose names are mentioned in the first column of the subjoined list No. 2 are wrongly stated in the said Voters' List, as shown in said list No. 2:—That the several persons whose names are set forth in the first column of the subjoined list No. 3 are wrongfully inserted in the said Voters' List, as shown in said list No. 3:—And that there are errors in the description of the property in respect to which the names respectively are entered on the Voters' List (*or stating other errors*), as shown in the subjoined list No. 4:—And take notice, that I intend to apply to the Judge in respect thereof, pursuant to the Statute in that behalf.

Dated the day of 18

JAMES SMITH,
Residence—Township of *Beby*.

Lists of Complaints mentioned in the above Notice of Complaint.

LIST NO. 1. (*shewing voters wrongfully omitted from the Voters' List.*)

NAMES OF PERSONS.	GROUNDS ON WHICH THEY ARE ENTITLED TO BE ON THE VOTERS' LIST.
James Tupper.....	Tenant to John Fraser, of N. ½ lot 1, 2nd Con.
Simon Beauclerk...	Owner in fee of N. W. ¼ lot 6, in 8th Con.
Angus Blain	Assessed too low—property worth $

LIST NO. 2 (*shewing voters wrongly named in Voters' List.*)

NAMES OF PERSONS.	POLLING SUB-DIVISION.	PART OF LIST.	THE ERRORS IN STATEMENT UPON VOTERS' LIST.
Joshua Townsend	2	1	Should be *Joseph* Townsend.
John McBean......	4	1	Should be John McBean the *younger*.
S. Connell..	3	2	Should be *Simon* O'Connell.
			&c., &c.

LIST NO. 3. (*shewing persons wrongfully inserted in Voters' List.*)

NAMES OF PERSONS.	POLLING SUB-DIVISION.	PART OF LIST.	STATEMENT WHY WRONGFULLY INSERTED IN VOTERS' LIST.
Peter White.......	4	1	Died before final revision of roll.
John May..	3	2	Tenancy expired—left the country.
David Walters	2	2	Assessed too high—property worth under $
			&c., &c.

LIST No. 4. (*shewing voters whose property is erroneously described in Voters' List, &c.*)

NAMES OF PERSONS.	POLLING SUB-DIVISION.	PART OF LIST.	ERRORS IN RESPECT TO PROPERTY OR OTHERWISE STATED.
Stephen Washburn.	3	2	Name should be in Subdivision No. 2.
Thomas Gordon.	2	1	Property should be W. ½ lot 7, in Con. 3.
Ronald Blue.	4	2	Should be described as owner, not tenant.

FORM 7.

(*Section 9.*)

CLERK'S REPORT IN CASE OF APPEALS AND COMPLAINTS TO THE JUDGE.

To His Honour the Judge of the County Court of the County of

The Clerk of the Municipality of states and reports that the several persons mentioned in column 1 of the Schedule below, and no others, have each given to him (*or* "left for him at his residence *or* place of abode," *as the fact may be*) written notice complaining of errors or omissions in the Voters' List for the said Municipality for 18 , on the grounds mentioned in column 2 of the said Schedule, and that such notices were received respectively at dates set down in column 3 of the said Schedule.

Dated, &c.

A. B.,
Clerk of the said Municipality.

Schedule.

1. NAME OF COMPLAINANTS.	2. ERRORS OR OMISSIONS COMPLAINED OF.	3. DATE WHEN NOTICE OF COMPLAINT RECEIVED BY CLERK.

FORM 8.

(*Section 9.*)

JUDGE'S ORDER APPOINTING COURT FOR HEARING COMPLAINTS AND APPEALS.

To , Clerk of the Municipality of the

Upon reading your Report and notification respecting the Voters' List for the said Municipality for 18 , pursuant to the Statute in that behalf, I appoint the of 18 , at the hour of at in the said County, for holding a Court to hear and determine the several complaints of errors and omissions in the said Voters' List, of which due notice has been given.

You are constituted Clerk of the Court.

You will advertise the holding of such Court, and post up in your office or the place in which the Council hold their sittings a list of all complaints of errors and omissions in the said Voters' List; and you will notify all parties concerned according to law.

Let the Assessor for the Municipality attend the sittings of the said Court, and let the original Assessment Roll of the Municipality for 18 , and the minutes of the Court of Revision for the Municipality for 18 , be produced before me or the acting Judge, on the day and at the place above mentioned.

Dated day of 18 .

Judge Co. Court Co. of

FORM 9.

(*Section 9.*)

NOTICE TO BE POSTED BY CLERK IN HIS OFFICE WITH LIST OF COMPLAINTS.

Notice is hereby given, that the Court will be held, pursuant to "*The Voters' Lists Act,*" at , on the day of 18 , at o'clock, for the purpose of hearing all complaints made against the Voters' List for the Municipality of for 18 , particulars of which complaints are shown in the subjoined Schedule.

All persons having business at the Court are hereby required to attend at the said time and place.

Dated, &c.

A. B.,
Clerk of the said Municipality.

Schedule.

NAME OF PARTY COMPLAINING.	NAME OF PERSON IN RESPECT TO WHOM APPEAL WAS MADE.	GROUNDS OF COMPLAINT ALLEGED.

FORM 10.

(*Section 9.*)

CLERK'S ADVERTISEMENT OF COURT IN NEWSPAPER.

Notice is hereby given that a Court will be held, pursuant to "*The Voters' Lists Act,*" by His Honour the Judge of the County Court of the County of , at , on the day of 18 , at o'clock, to hear and determine the several complaints of errors and omissions in the Voters' List of the Municipality of for 18 .

All persons having business at the Court are required to attend at the said time and place.

Dated, &c.

A. B.,
Clerk of the said Municipality.

FORM 11.

(*Section 9.*)

CLERK'S NOTICE TO PARTY COMPLAINING.

The Voters' List Act.

You are hereby notified that, pursuant to the Statute in that behalf, a Court for the Revision of the Voters' List, 18 , for the Municipality of , will be held by the Judge (*or* acting Judge) of the County Court of the County of , at , on the day of , 18 , at o'clock, at which Court all complaints duly lodged of any error or omission in the said List will be heard and determined. A list of said complaints is posted up in and you are hereby required to be and appear at such Court; and take notice, that the Judge may proceed to hear and determine the complaints, whether the parties complaining appear or not.

By order of His Honour the Judge of the County Court of the County of .

Dated day of 18 .

To

A person complaining of error in the said Voters' List. }.

A. B.,
Clerk of the Municipality of , and constituted Clerk of said Court.

FORM 12.

(*Section 9.*)

CLERK'S NOTICE TO PARTY COMPLAINED AGAINST.

"*The Voters' Lists Act.*"

You are hereby notified that, pursuant to the Statute in that behalf, a Court for the Revision of the Voters' List, 18 , for the Municipality of , will be held by the Judge (*or* acting Judge) of the County Court of the County of , at , on the day of , 18 , at o'clock, and you are required to appear at the said Court, for that has complained that your name is wrongly inserted in the said Voters' List ("because," &c., *state matter of complaint concisely*). A list of all complaints lodged is posted up in ; and take notice, that the Judge may proceed to hear and determine the said complaint, whether you appear or not.

By order of His Honour the Judge of the County Court of the County of

To

Entered on the said Voters' List.

A. B.,
Clerk of the said Municipality and constituted Clerk of the said Court.

FORM 13.

(*Section 10.*)

SUBPŒNA.

SEAL.

ONTARIO: County of , To WIT. } VICTORIA, by the Grace of God, of the United Kingdom of Great Britain and Ireland, Queen, Defender of the Faith.

To Greeting:

We command you, that, all excuses being laid aside, you be and appear in your proper person before our Judge of our County Court of the County of , at , on the day of , 18 , at o'clock in the noon, at a Court appointed, and there and then to be held, for hearing complaints of errors in the Voters' Lists for 18 , of the Municipality of the of , in the County of , and for revision of the said Voters' List, , then and there to testify to all and singular those things which you know in a certain matter (*or* matters) of complaint made and now depending before the said Judge, under "*The Voters' Lists Act*," wherein one is complainant, and which complaint is to be tried at the said Court Herein fail not.

Witness, His Honour , Judge of our said Court at the day of , in the year of our Lord one thousand eight hundred and .

A. B.,
Clerk.

FORM 14.

REPORT OF CLERK WHEN APPLYING FOR CERTIFICATE UNDER SECTION 11.

To the Judge of the County Court of the County of

I, , Clerk of the Municipality of , in the said County of , do hereby certify as follows:

That I did, on the day of , 18 , post up, and for a period of thirty days next thereafter keep posted up, in a conspicuous place in my office at , a true and correct printed copy of the Voters' List for the said Municipality of for 18 , made in pursuance of "*The Voters' Lists Act*," with the certificate required by section five of the said Act endorsed thereon.

That I did also duly deliver and transmit by post, by registered letter (*or* "by parcel post registered," *or*, "by book post"), the required number of similar printed copies of the said Voters' List, with my certificate endorsed, to each and all of the persons entitled to the same under sections three and four of said Act

That I did on the day of , 18 , cause to be inserted in the newspaper called the " ," published in , the notice required by section seven of the said Act.

That no person gave me nor did I receive any written notice of complaint and intention to apply to the Judge or Junior or acting Judge of the County Court of said County of in respect to the said Voters' List within thirty days after I, the said Clerk, had posted up the said List in my office, as directed by the provisions of the said Act.

And that to the best of my knowledge and belief, I have complied with the several requirements of the said Act, so as to entitle me to apply for certified copies under the eleventh section of the said Act; and I do hereby, in pursuance thereof, now apply to you the said Judge to certify three of the copies of the said List received by you as being the Revised List of Voters for the Municipality of the said of for the year of our Lord 18 .

Witness my hand this day of 18 .

————,
Clerk of the Municipality of
———— P. O.

39 V. c. 11, *Sched.*; 40 V. c. 10, s. 1.

FORM 15.

(*Section 11.*)

CERTIFICATE OF NO COMPLAINTS.

County of ——

A. B., Clerk of the Municipality of the of , having certified under his hand that no complaint respecting the List of Voters for said Municipality for the year 18 , had been received by him within thirty days after the first posting up of the same: and on application of the Clerk,

I, , Judge of the County Court of the County of in pursuance of the provisions of "*The Voters' Lists Act,*" certify that the annexed printed List of Voters, being one of the copies received by me from the said Clerk, under section three of the said Act, is the Revised List of Voters for the said Municipality for the year 18 .

Given under my hand and seal, at , this day of , 18 .

————
Judge.

FORM 16.

(*Section 12.*)

STATEMENT OF ALTERATIONS BY JUDGE.

Be it remembered, that upon a final revision and correction of the List of Voters of the Municipality of the of for the year 18 , pursuant to the provisions of "*The Voters' Lists Act,*" the following changes were duly made by me in the copies of the said list received by me from the Clerk of the said Municipality, viz.:

1. The following persons are added to the said List:

NAME.	POLLING SUBDIVISION.	PART OF LIST.	PROPERTY.

2. The following persons are struck off the said List:

NAME.	POLLING SUBDIVISION.	PART OF LIST.	PROPERTY.

3. The following changes are made in the property described opposite to the names of voters otherwise correctly inserted:

NAME.	POLLING SUBDIVISION.	PART OF LIST.	PROPERTY AS ORIGINALLY DESCRIBED ON LIST.	PROPERTY AS ALTERED.

4. The following changes are made in the names of voters incorrectly named:

NAME ORIGINALLY ON LIST.	POLLING SUBDIVISION.	PART OF LIST.	NAME AS ALTERED.	PROPERTY.

Witness my hand this day of A.D., 18 .

County Judge, County of

FORM 17.

(*Section 12.*)

CERTIFICATE OF JUDGE.

I, , Judge of the County Court of the County of , pursuant to the twelfth section of "*The Voters' Lists Act*," do hereby certify that the above (*as the case may be*) is a corrected copy of the List of Voters, for the year 18 , received by me from the Clerk of the Municipality of the of , according to my revision and correction thereof, pursuant to the provisions of the said Act.

Dated at , this day of , 18 .

Judge.

Form 18.

(*Section 20.*)

ORDER FOR PAYMENT OF COSTS.

"*The Voters' Lists Act.*"

In the matter of the Voters' List for the Municipality of , 18 , and of the complaint and appeal to the Judge of the County Court of the County of , by A. B., complaining of the name of C. D. being wrongly inserted in the said List (*or, as the case may be, stating in brief the nature of the complaint.*)

On proceedings taken before me, pursuant to the said Act, I find and adjudge that the name of the said C. D. was rightly inserted in the said List (*or*, "was wrongly inserted in the said List"), and order that the said A. B. do pay the said C. D. his costs occasioned by the said complaint (*or*, "and order that the said C. D. shall pay the said A. B. his costs incident to the said complaint,"—*or*, "and order that E. F., the Assessor of the said Municipality, being blameable for such wrong insertion, do pay the said A. B., his costs incident to the said complaint,"—*or, as the order may be, stating it in brief*), said costs to be taxed pursuant to the said Act.

Dated at , this day of 18 .

Judge.

Form 19.

(*Section 21.*)

WRIT OF EXECUTION.

VICTORIA, by the Grace of God of the United Kingdom of Great Britain and Ireland, Queen, Defender of the Faith.

To the Sheriff of the Greeting:

We command you that of the goods and chattels in your bailiwick of C. D., you cause to be made dollars, for certain costs which lately, by an order of His Honour , Judge of the County Court of , dated the day of , 18 , were ordered to be paid by the said C. D. to A. B., as and for his costs sustained by him on the trial of a complaint against the Voters' List for the Municipality of , in the said County, for 18 , made and prosecuted under the provisions of "*The Voters' Lists Act*," which said costs have been taxed and allowed at the said sum, as appears of record; and have that money before our Judge of our said Court at immediately after the execution hereof; and in what manner you shall have executed this our writ, make appear to our Judge aforesaid at immediately after the execution thereof, and have you there then this writ.

Witness, His Honour , Judge of our said Court, at , the day of , in the year of our Lord 18 .

A. B.,
Clerk.

Form 20.

(*Section 22.*)

ORDER FOR ASSESSMENT OF PERSONS OMITTED FROM ROLL, ETC.

In the matter of Assessment for the year 18 , in the Municipality of

The persons mentioned in the first column of the Schedules following not being assessed, or not being sufficiently assessed, on the Assessment Roll of the Municipality of , for the year 18 , and having been found entitled to vote, on proceedings taken before me, Judge of the County of , under "*The Voters' Lists Act*"—In pursuance of the twenty-second section of the said Act, it is adjudged that the said parties mentioned in the first column of the following Schedules respectively should have been assessed for the sums mentioned in the second columns respectively opposite their respective names, in respect to the land or other property or qualification mentioned in the third columns of the said Schedules respectively opposite the respective names of said parties, and it is ordered that the said parties should be assessed accordingly.

Dated the day of A.D., 18

———

Judge.

Schedule 1.

Column 1.	Column 2.	Column 3.
Names of persons liable to have been assessed on the Assessment Roll for the Municipality of for the year 18 , but not assessed.	Amount for which the parties should have been assessed.	Property in respect to which the liability to assessment exists.

Schedule 2.

Column 1.	Column 2.	Column 3.
Names of persons not sufficiently assessed on the Assessment Roll for the Municipality of , for the year 18 .	Amount for which the parties should be assessed in addition to the amount already on the Assessment Roll.	Property in respect to which the liability to assessment exists.

FORM 21.

(*Section 24.*)

APPLICATION TO JUDGE AGAINST DELINQUENT CLERK.

Pursuant to the twenty-fourth section of "*The Voters' Lists Act*," I, A. B., Clerk of the Peace for the County of , (*or*, "a person entitled to be named as an elector on the Voters' List for the Municipality of , for 18 ,") hereby inform His Honour the Judge of the County Court of the said County, that C. D., Clerk of the Municipality of , in the said County, has failed to perform the duties required of him as such Cleek by the said Act, in this, that he the said C. D. has not made out the Alphabetical List of Voters for 18 , for the said Municipality, within thirty days after the final revision and correction of the Assessment Roll thereof (*or*. "has not delivered or transmitted printed copies of the Voters' List for the said Municipality, for 18 , to and and or to any of them" *or, as the case may be, stating in brief the duty not performed*), according to the requirements of the said Act; and I apply to you the said Judge to enforce the performance of the duties aforesaid, and to take such other proceedings as may be necessary.

Dated at , this day of 18 .

A. B.,
Clerk of the Peace.

FORM 22.

(*Section 24, Sub-sec. 3.*)

SUMMONS.

"*The Voters' Lists Act.*"

In the matter of Voters' List for the Municipality of , in the County of , for 18 .

Whereas it appears by the application of A. B., the Clerk of the Peace for the said County (*or*, "a person entitled to be named as an elector on the said List"), made to me, in pursuance of the said Act, that you, C. D., the Clerk of the said Municipality, have failed to perform certain duties required of you by the said Act, in this that you have not made out the Alphabetical List of Voters for 18 , for the said Municipality, within thirty days after the final revision and correction of the Assessment Roll thereof (*or, as the case may be, following the application*); and whereas the said A. B. has applied to me to enforce the performance of the duties aforesaid;

You, the said C. D., are therefore hereby required to be and appear before me at my Chambers, in , on the day of , 18 , at the hour of , and then and there have with you and produce before me the Assessment Roll for 18 , for the said Municipality, and any documents in your custody, power or control, relating to the Assessment Roll, or to the Voters' List aforesaid; and then and there submit yourself for the examination on oath as may be required of you. Herein fail not at your peril.

Dated this day of

To C. D.,
Clerk of the Municipality of .

Judge.

THE

ONTARIO PROVINCIAL FRANCHISE.

THE LISTS.

AN ACT TO GIVE FINALITY TO VOTERS' LISTS AND FOR OTHER PURPOSES.

[*Assented to 7th March, 1878.*]

HER Majesty, by and with the advice and consent of the Legislative Assembly of the Province of Ontario, enacts as follows :

1. This Act may be cited as "The Voters' Lists Finality Act" (*a*). Short title.

2. In this Act unless there be something in the context repugnant to such a construction :— Interpretation.

(*a*) In 1858 the provisions of 16 Vic., c. 153, the first Canadian Act providing for the registration of voters, were re-enacted and the Assessment Roll made conclusive as to the right to vote. In 1874 the system of revision of the Voters' Lists by the County Judges was adopted in Ontario. The finality provision of the Act of 1858 had however been repealed by 32 Vic. c. 21, but the principle was again adopted in this Act.

See also report of Richards, C. J., in *Stormont case*, (Sept. 1871) recommending finality, 1 H. E. C 42, and 5 Leg. Ass. Journals, 1871-2, p. 6.

"Election"; "To vote"; "Corrupt Practices"; "Farmers' Son." (1.) The word "Election," the words "to vote," the words "Corrupt Practices," and the words "Farmers' Son," shall respectively have the meaning given thereto by section two of "The Election Act of Ontario" (*b*);

"Voter." (2.) The word "voter" shall mean a person entitled to vote, or to be named in the voters' list;

"List"; "Voters' List." (3.) The word "List," and the words "Voters' List," shall respectively mean the alphabetical list referred to in section two of "The Voters' Lists Act," or in section four of the Act passed in the fortieth year of Her Majesty's reign, and chaptered twelve, as the case may be (*c*);

"Scrutiny." (4.) The word "scrutiny" (*cc*) shall mean any scrutiny of the votes polled at an election within the meaning of sections seventy-two and the nine next succeeding sections of "The Controverted Elections Act of Ontario"; and

"Clerk of the Peace"; "County Judge." (5.) The words "Clerk of the Peace," shall mean the Clerk of the Peace for, and the words "County Judge" shall mean the Judge of the County Court for the County or union of Counties within which lies the municipality for or in respect of which the voters' list is made.

Certified voters' list conclusive **3.** Every voters' list which under this Act, or under sections eleven and twelve of "The Voters' Lists Act," or

(*b*) The first three expressions will be found in section 2 of the Election Act, as amended by the Franchise and Representation Act, 1885, s. 2, *ante*, but the expression "Farmers' Son," has disappeared from that section, the farmers' sons franchise having become merged in that of the "landholder's sons" class. As to what are "Corrupt Practices," see chapter thereon, *post*.

(*c*) These Acts are both merged in Rev. Stats., c. 9, *ante*.

(*cc*) Where by an election petition, the seat is claimed for the unsuccessful candidate, alleging that he had a majority of the legal votes polled, a scrutiny of the votes is entered upon. The enquiry into each vote is a separate case. The trouble and expense entailed by this system no doubt largely influenced the Legislature in passing this Act and thereby greatly narrowing the scope of the scrutiny.

under sections six or eight of "The Voters' Lists Act of 1876," was during the twelve months next prior to the passing hereof, or is hereafter certified by the County Judge, shall, upon any scrutiny, be final and conclusive evidence of the right of all persons named therein to vote at any election at which such list was or could have been legally used (*d*); except—

(1.) Persons guilty of corrupt practices (*e*) at or in re- Exceptions.

(*d*) The last named Act is consolidated in the Voters' Lists Act, Rev. Stats. cap. 9, ss. 11 and 12.

By Sec. 7 of the English Ballot Act, 1872, "at any election for a county or borough, a person shall not be entitled to vote unless his name is on the register of voters for the time being in force for such county or borough, and every person whose name is on such register shall be entitled to demand and receive a ballot paper, and to vote: Provided that nothing in this section shall entitle any person to vote who is prohibited from voting by any statute, or by the common law of Parliament, or relieve such person from any penalties to which he may be liable for voting." This section must be read with s. 79 of the Registration Act, 1843, which provides that "the register of voters shall be deemed and taken to be conclusive evidence that the persons therein named continue to have the qualifications which are annexed to their names respectively in the register in force in such election." It has been held under these sections that the register is conclusive, not only at the election, but on the election Judge at the trial of an election petition; see *Stowe* v. *Joliffe*, L. R. 9, C. P. 734; 43 L. J. Rep. C. P. 265; *Hayward* v. *Scott*, 5 C. P. D. 231. See also *Ryder* v. *Hamilton*, L. R. 4, C. P. 559; 38 L. J. C. P. 260. There is an appeal in certain cases from the revising barrister in England, as also from the revising officer when not a Judge under the Dominion Franchise Act, but there is no appeal from the County Judge under this Act; though he is subject to a mandamus to compel him to exercise his jurisdiction, and hear a case when proper notice of complaint has been given (even though he may have decided such a notice was insufficient), *McCullough and the Judge of Leeds and Grenville*, 35 U. C. Q. B. 449, and his proceedings are subject to be reviewed by the Superior Court on a *certiorari*, where he exceeds that jurisdiction *Regina* v. *Glamorganshire*, 12 Mod. 403, s. c. 1 Ld. Ray. 580; *Grenville* v. *College of Physicians*, 12 Mod 386; *Groenvelt* v. *Burwell*, 1 Ld. Ray. 213. The Judge may state a case for decision by the Court of Appeal under sec. 11, *post*; see also notes to secs. 11 and 31 of Dom. Fran. Act, *ante*.

(*e*) "*Corrupt practices.*"—Bribery, treating, undue influence, furnishing entertainment to meetings of electors, personation and subornation thereof, selling or giving liquors on polling day at taverns, etc., by tavern-keepers, betting, or providing money to bet, voting by prohibited persons, or procuring same to vote, paying for conveyance of voters to the polls, etc., as defined by the Elections and Controverted Elections Acts, and by the Common Law of Parliament. See further as to, chapters on Corrupt Practices and Penalties, *post*.

spect of the election in question on such scrutiny, or since said list was certified (*f*) by the County Judge as aforesaid.

(2.) Persons who, at any time subsequently to said list being certified by the County Judge as aforesaid, are or have been non-resident either within the municipality to which said list relates, or within the electoral district, for which the election is being held, and who by reason thereof are, under the provisions of "The Election Act of Ontario," incompetent and disentitled to vote (*g*).

(3.) [This sub-section is repealed by sec. 5 of the Voters' Lists Amendment Act, 1885].

(4.) Persons who, under sections four, five and six (*h*) of "The Election Act of Ontario" are disqualified and incompetent to vote.

[**4**, **5**, **6**, and **7**, refer only to lists based upon the Rolls of the year 1877, and are now of no importance].

8. It shall hereafter be the duty of the County Judge (*i*) so to arrange and proceed and so to fix the sittings of Judge to revise and certify within two

(*f*) "*Since said list was certified.*"—If the offence were committed before the list is certified, it could be inquired into and disposed of, on notice in the ordinary way, before the County Judge.

See notes to secs. 11 and 31 of Dom. Fran. Act, *ante*.

(*g*) Under sec. 7 of the Election Act, as amended by sec. 3 of the Franchise and Representation Act, 1885, (see *ante*) residents of the Electoral District are alone entitled to vote. Those qualifying in respect of real property as owners, tenants or occupants must be residents of the electoral district at the time of the final revision and correction of the assessment roll (subs. *Firstly*); those in respect of income or wages, or as householders must have resided continuously since the completion of the last revised assessment roll in the *municipality* (subs. *Secondly*, *Thirdly* and *Fourthly*); those as landholder's sons must have resided with their parents in the *municipality* for twelve months next prior to the return by the assessors of the assessment roll (subs. *Fifthly*)—and all must be so resident at the time of the election also.

(*h*) These sections are given with the Fran. and Rep. Act 1885, *ante*.

(*i*) "*The duty of the County Judge.*"—The section is directory and not imperative. It shall be the duty of the Judge to have the lists completed within the two months of the last day for complaints, but if he do not do so, the lists when completed will

the Court for the hearing of complaints against or in respect of any Voters' List, that such complaints shall be heard and determined, and said list finally revised, corrected and certified under "The Voters' Lists Act," within two months of the last day for making such complaints: Provided always, that nothing in this section contained, shall apply to any Voters' List specially provided for by the provisions of sections four, five and six of this Act.

months of last day for complaint.

9. To remove doubts it is hereby declared that any Farmer's Son entitled as such to be assessed or to have his name so entered in the Assessment Roll of any municipality, shall be so assessed and shall have his name so entered without any request in that behalf, unless he informs or notifies the assessor to the contrary; and any person entitled to be entered in such Assessment Roll or in the Voters' List based thereon, or to vote or to be a voter in the electoral district in which said municipality is situate, shall, in order to have the name of such Farmer's Son entered and inserted in such Assessment Roll, or List of Voters, as the case may be, have for all purposes the same right to apply, complain or appeal to any Court or to any Judge in that behalf, as such Farmer's Son would or can have personally, unless it is made to appear to the Court or Judge that such Farmer's Son actually dissents therefrom; and the Act passed in the fortieth year of the reign of Her Majesty, chaptered nine, and intituled "An Act to give the right of voting

Assessment and entry on roll of Farmer's Son.

be no less valid by reason of the delay. "There are abundant authorities to show, without the aid of this declaration that the naming of a time for the performance of a duty by a public officer within a certain time is to be considered as directory only to the officer, and not as a limitation of his authority," per Burton, J. A., in *Re Lincoln Election*, 2 Ont. A. R. 351; see *Rex* v. *Loxdale*, 1 Burr. 445; *Rex* v. *Sparrow*, 2 Strange 1,123; *Rex* v. *Inhabitants of Rufford*, 1 Strange 512; *Rex* v. *Justices of Leicester*, 7 B. & C. 6, s. c. D. & Ry. 772; *Pearce* v. *Morrice*, 2 A. & E. 96.

to Farmers' Sons in certain cases," shall be read and construed as if this section had been included therein at the time of the passing thereof (*j*).

Inspection and copies of documents.

10. Any voter, and any person entitled to be a voter; and any agent of such voter or person, shall have liberty at all reasonable times and under reasonable restrictions, to inspect and take copies of or extracts from assessment rolls, notices, complaints, applications and other papers and proceedings necessary or of use for the carrying out of the provisions of "The Assessment Act," "The Voters' List Act," and this Act; and the Clerk of the Municipality is to afford for the said purposes all reasonable facilities which may be consistent with the safety of the said documents, and the equal rights and interests of all persons concerned, and shall in regard to the matters aforesaid be subject to the directions and summary jurisdiction of the County Judge (*jj*).

Duty of Clerk.

11. In order to facilitate uniformity of decision without the delay or expense of appeals:

County Judge may obtain opinion from Court of Appeal or Judge thereof

(1.) Any County Judge may state a case on any general question arising or likely to arise, or expected to arise under "The Voters' List Act," or this Act, and may transmit the same to the Lieutenant-Governor in Council, who thereupon shall immediately refer the said case to the Court of Appeal or a Judge thereof for the opinion of such Court or Judge thereupon; or

Lieut.-Governor may obtain opinion.

(2.) The Lieutenant-Governor in Council may refer a case on any such general question to said Court of Appeal or a Judge thereof, for a like opinion.

(*j*) See sec. 6 of the Voters' Lists Am. Act 1885, which will be found in note to subs. 5 of s. 8 of the Voters' Lists Act, *ante*.

(*jj*) For fees payable for copies of list supplied by Clerk, see sec. 31 of the Voters' Lists Act, *ante*.

(3.) Immediately upon the receipt of such case it shall be the duty of such Court or Judge to appoint a time and place for hearing arguments (if any be offered) upon the points and matter involved in such case, of which time and place written notice shall be given by the Clerk of said Court, posting up a copy of such notice in the office of each one of the Superior Courts at Osgoode Hall in Toronto, at least ten clear days before the time appointed as aforesaid. Duty of Court or Judge.

(4.) At the time and placed fixed therefor as aforesaid, such Court or Judge shall hear argument upon the case by such and so many of the Counsel present (if any) as such Court or Judge may deem reasonable, and shall therepon consider the said case and certify to the Lieutenant-Governor in Council the opinion of the Court or Judge thereon; and such opinion shall thereupon be forthwith published in the *Ontario Gazette*, and a copy thereof sent to the Judge of each County Court. Argument. Opinion, publishing same.

(5.) The said Court of Appeal or a Judge thereof, may also give an opinion on any such question at the instance of any voter or voters, or person or persons entitled to to be voters, if said Court or Judge sees fit; and the proceedings with respect thereto shall be, as nearly as may be, the same as upon a case referred as aforesaid, but, in addition, such Court or Judge may require a deposit of money to cover the costs of hearing the question argued by Counsel, and may require such notice of the proceedings or any of them to be given to such person or persons as the Court or Judge may direct (*k*). Discretionary opinion by Court or Judge to voter. Proceedings.

(*k*) As the above section does not confer the necessary authority to render the decisions thereunder binding upon anybody, the provisions of the subsections have been of little or no practical utility. *Opinions*, not *judgments*, are, it will be observed, to be given in every case.

Clerk to give copies of list to Returning Officer.

12. The Clerk of the Peace or the Clerk of the Municipality who has the custody of a Voters' List, shall furnish copies thereof to the Returning Officer in four days after a written application thereof has been delivered to him personally or left for him at his proper office (*l*).

Production and custody of ballot papers on a recount.

13. In case of a recount of votes or ballot papers under section one hundred and seventeen and the five next succeeding sections of "The Election Act of Ontario," the Returning Officer shall, on a written notice from the Judge, produce the ballot papers at the time and place appointed for the recount, and the same shall continue in the custody of the Returning Officer; and he shall continue to be responsible therefor, subject to any directions which the Judge may give in respect of the said ballot papers (*m*).

Fraudulent insertion or omission, etc., on, or dealing with the roll.

14. Any person who wilfully or improperly inserts or procures or causes the insertion of any name in the assessment roll, or assesses or procures or causes the assessment of any person at too high an amount, with intent in either or any such case to give to any person not entitled thereto, an apparent right to vote at any election; or who wilfully inserts or procures or causes the insertion of any fictitious name in the roll, or who wilfully and improperly omits, or procures or causes the omission of any name from the assessment roll, or assesses or procures or causes the assessment of any person at too low an amount, with intent in either case to deprive any person of his right to vote, shall, upon conviction thereof before a Court of competent jurisdiction, be liable to a fine not exceeding two hundred dollars, and to imprison-

Penalty.

(*l*) For fees payable to the Clerk of the Peace for such copies, see sec. 31, subs. 2 of the Voters' Lists Act, *ante*.

(*m*) This section is supplementary to the provisions of the Election Act referred to.

ment until the fine is paid, or to imprisonment in the common gaol of the county or city for a period not exceeding six months, or to both fine or imprisonment, in the discretion of the Court (*n*).

15. Where it is provided by any by-law or contract under which the Clerk of any Municipality is appointed or employed, that the sum to be paid him by way of salary as such Clerk is intended expressly or impliedly to include payment for all duties which, as such clerk and under "The Voters' Lists Act" are to be performed by him, either in the preparation, publication and distribution of the list of voters under said Act, or before, upon or after the lodging with him of any complaint or appeal under said Act, or for any other act or work of whatsoever nature or kind required by the said Act to be done by him; then such clerk shall not, in respect of such duties or work, be entitled to or be allowed by the County Judge, nor shall there be taxed to him, any fee, payment, cost or charge whatsoever; but when it is not intended by such by-law or contract to provide for the performance of such above-mentioned duties, and work, then such clerk shall be entitled in respect thereof to the following but to no other fee or compensation, that is to say: Clerk's remuneration.

(1.) Two cents for the name of each person entered in the list of complaints and in respect to whom appeal was made.

(2.) Two cents for each such name entered in any necessary copy of said list of complaints.

(3.) Eight cents for each necessary notice to any party complaining or complained against.

(*n*) See also sec. 30 of The Voters' Lists Act, *ante*. As to form of action or proceeding to recover, the penalties prescribed, and the disposition thereof when recovered, see Interpretation Act, Rev. Stats. cap. 1, sec. 8, subs. 29.

(4.) Three dollars for each day's attendance on the sittings of the Court for the revision of the Voters' List.

(5.) And to the actual and reasonable disbursements (if any) necessarily incurred by him in serving the notices of complaint or appeal, when served by himself (*o*).

Constable's fees

16. The person acting as constable at the sittings of the Court for the revision of any Voters' Lists, shall as such constable be entitled to the following, but no other fees or compensation; that is to say:

(1.) The sum of one dollar and fifty cents for each day's attendance as such constable;

(2.) For the service of any process or notice including the service, the receipt and the return thereof, and all other services connected therewith when allowed by the Judge, a sum not exceeding ten cents per mile, one way for each mile actually and necessarily travelled to effect such service.

By whom and on what the Clerk and Constable shall be paid.

17. The compensation fixed by the two preceding sections shall be paid to the said clerk and constable respectively by the municipality, the list for which is the subject of investigation; and the amount of such compensation as certified by the Judge shall be so paid by the Treasurer of the said Municipality upon the production and deposit with him of the Judge's certificate.

(*o*) This section is given as amended by "The Voters' Lists Amendment Act, 1879," s. 6.

THE

QUEBEC PROVINCIAL FRANCHISE.

38 VIC., CAP. VII. (*a*).

[*Assented to 23rd February, 1875.*]

HER Majesty, by and with the advice and consent of the Legislature of Quebec, enacts as follows:

PRELIMINARY.

1. This Act shall be known and may be referred to and cited as: "The Quebec Election Act." Title.

It shall apply to every election of a member of the legislative assembly, whether the same be held at the time of a general election or to fill a vacancy. Application.

2. In interpreting this Act, unless it be otherwise provided, or unless there be in the context of its provisions something which indicates a different sense or requires another interpretation: Interpretation.

1. The word: "municipality" means every municipality of a parish or part of a parish, of a township or part of a township, of united townships, of a village, of a town, existing under the operation of the municipal code, and every town or city municipality, incorporated by charter or special Act; Municipality.

2. The word: "secretary-treasurer" includes the clerk of every town or city municipality; Secretary-treasurer.

(*a*) Only those portions of the Act which relate to the Franchise, are here given.

Owner.

3. The word: "owner" signifies any one who possesses real estate or whose wife possesses real estate whether as owner or usufructuary. Whenever one person has the mere ownership of real estate, and another has the enjoyment and usufruct thereof to his own use and benefit, the person who has the mere ownership of such real estate shall not be entitled to vote as owner thereof, and the usufructuary shall in such case alone have the right to vote, by reason of such real estate;

Occupant.

4. (*As amended by 39 Vict., cap. 13, s. 1*). The word: "occupant," signifies the person who occupies immovable property, otherwise than as owner, tenant or usufructuary, either in his own right or in the right of his wife, and who derives the revenue therefrom.

Tenant.

5. The word: "tenant" means as well the person who pays rent in money, as the person who is obliged to give to the owner a certain part of the revenues and profits of the real estate which he occupies; and such tenant must be *tenant feu et lieu*, save in case of the lessee of a shop, workshop or office;

Registrar.

6. The word: "registrar" means the registrar of the registration division, which comprises within its limits the electoral district in which the election is held. It also means the registrar of the registration division, comprised within the limits of such electoral district, or the limits whereof are the same as those of the electoral district;

Voting subdivision.

7. The term: "voting subdivision" means, for voting purposes, every municipality whereof the number of parliamentary electors entered on the list in force does not exceed three hundred: (1)

---

(1) See, nevertheless, sections 59 and 60 of the present law as amended by 39 V., c. 13, s. 8, which fix the number of two hundred electors to form a voting subdivision.

8. The words: "to vote" mean to vote at the election of a member of the legislative assembly of this province; To vote.

9. The expression: "electoral district" means any county or other place or portion of this province, entitled to return a member of the legislative assembly; Electoral district.

10. The term: "election officer" means the returning officer, the election clerk, and all deputy returning officers and poll-clerks, appointed for an election; Election Officer.

11. The term: "personal expenses" employed in relation to the expenditure of a candidate, respecting any election in which he is candidate, means all the reasonable travelling expenses of such candidate, and his reasonable expenses at hotels and other places to which he may repair, for the purposes of and in regard of such election. Personal Expenses.

3. Any form indicated by a capital letter in the various provisions of this Act, refers to the corresponding form contained in the schedule annexed to this Act. Forms.

Any of the forms contained in such schedule is sufficient in the case for which it is intended. Any other form having the same meaning, may be employed with equal effect.

4. Any reference to one or more sections indicated in the provisions of this Act, without mention of the Act or statute of which such sections form part, is a reference to the sections of this Act. Reference.

5. If the time fixed by this Act for the accomplishment of any proceeding or formality, prescribed by the provisions thereof, expires or falls upon a Sunday or legal holiday, the time so fixed shall be continued to the first day following, not a Sunday or holiday. Delay.

6. Every person before whom any oath must be taken or affirmation made, under the terms of this Act, is empowered, and shall be bound whenever the same is required of him, to administer such oath or affirmation, and to give a certificate thereof, without fee or reward. Oath.

FIRST PART.

PARLIAMENTARY (b) ELECTORS.

I.—CONDITIONS REQUISITE TO BE AN ELECTOR.

Entry on the list.

7. No person shall be entitled to vote at the election of a member of the legislative assembly of this province, unless, at the time of voting, he be an elector entered as owner, tenant or occupant, upon the list of electors in force.

Qualification of electors.

8. No person shall be entered upon the list of electors unless he fulfils the following conditions:

1. He must be of the male sex, of full age, and a subject of Her Majesty by birth or naturalization;

2. He must not be otherwise legally incapacitated;

3. He must be actually and in good faith owner or occupant of real estate, estimated according to the valuation roll in force, as revised, if it has been revised, even for local purposes only, at a sum of at least three hundred dollars in real value, in any city municipality entitled to return one or more members of the legislative assembly, and two hundred dollars in real value, or twenty dollars in annual value, in any other municipality, or

Be a tenant in good faith, paying an annual rent for real estate, of at least thirty dollars in any city municipality entitled to return one or more members of the legislative assembly, and of at least twenty dollars in any other municipality; provided that such real estate

(b) The word, "parliamentary," wherever used in the Act 38 Victoria, chapter seven, intituled: "An Act respecting the election of members of the Legislative Assembly of the Province of Quebec," shall be held and construed to mean and apply to the election of members of the Legislative Assembly of Quebec only.—*40 Victoria, cap. 27, sec. 1.*

be estimated according to such valuation roll, in real value at, at least three hundred dollars in any municipality entitled to return one or more members of the legislative assembly, and two hundred dollars in any other municipality.

9. Whenever two or more persons are co-owners, co-partners in the property or possession, co-tenants or co-occupants of any real estate valued at an amount sufficient for the share of each to confer upon him the electoral suffrage, each of such persons shall be deemed to be an elector in conformity with this Act, and entered upon the list of electors. He whose share does not amount to the value required for the electoral suffrage shall not be so entered nor be an elector.

Co-owners; co partners; co-tenants, and co-occupants.

The same rule applies to co-tenants, respecting the amount of rent which they pay.

10. Nevertheless, if the real estate is owned or occupied by a corporation, no one of the members of the corporation shall be an elector nor entered upon the list of electors, by reason of such real estate.

Corporation.

II. PERSONS WHO CAN NEITHER BE ELECTORS NOR VOTERS.

11. The following persons can, in no case, be electors, or vote:

Persons disqualified to vote.

1. The judges of the court of Queen's Bench and of the superior court, the judge of the vice-admiralty court, the judges of the sessions, district magistrates, recorders;

2. Officers of the customs, clerk of the Crown, clerks of the peace, registrars, sheriffs, deputy-sheriffs, deputy-clerks of the crown and the officers and men of the provincial or municipal police force;

3. Agents for the sale of crown lands, post-masters in cities and towns, and all officers employed in the collection of any duties payable to Her Majesty, in the nature

of duties of excise, including collectors as well of federal as of local revenue.

If any of the persons set forth in this section, vote save in the case of section 205 (*c*) he shall incur a penalty of not more than five hundred nor less than one hundred dollars, or imprisonment not exceeding twelve months in default of payment, and his vote shall be null and of no effect.

III. LIST OF PARLIAMENTARY ELECTORS.

1. *Preparation of the List.*

Time and mode.

12. The secretary-treasurer of each municipality shall, between the first and fifteenth days of the month of March in each year, make in duplicate a list, in alphabetical order, of all persons who, according to the valuation roll then in force in the municipality for local purposes, and as revised, if it has been revised even for local purposes, appear to be electors by reason of the real estate possessed or occupied by them, within the municipality (*d*).

Distinction to be made.

13. The secretary-treasurer, in drawing up the list of electors, shall distinguish the persons who appear to be qualified as owners, from those who appear to be qualified as tenants or occupants, and shall specify the real estate through which such persons are electors.

Omissions.

14. (*As amended by 39 Vict., cap. 13, sec. 2.*) The secretary-treasurer shall omit from the list of electors, every person who, under sections 11, 267 and 270 or any other legal provision whatsoever, is not then entitled to vote (*e*).

(*c*) Sec. 205 provides for a casting vote by the Returning Officer.

(*d*) Amended as to Gaspé and Bonaventure.

(*e*) S. 257 provides for disqualification of candidate for seven years, where corrupt practices committed by or with his actual knowledge and consent. S. 270 disqualifies for seven years any other person found guilty of a corrupt practice.

15. If any municipality is situated partly in one electoral district and partly in another, the secretary-treasurer shall prepare in the same manner, for each of such electoral districts, an alphabetical list of the persons who are electors therein. Case of two lists.

16. If the municipality is divided into voting subdivisions under sections 59, 60 or 61, the secretary-treasurer shall divide the list into as many parts as there are voting subdivisions in the municipality. Division of the list.

Each such part, the title whereof shall be the name, number or description of the voting subdivision to which it relates, shall only contain the alphabetical list of the electors of such voting subdivision.

17. If a person is an elector, in one and the same municipality from more than one parcel of real estate, or from more than one title, his name shall nevertheless be entered but once on the list of electors of the municipality. Name of electors only entered.

If the list is drawn up by subdivisions and one person is an elector in more than one subdivision, his name shall be inserted in one subdivision only; and if such person is an elector in the subdivision of his domicile, his name shall be entered on the list for such subdivision.

18. In the case of section 17, if a person is an elector in more than one electoral district, his name shall be entered in the list of each electoral district, in which he is an elector, according to the rules laid down in the preceding section. Case of a person being elector in several electoral districts.

19. The secretary-treasurer shall certify the correctness of the list of electors by him made, by the following oath, taken before a justice of the peace: Attestation.

"I (*name of the secretary-treasurer*) swear that, to the best of my knowledge and belief, the foregoing list of electors is correct, and that nothing has been inserted Oath.

therein or omitted therefrom, unduly or by fraud: So help me God."

Each duplicate list must be attested separately under the foregoing oath.

Deposit of the list.

20. One of the duplicates of the list so attested shall be kept in the office of the secretary-treasurer, at the disposal and for the information of all persons interested.

Notice.

21. The secretary-treasurer, on the day upon which he shall take the oath required by the section before the last, shall give and publish public notice, setting forth that the list of electors has been prepared according to law, and that a duplicate thereof has been lodged in his office, at the disposal and for the information of all persons interested.

Such notice shall be given and published in the same manner as notices for municipal purposes in the municipality in which the list has been prepared.

Form.

22. The list of electors may be drawn up in accordance with form A.

Clerk *ad hoc*.

23. If the secretary-treasurer has not made the alphabetical list of electors, or has not given and published the notice required by section 21, in the first fifteen days of the month of March, then the judge of the superior court for the district, or in the event of the absence of the district judge, or of his inability to act, the district magistrate, on summary petition from the mayor, the registrar or other person entitled to be entered as an elector in the municipality, shall appoint a clerk *ad hoc* to prepare the alphabetical list of electors.

Responsibility of the secretary treasurer.

24. The secretary-treasurer shall be personally liable for the costs incurred on such petition, and for those incurred in drawing up the list by the clerk *ad hoc*, unless the judge or the district magistrate, for special reasons, deem it advisable to order otherwise, and in such case, the costs shall be left to their discretion.

The secretary-treasurer may however draw up and prepare the list, so long as the clerk *ad hoc* shall not have been appointed.

25. The clerk *ad hoc* shall proceed, within fifteen days after notice of his appointment, to the preparation of the list of electors. He shall, for such purpose, become an officer of the municipal council, and shall have the same powers to exercise, and the same duties to discharge, as the secretary-treasurer of the municipality, and shall do so under the same penalties in the case of default or neglect on his part. Duties of the Clerk ad h

26. (*As replaced by 39 Vict., cap. 13, sec. 3*). The mayor and the officers of the council, in so far as the same are incumbent upon them, shall be bound to deliver to the clerk *ad hoc*, on his demand, the valuation roll which is to avail as the basis of the list of electors under a penalty not exceeding two hundred dollars, or in default of payment, of imprisonment not to exceed six months. Duties of the mayor, &c.

2. *Examination and putting into force of the list.*

27. (*As replaced by 39 Vict., cap. 13, sec. 4*). The list of electors may be examined and corrected by the council of the municipality, in the thirty days next after the publication of the notice given under section 21, upon complaint in writing, to such effect under either of the two sections following and not otherwise. Examination.

28. Any person who deems himself aggrieved either by the insertion in, or omission of his name from the list, may, either by himself or through his agent, file a complaint in writing to such effect, within the fifteen days next after the publication of the notice given under section 21. Complaint in writing.

29. (*As replaced by 39 Vict., cap. 13, sec. 5.*) Any person believing that the name of any person entered on the list, should not have been so entered, owing to his Idem.

not possessing the qualifications required for an elector, or believing that the name of any other person, not entered thereon, should be so entered owing to his possessing the qualifications required, may file a complaint in writing to such effect, within the same delay of fifteen days.

Notice.

30. The Council, before proceeding to any examination or correction of the list of electors, shall cause to be given through the secretary-treasurer, the clerk *ad hoc*, or any other person, public notice of the day and hour at which such examination shall begin.

He shall also, previous to taking into consideration the complaints in writing filed in the office of the council, with respect to the list of electors, cause a special notice to be given to every person, the insertion or omission of whose name upon the list is demanded.

The public notice and every special notice required by this section shall be of five days' duration; and they shall further be given and published or served, in the same manner as notices for municipal purposes in the municipality within which the list has been prepared.

Examination and hearing.

31. The council on proceeding to the examination of the list shall take into consideration all the complaints in writing relating to the said list, and hear all persons interested.

Decision.

32. The council by its decision on each complaint, may confirm or correct each of the duplicates of the list.

Fraudulent title.

33. If, upon proof, the council is of opinion that a property has been leased, assigned or made over under any title whatsoever, with the sole object of giving to a person the right of having his name entered on the list of electors, it shall strike the name of such person from the said list, upon complaint in writing being made to that effect.

Corrections to be authenticated.

34. Every insertion, erasure or correction whatsoever of the list, in virtue of the two preceding sections, shall be authenticated by the initials or *paraphe* of the presiding officer of the council.

35. The list of electors shall come into force at the expiration of the thirty days following the notice given in virtue of section 21, as it then exists, and shall remain in force until the month of March next, and thereafter until a new list is made and put in force under the authority of this act. Duration of the list.

If there is an appeal to a judge of the superior court or to a district magistrate, in districts in which there is no judge of the superior court, touching a portion of the list, such portion of the said list shall remain in force notwithstanding such appeal, until the final decision of the court, before which the said petition in appeal is pending.

36. Every list of electors so put in force shall, during the whole period in which it remains in force, be deemed the only true list of parliamentary electors, within the territorial division to which it relates, even although the valuation roll which has served as the basis of such list be defective or shall have been quashed or set aside; saving nevertheless any correction made under section 44. Value of the list.

37. It shall be the duty of the secretary-treasurer, as soon as the list of electors has come into force, to insert at the end of such list, on the duplicates thereof, the certificate set forth in form B. Certificate of the sec.-treas.

38. One of the duplicates of the list of electors shall be kept in the archives of the municipality, and shall there remain of record. One duplicate remains in the archives, the other is transmitted to the registrar.

The other duplicate shall be transmitted to the registrar of the registration division in which is situated the municipality, within eight days following the day upon which such list shall have come into force, by the secretary-treasurer or by the mayor, under a penalty of two hundred dollars, or of imprisonment of six months in default of payment, against each of them, in case of contravention of this provision.

Nevertheless the transmission of the duplicate of the said list to the registrar after the delay prescribed by this section, or the fact of the same not having been transmitted, shall not have the effect of invalidating such list.

If a copy. **39.** If, in lieu of the duplicate required by the preceding section, a certified copy of the list has been transmitted to the registrar, such copy shall be deemed to be the duplicate required, and shall have the same effect as if the duplicate has itself been transmitted.

Duplicate remains of record. **40.** All duplicates or copies of lists of electors transmitted to the registrar under the two preceding sections, shall be preserved by such officer, and shall remain of record in his office.

The registrar, on receipt of the said duplicates or copies, shall enter upon each the date of the reception thereof.

3. *Appeal to judge of the superior court or district magistrate.*

38 Vic., c. 7, sec. 41, as replaced by 43-44 V., c. 15, s. 1, amended. **41.** *(As replaced by 43-44 Vict., cap. 15, sec. 1, and amended by 46 Vict., cap. 2, sec. 1.)* Any elector of the electoral division may appeal from any decision of the council, confirming, correcting or amending the list, to the judge of the superior court of the district within fifteen days following such decision, by means of a petition in which are briefly set forth the reasons of appeal.

Proceedings suspended until security given. The respondent may, in all such appeals, obtain a suspension of the proceedings until the appellant has given such security as may be considered necessary in the discretion of the court or judge, or deposited in the hands of the clerk of the court, such sum as may be specified by the court or judge for the payment of the costs on such appeal.

42. (*As replaced by 39 Vict., cap. 13, sec. 7.*) If the council has neglected or refused to take into consideration within the time prescribed, a complaint duly filed, any person may appeal to such judge therefrom, in the manner and within the delay prescribed in the preceding section. Idem.

43. A copy of the petition in appeal shall be served upon the secretary-treasurer of the municipality, who shall immediately give special notice thereof to the mayor, and public notice to the parties interested. Service.

44. The judge of the superior court shall have full power and authority to hear and decide such appeal, in a summary manner on any day which he shall fix, and shall proceed without delay, from day to day, in term or in vacation. Power of the court.

Such appeal shall have precedence over other causes.

45. He may also order that further notice be given to any of the parties to the cause, summon before him and question under oath or affirmation any party or witness, and require the production of any document, paper or thing. He shall possess all the powers conferred upon the superior court in relation to matters pending before that court. Idem.

46. No proceedings on such appeal shall be annulled for defect of form. Defect of form.

47. The costs of appeal shall be taxed at the discretion of the judge for or against such of the parties as he shall deem advisable, and shall be recoverable under a writ of execution issued in the usual manner. Costs.

48. The decision of the judge shall be final. Decision.

49. The secretary-treasurer and the registrar shall, each, correct the duplicate of the list of electors in his possession, according to the decision of the court, immediately upon authentic copies thereof being served upon them. Correction.

Districts where there is no resident judge.

50. In any district in which there is no resident judge of the superior court, the appeal specified in sections 41 and 42, may moreover be brought before the district magistrate for such district in the same manner and with the same effect as before the judge of the superior court.

4. *Miscellaneous Provisions.*

Case of alteration.

51. If, at any time it is made to appear to any judge of the superior court, in term or in vacation, that the secretary-treasurer of any municipality, or the registrar of the registration division, have altered or falsified, or have permitted to be altered or falsified the duplicate of the list in their possession, the judge shall require the secretary-treasurer, the registrar and every person having the custody of the valuation roll, which served as the basis of the list, to appear before him and to produce the rolls and lists in their possession.

Power of the judge or magistrate.

52. At the time and place fixed for the appearance of such persons, the judge, after having examined the duplicates of the list produced by the secretary-treasurer and the registrar, together with the valuation roll, shall, with or without further proof, make the alterations or corrections, which he shall deem necessary, to render the duplicate so altered or falsified, accurate and faithful.

Sec.-treas. to deliver copies.

53. It shall be the duty of the secretary-treasurer of every municipality and of the registrar of every registration division having the custody of a list of electors, to deliver certified copies thereof to any person applying therefor, and offering to pay for the cost of any such copy, three cents for every ten electors entered on the list.

Sec.-treas. shall furnish the list *gratis*.

54. The secretary-treasurer of every municipality shall furnish *gratis* on demand, to every deputy returning officer acting within the limits of the municipality, a certified copy of the list of electors to avail at the election, or of that part of such list, which relates to the locality for which he acts as deputy returning officer.

55. The cost of all copies of the list of electors given by the registrar, in consequence of the secretary-treasurer having refused or neglected to furnish the same, under the preceding section, may be recovered from the secretary-treasurer or the corporation whose officer he is, either by the registrar who has given the copies, or by the returning officer or deputy returning officer who shall have procured the same. Recourse in case of refusal. Penalty.

56. *(As replaced by 40 Vict., cap. 27, sec. 1.)* Every secretary-treasurer, who has refused or neglected to make the alphabetical list of electors, as required by this Act, or who having made the list, has wilfully inserted therein or omitted therefrom, any name which should not have been so inserted or omitted, shall incur a penalty not exceeding five hundred dollars, or imprisonment not exceeding twelve months in default of payment. Penalty.

57. *(As replaced by 40 Vict., cap. 27, sec. 1.)* Every person having the custody of elector's lists and whose duty it is to deliver copies thereof, who shall have made any insertion or omission at in the preceding sections in the copies furnished by him, shall incur the penalty prescribed in the preceding section. Idem.

58. Every list of electors made for any municipality, and in force at the time of the coming into force of this Act, shall continue, even although the valuation roll which has served as basis for such list is defective or is quashed or annulled, to avail and to remain in force until it is replaced by a new list of electors made under the authority of this act. Old lists.

IV. DIVISION OF THE MUNICIPALITY INTO VOTING SUB-DIVISIONS.

59. *(As amended by 39 Vict., cap. 13, sec. 8.)* Whenever in any municipality, the number of electors shall ex- Division by the council into voting subdivisions.

ceed two hundred, it shall be the duty of the council of such municipality to divide, by a by-law made in the ordinary way, the municipality into voting subdivisions so that there shall not be more than two hundred electors in each voting subdivision.

The limits of these subdivisions shall be well defined and shall not divide any real estate under which an elector is entitled to vote.

New division. **60.** (*As amended by 39 Vict., cap. 13, sec. 8.*) Whenever any one of such voting subdivisions shall contain more than two hundred electors, it shall be the duty of the council to subdivide by by-law, such voting subdivision, into others not containing more than two hundred electors each.

Idem. **61.** The council may always, and at any time, for the greater convenience of the electors, amend or repeal any by-law made under the two last sections, and may make a new division as provided by section 59.

Appeal. **62.** No by-law made under the three preceding sections shall be appealed from the county council.

Old voting subdivisions. **63.** Every by-law or municipal order dividing a municipality into voting subdivisions or other analogous subdivisions, in force upon the coming into effect of this Act, shall remain in force until the same is replaced or repealed under the authority of this Act.

List of electors, Montreal. **64.** The list of municipal electors of the city of Montreal as annually drawn up, revised and closed, under the authority of the Acts now in force in relation to the same, shall be for all purposes, the list of parliamentary electors, (1)—including therein such persons as shall have been struck from the municipal list for default of payment of municipal taxes within the delay perscribed.

---

(1) That is to say, for the election of members of the Legislative Assembly of the Province of Quebec (as interpreted by 40 Vic., cap. 27, s. 1).

SCHEDULE A.

FORM MENTIONED IN THE 22ND SECTION.

PROVINCE OF QUEBEC,
MUNICIPALITY OF (*the parish of St. James*, in the County of Levis).

LIST OF PARLIAMENTARY ELECTORS.

Surnames.	Names.	Occupations.	Proprietors, tenants, or occupants.	Description of immoveable.
		Voting Sub-Division *number one.*		
Aubin	Jean-Baptiste	Farmer	Proprietor	*Des Pins* concession.
Bédard	Joseph	Merchant	Tenant	Township Ely, 3rd range, No. 19.
Charette	Jacques	Gentleman	Occupant	Côte St. Michel.
		Voting Sub-Division *number two.*		
Araud	Paul	Notary	Proprietor	St.-Amable street, No. 4.
Béland	Jérémie	Advocate	Tenant	St.-Peter street, No. 10.
Carreau, sr	Homère	Shoemaker	Occupant	" " No. 11.
Carreau, jr	Homère	Blacksmith	Proprietor	St.-Paul " No. 5.

Made in duplicate this day of the month of eighteen hundred and

I, P. P., swear that to the best of my knowledge and belief, the foregoing list of electors is correct, and that nothing has been inserted therein or omitted therefrom, unduly or by fraud: So help me God.

Sworn this day of 18 , before the undersigned F. F., Justice of the Peace,

P. P.,
Secretary-Treasurer.

If the Cadastre in the municipality has been completed, the description of the immoveable by the number given in the Cadastral plan and book of reference will be sufficient.

The list of electors shall be made in duplicate, that is to say: the Secretary having correctly prepared and made a clean copy of the list of electors, shall make another exactly similar to the first.

The Secretary-Treasurer shall take two distinct oaths, one oath on one duplicate, and the other oath on the other duplicate. The two oaths shall be taken on the same day.

The Secretary-Treasurer shall, on the same day, give the notice required by section 21 in the manner ordinarily in use for municipal matters, and at the expiration of the 30 days next after such notice, he shall place at the end of the list on each duplicate the certificate given in the following form.

B.

FORM MENTIONED IN SECTION 37.

I, the undersigned, P. P., Secretary-Treasurer, certify, on my oath of office:

1. That I have given the notice required by section 21 of the *Quebec Election Act.*

2. That, from the date of such notice, one of the duplicates of the above list remained in my office at the disposal of all persons interested.

3. That this list has been examined (and corrected, *if it has been corrected*) by the Council of this Municipality, within the thirty days next after the said day (*date of publication of notice required by section 21*) that is to say: at the sittings of the Council held on the (*days when sittings were held*), and that the corrections (*if there were any made*) were initialed by B. B., Mayor (or C. C., Councillor, presiding in the absence of the Mayor, *as the case may be*);

(*Or if the list has not been examined*),

That this list has not been examined by the Council of this Municipality within the thirty days after the said day (*date of publication of the notice required by section 21*);

4. That the above list of electors thus came into force on the day of the month of eighteen hundred and , being the thirtieth day after the (*date of publication of notice required by section 21*).

Made on both duplicates of the list this day of the month of 18 .

P. P.,
Secretary-Treasurer.

THE

NEW BRUNSWICK

PROVINCIAL FRANCHISE.

CON. STATS. OF NEW BRUNSWICK, CAP. 4 (*a*).

1. Every male person of the age of twenty-one years or upwards, being a British subject, not subject to any legal incapacity, who shall have been assessed for the year for which the registry is made up, in respect of real estate to the amount of one hundred dollars, or personal property, or personal and real amounting together to four hundred dollars, or four hundred dollars annual income, shall be qualified to vote for Representatives of the County or City for which he shall be so assessed; if there be no assessment for the Parish in any year, then the possession of the qualification shall of itself be sufficient. **Qualification of electors.**

2. The County Councillors of each Parish, with another person appointed therefor by the County Council, shall be the Revisors for their respective Parishes; provided that where there are three Councillors for a Parish they shall be the Revisors, and where there are more than three Councillors for a Parish the County Council shall select three of such Councillors to be Revisors. **Revisors.**

3. In the Cities of Fredericton and Saint John, or any incorporated Town, being in itself a Parish, any three or more of the Aldermen and Councillors to be appointed in each year by the respective Councils of such Cities or **Revisors in Saint John, Fredricton and incorporated Towns, being Parishes.**

(*a*) Only those portions of the statute which relate to the Franchise are here given.

Towns, shall annually revise the list of electors qualified to vote therein at County elections, in the manner and at the times herein prescribed.

Assessors to furnish Revisors with Assessment List.

4. The Assessors of every Parish shall, on or before the first day of August in each year, deliver to the Revisors a copy of the assessment list for the Parish; or if they have not received any warrant therefor, make out a list of the names of all persons possessed of real or personal estate, or income, in the form following, and deliver it to the Revisors:

	Real Estate in the Parish of Inhabitant.	Personal Estate of Inhabitant.	Real Estate of Non-resident.	Annual Income.
A. B. ..	$100 00	$ 0 00	$ 0 00	$ 0 00
C. D. ..	0 00	400 00	0 00	0 00
E. F. ..	0 00	0 00	100 00	0 00
G. H.	0 00	0 00	0 00	400 00

5. The Revisors (*b*) shall before the first day of September of each year, meet and prepare from the assessment list an alphebetical list of the qualified electors in their Parish, distinguishing the resident from the non-resident, and affixing the place of residence of the non-resident when known, and on or before the first day of September in each year, post up a copy of the said list in three of the most public places in each polling district of their Parish, with the following notice:

"The Revisors will meet at , in the Parish of , on the twenty-fifth [*if Sunday say* twenty-

(*b*) A bill was introduced at the session of the Legislature of 1885, which provided among other things for the appointment, by the Lieut.-Governor in Council, of a Revising Commissioner or Barrister for each county, to whom appeals from the Revisors might be had, but the bill did not become law.

sixth] day of October *(c)* next, at o'clock, A.M., to revise the list of electors for the Parish of and any person claiming to add to or strike off a name from the list, must give notice thereof, with the cause of objection, to either of us, on or before the first day of October next, and also notify every person proposed to be struck off.—Dated the day of , 18 .

Revisors to meet and prepare Electoral Lists; notice of meeting to revise list.

A. B. }
C. D. } *Revisors."*
E. F. }

6. The Revisors shall, on or before the tenth day of October in each year, post up in the said three most public places of the polling district, an alphabetical list of the persons proposed to be added or struck off respectively, with a notice appropriate to each list, to the effect following:—

Changes proposed and time of hearing to be posted.

"The Revisors will on the twenty-fifth [*if Sunday, say* twenty-sixth] day of October (*c*) instant, at in the Parish of , adjudicate upon the propriety of adding (*or* striking off, *in case of striking off,*) the foregoing names to (*or* from) the list of qualified voters. —Dated the day of October, 18 .

A. B. }
C. D. } *Revisors."*
E. F. }

7. The person who proposes to strike a name from the list, shall, on or before the first day of October, give notice in writing to the party objected to, either personally or by leaving it at his last or usual place of abode, and shall prove on oath the giving the notice to the satisfaction of the Revisors before they hear the objection.

Objectors to notify parties objected to.

8. At the time and place appointed, the Revisors shall

(*c*) By cap. 14 of the Stats. of 1879, s. 1, when the 25th Oct. falls on the same day on which the election of Councillors for any Municipality is to be held, there shall be substituted in the notices provided by secs. 5 and 6 above, the words "*twentieth* day of October" instead of "twenty-fifth day of October."

Revised list to be sent to the County Secretary.

attend and correct the lists, and shall, with all convenient dispatch, make out an alphebetical list of the resident electors of each polling district of the Parish, and of the non-resident electors, stating the residence when known, and on or before the tenth day of November in each year, transmit the same to the County Secretary.

Mode of revision. Firms, members of, may vote; when.

9. The Revisors shall add to or strike off from the list the name of any person whose qualification or disqualification is satisfactorily proved to have existed at the date of the last assessment, or date of the list to be made up by the Assessors in the event of no assessment, if notice have been given to a revisor of the claim on or before the first day of October, and in case of disqualification, they prove to the satisfaction of the Revisors that notice in writing has been given to the party objected to within the same period. When a firm is assessed in respect of property or income sufficient to give each member a qualification, the several persons composing such firm shall be inserted on the list.

Incorrect Lists, neglect to revise; penalty for.

10. If the Assessors neglect to make up and deliver the list, or wilfully deliver an incorrect list, or if the Revisors neglect to revise the list so delivered, or wilfully transmit an incorrect list, for every neglect or wilful delivery or transmission of an incorrect list each Assessor or Revisor so contravening this Chapter shall pay a fine of eighty dollars, which any person may recover with costs, and each day a list is delayed shall be a separate contravention hereof.

Eldon, resident voters of, may have their names on List for Addington.

11. Any duly qualified voter resident in the Parish of Eldon, in the County of Restigouche, and possessed of a freehold estate situate in the said Parish of the value of one hundred dollars, may have his name placed on the list for the Parish of Addington in the following manner, —such voter shall, on or before the twenty-fifth day of October in each year, make and subscribe before the Revisors of the Parish of Addington, or one of them, the

following affidavit under oath, which oath the said Revisors or any one of them are hereby authorized to administer:

"I, A. B., do hereby make oath and say, I am a British subject of the full age of twenty-one years, I reside in the Parish of Eldon, in the County of Restigouche, and am possessed of a freehold estate therein of the full value of one hundred dollars, and that I am not subject to any legal incapacity."

And such Revisors shall thereupon add the name of the voter to the said list before transmitting the same to the County Secretary, and such person shall be dealt with as if he was a resident elector of Addington.

Sheriff to direct County Secret'ry in making copies of Lists for polling districts; how made up.

12. The Sheriff of the County shall, on or before the tenth day of December in each year, attend at the office of the County Secretary to ascertain the non-resident and resident electors who may be qualified to vote in more than one Parish, and the Secretary shall, under his direction, make a copy of the list of each polling district, with the name of any non-resident elector marked as such, who may have selected that poll. He shall make an alphebetical list of the remaining non-resident electors. Whenever a non-resident elector shall notify the Sheriff in writing of his selection of a particular poll, his name shall be inserted and continued in the list of that poll until he becomes disqualified, or direct otherwise. If it appear by the list that a resident elector of any Parish is returned qualified to vote in any other, his name shall be only inserted on the list of the polling district in which he resides (*d*).

Sheriff to sign Lists. Secretary to send copy to Town Clerk.

13. The list shall be made up and signed by the Sheriff, and deposited with the County Secretary on or before

(*d*) By cap. 15 of the Stats. of 1879, the duties to be performed by the Sheriff under secs. 12 and 13 are to be performed, as to the County of York, by the Warden of that County.

the twenty-fourth day of December in each year, and shall be the Register of electors for the County for which they are so made for the year commencing with the first day of January following; and the County Secretary shall send a copy of the list for each polling district to the Clerk of the Parish for which such poll is held, on or before the thirtieth day of December in each year, for inspection by any elector (*d*).

On default, last Register to be used.

14. If from any cause the Register of electors for any polling district is not made up in any year, the register last made up shall be used in its stead for the purpose of elections.

Lists for Saint John City; revision of.

15. The list of electors for the City of Saint John shall be revised and corrected by the Aldermen and Councillors at the time therein prescribed, and the Common Council may regulate the same by bye-laws not inconsistent with this Chapter; and the name of every freeman of the City not included therein, assessed in the sum of one hundred dollars, shall be added to and inserted in the list, and when it is corrected, and an alphabetical list of every Ward or polling district made up, it shall be signed by the Mayor, filed with the City Clerk, and be the Register of electors for the said City.

Witnesses concerning qualification: attendance, examination, fees

16. The Revisors shall have power to summon witnesses to attend at the time and place appointed, to give evidence as to the qualification or disqualification of any person, and to administer an oath, and examine the parties and such witnesses on oath; and every person so summoned who shall neglect to attend without good cause shewn therefor to the Revisors, or attending shall refuse to be sworn or give evidence, shall be liable to a penalty of twenty dollars; and every witness attending shall be entitled to receive the same fees and travelling charges as witnesses attending before Justices of the

---

(*d*) See note on preceding page.

Peace in civil suits, to be paid by the person at whose instance the respective witnesses may be summoned.

Compensation to Officers for preparing Lists.

17. The County Council shall allow the Sheriff, County Secretary, Warden, Assessors, Revisors, and any other person required by them to assist in preparing the Register of electors, a reasonable compensation for their services, and any necessary expenses incurred, and charge the amount thereof on the County funds.

THE

NOVA SCOTIA PROVINCIAL FRANCHISE.

(48 VICTORIA, CAP. 2.)

[*Passed the 24th day of April, A.D. 1885.*]

BE it enacted by the Governor, Council, and Assembly, as follows:

Who entitled to vote.

1. The following persons, if of the full age of twenty-one years and subjects of Her Majesty by birth or naturalization, and not disqualified by any section of this Act or otherwise by law prevented from voting, shall be entitled to have their names entered upon the list of electors provided for by the thirteenth section of chapter four of the Revised Statutes, fifth series, and if so entered shall be entitled to vote at elections of members to serve in the House of Assembly, that is to say:

(*a*) Every male person who, at the time of the last assessment, shall have been assessed in respect of real property to the value of one hundred and fifty dollars, or in respect of personal property, or of personal and real property together, to the value of three hundred dollars.

(*b*) Every male person who, at the time of the last assessment, shall have been in possession of real or personal property, or of personal and real property together, of the respective values mentioned in the preceding subsection, and shall have been by law specially exempted from taxation.

(*c*) Every male person who, at the time of the last assessment, shall have been a *bonâ fide* yearly tenant of real property of the value of one hundred and fifty dollars where the assessment on real property was by law levied upon the owners thereof, or the assessed value of whose personal property combined with that of the real property so occupied by him as a yearly tenant shall have been three hundred dollars or upwards.

(*d*) The son of every person qualified under the preceding subsections, if such person at the time of the last assessment shall have been in possession as owner or yearly tenant of sufficient property to qualify more than one voter, and if such son shall have resided in the residence or dwelling of his father, or on property owned by his father within the assessment district, for at least one year next prior to said assessment.

(*e*) The son of every widow if such widow, at the time of the last assessment, shall have been in possession, as owner or yearly tenant, of sufficient property to give a qualification to vote, if such son shall have resided in the residence or dwelling of his mother, or on the property owned by his mother within the assessment district, for at least one year next prior to said assessment.

(*f*) Every person who, at the time of the last assessment, shall have been entitled to be assessed as in subsection (*a*) mentioned, or shall have been qualified under any of the preceding subsections, and whose name shall have been omitted from the assessors' returns.

Where more than one resident son.

2. If in either of the cases mentioned in subsections (*d*) and (*e*) of the first section of this Act, there are more sons than one so resident, and if the property is not of

sufficient value if divided between them to give a qualification to vote to the father and all the sons, where the father is living or to the sons alone where the mother is a widow, then the right to vote under this Act shall belong to and be the right only of the father and such of the eldest or elder of said sons to whom the value of the property will when divided between them give the qualification to vote; and if the property is not sufficient value if divided between the father (if living) and one son, to give each a qualification to vote, then the father shall be the only person entitled to vote in respect of such property.

Occasional absence not to disqualify.

3. Occasional or temporary absence of the son from the residence or property of the father or mother for not more in all than four months in the year, shall not disqualify such son as a voter under this Act. The time spent by mariners and fishermen in the prosecution of their occupation, and by students at institutions of learning within the Dominion of Canada, shall be considered time spent at home.

Duty of Assessors.

4. The assessors of each assessment district shall on or before the twentieth day of January in each year deliver to the revisors a copy of the assessment rolls for the polling districts within the revisal section, and they shall also deliver to the revisors a list of persons exempt from taxation, with a statement of the value of the property of every such person, and also a list of such sons as are by this Act entitled to be placed on the voters' lists. The returns delivered to the revisors shall be in the form prescribed in the schedule to this Act, or in such other form as will most conveniently furnish to the revisors the information necessary for the making up of the list of voters in accordance with the intention of this Act,

and the City Clerk of Halifax, the Clerk of every incorporated Town, and the Clerk of every Municipality, shall at the cost of such city, town, or municipality, furnish the assessors with such blank books or forms as may be required for the purpose of collecting the information and making the returns.

5. Whenever two or more persons are either as business partners, joint tenants, tenants in common, or by any other kind of joint interest, the owners or yearly tenants of any real property, or the joint owners of any personal property, or of real and personal property together, the names of each of such persons shall be entered in the assessors' returns and the property apportioned among them to the best of the assessors' judgment (*a*) and such apportionment shall have the same force and effect respecting the qualifications of voters as if each of such persons had been individually assessed in the amount set opposite their respective names; but where property is held by a body corporate no one of the members thereof shall be entitled to vote or be entered on the list of voters in respect of said property. **Cases of business partners, etc.**

6. The assessors shall mark on their returns opposite each name the number of the polling district in which the property of the elector is situate and the residence of such elector. **Returns, what to contain.**

7. Persons qualified under this Act as voters in respect of personal property or as sons shall only be placed upon the list as voters and vote in the polling district in which they reside, and persons qualified as voters in respect of real property, or of real and personal property together, shall only be placed on the voters' list and vote in the polling district where the real property in respect of **Voters, how placed on list.**

(*a*) See *ante*, note *(w)* p. 39, and note *(op)* p. 100.

which they are qualified is situate; but when the real property is partly within one polling district and partly within another, although all within one electoral district, the person qualified in respect thereof shall be entitled to be placed upon the list of voters and to vote in either of such polling districts for which he may at the time of the revision of the lists desire to be registered as the voter.

Assessors to make careful inquiry.

8. It shall be the duty of the assessors to make a careful inquiry as to the qualifications of all persons who apply or on whose behalf application is made to have their names placed on the returns, and if any assessor, wilfully or through failure to make proper inquiries, returns as a qualified voter any person who is not qualified, or fails to return any person qualified under the provisions of this Act, such assessor shall be liable to a penalty of forty dollars, which may be recovered before any two justices of the peace or any police or stipendiary magistrate, upon the information or complaint of any elector or person qualified to be an elector under the provisions of this Act; and any person who wilfully gives false information to the assessors for the purpose of having placed in their returns of qualified voters the name of any person not qualified, or of having the name of any person qualified omitted from the returns, shall be liable to a like penalty, which may be recovered by the like persons and in the same way as penalties of assessors.

Allowance to Assessors.

9. The City Council of Halifax, the Council of every incorporated Town, and the Council of every Municipality shall, out of the funds under their control, make reasonable allowance to the assessors for any additional duty imposed on them by the provisions of this Act.

10. Until the completion of voters' lists under the provisions of this Act, the qualification of electors in elections for the House of Assembly shall be the same as it is at the time of the passing of this Act. Qualification of Electors.

11. Sections nine, fourteen and fifteen of chapter four of the Revised Statutes, fifth series, and any section of said chapter, or any enactment inconsistent with the provisions of this Act, are hereby repealed. Inconsistent law repealed.

12. This Act may be cited as "The Franchise Act, 1885." Short title of Act.

SCHEDULE.

ASSESSORS' RETURNS FOR ELECTORAL LISTS, POLLING DISTRICT No. , COUNTY OF

Assessment Roll.

NAME.	Real Estate of Residents within County.	Personal Estate of Residents within County.	Real Estate of Non-residents.	Personal Estate of Non-residents.	Number of Polling District in which Real Estate is situate.	Number of Polling District in which Personal Estate is.	Residence.
A. B.	$200 00	$ 0 00	$ 0 00	$300 00	Eleven.	Nine.	
C. D.	0 00	300 00	200 00	0 00	Nine.	Eleven.	

Persons Exempt from Taxation.

NAME.	Real Estate of Residents within County.	Personal Estate of Residents within County.	Real Estate of Non-residents.	Personal Estate of Non-residents.	Number of Polling District in which Real Estate is situate.	Number of Polling District in which Personal Estate is.	Residence.
A. B.	$200 00	$ 0 00	$ 0 00	$300 00	Eleven.	Nine.	
C. D.	0 00	300 00	200 00	0 00	Nine.	Eleven.	

Bonâ fide Yearly Tenants, where assessment is by law levied on the owner of Real Property.

NAME.	Real Estate occupied by yearly tenant.	Personal Estate of yearly tenant.	Number of Polling District in which Real Estate is situate.	Number of Polling District in which Personal Estate is.	Residence of owner of Real Estate.	Residence of yearly tenant.
A. B	$300 00	$ 0 00	Nine.	Eleven.		
C. D.	100 00	250 00	Eleven.	Nine.		

Apportionment of Property by Assessors under the provisions of Section 5 of the Franchise Act, 1885.

Firm, Business or other name.	Individual Names.	Real Estate of residents within County.	Personal Estate of residents within County.	Real Estate of non-residents.	Personal Estate of non-residents.	Number of Polling-District in which Real Estate is situate.	Number of Polling District in which Personal Estate is.	Amount apportioned to each individual.			Residence.
								Real.	Personal.	Total.	
Roe & Co...	A. B....	$200 00	$500 00	$200 00	$500 00	Nine.	Eleven.	$150	$200	$350	
	C. D....							50	300	350	
Doe & Co....	E. F....	$500 00	$200 00	$500 00	$200 00	Eleven.	Nine.	350	150	500	
	G. H....							150	50	200	

Sons to be entered on Voters' List.

Name of Father (or Mother, if a widow).	Value of Real Property owned, or occupied as yearly tenant.	Value of Personal Property.	Number of Polling District in which Real Property is situate.	Number of Polling District in which Personal Property is.	Residence of Father (or Mother, if a widow).	Number of Sons qualified to vote.	Names of Sons qualified.
A. B............................	$450 00	$ 0 00	Nine.	Eleven.		Two.	E. F. / G. H.
C. D. (widow)................	0 00	600 00	Eleven.	Nine.		Two.	H. I. / J. K.

THE

MANITOBA PROVINCIAL FRANCHISE.

AN ACT RESPECTING THE LEGISLATIVE ASSEMBLY AND THE REPRESENTATION OF THE PEOPLE THEREIN (*a*), (CONSOLIDATED).

HER Majesty, by and with the advice and consent of the Legislative Assembly of Manitoba, enacts as follows:

EXPLANATORY.

I. This Act may be known and cited as "The Act respecting the Legislative Assembly." 38 V. c. 2, s. 1. **How Act cited.**

II. This Act shall apply not only to the Legislative Assembly, but also to every election of every member thereof, whether the same be held at the time of the general election or to fill a vacancy in the Legislative Assembly. 38 V. c. 2, s. 1. **Application of Act.**

III. In interpreting this Act, unless it be otherwise provided, or unless there be in the context something which indicates a different sense, or requires another construction; **Interpretation.**

(*a*) Only those portions of the Act are here given which relate to the Franchise and the Voters' Lists.

"The Province" "this Province" (1.) The words "the Province" or "this Province" mean the Province of Manitoba; and the words "Legislative Assembly," mean the Legislative Assembly of Manitoba;

Owner. (2.) The word "owner" signifies proprietor in his own right;

Occupant. (3.) The word "occupant" signifies the person who occupies immovable property otherwise than owner, but who enjoys the revenue and profits arising therefrom;

Tenant. (4.) The word "tenant" means as well the person who pays rent in money as the person who is obliged to give to the owner a certain part of the revenues and profits of the real estate which he occupies;

Electoral division. (5.) The words "electoral division" mean any place or portion of this Province entitled to return a member of the Legislative Assembly;

Election officers (6.) The term "election officers" means the returning officer, the election clerk, and all deputy returning officers and poll clerks appointed for an election;

Executive Council. (7.) The words "Executive Council" mean the Executive Council of the Province of Manitoba, and the words "Lieutenant-Governor" mean Lieutenant-Governor in Council;

Personal expenses. (8.) The term, "personal expenses," employed in relation to the expenditure of a candidate, in respect of any election in which he is a candidate, means all the reasonable travelling expenses of such candidate, and his reasonable expenses at hotels, and other places, to which he may repair, for the purposes of, and in regard of such election. 38 V. c. 2, s. 2.

Capital letter refers to form. IV. Any form indicated by a capital letter, in the various provisions of this Act, refers to the corresponding form contained in the schedule annexed to, and forming part of this Act, and any of the forms contained in such schedule shall be sufficient for which it is intended; but any other form, having substantially the same meaning may be employed with equal effect. 38 V. c. 2, s. 3.

V. Any reference to one or more sections indicated in the provisions of this Act, without mention of the Act or statute of which such sections form part, is a reference to the sections of this Act. 38 V. c. 2, s. 4. Reference.

VI. If the time fixed by this Act for the accomplishment of any proceeding or formality, prescribed by the provisions thereof, expires or falls upon a Sunday or legal holiday, the time so fixed shall be continued to the first day following not a Sunday or holiday. 38. V. c. 2, s. 5. Time fixed falling on Sunday or holiday continued to next day.

VII. Every person before whom any oath must be taken or affirmation made, under the provisions of this Act, is empowered and shall be bound, whenever the same is required of him, to administer such oath or affirmation, and to give a certificate thereof without fee or reward. 38 V. c. 2, s. 6. Person to administer oath and give certificate without fee

VOTERS' LISTS.

XXXIV. The list of electors now or hereafter compiled according to law, certified and returned to the clerk of the executive council, by the clerks of the respective municipalities, incorporated cities and towns, shall be held and taken to be the electoral lists of the Province, and of the several electoral divisions thereof, until the same are superseded by new or succeeding lists, certified and returned to the clerk of the executive council as hereinafter provided. List of electors to be certified and returned to clerk of E. C.

Clerk to make alphabetical list.

XXXV. On or before the fifteenth day of August in each year, the clerk of the municipality of each city, town or municipality shall make a list in alphabetical order of all persons who, according to the valuation roll then in force in the municipality for local purposes and as then revised for local purposes, appear to be electors by reason of the real estate possessed or occupied by them as tenants or otherwise within the city, town or municipality.

List to distinguish owners or lessees.

XXXVI. The clerk, in drawing up the list of electors, shall distinguish the persons who appear to be qualified as owners from those who appear to be qualified as lessees or occupants; and shall specify the persons who reside in such city, town or municipality, from those who are not residents therein.

Clerk to omit from list any person not entitled to vote.

XXXVII. The clerk shall omit from the list of electors every person who under cap. three, section sixty-five of the consolidated statutes, is not entitled to vote.

When municipality is partly in one division and partly in another.

XXXVIII. If any municipality is situated partly in one electoral division and partly in another, the clerks of each municipality shall prepare in the same manner for each of such electoral divisions, an alphabetical list of the persons who are electors therein.

When a person is an elector in more than one ward.

XXXIX. If a person is an elector in more than one ward in an electoral division, his name shall be entered in the list of each ward of such electoral division in which he is an elector.

Clerk to certify to the correctness of list.

XL. The clerk shall certify the correctness of the list of electors by him made by the following oath, taken before a justice of the peace:

Oath.

"I (*name of Clerk*) swear, that, to the best of my knowledge and belief, the foregoing list of electors is correct, and that nothing has been inserted therein, or omitted therefrom, unduly or by fraud: So help me God."

XLI. Each list must be attested under the foregoing oath. The list so attested shall be kept in the office of the clerk, at the disposal, and for the information of all persons interested.

Each list to be attested.

XLII. The clerk, on the day upon which he shall take the oath required by this Act shall give and publish public notice, setting forth that the list of electors has been prepared according to law, and has been lodged in his office, at the disposal and for the information of all persons interested; and it shall be the duty of the clerk, on or before the twenty-fifth day of August, to post up in every postoffice and schoolhouse in the municipality, and in the office of the clerk of the county court for the municipality a certified copy of said list: provided always such clerk shall furnish to any person on application for the same a certified copy of such list on payment of five cents for every ten names therein.

Clerk to publish public notice.

Proviso.

XLIII. If the clerk has not made the alphabetic list of electors required by this Act, then the judge of the county court, on summary petition from the warden, or mayor, or councillor, or other person entitled to be entered as an elector, shall appoint a clerk *ad hoc* to prepare the alphabetical list of electors.

When clerk has not made alphabetical list.

XLIV. The clerk shall be personally liable for the costs incurred on such petition, and for those incurred in drawing up the list by the clerk *ad hoc*, unless the judge, for special reasons, deem it advisable to order otherwise, and in such case the costs shall be left at his discretion.

Clerk to be liable for costs.

XLV. The clerk *ad hoc* shall proceed, within fifteen days after notice of his appointment, to the preparation

Clerk to prepare list within 15 days of his appointment. of the list of electors. He shall, for such purpose, become an officer of the municipal council, and shall have the same powers to exercise and the same duties to discharge as the clerk of the municipality, and shall be subject to the same penalties in case of default or neglect on his part.

Mayor or Warden to deliver to clerk the valuation roll.

XLVI. The mayor, warden and the officers of the council, in so far as the same is incumbent upon them, shall, under the penalties prescribed by this Act, be bound to deliver to the clerk *ad hoc* on his demand, the valuation roll which is to avail as the basis of the electoral list.

When a name has been omitted from the voters' lists.

XLVII. Any person whose name has been omitted from the voters' list so compiled and posted as aforesaid, may by himself or his agent within one month thereafter, notify the clerk of the municipality of such division of his intention to apply at the next sitting of the county court having jurisdiction in said municipality to have his name added to said list, and any elector finding that any name or names have been wrongfully put on said list may notify the clerk of the municipality that he intends to apply at the next sitting of the county court to have such name or names struck off said list; and in that case he shall notify the person whose name he asks to be struck off at least five days before the sitting of the county court of such, his intended application, and the clerk of the municipality in each of the cases aforesaid shall post and keep posted up in his office a list of the names of persons in said notices from the time they are so received by him until the sitting of the court aforesaid, and shall also send to the clerk of the county court for said municipality copies of said notices, and the clerk of the county court shall also post up and keep posted, in his said office, a list of the names of the persons contained in said notices from the time of receiving the same until the sitting of the court aforesaid.

XLVIII. The judge of the county court having jurisdiction in said municipality shall take into consideration all the complaints in writing relating to the said list, and hear all persons interested, and the clerk of the said county court shall within one week make a return to the clerk of the municipality of the names which shall be so added or struck off by the said judge and shall add to, or strike off the said list, the names so added or struck off as aforesaid. Judge to take into consideration all complaints in writing.

XLIX. The list of electors shall come into force from and after the revision and return thereof to the clerk of the executive council as hereinafter provided, and shall remain in force until a new list is made and returned as aforesaid. When list shall come into force.

L. It shall be the duty of the clerk as soon as the list of electors has been revised to insert at the end of such list, the certificate set forth in form A. Clerk to insert certificate in form A.

LI. The list of electors shall be kept in the archives of the city, town or municipality, and shall there remain on record.

LII. A duplicate thereof shall be transmitted to the clerk of the executive council within eight days following the day upon which such list shall have been revised by the clerk, or by the mayor, or warden, under a penalty of two hundred dollars or of imprisonment for six months in default of payment, against each of them, in case of contravention of this provision. Duplicate to be transmitted to the clerk of the E. C.

LIII. Nevertheless the transmission of the said list to the clerk after the time prescribed by this Act, shall not have the effect of invalidating such list. If after time not to invalidate.

Clerk of E. C. to preserve such lists.

LIV. All lists of electors transmitted to the clerk of the executive council, or posted up in the office of the clerk of the county court, shall be preserved by such officer, and shall remain on record in his office. The clerks on receipt of the said lists shall enter upon each the date of the reception thereof.

Costs of revision

LV. The costs of revision of the voters' list shall be taxed at the discretion of the Judge, for or against such of the parties as he shall deem advisable, and shall be recoverable under a writ of execution issued in the usual manner.

Judge's decision final.

LVI. The decision of the judge shall be final.

Clerks to correct list.

LVII. The clerks shall each correct the list of electors in his possession according to the decision of the court.

When list has been altered or falsified.

LVIII. If at any time it is made to appear to any judge of the county court, in term or in vacation, that any of the persons having the custody of the lists of electors have altered or falsified, or have permitted to be altered or falsified, the said lists in their possession, the judge shall require the said person or the person having the custody of the valuation roll, which served as the basis of the lists, to appear before him and to produce the rolls and lists in their possession.

After examination by judge.

LIX. At the time and place fixed for the appearance of such persons, the judge after having examined the duplicates of the lists produced by the clerk, together with the valuation roll, shall, with or without further proof, make the alterations or corrections which he shall deem necessary, to render the lists so altered or falsified, accurate and correct.

LX. Every clerk of a city, town or municipality, who has refused or neglected to make the alphabetical list of electors as required by this Act, shall incur a penalty not exceeding two hundred dollars, or imprisonment, not exceding six months, in default of payment; any clerk who, having made the list, has wilfully inserted therein, or omitted therefrom, any name which should not have been inserted therein or omitted therefrom, or who has otherwise altered or falsified the same, so that it ceases to be or is not an exact and correct list of all the electors entitled to be entered therein, shall incur a penalty not exceeding two hundred dollars, or imprisonment not exceeding twelve months, in default of payment; nevertheless, any person who, under section three of the consolidated statutes of Manitoba, although entered on any such list of electors is disqualified from voting, shall not be entitled to vote.

When clerk has refused to make alphabetical list

Penalty.

Clerk omitting or inserting any name.

Penalty.

QUALIFICATION OF ELECTORS.

Conditions requisite to be an Elector.

LXI. No person shall be admitted to vote at the election of a member of the Legislative Assembly of this Province unless his name appears at the time of the voting on the list of electors then in force; and no person shall be entered upon the list of electors for any electoral division unless he fulfils the following conditions, that is to say:

Entry on list.

(1.) He must be of the male sex, twenty-one years of age, and a subject of Her Majesty by birth or naturalization;

(2.) He must not otherwise be legally incapacitated;

(3.) He must have been, in such electoral division for

a period of at least three months, actually and in good faith, owner of real estate of the value of one hundred dollars or upwards, or tenant for the year or by the year of real property of the value of two hundred dollars and upwards, under an annual rent of at least twenty dollars, or the occupant and *bona fide* householder, by the residence of himself, or of himself and family, if he have any, on land in the electoral division of the annual value of at least twenty dollars. 38 V. c. 2, s. 9.

Two or more persons co-tenants or co-owners allowed to vote.

LXII. Whenever two or more persons are co-owners or co-tenants or co-occupants of any real estate valued at an amount sufficient for the share of each to confer upon him the right to vote, each of such persons shall be deemed to be an elector under this Act, and shall be entered upon the list of electors; but he whose share does not amount to the value required to confer the right to vote, if any be in such position shall not be so entered nor be an elector; and the same rule shall apply to co-tenants respecting the amount of rent which they may jointly and severally pay. 38 V. c. 2, s. 9.

Members of corporation not allowed to vote

LXIII. Nevertheless if the real estate is owned or occupied, by a corporation, no one of the members of the corporation shall be an elector, nor entered upon the list of electors, by virtue thereof. 38 V. c. 2, s. 10.

Persons entitled to vote.

LXIV. All persons answering the conditions aforesaid, and whose names, under the provisions of this Act, shall appear and be contained on the said revised electoral lists and who are not otherwise disqualified according to law, shall be entitled to vote at elections of members to serve in the Legislative Assembly of Manitoba. 35 V. c. 5, s. 1.

QUALIFICATION OF ELECTORS.

Persons who cannot be Electors.

LXV. The following persons can in no case be electors, or vote: Persons who can neither be electors nor voters.

(1.) The judges of the court of the Queen's Bench and of the county court, and the recorders of cities;

(2.) Clerks of the crown and peace, registrars, sheriffs, deputy sheriffs, and clerks of the county court;

(3.) Indians or persons of Indian blood, receiving an annuity from the crown, so long as said Indians or persons of Indian blood receive such annuity; and if any of the persons set forth in this section vote, he shall be liable to a penalty not exceeding five hundred dollars, or to imprisonment for a period not exceeding twelve months in default of the payment of the penalty imposed, and his vote shall be null and void. 38 V. c. 2, s. 11. Persons excluded from voting. Penalty on persons voting not entitled to vote.

FORM A.

LIST OF ELECTORS.

For that portion of the Electoral Division No. , or situate in the Municipality of for the year 188 ,

Names of Electors in Alphabetical order.	Profession.	No. of lot upon which qualified.	City, town or parish	Section.	Township.	Range.	Owner.	Lessee.	Occupant.	Resident.	Non-resident.	Residence of Non-residents when known.	Remarks.

I, make oath that to the best of my knowledge and belief, the list of electors above mentioned is correct and according to law, and that nothing has been entered thereon or omitted therefrom unduly or fraudulently. So help me God.

Sworn before me at in the County of in the Province of Manitoba, this day of A.D. 18

J.P. A. B., *Clerk.*

THE
BRITISH COLUMBIA
PROVINCIAL FRANCHISE. (a)

AN ACT TO MAKE BETTER PROVISION FOR THE QUALIFICATION AND REGISTRATION OF VOTERS.

[*Assented to 19th May, 1876.*]

HER Majesty, by and with the advice and consent of the Legislative Assembly of the Province of British Columbia, enacts as follows:—

1. The "Qualification and Registration of Voters Act, 1875," shall be and is hereby repealed. **Repeals former Act.**

2. Every male of the full age of twenty-one years, not being disqualified by this Act or by any other law in force in this Province, being entitled within this Province to the privileges of a natural-born British subject, having resided in this Province for twelve months, and **Who may vote at Elections for Legislative Assembly.**

(a) By sec. 9 of the Dominion Franchise Act, besides the persons who are entitled to be registered under that Act, every person who *at the time of the passing of the same*: (1) Is of age and not disqualified; (2) Is a British subject, resident in the Province, and entitled to vote by the existing Provincial laws, is entitled to be registered under the Dominion Act. Only those of age when the Dominion Act was passed (20th July, 1885), and otherwise qualified at that date can qualify under the Provincial Act to vote at Dominion elections. If they cannot so qualify they must do so under the provisions of the Dominion Act. By this arrangement no one is disfranchised who has hitherto voted, while the gradual adoption of the franchise as in the Dominion Act is provided for, for Dominion elections.

in the Electoral District in which he claims to vote for two months of that period immediately previous to sending in his claim to vote as hereinafter mentioned (*b*), and being duly registered under the provisions of this Act, shall be entitled to vote at the Election of a Member or Members of the Legislative Assembly: Provided that no person shall be entitled to be registered as aforesaid, who shall have been convicted of any treason, felony, or other infamous offence, unless he shall have received a free or conditional pardon for such offence, or have undergone the sentence passed upon him for such offence.

Who may be elected a member of the Legislature.

3. No person shall be capable of being elected a Member of the Legislature who shall not be duly registered or entered on the Register of Electors for some Electoral District of the Province according to the provisions of this Act at the time of his election, and who shall not have been resident within this Province for one year previous to the date of his election; and no person shall be capable of being elected a Member to serve in the Legislative Assembly who shall be a Minister of any Religious Denomination, whatever may be his title, rank, or designation.

Who shall not vote at elections

4. No Judge of the Supreme Court or of the County Courts, no Stipendiary Magistrate, no Constable or Police Officer, Sheriff or Deputy Sheriff, or Returning Officer, except in cases to be hereafter provided, shall be entitled to vote at any election of a Member of the Legislature. (See 46 Vic. c. 34, s. 2).

Polling Divisions

5. It shall be lawful for the Lieutenant-Governor in Council, from time to time, to fix a polling place or polling places in each Electoral District; or, if in the opinion of the Lieutenant-Governor in Council it is advisable, to

---

(*b*) Under the Dominion law however non-resident owners may be registered, and may vote; See Dom. Fran. Act, s. 3, subs. (3); and sec. 4, subs. (3). See also Act of 1875, *post*; also Dom. Fran. sec. 2, "Person,"; and sec. 11, subs. (*c*), *ante*.

divide any Electoral District into any number of Polling Divisions, and to assign to each such Polling Division a polling place, in such manner as to enable each voter, so far as practicable, to have a polling place within a convenient distance of his residence; and such polling places and the boundaries of such Polling Divisions shall be proclaimed in the British Columbia Gazette; and every such Polling Division to alter and vary, as in his discretion he may think fit.

6. The existing Polling Divisions shall be deemed to be Polling Divisions established by virtue of this Act, and shall be continued as such Polling Divisions until altered or varied by the authority hereof. Polling Divisions now established to be continued.

7. The Lieutenant-Governor in Council shall appoint for each Electoral District, or for any Polling Division of such District, as may be required from time to time, a person to be Collector, and the duties of such Collector shall be as follows:— Appointment of Collector, and his duties.

(a) He shall furnish to any one applying for the same, any of the first three forms in the Schedule hereto, without charge:

(b) To receive from any person offering the same, a notice of claim to vote in the Form A in the Schedule hereto, and to insert the name of such person in a list of persons claiming to vote, which list shall be posted up in the office of such Collector, and a copy thereof shall be placed in some conspicuous place on the outside of the door of such office; and such list shall be according to the Form D in the Schedule hereto:

(c) After such name shall have been inserted for two months in such list of persons claiming to vote, without any written objection thereto as hereinafter mentioned, the Collector shall enter such name upon the Register of Voters for the Electoral District, or

Polling Division thereof, for which such Collector shall have been appointed; and if he shall have reason to believe that there exists any valid objection to the name of such person being placed on the said Register, he shall write opposite the name of such person in the said Register the word "objected"; and the Collector shall post a copy of such Register once in every four months on the door of the principal Court House in such Electoral District, and shall also transmit to any Returning Officer appointed for such district, whenever an election shall be held therein, for a Member to serve in the Legislative Assembly, a copy of the Register of Voters, as it exists at the time of such election, and shall deliver written or printed copies thereof to all persons applying for the same, on payment therefor at the rate of twenty-five cents for one hundred names:

(*d*) Upon receiving, during such two months, from any elector a written objection, stating the reasons therefor, to such name being placed upon the Register of Voters (which objection may be in the Form B in the Schedule hereto) the Collector shall forward a notice, through the post office or in such manner as he may deem advisable, to the person whose claim is objected to, stating the fact of such objection, the name of the person objecting, the ground of such objection, and that the claim and objection will be heard at a time and place to be named by the Collector in such notice; and such notice shall be posted, or left with the person objected to, not less than thirty days before the time fixed for the hearing of such claim and objection:

(*e*) To hear all such claims and objections and to decide whether the name of the person objected to shall be placed on the Register of Voters or not; and if such decision be in the affirmative, to place such name on the Register of Voters accordingly:

(*f*) On the first Monday of August, in each and every year, the Collector shall hold a Court of Revision, of which two months' notice shall be given by him; such notice to be published in the British Columbia Gazette, and copies of such notice shall be posted in the office of such Collector, and on the door of the principal Court House of the Electoral District, and in not less than three conspicuous places within the district, for which, or for the Polling Division whereof, he shall have been appointed:

(*g*) Upon the holding of such Court, it shall be the duty of such Collector to hear and determine any or all objections against the retention of any name or names on the Register of Voters; provided notice of every objection, and the reason therefor, which may be in the form B in the Schedule hereto, shall have been given to the Collector, by the person objecting, thirty days previously to the holding of such Court, and that the Collector shall have forwarded, twenty-one days before the holding of such Court, a notice, through the Post Office, or in such manner as he may deem advisable, to the person objected to, stating the fact of such objection, the ground thereof, and that the same will be heard at the holding of such Court. It shall also be the duty of such Collector to strike off the Register of Voters all names thereon of persons who shall be dead, or shall have ceased to reside in the Province of British Columbia.

Revised Register.

8. The Register of Voters so revised, with any additions thereto as aforesaid or amendment made under authority of section 1 of the "Qualification and Registration of Voters Act (1876) Amendment Act 1884,"

shall be the Register of Voters for the Electoral District, or Polling Division thereof, for which such Collector shall have been appointed, until the Register shall be again revised. (See 47 Vic. c. 34 s. 2).

Registers now in force to be deemed Revised Registers.

9. The several Registers of Voters now in force shall be deemed to be revised Registers made by authority hereof; provided, that if the name of any person is improperly placed upon the Register of Voters, the vote of such person shall, notwithstanding his name appears upon the Register of Voters, be null and void, and shall not be counted.

Appeal from decision of Collector.

10. Any person dissatisfied with the decision of the Collector may have the same reviewed before any County Court holden within the Electoral District, or Polling Division thereof, for which such Collector shall have been appointed; or, in case there shall be no such County Court, then to the County Court holden nearest to such District or Polling Division thereof as aforesaid, by giving to the Collector a notice of review, which may be in the form C in the Schedule hereto, within six days after such decision shall have been rendered. Such notice shall also be served, within such time, upon the elector objecting, or the person whose claim to vote shall have been allowed, as the case may be; and such notice shall be given ten days before the hearing of such review, or at such other time as the County Court Judge shall appoint, and the case shall be heard at one of the usual sittings of such County Court, and the Judge shall either affirm or dismiss such appeal, and make such order as to the costs thereof and generally as to the premises as he may deem just, and may enforce the same as and in the same way as a judgment of the Court is usually enforced. Provided, always, that every such decision of any such County Court Judge may be appealed from to the Supreme Court of British Columbia;

and all the proceedings concerning such appeal shall be conducted as nearly as may be according to the provisions of the "County Courts Amendment Ordinance, 1870." And the Collector, on any such review, shall regard and be governed, as to placing, retaining, or removing any name on or from the Register of Voters, by the decision of the County Court Judge, or if such decision shall be reversed by the Supreme Court, then by the decision of the Supreme Court. (Provided, however, that with respect to the Electoral Districts of Kootenay and Cassiar, the revision hereinbefore mentioned, instead of being made to, taken or held before a County Court, shall be made to, taken or held before any two Justices of the Peace residing in such district, the Collector not being one of such Justices, 42 Vic. c. 22 s. 3).

11. Any person whose name is not upon the Register of Voters as aforesaid, shall not be entitled to vote at any election for a member or members to serve in the Legislative Assembly. No person to vote whose name is not registered.

12. The Lieutenant-Governor in Council may, from time to time, fix such remuneration to be paid to the Collectors appointed under this Act, as may be found necessary or desirable for the purpose. Remuneration of Collector.

13. Any person making a claim to vote as aforesaid, knowing any statement therein contained to be false, shall, upon conviction of any such offence, either before the nearest Stipendiary Magistrate in the Electoral District or Polling Division, or before any Justice of the Peace in such District or Polling Division, be liable to a penalty not exceeding fifty dollars, to be recovered in a summary way, and in default of payment thereof shall be imprisoned for any period not exceeding two months. Penalty of false declaration.

14. Any person whose name shall be on the Register of Voters for any Electoral District, or Polling Division thereof, may vote at any election for a member to serve Voter may vote in one but in no other Polling Division, and must not vote

in two Electoral Districts.

in the Legislative Assembly for such District in any one (but no other) Polling Division of such Electoral District; and, at any General Election, no person shall be entitled to vote in more than one Electoral District; and any person contravening any of the provisions of this section shall be liable to a penalty not exceeding fifty dollars, to be recovered in a summary way before any Justice of the Peace, and in default of payment thereof shall be imprisoned for any period not exceeding one month.

Any person whose name is on two registers shall not vote.

15. Any person whose name is on the Register of Voters of two or more Electoral Districts, who shall permit his name to remain on more than one Register, shall have no right to vote at any election of a member to serve in the Legislative Assembly; and if such person shall vote while his name remains on the Register of more than one Electoral District, he shall be liable to a penalty of fifty dollars, to be recovered in a summary way before any Justice of the Peace, and in default of payment thereof shall be imprisoned for any term not exceeding one month.

Penalty for voting while his name is on two registers.

No person to send in claim to vote while his name is on any register.

16. No person whose name is on the Register of Voters for an Electoral District shall send in his claim to vote in any other Electoral District, until he shall have caused his name to be removed from such Register; and if any person shall act contrary to the provisions of this section, he shall forfeit and pay a sum of money not exceeding fifty dollars, to be recovered before any Justice ef the Peace, or in default of payment thereof shall be imprisoned for any term not exceeding one month.

Penalty.

Any person may have his name removed from register.

17. The Collector of any Electoral District or Polling Division thereof shall remove the name of any person whose name is on the Register of Voters for such district, on the written request of such person and proof that

such request was deposited in the post office in a prepaid letter addressed to the Collector, or proof that such request was personally delivered to him shall be deemed proof that the name of such person has been removed from the Register.

18. Every Collector shall, on or before the first day of September in each year, transmit to the Registrar of the Supreme Court, at Victoria, a copy of the Register of Voters for the Electoral District or Polling Division thereof for which such Collector shall have been appointed, as such register shall exist at the time of transmission; and such copy shall be certified under the hand of the Collector, and shall be dated; and every copy of any such copy register, signed and certified by the Registrar of the Supreme Court, may be used as the original register, whenever such original register is lost or destroyed; and any one may obtain from the Register of the Supreme Court a copy of any such copy register, on paying therefor according to the rates taken in the Supreme Court for office copies.

Register of Voters to be transmitted to Supreme Court.

19. Any Collector of any district or division who shall wilfully refuse or neglect to make out any list, or who shall wilfully neglect to insert therein the name of any person who has given due notice of claim; or who, in making out the List of Voters, or the Register of Voters for any district or division, shall wifully and without any reasonable cause omit the name of any person duly qualified to be inserted in such lists, or who shall wilfully and without reasonable cause insert in any such lists the name of any person not duly qualified; or who shall wilfully refuse or neglect to publish any notice, or lists, or copy of the Register of Voters, or part of the Register of Voters relating to his division, at the time and in the manner required by this Act; or who shall wilfully refuse or neglect to deliver to the Returning

Collector neglecting his duties liable to penalty.

Officer the copy of the Register of Voters as required by this Act; or who shall wilfully refuse or neglect to attend the Court for revising the Lists of Voters of his district or division; or who shall wilfully commit any breach of duty in the execution of this Act shall, for every such offence, be liable to pay, by way of fine, a sum of money not exceeding fifty dollars, to be imposed by and at the discretion of any Justice of the Peace, or to imprisonment for any term not exceeding three months. Provided, always, that nothing herein contained, as to any fine as aforesaid, shall affect or abridge any right of action against any Collector or other person which he may incur under or by virtue of this Act, or any law for the time being in force in this Province.

Interpretation and construction clause.

20. Where in any Act heretofore passed reference is made to the "Qualification and Registration of Voters Act, 1871," or to the "Qualification and Registration of Voters Act Amendment Act, 1872," such reference shall not be deemed to have reference to such Acts respectively, but shall be deemed and construed to have reference to this Act; and where, in the "Election Regulation Act, 1871," the words "Registrar of Voters for the district" occur, they shall be deemed and construed to mean the "Collector or Collectors of Voters for the district."

Short Title.

21. This Act may be cited for all purposes as the "Qualification and Registration of Voters Act, 1876."

By section 1 of "An Act relating to an Act to make better provision for the Qualification and Registration of Voters," (1875), which is still in force, it is enacted:

1. No Chinaman or Indian (*a*) shall have his name placed on the Register of Voters for any Electoral District, or be entitled to vote at any election of a Member to serve in the Legislative Assembly of this Province. Any Collector of any Electoral District or Polling Division thereof, who shall insert the name of any Chinaman or Indian in any such Register, shall, upon conviction thereof before any Justice of the Peace, be liable to be punished by a fine not exceeding fifty dollars, or to be imprisoned for any period not exceeding one month.

Chinamen and Indians shall not vote, and Collector shall be fined if he inserts their names on Voters List.

By an Act to amend the Qualification and Registration of Voters Acts (18th February, 1884), it is enacted:

1. In the event of any person whose name is on the Register of Voters for any Electoral District, or Polling Division thereof, changing his residence, or changing or abandoning his profession, trade, or calling, it shall be lawful, notwithstanding anything contained in any law to the contrary, for the Collector of such Electoral District or Polling Division thereof, and he shall, upon the written request of any such person, and upon proof satisfactory to the Collector that the person making the request is the same person whose name is on the Register of Voters, amend the Register of Voters so far as to correct the description of residence, or profession, trade or calling entered therein.

Collector of Votes to correct the register as to residence and occupation when requested in writing so to do.

(*a*) See Dominion Franchise Act, sec. 2, subs. "Person," and sec. 11, subs. (c) *ante*.

SCHEDULE.

Form A.

FORM OF NOTICE TO BE GIVEN TO THE COLLECTOR.

To the Collector of the Electoral District of (or Polling Division of the Electoral District of).

I claim to have my name inserted in the Register of Voters for the Electoral District of (*or* *Polling Division of the Electoral District of*) in virtue of my being a British Subject of the full age of 21 years, having resided in this Province for twelve months, and in the Electoral District of two months immediately previous to the date hereof, and not being disqualified by any law in force in this Province.

Dated at in the Province of British Columbia, this day of A. D. 18 .

(Signed), A. B.

(*Claimant to state his Christian name and surname at full length, and add his residence, and his profession, trade or calling.*)

NOTE.—By Section 13 any person making a claim to vote, knowing any statement therein contained to be false, shall upon conviction of any such offence be liable to a penalty not exceeding $50, or in default of payment, shall be imprisoned for any period not exceeding 2 months.

Form B.

FORM OF NOTICE OF OBJECTION, TO THE COLLECTOR.

To the Collector of

I object to the name of W. S., of (*describe person objected to as he is described in the list of persons claiming to vote, or Register of Voters, as the case may be*) being placed (*or retained*) on the Register of Voters for the Electoral District of (*or the* *Polling Division of the Electoral District of*), on the following grounds, (*here specify the grounds of objection.*)

(Signed), C. D.

(*Objector to state here his qualification, his profession, trade, or calling, and residence*).

Dated the day of A.D. 18 .

FORM C.

FORM OF NOTICE OF REVIEW.

To the Collector of

I hereby give you notice that on the day of 18 , before the County Court of British Columbia, to be holden at , I intend to have reviewed your decision, made on the day of , 18 , whereby you allowed *(or disallowed)* the name of to be placed on the Register of Voters for , *(or whereby you removed or refused to remove the name of from the Register of Voters for .)*

Dated the day of , A.D. 18

(Signed), E. F.

(Objector to here state his qualification, his Profession, trade, or calling, and residence).

FORM D.

FORM OF LIST OF PERSONS CLAIMING TO VOTE.

Electoral District of
(or Polling Division of the
Electoral District of).
TO WIT:

LIST OF PERSONS CLAIMING TO VOTE IN THE ELECTORAL DISTRICT OF , (OR POLLING DIVISION OF THE ELECTORAL DISTRICT OF).

No.	Christian name and surname of the Claimant at full length.	Residence of Claimant, (If in a city or town, the name and side of the street upon which he resides, and the names of the nearest cross streets between which his residence is situate).	Profession, trade, or calling.

THE

PRINCE EDWARD ISLAND

PROVINCIAL FRANCHISE. (a)

THE qualifications of voters for members of the House of Assembly, as required by the Act of the twenty-fourth year of the reign of her present Majesty, chapter thirty-four, are in substance as follows, namely: (See also 45 Vic. c. 1).

Who may vote. Every voter must be a male person of the age of twenty-one years, a British subject, not subject to any legal incapacity, and must have been duly qualified for at least twelve calendar months next before the date of the writ of election (*b*); and must, in addition, be entitled to one or more of the following qualifications: First, for a town and royalty (excepting Princetown and royalty),

---

(*a*) This statement of qualification of voters forms part of the "Election Poll Notice" supplied by the Provincial Act. By virtue of sec. 9 of the Dominion Franchise Act, the franchise as here stated, still governs to a certain extent in Dominion Elections, and in addition, any persons entitled to be registered under that Act, but not under the Provincial laws, are entitled to the Franchisein such elections in this Province. (See "owner" and "occupant" in right of wife, "farmer's son," "son of an owner of real property," "income," etc. Dominion Franchise Act, pp. 7, 8, 14, 15, 18, 19, 26, 28, 29, 30, 31, 32, 34, etc.) But only those entitled "*at the time of the passing*" of the Dominion Act, (20th July, '85,) to vote under the Provincial law, can be registered under the Dominion Act, unless they can also qualify under the latter Act; see Dom. Fran. Act.

(*b*) As the Dominion lists must be completed before an election can be held upon them, and such completion must in most cases necessarily take place before the Writ of Election issues; (see 57 of Dom. Fran. Act, *ante*,) it is plain, that residence for

must own a freehold estate, consisting of one whole water, common, town or pasture lot, or a freehold estate, of the clear yearly value of forty shillings, consisting of a dwelling house, warehouse, shop, or other building, or of a farm or piece of land: or must be in the *bona fide* use and occupation or actual possession of any dwelling house, warehouse, shop, or other building, or any farm or piece of land, of the clear yearly value of forty shillings (c) the qualification to be within the town, common, or royalty, save and except as aforesaid; or who shall be an occupier of eight acres of the reserved lands as regards a vote for Georgetown. Second, for an electoral district, must own a freehold estate of the clear yearly value of forty shillings, consisting of any warehouse, shop or other building, or any farm or piece of land, or must be in the *bona fide* use and occupation or actual possession of any such last mentioned premises. Third, for either town or electoral district, the performance of statute labor, or payment of the commutation money for the last year the same shall have become due, next, before the day of holding the said election, together with the overseer's certificate, and a twelve months' residence in the polling division; or holding situation exempting from statute labor by Act of Assembly.

Fourth, for the City of Charlottetown and the Common thereof, and the Town of Summerside, the payment of the Provincial Poll Tax for the year immediately preceding the tests of the Writ of Election, together with

Charlottetown and Summerside.

the period named, (*i. e.*, down to date of writ) cannot be proved at the time of revision. Yet, it would not seem to have been the intention of the Dom. Franchise Act to exclude all persons who cannot qualify under that Act for this reason. (See Dom. Fran. Act, 9).

(c) Where the premises constituting a property qualification shall be owned or occupied by joint tenants, or occupants, tenants in common, co-parceners, or co-partners in trade, then not more than one of either of such description of persons, respectively, shall vote thereon, unless their individual interest therein shall be of the yearly value of forty shillings. 24 Vic., (P. E. I.) c. 34, s. 14.

Poll tax qualification.

the Collector's certificate, and a residence in Charlottetown, Common and Royalty, or the Town of Summerside, of twelve months, and in the polling division for which he claims to vote, a residence of one month next before the Writ of Election.

Where no Provincial Poll Tax.

Fifth, for the City of Charlottetown and the Common thereof, and the Town of Summerside, where no Provincial Poll Tax is imposed, and where the voter is liable to pay Civic Poll Tax, the payment thereof in full, or of seventy-five cents on account where such Poll Tax exceeds the said sum. Such Poll Tax to be for the year immediately preceding the tests of the Writ of Election, together with the Collector's certificate, and a residence in Charlottetown, Common and Royalty, or the Town of Summerside, of twelve months, and in the polling division for which he claims to vote, a residence of twelve months next before the Writ of Election.

Cestui qui trust.

Every mortgagor or *cestui qui trust* in actual possession by himself, or his tenant, of real estate, of the yearly value of forty shillings, dower land set off and reduced into possession and value forty shillings per year.

Yearly value how estimated.

The clear yearly value as aforesaid to be estimated by the annual value of the buildings, or by the value of agricultural or other produce yielded by the land *(d)*.

Perjury.

Wilfully, falsely and corruptly swearing to any of the oaths prescribed by the Act, or procuringor suborning any person so to do, is punishable with the pains and disabilities inflicted on persons guilty of wilful and corrupt perjury.

(*d*) If the fee simple value amounts to £35, though the annual rent does not amount to 40 shillings, the person in possession is nevertheless entitled to vote. See 24 Vic., (P. E. I.) c. 34, s. 15.

THE

NORTH-WEST TERRITORIES

FRANCHISE.

QUALIFICATION OF VOTERS AND OF CANDIDATES AT ELECTIONS OF MEMBERS TO SIT IN THE COUNCIL OF THE NORTH-WEST TERRITORIES.

SECTIONS Seventeen and Eighteen of 43rd Victoria, Chapter 25, known as "The North-West Territories Act, 1880," reads as follows :

17. The persons qualified to vote at such election shall be the *bona fide* male residents and householders of adult age, not being aliens or unenfranchised Indians, within the electoral district, and shall have respectively resided in such electoral district for at least twelve months immediately preceding the issue of the said writ. Who may vote.

18. Any person entitled to vote may be elected.

VOTERS' LISTS.

(Extracts from Proclamation of Lieutenant-Governor, dated 5th February, 1881.

17. Should the Lieutenant-Governor not see fit to appoint an Enumerator or Enumerators to make Lists of Appointment of Enumerators.

the electors in the Electoral District, the Returning Officer, conjointly with the nearest member of the Council of the North-West Territories, or with any two Justices of the Peace, or one Justice of the Peace and a Notary Public, or with any one of them resident in or near the Electoral District, and two electors of such District, neither of the number being a candidate, shall appoint under their hand a competent and reliable person to be Enumerator for any one or more polling divisions of such District; and the Returning Officer shall see that no polling division is omitted to be included in one or other of such appointments.

Enumerator to compile lists.

18. It shall be the duty of each such Enumerator, immediately after nomination day, should a poll be granted, to carefully compile a list of all the persons qualified as electors to vote at the election then pending, for the polling division, or each of the polling divisions, for which he has been appointed; and to make three plainly written copies of the same, with the names of voters alphabetically arranged, and giving the occupation and residence of each voter, as required in the form supplied to him by the Returning Officer.

Completion and posting up of list.

19. Each Enumerator shall complete, date at his place of residence, and sign the copies of the Voters' List or Lists, as aforesaid, four days before polling day: two of the said copies for each polling division he shall forthwith post up in two of the most public places within such polling division, and the other he shall retain for revision.

Additions and alterations.

20. Should any Enumerator, at any time after posting up any Voters' List and before polling day, be fully satisfied from representations made to him by any credible person, that the name of any qualified voter has

been omitted from the Voters' List of the polling division to which such voter belongs, he may add such name to the copy of the List in his possession below his own signature; should the Enumerator, in like manner, be fully satisfied that there is on the List the name of any person who is not qualified as a voter in such polling division, he may draw erasing lines through such name and write his own initials opposite thereto in the column for "remarks"; and should the Enumerator find the occupation or residence of any voter to be inaccurately stated in the List, he may make the necessary alteration and affix his initials thereto.

21. Every Enumerator, having revised and corrected such retained copy of each Voters' List compiled by him, if he deem such correction necessary, as provided in the last preceding section, shall write at the foot of such copy and close to the last name thereon, on the day immediately preceding polling day, a certificate in the following form: **Enumerator's Certificate.**

> I certify that the above is a correct List of the Voters in Polling Division No. (or other designation) of the Electoral Division of as revised (or if no correction be made, as finally approved) by me this day of 18 .
>
> (Signature) A. B.,
> *Enumerator.*

22. Every such Voters' List so certified by the Enumerator, he shall deliver forthwith, or before eight o'clock in the morning of polling day, to the Deputy Returning Officer for the polling division named therein; and such List as received by such Deputy Returning Officer, shall be the Voters' List for such polling division, subject to be further corrected on polling day as hereinafter provided. **Delivery of lists to Deputy Returning Officer.**

23. It shall be the duty of the Returning Officer to

cause to be posted up with the Election Notice, a hand-bill in the following form :

INFORMATION TO ELECTORS.

Handbill.

The following is the Qualification of Electors as perscribed by the Parliament of Canada :

(Here insert Qualification.)

If any Elector find that his name is not on the Voters' List of the polling division to which he belongs, he can apply to the Enumerator, on any day before polling day, and if the Enumerator objects to add his name to the said List, he can require the Deputy Returning Officer, on polling day while the Poll is open, to cause his name to be placed on the List, by taking before that officer the following oath :

(Here insert Oath No. 1.)

Each Elector can only vote at one polling station, and for one candidate.

Any Elector wishing to record his vote, shall, in his turn, while the poll is open, go up to the Deputy Returning Officer, give his full name, occupation, and place of residence, state for which candidate he votes, and answer such questions and take such oaths as the Deputy Returning Officer may lawfully put to him.

Every Elector after having voted ought to go away quietly from the polling station.

(Signature), A. B.,
Returning Officer.

Dated 18

OATHS TO BE TAKEN BY VOTERS.

Oaths.

30. Every Deputy Returning Officer shall administer to any elector, if required, either one or both of the following oaths :

No. 1.

You do swear that you are a bona fide male resident and householder within this polling division of this Electoral District, that you are twenty-one years of age, that you are not an alien or an unenfranchised Indian, and that you have resided in this Electoral District for at least twelve months preceding the date of the issue of the writ for this election. So help you God.

No. 2.

You do swear that you have not received any money or other reward, nor have you accepted any promise made to you, directly or indirectly, to induce you to vote at this election ; and that you have not before voted at this election, either at this or any other polling station. So help you God.

31. The Deputy Returning Officer shall, while the poll is open, if required by any elector whose name is not on the Voters' List, administer to such elector Oath No. 1: and such oath having been taken, the Deputy Returning Officer shall at once cause such elector's name to be added to the Voters' List, with the word "sworn" written thereafter. **Addition of name to list.**

32. Every person whose name is on the Voters' List, unless sworn as in the last preceding section provided, before being permitted to vote, if required by any candidate, agent or elector, shall take oath No. 1; and if he refuse to take the same his name shall be erased from the Voters' List, and the words "refused to be sworn," written thereafter. **Swearing voters.**

33. Every voter shall be entitled to vote whose name is on the Voters' List after the said List has been corrected as provided in the next two preceding sections; but if any such voter, when required by the Deputy Returning Officer, or by any candidate, agent, or elector, refuse to take Oath No. 2, he shall not be permitted to vote, and if his name has been entered in the Poll Book, it shall be erased, and the words "refused to take Oath No. 2" written thereafter. **Voters on list entitled to vote.**

PART II.

THE ELECTION LAWS.

CHAPTER I.

CORRUPT PRACTICES.

Under Dominion Laws.

Corrupt Practices according to the Dominion Controverted Elections Act (*a*) mean Acts in reference to Elections, which are declared to be corrupt practices by "The Dominion Elections Act, 1874," or any other Act of the Parliament of Canada, or recognized as such by the common law of Parliament. The offences declared to be corrupt practices by the Elections Act (*b*) are bribery, treating and undue influence, as defined by that or any other Act of the Parliament of Canada, personation or the inducing any person to commit personation, or any wilful offence against certain specified sections of the act; which include, besides definitions of the above mentioned offences, (*c*), the giving or causing to be given to any voter on the nomination day or day of polling, on account of such voter having voted or being about to vote, any meat, drink or refreshment (*d*), and the hiring, paying or promising to pay for conveyance of voters to or from the poll (*e*).

(*a*) 37 Vic., c. 10 s. 4; cap Oa. s. 2 of new Revised Act as in Commissioners' Report.

(*b*) 37 Vic., c. 9, s. 98; Revised Act, s. 92.

(*c*) See ss. 92, 93, 94, 95 and 97.

(*d*) See last clause of sec. 94.

(*e*) See sec. 96.

Under Ontario Laws.

Under the Controverted Elections of Ontario (*f*), and the Election Law Amendment Act, 1884, the term "Corrupt Practices" covers not only the above offences, but also the furnishing drink or other entertainment to any meeting of Electors, assembled for the purpose of promoting such election (*g*), the selling or giving of spirituous or fermented liquor or strong drink at any hotel, etc., during the hours of polling (*h*); betting, or the participation therein, by a candidate upon the result of the election in the electoral district or in any part thereof, or on any event or contingency relating to the election (*i*), providing money to be used by another in such betting (*j*), betting by any person for the purpose of influencing an election (*k*); voting by prohibited persons or inducing or procuring them to vote (*l*).

Effect of corrupt practices on election.

Proof of corrupt practices by a candidate or his agent necessarily involves the avoidance of the election, and, if the candidate be personally guilty, his personal disqualification, whether the election be under Dominion or Ontario laws, unless in the latter case the Judges exercises a saving power given them under certain circumstances by the Ontario Election Act (*m*).

(*f*) Rev. Stats. Ontario, c. 11, s. 2, subs (6); 47 Vic., c. 4.

(*g*) Rev. Stats., c. 10, s. 151.

(*h*) Sec. 157. This offence is confined to hotel-keepers, etc., though a candidate present and participating in such offence will be disqualified, as having suffered a corrupt practice to be committed by or with his actual knowledge and consent. See *post*; *Lennox* 2 Ont. El. Cases 41; *N. Wentworth*, 1 H. E. C. 343.

(*i*) 47 Vic., c. 4, s. 3 (Ont.).

(*j*) *Ib.* subs. (2).

(*k*) *Ib.* subs. (3).

(*l*) *Ib.* Section 4.

(*m*) Sec. 162 of the Rev. Stats. Ontario, c. 10: see further, as to effects of corrupt practices, chapter on Penalties, *post*.

BRIBERY.

By the Dominion Elections Act 1874 (*mx*), sec. 92, the following persons shall be deemed guilty of bribery, and shall be punishable accordingly :—

Definitions. Persons guilty of bribery under Dominion Act.

(1.) Every person who directly or indirectly, by himself, or by any other person on his behalf, gives, lends or agrees to give or lend, or offers or promises any money, or valuable consideration, or promises to procure or to endeavour to procure, any money or valuable consideration, to or for any voter, or to or for any person, on behalf of any voter, or to or for any person in order to induce any voter to vote, or refrain from voting, or corruptly does any such act as aforsaid on account of such voter having voted or refrained from voting at any election ;

Bribers.

(2) Every person who, directly or indirectly, by himself, or by any other person on his behalf, gives or procures, or agrees to give or procure, or offers or promises any office, place or employment, or promises to procure, or to endeavour to procure any office, place or employment, to or for any voter, or to or for any other person in order to induce such voter to vote, or refrain from voting, or corruptly does any such act as aforesaid, on account of any voter having voted or refrained from voting at any election ;

(3.) Every person who directly or indirectly, by himself or by any other person on his behalf, makes any gift, loan, offer, promise, procurement, or agreement as aforesaid, to or for any person, in order to induce such person to procure or endeavour to procure the return of

---

(*mx*) 37 Vic. c. 9, s. 92. Cap. No. s. 85 of the Act as revised by the Commissioners.

any person to serve in the House of Commons, or the vote of any voter at any election;

(4.) Every person, who, upon or in consequence of any such gift, loan, offer, promise, procurement or agreement procures or engages, or promises or endeavours to procure the return of any person to serve in the House of Commons, or the vote of any voter at any election;

(5.) Every person who advances or pays, or causes to be paid, any money to or for the use of any other person, with the intent that such money or any part thereof shall be expended in bribery, or corrupt practices at any election, or who knowingly pays or causes to be paid, any money to any person in discharge or repayment of any money wholly or in part expended in bribery or corrupt practices at any election;

And any person so offending shall be guilty of a misdemeanor, and shall also be liable to forfeit the sum of two hundred dollars, to any person who shall sue for the same, with full costs of suit (*n*): provided always, that the actual personal expenses of any candidate, his expenses for actual professional services performed, and *bona fide* payments for the fair cost of printing and advertising, shall be held to be expenses lawfully incurred, and the payment thereof shall not be a contravention of this Act.

Bribees. By Section 93 of the same act (*o*), the following persons shall be deemed guilty of bribery, and shall be punishable accordingly:—

(1.) Every voter who, before or during any election, directly or indirectly, himself or by any other person on

(*n*) See chapters on Penalties, *post*. These acts on the part of a candidate or his agent, void his election.

(*o*) See s. 86 of the revised Act.

his behalf, receives, agrees or contracts for any money, gift, loan or valuable consideration, office, place or employment, for himself or any other person, for voting or agreeing to vote, or for refraining or agreeing to refrain from voting at any election ;

(2) Every person who, after any election, directly or indirectly, himself or by any other persons on his behalf, receives any money or valuable consideration for having voted or refrained from voting, or having induced any other person to vote or refrain from voting at any election ;

And any person so offending shall be guilty of a misdemeanor, and shall also be liable to forfeit the sum of two hundred dollars to any person who shall sue for the same, together with full costs of suit *(p)*.

The definitions in the Ontario Act are the same *(q)*. Ontario Act.

Bribery is also an offence at common law *(r)* ; as is also the mere offer of a bribe *(rr)*. Common law offence.

If the money or other consideration be given *before* the vote is given, it is *ipso facto*, bribery, *i.e.*, the presumption will be that it is bribery unless the contrary be shewn ; but if it be given *after* the vote is polled, it must be shewn to have been done "corruptly." "Where the legislature has not introduced the word 'corruptly' *(s)*, and the natural and reasonable inference from the act is that it was an act done for the purpose contemplated, the legislature has treated it as corrupt without mentioning

Before the Election.

After the Election.

(p) See chapter on Penalties, *post*.

(q) Rev. Stats. Ont. c. 10, secs. 149 and 150. The proviso to sec. 149 has however been amended by 42 Vic. c. 4, s. 19, (Ont.)

(r) *The King* v. *Pitt*, 3 Burr. 1,338 ; *Regina, ex rel. McKeon* v. *Hogg*, 15 U. C. R. 140 ; *Regina* v. *Bunting*, 7 Ont. R. 524.

(rr) *Rex* v. *Vaughan*, 4 Burr, 2,500.

(s) As in the first part of subs. 1 of sec. 92, *ante*.

anything more about it; but in those cases (*t*), in which it seems intended that the Court should not infer the purpose simply and solely from the act, it has introduced the word 'corruptly'" (*u*).

Offers.

An *offer* is as bad as the actual payment of money (*v*). The offer will equally amount to bribery, even though the thing offered be of no value (*w*). But the *evidence* to prove an unaccepted offer is required to be stronger and more exact than that required to prove a bribe actually given or accepted (*x*). A statement, however, that an offer to bribe was made in jest will be received with great suspicion. A briber may make an offer, which he intends should be taken seriously, and then, in the event of its not being accepted, shelter himself afterwards with the plea that it was only in jest (*y*). The payment of a legal debt due a voter may be bribery. "It is always open to inquire, under statutes of this nature, whether the debt was simply paid in accordance with the legal obligation to pay it, or whether it was in fact paid or secured in order to induce the elector to vote or refrain from voting" (*z*). Bribery is not confined to

Payment of debt.

(*t*) As in the latter part of subs. 1 of sec. 92, *ante.*

(*u*) *Limerick*, 1 O'M. & H. 262. See also *Stroud*, 2 O'M & H. 184; *Harwich*, 3 O'M. & H. 70; *Cooper* v. *Slade*, 27 L. J. Q. B. 451; 6 H. L. C. 746.

(*v*) *Coventry*, 1 O'M. & H. 107; *Staleybridge*, *Ib.* 66.

(*w*) *Bewdley*, 44 L. T. N. S. 283. The following words by a candidate to an elector at an election:—"*Si tu n'est pas mal à main pour moi je ne le serai pas pour toi,*" were held not to constitute a corrupt offer within the Act, and the words made use of on such occasions should be interpreted, not according to what the party addressed understood by them, but according to what the candidate means, *Robillard* v. *Le Cavalier*, 7 L. R. 662, s. c. 1877, (Que.); see also *N. Victoria*, 1 H. E. C. 252, *Halton*, *Ib.* 736.

(*x*) *Cheltenham*, 1 O'M. & H. 64; *Mallow*, 2 O'M. & H. 22; *Carrickfergus*, 3 O'M. & H. 92; *S. Grey*, 1 H. E. C. 52; *E. Toronto*, 1 H. E. C. 70; *Cimon* v. *Perrault*, 10 L. R., (Que.) 651; *Hebert* v. *Hannington*, 6 All. (N. Br.) 536, and other cases in H. E. C.

(*y*) *N. Middlesex*, 1 H. E. C. 380.

(*z*) *Per* Burton, J. A., in *N. Ontario*, 1 H. E. C. 341; *Cooper* v. *Slade*. 6 H. L. C. 746; *Halton*, 1 H. E. C. 736.

the actual giving of money. Where a grossly inadequate price has been paid for work or for an article, it is clearly bribery (*a*). Paying inadequate price.

An offer to vacate a seat in a Town Council in favor of a voter is an offer to procure an "office" within subs. 2 of sec. 92, *supia* (*b*). Offer of seat in a Council.

Besides *direct* bribery, there are indirect modes of paying or offering money or other valuable consideration, which may be equally held to be bribery. Indirect bribery.

A candidate's appeal to his business as being a benefit generally to the community, or to certain classes of it, or to the employment of his capital in a manner promoting the prosperity of the constituency, if honestly and truly made, is not prohibited (*c*). Nor is a statement by a candidate in a public speech, in reply to a charge by his opponent of having no influence, "that he had had influence to procure more appointments for the electors of the county than any member" (*d*). Appeals to interest.

If gifts and subscriptions for charitable purposes, made by a candidate who is in the habit of subscribing liberally to charitable purposes, are not proved to have been offered or made as an inducement to, or on any condition that, any body of men or any individual should vote or act in any way at an election, or on any express or implied promise, or undertaking that such body of men or individual would, in consequence of such gift or subscription, vote or act in respect to any future election, then such gifts or subscriptions are not a corrupt practice within the meaning of that expression as defined by Charitable gifts

(*a*) *Cornwall*, 1 H. E. C. 547 ; *Cornwall*, (3), 1 H. E. C. 803.

(*b*) *Waterford*, 2 O'M. & H. 25.

(*c*) *Per* Draper, C. J., in *W. Peterboro'*, 1 H. E. C. 277.

(*d*) *Jacques Cartier*, 2 Sup. Ct. 216.

the Elections and Controverted Elections Acts 1874 (*e*). It may be "charity stimulated by gratitude or hope of favours to come" (*f*). But a gift, professedly out of public charity or liberality, even where the person to whom it is paid states that it has no influence so far as he is concerned with regard to the election, may be such bribery as, even although not given in the candidate's presence, but with his knowledge by an agent, to make him personally guilty of a corrupt practice (*g*).

Promise to lay sidewalks.

A promise by a candidate that, if elected, he would lay sidewalks at his own expense in the municipality is a corrupt promise and will avoid an election (*h*).

Colorable employment of Voters.

The employment of voters in and about the election is forbidden by s. 11 subs. (*b*) of the Dominion Franchise Act and sec. 73 of the Dominion Elections Act, the penalty being the disqualification of such persons from voting (*i*). To make the offence a corrupt practice, however, sufficient to avoid the election, it is necessary to show that the employment is *colorable*—in other words, that it amounts to bribery. Formerly the practice prevailed in England of employing on behalf of a candidate large numbers of persons termed "watchers" *i.e.*, persons (voters) to watch the polls, the excuse being that breaches of the peace or other troubles were feared, and it was necessary to thus provide against such contingencies—"to pay men for what is called watching, but in reality doing nothing" (*j*). The colorable employ-

"Watchers."

(*e*) *S. Ontario*, 3 Sup. Ct. 641.

(*f*) *Per* Willes, J., in *Westbury case*, 1 O'M. & H. 47; and see *Windsor*, 2 O'M. & H. 90; but see *Stafford*, 1 O'M. & H. 230; *S. Huron*, 24 U. C. C. P. 488; *Mallow*, 2 O'M. &. H. 22; *Northallerton*, 1 O'M. & H. 173; *Belfast*, *Ib.* 282.

(*g*) *Megantic*, 9 Sup. Ct. 279.

(*h*) *Robert* v. *Bertrand*, 2 L. N. 198, S. C. R. 1879 (Que.).

(*i*) The Ontario law is similar; see Rev. Stats. Ont., c. 10, s. 5; 41 Vic. (Ont.), c. 21, s. 3, subs. 4.

(*j*) *Bewdley*, 1 O'M. & H. 20.

ment of voters in this way, whether to secure their votes or to prevent their voting for the opposite party was held to be a corrupt practice (*k*); and the same rule applies in Canada (*l*). Whether the employment was colorable or not is a question of fact, and the number of persons employed, the proportion of those persons who were voters, the class and amount of work done, and the amount of payment in proportion thereto, are circumstances to be considered in relation thereto, (*m*). The Election Act, it may be remarked, makes full provision for the preservation of order at Elections by the returning officer, who should be applied to in case trouble is anticipated (*n*), and the Ontario Act does the same (*o*).

Canvassers and orators. The question of the effect of the employment of canvassers and speakers upon an election is a very important one for the candidate, and unfortunately the law cannot be said to be in a satisfactory condition of certainty upon the point, so far, at all events, as Dominion elections are concerned. Under an Act of the Quebec Legislature, similar to the Dominion Act, it was held by the Quebec Courts that the employment and payment *bona fide* of an elector as canvasser was not a corrupt practice (*p*). **Quebec law.** The Quebec Legislature promptly met this, by an amendment of their Act, making the payment of canvassers a corrupt practice (*q*). No such amendment has however been made to the Dominion or Ontario Acts, but it has been established in several

(*k*) *Bewdley*, 1 O'M. & H. 20, also *Nottingham*, 1 O'M. & H. 246; *Boston*, 3 O'M. & H. 151; *Oxford*, 3 O'M. &. H. 155; *Salisbury*, 3 O'M. & H. 134; *Salisbury*, 4 O'M. & H. 22.

(*l*) *Charlevoix case*, 5 Sup. Ct. 133.

(*m*) See also *Durham*, 2 O'M. & H. 137.

(*n*) See 37 Vic., c. 9, s. 81, *et seq.*; see also *Charlevoix case*, 5 Sup. Ct. 133.

(*o*) Rev. Stats. Ont., c. 10, s. 135 *et seq.*

(*p*) *Quebec East case*, 1 Q. L. R. 295; *Gingras* v. *Sheyn*, 1 Q. L. R. 205.

(*q*) 39 Vic. c. 13, s. 19, Que.

Ontario provincial cases that the *bona fide* employment of canvassers and persons to distribute cards and placards is not illegal (*r*); and Cameron, C. J., in a recent case states that he can see no distinction between the employment of an orator or public speaker, so called, and a canvasser (*s*). As the Ontario Court of Appeal, the court of final resort in regard to Ontario Provincial cases, has come to a decision upon the subject (*t*), it may be considered that the law, at all events as regards the employment of canvassers, is settled, so far as elections for the Ontario Legislature are concerned. The law with regard to Dominion Elections must however be referred to.

Ontario law.

North Ontario case. Armour, J.

Mr. Justice Armour in the *North Ontario (Dominion Election) Case* (*u*) held that the payment of canvassers and orators was within subsection 3 of section 92 of the Elections Act, which declares that "every person who directly or indirectly, by himself or by any other person on his behalf makes any gift, loan, offer, promise, procurement, or agreement as aforesaid, to or for any person, in order to induce such person to procure or endeavour to procure the return of any person to serve in the House of Commons, or the vote of any voter at any election is to be deemed guilty of bribery"; and that such payment was not covered by the proviso at the end of the section, which provides "that the actual personal expenses of any

(*r*) *E. Toronto*, 1 H. E. C. 70; *W. Toronto*, 1 H. E. C. 97; *Lennox*, 2 Ont. El. Cases, 41.

(*s*) *Lennox*, 2 Ont. El. Cases, p. 69. It is evident that Cameron, C. J., was in error when he stated, (p. 68) that the majority of the Judges of the Supreme Court, who gave judgment in the *N. Ontario* case, decided in favor of the legality of paying canvassers, as will presently appear, though that may be the ultimate decision of the Court, when the matter comes squarely before them.

(*t*) *Ibid.*

(*u*) 1 H. E. C. 785.

candidate, his expenses for actual professional services performed, and *bona fide* payments for the fair cost of printing and advertising, shall be held to be expenses lawfully incurred, and the payment thereof shall not be a contravention of this Act (*v*)." The learned judge held that the English authorities, in favor of the legality of such payment (*w*), were inapplicable to this country, the proviso in the English Act being wider than that in our Act, the English proviso as contained in the C.P.P. Act, 1854 being "Provided always, that the aforesaid enactment shall not extend to or be construed to extend to any money paid or agreed to be paid for or on account of any legal expenses *bona fide* incurred at or concerning any election." The learned judge therefore came to the conclusion that the hiring of canvassers and orators was, *per se*, bribery (*x*).

The *North Ontario* case was carried to the Supreme Court, but though the decision of Armour J. was reversed, the judgment of the majority of the judges of the Supreme Court did not turn altogether upon the questions of law involved in it, though the opinions of some of the individual judges were given. Sir William *Supreme Court.*

(*v*) By sec. 125 the words "personal expenses" are interpreted to include "the reasonable travelling expenses of such candidate, and the reasonable expenses of his living at hotels, or elsewhere, for the purpose of and in relation to such election." The proviso in the Ontario Act was formerly the same as that in the text, but it was widened immediately after the decision of Armour, J., by 42 Vic. c. 4, s. 19, (Ont.).

(*w*) See *Coventry*, 1 O'M. & H. 101; *Tamworth*, 1 O'M. & H. 109, and earlier cases therein cited. The decision of Armour, J., appears contrary to the conclusions arrived at by Richards, C. J., in *West Toronto*, 1 H. E. C. 108.

(*x*) The learned Judge says, (H. E. C. p. 801). "It may be that this proviso in our Act does not cover every expenditure that may legally be made, but if any expenditure made outside of that permitted by the proviso should happen to be covered by the express words of the clauses relating to bribery, such expenditure will inevitably amount to bribery," and the hiring of canvassers and orators being, in his opinion, outside of what is permitted by the proviso, and within the very words of subs. 3, he held it bribery.

Ritchie, C. J. Ritchie, C. J., said (*y*) he would not discuss "whether or not, under the law as it now is, candidates may, or may not legally employ and pay for the expenses and services of canvassers and orators to place their views and the views of their party before the electors individually or collectively at public meetings, with a view of influencing the constituency in favour of a particular candidate, or of inducing the public to look favorably on any particular policy either of the great parties in the country may be upholding." As he held that, in the case under consideration, the candidate had merely promised to pay the expenses of the speaker *conditionally on its proving to be legal to do so*, and had after the election declined to pay such expens s, and was therefore not within the section—he deemed it unnecessary to consider the broad *Henry, J.* legal question. Mr. Justice Henry arrived at the same conclusion on the facts and said (p. 484) "Taking this view of the evidence it is unnecessary to give any opinion as to the legal bearing of the question, whether it would be against the provision of the subsection mentioned if a candidate *bona fide* agreed to pay the travelling expenses of one of his supporters to address meetings on his behalf. If, however, it be done to procure the support or influence of a party or his friends, it *Fournier, J.* would no doubt be within it." Mr. Justice Fournier quotes with approval the language of Mr. Justice Willes in the *Coventry* case (*z*), and that of Chief Justice Meredith in the case of *Gingras v Sheyn*, (*a*) and thinks that s. 73 shews that the legitimate expenditure of a candidate is not restricted to those expenses mentioned in the proviso to s. 92—the only penalty for other

(*y*) 4 Sup. Ct. p. 463.
(*z*) 1 O'M. & H. 101.
(*a*) 1 Q. L. R. 205.

expenditure of the class under consideration being, in case of the employee being a voter, the loss of his vote. He moreover seems to consider the "professional services" of an advocate embrace services as an election orator; and that both canvassers and orators may legally be employed by the candidate. The fact that the Dominion Election Law remains the same as was the law of Quebec when the *Quebec East case* (*b*) was decided, makes applicable, in the opinion of the learned judge, the judgment of Chief Justice Meredith (*c*). Judge Fournier arrives at the conclusion that the promise to pay his personal expenses to the voter, in the case before him, for assisting at public meetings, in the discussion of public questions, as a political speaker, was not illegal within the statute. Mr. Justice Taschereau, on the other hand, says "I am of opinion, with Mr. Justice Armour, who presided at the trial in this cause, that the hiring of electors as orators and canvassers is within the very words of sub. sec. 3 of sec. 92 of the Election Act, and is therefore bribery." Touching the question on which the judgments of the Chief Justice and Henry J. were based, namely, the statement of the candidate that his promise was conditional upon the payment being legal, he says, "whether he thought it to be so or not does not make any difference. Corrupt practices in elections would easily be committed with impunity if courts of justice required their perpetrators to acknowledge under oath that they have acted with the intention to violate the law, before finding them guilty." Regarding the Quebec decisions, the same learned judge says, *Taschereau, J.*

(*b*) 1 Q. L. R. 295.

(*c*) He also quotes the judgment in *Benoit et al.* v. *Jodoin* 19 L. C. Jur. 185, to shew that the Quebec Court considered the *bona fide* payment of expenses of orators as legitimate.

"The *Quebec East* election has been referred to as holding that the payment of canvassers is not a corrupt practice, under a statute similar to the one which rules this case. It is true, that it was so held in the case referred to, but what clearly shows that this decision was entirely opposed to the intentions of the legislature by which it was enacted is, that a few weeks after this decision they passed a special enactment, by which it was expressly ordered that the payment of canvassers shall be corrupt practices; and this, no doubt, to meet the point decided in the *Quebec East* election." Mr. Justice Gwynne, after commenting upon the facts, says (*d*), "the secrecy attending the whole transaction and the evidence generally in my opinion, warrant the conclusion that notwithstanding that H. may have expressed to the appellant his opinion that payment for such services was legal, the appellant himself entertained grave doubts as to the correctness of this opinion; but however this may be, the appellant's belief in the correctness of the opinion will not exempt him from responsibility; if the opinion be not sound and the act be declared by law to be bribery and corruption." He further considers that the judgment of Armour J. is not at variance with the English decisions which hold that the *bona fide* employment of persons as canvassers to ascertain the votes of the constituency, although, in the course of their employment, they had to recommend the candidate employing them, is not within the act; "for," says his lordship, "there is a great difference between the case of a person being employed to ascertain how the voters would vote, being paid for that service, as the *bona fide* consideration for that payment, although the

Gwynne, J.

(*d*) At p. 490.

persons so employed should recommend the voters to vote for their employer, and the case of a person being employed for the express purpose of inducing, persuading and endeavouring to procure the voters to vote for his employer upon a promise of payment to be made o the person so employed for such services. If, under the guise of employment as ordinary canvassers, persons are in fact employed and paid, or promised payment, for rendering services, such as H. was employed to render here, I see no reason why the person so employing them and paying or promising payment, for such services should not (within the express provisions of the act) be deemed guilty of bribery. It would be a mockery of justice and a reproach upon common sense to hold the promise of payment, to a poor voter, of his expenses in coming to the poll to record his vote (otherwise perhaps conscientiously given), to be bribery, and the promise of payment to the witness of his expenses, in consideration of his going through the electoral division using all his influence, by the exercise of his persuasive and oratorical powers, and of his local and professional influence, to procure the return of the appellant, not to be. Indeed, as was pointed out by the learned judge in his judgment, bribery of influence is more extensive, more effectual and more pernicious than the bribery of a voter merely to give his vote. It is difficult to conceive any conduct more odious and corrupt than that of the advocate who, by his oratorical powers, and the extent of his acquaintance with the electors which the practice of his profession among them had given him, while concealing the fact that his praise and his advocacy was purchased, should, under the assumed character of an independent elector disinterestedly and conscientiously in the public

Bribery of influence.

interest supporting a particular candidate, exert his influence by persuading his fellow electors to vote for the man whom, in truth, he was serving under a contract of hiring. But the letter of the Act is clear and we have no right to cripple the Act by depriving this section (subs. 3) of the smallest particle of its literal force and effect. Parliament has deemed it necessary to enact this peremptory provison, in order to secure the utmost purity in the election of members to serve in parliament, and to make them in reality, as in name, the freely chosen representatives of an independent people. And, undoubtedly, the promise to pay H. even his expenses attending his rendering the services which the appellant admits he agreed to render, does come within the letter of the clause, unless it comes within the protection of the proviso," which the learned Judge then quotes, adding, " Now, that services of this nature should not be held to come within the term 'actual professional services,' the honor of the profession and electoral purity, which it was the express object of this Act to secure, alike require." Such were the views of Mr. Justice Gwynne as declared in his judgement. Mr. Justice Strong, the only other member of the Court, was not present when the case was argued, nor when judgment was delivered.

The very great importance to candidates of the questions discussed, is the only excuse offered for reviewing at such length, in a work such as this, the judgments of the individual Judges of the Supreme Court. It is unfortunate that no more definite result can be arrived at as to the state of the law upon the important subject of the legality or illegality of employing or paying the expenses of speakers and canvassers, than a consideration of this case yields. Until a decision is arrived at, and so long as the statute remains unaltered, there can be no certainty upon these points as regards elections for the House of Commons.

From the *North Ontario* case, the candidate is, however, safe in arriving at this conclusion—that the *colorable* (in other words *corrupt*) employment of voters, either as speakers or canvassers is a corrupt practice, a result previously involved in the English decisions.

As to whether even the personal expenses of a speaker or canvasser may be promised *bona fide* to be paid, without the risk of avoiding the election being incurred, the judgments do not afford sufficient *data* from which to hazard a decided opinion; though the words of the statute, that the promise must be made *in order to induce* the person to endeavor to procure the return, &c., to constitute bribery under subs. 3, would seem to warrant the exclusion of promises which would not and are not intended to form any *inducement*. The promise of payment of actual and reasonable personal disbursements of a speaker or canvasser when engaged in the campaign could hardly, it is submitted, be regarded as an *inducement* held out to him to endeavor to procure the return of a candidate, though the payment thereof is not covered by the proviso any more than are the rent of halls and other reasonable payments, which have, however, been generally regarded as legitimate. Some further indication of the opinion of the Court is afforded by the *Berthier case* (e) in which Sir William Ritchie, C. J., *Berthier case.* says (p. 120), "As to the *Chalut* case, I think this was nothing more than a *bona fide* payment of the expenses of *Chalut*, and was neither colorable nor corrupt." While

(e) 9 Sup. Ct. 102.

Strong, J., says (p. 129), "The conduct of the respondent and his agents in this (*Chalut's*) case seems to me entirely free from any taint of illegality. Mr. *Chalut* was a warm supporter of the respondent, and the chairman of his principal committee. He was asked to go to a parish at some distance to canvass and make arrangements for the election, and $20 were sent him by the respondent for his expenses, and $5 by Mr. *Tranchemontagne*, a member of the committee. I can see no objection to this. The money was not an unreasonable indemnity for the expenses and the loss of time of a professional man—a notary—for some four days. It is not and could not have been pretended that it was a colorable payment, cloaking a bribe, and I know of no law which prohibits the *bona fide* employment of electors for lawful purposes incidental to the election. The case was rightly dismissed by the Court below." Mr. Justice Gwynne says, regarding the *Chalut* case, "There cannot be entertained a doubt that the money given to this gentleman, who was president of the respondent's committee, and one of the most zealous of his supporters, was given by way of remuneration for his travelling expenses to an outer part of the electoral division, and his services as a lawyer in organizing a canvass upon behalf of the respondent in such part of the division; a purpose in itself quite legal and proper. There is no pretence of anything illegal having been done by Mr. *Chalut* in pursuance of the commission entrusted to him; if there had been, the charge would have been presented in a different shape, but that it was given, as charged, for the purpose of corrupting Mr. *Chalut* there does not appear to be any foundation whatever, nor, therefore, any for calling in question the finding of the learned Judges upon this charge."

It is to be observed that the question of the employment of non-voters, whether resident within or outside the constituency, is not, in these cases, discussed. The promise made to "*any person* in order to induce such person to endeavor to procure the return," &c., being within the wording of the Act, it would seem to follow that the employment of such a person would be illegal, if that of a voter is. The "bribery of influence" as defined by Armour, J., may, it is presumed, be as effectively practised by the employment of an influential outsider, as by the engagement of an uninfluential elector in the constituency. In the *Berthier case* mention is made of a "*paid agent*, not a voter, having no connection with the election or with the respondent beyond this, that he was brought from Montreal and employed to make a speech on the Sunday after mass at the church door at *St. Damien*" (*f*). No question seems, however, to have been raised as to the legality of the employment of this person, the sole question apparently being as to whether he was an agent for whose acts the candidate would be responsible. It is worthy of notice, however, that no remark fell from the learned Judges respecting the legality or illegality of his employment.

Employment of non-voters as orators and canvassers.

With regard to the point upon which the judgment of the Supreme Court really turned in the *North Ontario* case, namely, as to the precise nature of the promise made by the candidate, a word may be said. The majority of the Court would seem to have arrived at the conclusion that to promise to pay a voter such expenses as might be afterwards ascertained to be *legal* would not be within the mischief of the Act. To make promises

Conditional promises; to be avoided.

(*f*) *Berthier*, 9 Sup. Ct. *per* Strong, J., p. 131.

of this description, however, whether in feigned or real ignorance of the law, should be avoided by candidates (*g*).

Betting and supplying money for betting.

Inducing an elector to bet in favor of a candidate for whom the other party to the wager desires to obtain his vote or influence, in order to obtain such vote or influence, has been held to be bribery, and, when practised by an agent of the candidate, to avoid the election of such candidate, as has also a similar device to induce the voter to refrain from voting against the candidate by inducing him to bet that he will not vote—even in a case where the agent denied any corrupt intent and the voter stated that he had formed the resolution not to vote before he made the bet (*h*). Similarly the procuring a man's vote or influence for a candidate by supplying him with money with which to bet in favor of such candidate, the profits on such betting to be divided with or retained by the person to whom the money is supplied, is a corrupt practice—and one of a far-reaching character (*i*). By the Ontario Statute 47 Vic., c. 4, s. 3, which will be found on a subsequent page, the principles enunciated as above have been put in the form of a legislative enactment, as regards the Ontario Provincial Elections.

Payment of taxes of voter.

The advancing money to income voters, to pay their taxes, when the payment of such taxes was essential to entitle them to vote, has been held to be bribery (*j*). Under the Ontario Franchise and Representation Act,

---

(*g*) See Rev. Stats. Ont, c. 10, s. 162, referred to *post*, under "Corrupt practices under Ontario Acts," as amended by 47 Vic., c. 4, s. 48; and 48 Vic., c. 2, s. 18 (Ont.).

(*h*) *West Northumberland*, 2 Ont. El. Cases, 32, reversed on appeal by Supreme Court, 10 Sup. Ct. 635, the latter Court holding in effect, such offence to be *per se* bribery. See also *West Middlesex* (1) *Provincial Election case*, 1883; *Herbert* v. *Hannington*, 6 All. (N. Br.) 530.

(*i*) *Lincoln* (2), 1 H. E. C. 489; *South Norfolk*, 1 H. E. C. 660.

(*j*) *Lincoln* (2), 1 H. E. C. 489.

1885, however, it is no longer necessary that an income voter shall have paid his taxes to entitle him to vote (*k*).

Payment for loss of time.

Payment of voters for loss of time is also another form of indirect bribery (*l*). And it has in England been held to be bribery where an employer gives a holiday to his workmen on the polling day, paying their wages as usual (*m*).

Employing relations of voter, etc.

Evasions of the Act, such as employing the relations of electors on unreasonable terms, or for mere nominal duties, giving money or presents to the wives or children of voters, &c., will also amount to bribery (*n*).

General bribery.

Where bribery is practised to such an extent that the corruption is general, the election will be void at common law, even where no agency is proved (*o*).

Time when act committed immaterial.

It is immaterial at what period the gift or offer was made. "Much stress was laid upon the time of revision, as if for a moment the idea seemed to pervade the minds of some parties that bribery is less bribery because it was committed two months or two years before an election. Any act committed previous to an election, no matter at what distance of time, with a view to influence a voter at the coming election, whether it is one, two or three years before, is just as much bribery as if it was committed the day before the election, or the day of the election; nay, more, if a man commits bribery on the first week of a parliament, and if he sues for the suffrages of that constituency in the last week of the seven years

(*k*) Ont. Act, 48 Vic., c. 2, s. 4.

(*l*) *Taunton*, Judgments 353; 1 O'M. & H. 183; *Staleybridge*, 1 O'M. & H. 67; *Simpson* v. *Yeend*, 4 L. R. Q. B. 626; 38 L. J. Q. B. 313; 21 L. T. 56.

(*m*) *Gravesend*, 44 L. T. N. S. 64; 3 O'M. & H. 84.

(*n*) *Cheltenham*, Judgments, 51; *Halton*, 1 H. E. C. 283.

(*o*) *Lichfield*, 1 O'M. & H. 26; *Beverly*, *Ib.*, 147; *Stafford Ib.*, 234; *Drogheda*, *Ib.*, 257; *Guildford*, *Ib.*, 15; *Bridgewater*, *Ib.*, 115.

which precede the dissolution, that act committed six years before can be given in evidence against him, and his seat will not hold an hour" (*p*).

TREATING.

Definition. By the Dominion Elections Act, 1874, s. 94 (*q*), every candidate who corruptly, by himself or by or with any person, or by any other ways or means on his behalf, at any time either before or during any election, directly or indirectly gives or provides, or causes to be given or provided, or is accessory to the giving or providing, or pays wholly or in part any expenses incurred for any meat, drink, refreshment or provision to or for any person, in order to be elected or for being elected, or for the purpose of corruptly influencing such person or any other person to give or refrain from giving his vote at such election, shall be deemed guilty of the offence of treating, and shall forfeit the sum of two hundred dollars to any person who shall sue for the same, with full costs of suit, in addition to any other penalty to which he may be liable therefor under any other provision of this Act: and on the trial of an Election Petition, there shall be struck off from the number of votes given to such candidate, one vote for every person who shall have voted and is proved on such trial to have corruptly accepted or taken any such meat, drink, refreshment or provision: And the giving or causing to be given to any voter on the nomination day or day of polling on account of such voter having voted or being about to vote, any meat, drink or refreshment, or any money or ticket to enable such voter to procure refreshment, shall be deemed an

(*p*) *Sligo*, judgments, 144; 1 O'M. & H. 302.

(*q*) See chapter *Na*. sec. 87 of Statutes as revised by commissioners.

unlawful act, and the person so offending shall forfeit the sum of ten dollars for each offence to any person suing for the same, with full costs of suit.

By section 98, Treating (defined in the first part of the above section), or any *wilful* offence against the latter part of the section are declared "corrupt practices." A corrupt practice.

Though section 2 subsection 6 of the Ontario Controverted Elections Act (r) makes "Treating" as defined by that or any act of the Legislature of the Province or by common law, a "corrupt practice," singularly enough the offence of treating, *eo nomine*, is not defined by that Act nor by the Ontario Election Act, but sections 152 and 153 of the latter Act declare the offences defined by section 94 of the Dominion Act (as above), in almost identical language, to be "corrupt practices," and it seems to have been assumed in most cases under the Provincial Acts that these offences were within the definition of corrupt practices contained in the Controverted Elections Act, and therefore sufficient to void an election (s). The Ontario Act

The use of the word "candidate" does not confine the operation of the section to acts done after the dissolution (t). "Candidate."

To avoid the election the treating must have been done *corruptly* (u)—"'corruptly' means an act done by Must be done with corrupt intent.

(r) Rev. Stats. Ont., c. 11.

(s) The omission is pointed out by Osler, J. A., in the *N. Ontario* (Prov'l.) case, 2 Ont. El. cases p. 17; and by Patterson, J. A., in the *W. Simcoe* case, (1883) not yet reported, in which latter case it was held that the offence defined in s. 153 was not covered by a general charge in the petition of Corrupt Practices under the "*Controverted Elections Act.*" Further and more important differences between the Dominion and Ontario Acts are pointed out further on.

(t) *Youghal case*, 1 O'M. & H. 293.

(u) *Jacques Cartier*, 2 Sup. Ct. 245.

a man knowing that he is doing what is wrong, and doing it with an evil object." (*v*).

Nomination or polling day.

The giving of meat, drink or refreshment on nomination or polling day, under the latter part of section 94, must, in order to affect the election, be coupled in some manner with "such voter having voted or being about to vote" (*w*) and must under the Dominion Act be a "wilful" (*x*) offence, and though the word "wilful" does not appear in sec. 153 of the Ontario Act (*y*) the effect is the same (*z*).

Amount of treating not material.

The *amount* of the treating is not material, if it be done for the purpose of influencing voters (*a*).

Treating in compliance with custom.

Treating, when done in compliance with a custom prevalent in the country and without any corrupt intent, will not avoid an election; though one glass of liquor given with a view of influencing a vote will avoid the election (*b*). The general practice which prevails here of persons drinking in a friendly way when they meet would require strong evidence of a profuse expenditure of money in drinking to induce a judge to say that it was corruptly done, so as to make it bribery or treating at common law (*c*).

(*v*) *Bradford*, 1 O'M. & H, 37 ; *Tamworth*, *Ib.* 83 ; *N. Norfolk*, *Ib.* 242 ; *Coventry*, *Ib.* 106 ; *Bodmin*, *Ib.* 125 ; *Glengarry*, 1 H. E. C. 8 ; *N. Middlesex*, 1 H. E. C. 376 ; *N. Ontario*, 1 H. E. C. 786 ; *S. Norfolk*, 1 H. E. C. 660.

(*w*) Per Richards, C. J., in *Jacques Cartier*, 2 Sup. Ct. 242 and 245 ; per Meredith, C. J., in *Portneuf*, 2 Q. L. R. 268 ; Blake, V. C., in *East Elgin*, 1 H. E. C. 769 ; *N. Victoria* (2) 1 H. E. C. 703 ; 37 U. C. Q. B., Richards, C. J., p. 244.

(*x*) See however, as to meaning of "wilful," *Selkirk*, 4 Sup. Ct. 494.

(*y*) Rev. Stats. Ont., c. 10.

(*z*) *Lennox*, 2 Ont. El., C. 41.

(*a*) *Hebert* v. *Hannington*, 6 All. (N. Br.) 530.

(*b*) Per Strong, V. C., in *Welland*, 1 H. E. C. 47 ; but see Rev. Stats. Ont., c. 10, s. 162.

(*c*) Per Richards, C. J., in *Kingston*, 1 H. E. C. 625 ; *N. Ontario*, 2 Ont. El. Cases 1 ; but see remarks of Richards, C. J., in *Jacques Cartier*, 2 Sup. Ct. 247.

As the offence of treaitng is one of *intent*, a distinction has been made in favor of a candidate whose occupation and habit at all times led him to treat at taverns and who treated to a less extent during his canvass than was his habit, and not apparently for the purpose of ingratiating himself with the electors (*d*). The same distinction has been drawn in favor of an agent, who had been a candidate for various offices for twenty years prior to the election in question, and had freely employed treating as an element in his canvassing, and had become an agent of the respondent, and treated extensively, as was his common practice during the election (*e*). In both of the cases referred to the treating was held not a corrupt practice, though the same amount of treating, if practised by one not theretofore given to the practice, would have been sufficient to have avoided the election (*f*). If, however; the evidence leads to the conclusion that the candidate treats indiscriminately in order to make for himself a reputation for good fellowship and hospitality, and thereby to influence voters to vote for him, it would, according to the opinion of Spragge, C., as expressed in the North Middlesex case (*g*), be considered a species of bribery which would avoid the election. Blackburn, C. J., said (*h*), "I think, however, the intention by such means to gain popularity and thereby to affect the election, or even if the case is, as very often perhaps it is, that persons are afraid that if they do not provide entertainment and drink to secure the strong

Ordinary habit of person treating, will be considered to show absence of corrupt intent.

Indiscriminate treating.

(*d*) *North Middlesex*, 1 H. E. C. 376.

(*e*) *East Elgin*, 1 H. E. C. 769.

(*f*) *Ibid.*

(*g*) *North Middlesex*, 1 H. E. C. 376.

(*h*) *Wallingford*, 1 O'M. & H. 58, quoted in *Mallow*, 2 O'M. & H. 22, and in *N. Middlesex*, 1 H. E. C. 376; but see as to such treating by an agent, *E. Toronto*, 1 H. E. C. 90-91.

interest of the publicans and of the persons who take drink whenever they can get it for nothing (who are always a numerous body) they will become unpopular, and they therefore provide it in order to affect the election, when there is an intention in the mind either of the candidate or his agent to produce that effect, then I think that it is corrupt treating, and the seat ought to be considered vacated."

Giving meals on polling day,

Though the giving of free dinners to electors who had come a long distance in severe winter weather, in the absence of evidence that it was done for the purpose of influencing the election, either by their voting or not voting or because they had voted, has been held not to entitle the petitioner to have the votes of such as voted for the respondent struck off under the first part of section 94, it does not necessarily follow that such an act might not be held a corrupt practice sufficient to void the election under the latter part of the section and of section 98 (*i*). The systematic giving of meals to electors without some such excuse as was afforded in the *North Victoria* case would indicate that the act was done *wilfully* and *corruptly* and would avoid the election (*j*).

to be avoided.

Sufficient has been said to show that the giving of meals or other refreshments to voters on nomination or polling day is to be avoided. Indeed it is well to avoid treating during the contest altogether (*k*).

After the Election.

If meat and drink be given *after* the election, it must be connected with something done before the election to make it corrupt treating. "The treating which the Act calls corrupt as regards a bygone election, must be con-

(*i*) *N. Victoria*, (2) 1 H. E. C. 671 ; 37 U. C. Q. B. 244 ; Richards, C. J., in *Jacques Cartier*, 2 Sup. Ct. 242.

(*j*) *York County W. Riding*, (*Southern Div.*) 1 O'M. & H. 215.

(*k*) Remarks of Richards, C. J., in *Jacques Cartier*, 2 Sup. Ct. p. 247.

nected with something which preceded the election—must be the complement of something done or existing before, calculated to influence the voter while the vote lies in his power: an invitation given before to an entertainment to take place afterwards, or even a promise to invite, or a practice of giving entertainments after an election which it may be supposed the voters would calculate on if followed up by the treat afterwards, give it the character of corrupt treating" (*l*).

The offence of treating under the first part of section 94 (*m*) is not confined to the giving of refreshments to electors, the words being "any person." The treating of non-electors may be illegal and corrupt just as much as the treating of voters (*n*). Women may be the subject of treating, with a view to their influencing the votes of their fathers, brothers, sweethearts, etc (*o*). **Treating not confined to electors.**

Where refreshments are supplied in such quantities as to produce general corruption of the constituency, this general treating will render the election void at common law, even if no agency be proved (*p*). **General treating.**

Treating meetings of Electors under Ontario Law.

There are two offences declared to be corrupt practices under the Ontario Acts not declared to be so by the Dominion Act (*qq*). One of them is that defined by section 151 of the Election Act of Ontario (*q*), which is as follows:

(*l*) Per Lush, J., *Brecon*, 2 O'M. & H. 45, approved of by Grove, J., *Poole*, 2 O'M. & H. 125; see also *Harwich*, 3 O'M. & H. 71.

(*m*) 37 Vic. c. 9, s. 94.

(*n*) *Longford*, 2 O'M. & H. 15; *Bewdley*, 1 O'M. & H. 19, 58 and 59.

(*o*) *Tamworth*, 1 O'M. & H. 86.

(*p*) *Ibid*, 15.

(*q*) Rev. Stats. Ont., c. 10.

(*qq*) Somewhat similar provisions are contained in secs. 87 and 91 of the Dom. Elections Act, but they are not declared to be corrupt practices.

Offence defined.

"No candidate for the representation of any Electoral District shall, nor shall any other person, either provide or furnish drink or other entertainment at the expense of such candidate or other person to any meeting of electors assembled for the purpose of promoting the election previous to, or during such election, or pay or promise or engage to pay for any such drink or other entertainment, except only that nothing herein contained shall extend to any entertainment furnished to any such meeting of electors by or at the expense of any person or persons at his, her or their usual place of residence.

Penalty.

2. Every person offending against the provisions of this section shall incur a penalty of one hundred dollars."

A corrupt practice.

By section 2 subsection 6 of the Controverted Elections Act of Ontario (*r*), any violation of the above section is made a corrupt practice.

Not a question of intent.

As this section stood prior to 1873, it contained the words, "with intent to promote his election," and "with intent to promote the election of any such candidate" (*s*). These words were struck out and the clause re-enacted as it now stands in 1873. This change did away with the necessity of showing a corrupt intent, and a violation of the section being now, by section 2 subsection 6 of Revised Statutes, cap. 11, made a corrupt practice, it follows that the violation of the section is complete without any evidence of intent (*ss*). The offence, if not committed by the candidate, must be shown to have been committed by an *agent* in order to affect the election under section 158 of the Election Act (*t*).

(*r*) Rev. Stat. Ont. c. 11.

(*s*) See Act of 1868.

(*ss*) Though to disqualify candidate such intent must be shewn ; see 48 Vic. c. 2, s. 18, *post*.

(*t*) *N. Victoria*, 1 H. E. C. 252 ; *Halton*, 1 H. E. C. 283 ; *N. Ontario*, 1 H. E. C. in appeal, p. 343 ; *W. Wellington*, 1 H. E. C. 231 ; *E. Middlesex*, 1883, not yet reported.

By a recent decision of the Court of Appeal (*u*) it has been finally decided that committee meetings, as well as public meetings, are within the section. The treating of persons casually met at a tavern, however, is not a meeting of electors under the section (*v*). Committee meetings.

The meeting of electors for the nomination of candidates is a "meeting assembled for the purpose of promoting the election"; though where, after the business for which the electors had assembled was over, the electors left the building in which the meeting was held and dispersed to various taverns, at which their vehicles had been put up, and then before leaving for home treated each other; and at one of the taverns the respondent himself partook of a treat, this was held not to be a violation of section 151 (*w*). But where an agent of a respondent, on the day of nomination, while the speaking was going on, treated a large number of persons at a tavern across the street from the place of nomination, for which he paid $7 or $8, it was held a treating of a meeting of electors to promote the election, and although the agent was not actuated by any corrupt motives in giving the treat, the act was held to be one which came within the meaning of the statute as a corrupt practice (*x*). A similar decision was given where an agent, after a public meeting went with a number of electors from the place of meeting to a tavern and there treated many times, as did also a supporter of the opposing candidate (*y*); though where such a meeting had dispersed an hour before, a treat by a candidate to a number of the electors at a neighbouring tavern was Nomination meetings

(*u*) *East Middlesex Provincial Election 1883*, not yet reported.

(*v*) *London*, 1 H. E. C. 214; *Dundas*, *Ib.* 205: *N. Ontario*, 2 Ont. El. C. 1.

(*w*) *N. Middlesex*, 1 H. E. C. 376.

(*x*) *Dundas*, 1 H. E. C. 205.

(*y*) *E. Peterboro'*, 1 H. E C. 245.

Candidate treating meeting.

held not within the Act (*z*). Where a candidate was found to have violated the section, though ignorant of the legal effect of the Act, he was held not to come within the provisions of the saving section 162, in that he did not come within the other provisions of that section, and was disqualified (*a*).

Selling or giving liquor on polling day under Ontario Law.

Offence defined.

By Section 157 of "The Election Act of Ontario" (*b*), "no spirituous or fermented liquors or strong drink shall be sold or given at any hotel, tavern, shop or other place within the limits of the polling subdivision, during the polling day therein or any part thereof, under a penalty of one hundred dollars for every offence; and the offender shall be subject to imprisonment not exceeding six months at the discretion of the Judge or Court, in default of payment of such fine."

A corrupt practice.

By section 2, subsection 6 of The Controverted Elections Act (*c*) any violation of the above section during the hours of polling is made a corrupt practice.

This is the second of the two treating offences above referred to as being made corrupt practices by the Ontario but not by the Dominion law (*d*).

Nature of treat.

The nature of the treat, as for instance where made in a bar-room the evidence shewing that decanters were put

(*z*) *Dundas*, 1 H. E. C, 245.

(*a*) *Muskoka Provincial Election, 1883*, not yet reported—but see 48 Vic., c. 2, s. 18 *post*.

(*b*) Rev. Stats. Ont., cap. 10.

(*c*) Rev. Stats. Ont., c. 11.

(*d*) Sec. 91 of 37 Vic., c. 9, makes the same thing an offence punishable by fine and imprisonment, but it is not made a corrupt practice by that or any other Dominion Act.

down, may be in itself sufficient to raise a presumption that the treat was of spirituous liquors (*e*).

Four conclusions have been arrived at by the Court of Appeal with regard to the above section (157): **Conclusions of Court of Appeal on s. 157.**

1. That the words "or other place" in the section apply only to places "*ejusdem generis*" with those specified in the section (e.g. saloons, etc.), and that giving liquor in a blacksmith shop does not come within the section (*f*) nor constitute corrupt practice, unless done with a corrupt intent, or unless it is in some way connected with the voter's "being about to vote or having voted" (*g*). **Offence confined to hotels, etc.**

2. That the penalty contained in the section applies only to the keeper of the house, so that "no agent of the candidate will, by giving liquor to any person within the prohibited hours, be guilty of a corrupt practice avoiding the election, unless he is the keeper of such house" (*h*), or unless he comes within one of the preceding sections by giving it with a corrupt intent, or "on account of such voter being about to vote or having voted." **Only applies to agents who are hotel keepers, etc.**

3. If a candidate participate in or is in any way party to a treat in a tavern during polling hours, a corrupt practice is committed "with the actual knowledge and consent of the candidate" and his election is thereby avoided and himself disqualified (*i*); though corrupt intent is now necessary to cause disqualification of the candidate under 48 Vic. c. 2, s. 18. **If candidate participate.**

(*e*) *North Victoria*, 1 H. E. C. 252.

(*f*) *Lennox*, 2 Ont. El. Cases, 41; *S. Ontario*, 1 H. E. C. 420.

(*g*) Under secs. 152 and 153.

(*h*) Per Moss, J. A., in *S. Ontario*, 1 H. E. C., p. 457; *Lennox*, 2 Ont. El. Cases, 41—or person acting for the keeper, per Patterson, J. A., in *S. Ontario*.

(*i*) *N. Wentworth*, 1 H. E. C. 343; *N. Grey*, 1 H. E. C. 362; *S. Ontario*, 2 Ont. El. Cases, per Burton, J. A., p. 446.

Immaterial whether person treated a voter or not.

4. It matters not whether the person to whom the liquor is sold or given be a voter or not; "the offence does not depend upon the character of the person treated" (*j*).

Corrupt Practices by Treatiug under Ontario Law Summarized.

Cameron, C. J.

Chief Justice Cameron summarizes the cases in which the use of liquor is made a corrupt practice as follows (*k*):

Corrupt treating.

"*First.* When it is given at any time to induce an elector to vote or refrain from voting.

On account being about to vote, or having voted.

Second. When it is given to a voter on nomination or polling day, anywhere, on account of his being about to vote or having voted.

Treating meetings of electors.

Third. Furnishing it to a meeting of electors assembled to promote the election at any time or any place, except at the usual place of residence of the candidate or person furnishing it.

Selling or giving on Polling day.

Fourth. Selling or giving it within a polling subdivision on polling day, contrary to sec. 157.

All the provisions except the last extend to any kind of drink or refreshment, and to any place, while the last alone is restricted to strong drink, and applies to the selling or giving liquor to a non-voter as well as voter," (and, it may be added, only to giving or selling in a hotel, etc., by the keeper, or person acting as keeper, of the hotel, etc.).

Advice to Agents as to Treating.

Warning.

"It cannot be too seriously impressed on all those who may be in any way acting to further the election of a

(*j*) *S. Ontario*, per Draper, C. J., Patterson and Moss, J. J. A.

(*k*) *Lennox*, 2 Ont. El. Cases, at p. 67.

candidate, and who can properly be considered agents, the absolute necessity of avoiding the furnishing of refreshments to electors during the contest, whatever may be their motive in doing so. When a course of conduct which, in view of surrounding circumstances, may bear a favourable construction, but is considered open to serious objections, is followed after repeated warnings, Courts and Judges will feel less inclined to put the favourable construction on such conduct, and will have less hesitation in deciding that parties who will persist in acting recklessly after repeated warnings, intend to act illegally" (*l*).

UNDUE INFLUENCE.

The 95th section of the Dominion Elections Act, 1874 (*m*) is as follows:

"Every person who, directly or indirectly, by himself or by any other person on his behalf, makes use of, or threatens to make use of any force, violence or restraint, or inflicts, or threatens the infliction by himself, or by or through any other person, of any injury, damage, harm or loss, or in any manner practises intimidation upon or against any person, in order to induce or compel such person to vote or refrain from voting, or on account of such person having voted or refrained from voting at any election, or who by abduction, duress or any fraudulent device or contrivance, impedes, prevents or otherwise interferes with the free exercise of the franchise of any voter, or thereby compels, induces or prevails upon any voter either to give or refrain from giving his vote at any election, shall be deemed to have committed the

Offence defined.

(*l*) Per Sir W. B. Richards, C J., in *Jacques Cartier*, 2 Sup. Ct. at p. 247.

(*m*) Cap. No. sec. 88 of statutes as revised by Commissioners.

offence of undue influence, and shall be guilty of a misdemeanor, and shall also forfeit the sum of two hundred dollars to any person suing for the same, with full costs of suit.

A corrupt practice.

By section 98 undue influence is made a corrupt practice.

Same under Ontario Acts.

Section 155 of the Election Act of Ontario (*n*) is identical in terms, except that the offence is not declared to be be a misdemeanor, and costs of suit for the penalty are not provided for in the section. Section 2, subsection 6 of The Controverted Elections Act of Ontario (*o*) makes the offence a corrupt practice.

Proper definition.

"The proper definition of that undue influence which was dealt with in 17 and 18 Vic., c. 10?, s. 5" (identical in terms with the above) "is using any violence or threatening any damage, or resorting to any fraudulent contrivance to restrain the liberty of a voter, so as either to compel or frighten him into voting or abstaining from voting otherwise than he freely wills" (*p*).

Whatever, under ordinary circumstances, it is bribery to promise, it is intimidation to threaten the deprivation of (*q*).

Cases within the section.

Among the acts and threats which will come within the section are: Withdrawal of custom from a tradesman or other person; Eviction of a tenant voter; Threats by fellow workmen; Dismissal from employment; Abduction of or fraud on voter; Inciting mobs or paying men to interfere with persons going to the polls.

Withdrawal, or threat of with-

"Whether the ill-treatment be violence or damage done by the removal of custom, or business, or employ-

(*n*) Rev. Stats. Ont., cap. 10.

(*o*) Rev. Stats. Ont., cap. 11.

(*p*) Per Willes, J., in *Lichfield*, 1 O'M. & H. 52.

(*q*) *Westbury*, 1 O'M. & H. 52.

ment, is immaterial; if it is done with a view to affect a voter or interfere with the free exercise of the franchise, it is within the prohibition" (*r*).

drawal of custom.

"Undoubtedly, when the election is over, a man may employ whom he pleases; but to make use of it as a threat during an election to withdraw his custom in order to influence the election, is, I think, as clearly an infraction of the 5th section of the Act as it would be if a landlord were to say to his tenant, 'If you do not vote so-and-so I will turn you out of your house'" (*s*).

Eviction, or threatened eviction of tenant.

The subject of undue ecclesiastical influence has been fully considered in this country as well as in Great Britain in a number of cases. "The principle of all the decisions in these cases is that the priest must not appeal to the fears of his hearers, nor say that the elector who votes for such a candidate will commit a sin, or incur ecclesiastical censures, or be deprived of the sacraments" (*t*). The prohibition applies to utterances of the clergy both in and out of the pulpit. Keogh, J., in the *Galway (County) case*, ruled that the clergy were justified in exerting their legitimate influence over the minds of their congregations; but he said: "Undue influence would be used if ecclesiastics make use of their powers to excite superstitious fears or pious hopes: to inspire, as the object may be best promoted, despair or confidence; to alarm the conscience by the horrors of eternal misery, or support the drooping spirits by unfolding the prospect of eternal happiness—that good or evil which is never to end. . . . . He had to consider the case very fully at

Spiritual intimidation.

(*r*) *Blackburn*, judgments, 11.

(*s*) *Per* Campbell, C. J., in *Reg.* v. *Barnwell*, 5 W. R. 558; see also *Windsor*, 2 O'M. & H. 90; *Petersfield*, 2 O'M. & H. 54. Where a landlord said to a number of his tenants, "If you can vote for my friend, Captain T., I shall be delighted if you will do so; if you cannot vote for him at all events stay at home and do not vote against him"; this was held not to exceed the bounds of legitimate influence, *Galway*, 2 O'M. & H. 54.

(*t*) *per* Taschereau, J., in *Charlevoix*, 1 Sup. Ct. 195.

Drogheda (*u*), and there the election was declared void, not only by reason of general intimidation, but because of undue ecclesiastical influence brought home to the sitting member and his agent in one particular case" (*v*).

"In the proper exercise of his influence on electors, the priest may counsel, advise, recommend, entreat, and point out the true line of moral duty, and explain why one candidate should be preferred to another, and may, if he think fit, throw the whole weight of his character into the scale: but he may not appeal to the fears or terrors or superstition of those he addresses. He must not hold out hopes of reward here or hereafter, and he must not use threats of temporal injury, or of disadvantage, or of punishment hereafter. He must not for instance threaten to excommunicate, or to withold the sacraments, or to expose the party to any other religious disability, or denounce the voting for any particular candidate as a sin, or as an offence involving punishment here or hereafter. If he does so with a view to influence a voter, or to affect an election, the law considers him guilty of undue influence" (*w*). The prohibition applies to priests and ministers of all churches and sects (*x*).

Applies to all priests and ministers.

Change in English Act.

These decisions so accorded with the will of Parliament that in re-enacting the above section in 1883 (*y*) the words "temporal or spiritual" were inserted before the word "injury," to insure the same interpretation prevailing in future.

Priesthood

In the *Charlevoix* case (*z*), a claim of immunity on the

(*u*) Judgments pt. ii., p. 320.

(*v*) Judgments, 66.

(*w*) Per Fitzgerald, J., in *Longford*, 2 O'M. & H. 16; see also *Tipperary*, 2 O'M. & H. 31.

(*x*) *Galway* (*County*) Judgment, per Keogh, J., and 2 O'M. & H. 56; see also *Galway* (*Town*) *case*, judgments 347; *Hamilton* v. *Beauchesne*, 3 Q. L. R. 75, S. C. 1876.

(*y*) See C. I. & P. P. Act 1883, s. 2.

(*z*) 1 Sup. Ct. 195.

part of the priesthood for utterances in the pulpit, except from the jurisdiction of ecclesiastical courts, was set up and held good by Mr. Justice Routhier, but, by a unanimous judgment, the Supreme Court of Canada reversed this decision and held that, even where they spoke in accordance with a pastoral letter of the Archbishop and bishops of Quebec they were amenable to the civil courts and to the election laws.

amenable to Civil as well as Ecclesiastical Courts.

Where fellow-workmen ill-treat one another, or expel one another from the common place of employment, they are guilty of the offence of undue influence (*a*); as they would be also, it is conceived, were they to expel or threaten to expel a member from a non-political association or trades-union on account of his voting or being about to vote in a particular manner.

Threats, etc., by fellow workmen

Expelling or wrongfully discharging voters shortly before a parliamentary election, in consequence of their politics being different from those of their employers amounts to undue influence (*b*). Threatening to procure the discharge of Government employees for a similar reason would also constitute the offence (*c*).

Dismissal from employment.

Using open force, or abducting a voter is also prohibited by the section. Two agents of the respondent gave a voter whiskey on polling day, and took him in a boat to an island, where they stayed for some time. One of the agents then left, and the other sent the voter to another part of the island for their coats. During his absence the latter agent left the island with the boat, but the voter got back in time to vote, being sent for by the opposite party: *Held*, that the two agents were guilty of undue influence (*d*).

Abuduction of, or fraud on voter.

(*a*) *Blackburn*, 1 O'M. & H. 204.

(*b*) *Blackburn*, Judgments, 16; *Westbury*, 1 O'M. & H. 51.

(*c*) See *Welland*, 1 H. E. C. 187.

(*d*) *North Ontario*, 1 H. E. C. 785.

Cards and circulars intended to deceive.

It was held in the *Gloucester* case, 1873 (*e*), by Blackburn, J., where cards had been sent round to voters containing directions how to vote, that if a fraudulent intention could be inferred from the wording on the card, it would bring the case within the section, whether the voter had been influenced thereby or not; that a fraudulent device to prevent a voter voting a certain way, whether successful or not, was contrary to the Act—for instance, if a voting card was intended to induce persons to believe that they could not vote for A, and that their vote would only be valid if they put a cross opposite the name of B. In the *East Northumberland (Ontario Provincial)* case (*f*), however, there were three candidates, F, W and C. A night or two before the polling some letters or circulars were sent by a member of F's agents to different leading men, stating that W, an independent candidate, had despaired of success and wanted his friends to vote for C, a report which W denied. Mr. Justice Gwynne says: "It is in my judgment distinguishable from the *Gloucester* case, which is the only case reported having any resemblance to the present. There the Act complained of was one which, if it had been designed with the intent imputed, would have been calculated to have the effect of misleading persons, without any exercise of judgment, to place their mark on the ballot paper, opposite the respondent's name only, and so have been calculated to make persons, by a trick and deception, vote for a candidate for whom at the time of voting they did not intend to vote. In the case before me, the most that can be said is (assuming the statement in the circular to be false, to the knowledge of the parties issuing it) that they were by a falsehood appealing to the electors to exercise their judgment in the voting for the friend of the parties issuing the circular."

(*e*) 2 O'M. & H. 60.
(*f*) 1 H. E. C. 390.

Candidates and their friends, however, who desire to regard the law, should be careful that no cards or circulars containing misleading statements are sent out. Advice to candidates and friends.

An agent inciting a mob to prevent persons voting, though it may not amount to general intimidation, is guilty of the offence of undue influence (*g*). Inciting mob.

Where persons are hired to come from other places into the constituency by a candidate or his agent, for the purpose of intimidating the opposite party, it will avoid his election (*h*). Hired intimidators.

Though bodies of men may be introduced from other places as a defensive force, if done merely to prevent intimidation by others, it is a highly dangerous step to take, and one which should only be adopted under extreme circumstances (*i*). Hiring defensive force.

A mere attempt by an agent, to intimidate a voter, even though unsuccessful, will, it has been held, avoid an election (*j*); though when the agent of a candidate in the polling booth, in presence of the deputy returning officer, told a voter who claimed to vote on his wife's property, that he could not vote unless the property was his own, and on the oath being read over, by the deputy returning officer, the agent told the voter he could not take it, the agent believing, at the time what he said was true, and the voter in consequence of the doubt raised did not vote, Draper, C. J. A., declined to hold that a case of undue influence by intimidation had been made out (*k*). Attempt to intimidate.

General intimidation of any kind, if it goes to the extent of influencing the body of voters and preventing the General intimidation.

(*g*) *Stafford*, Judgments, 295; 1 O'M. & H. 229.

(*h*) *Longford*, 2 O'M. & H. 12.

(*i*) *Ibid*; if they be voters colorable employment in this way amounts to bribery, *Charlevoix*, 5 Sup. Ct. 150, see *ante*.

(*j*) *Northallerton* 1 O'M. & H. 173, per Willes, J; *N. Ontario*, 1 H. E. C. 304, per Wilson, J.

(*k*) *Halton*, 1 H. E. C. 283.

real freedom of election, will render void an election at common law without proof of agency *(l)*.

Rioting.

This rule applies to general rioting even where the respondent polled an actual majority of the registered voters *(m)*.

General intimidation of Crown debtors.

It would apply also where, in a constituency composed largely of debtors to the Crown on Crown Lands, an organized and general system existed, leading the electors to believe that supporters and opponents of the Government would be differently dealt with, so as to create any grounds of apprehension in their minds (*n*).

General spiritual intimidation.

It applies also in cases of general spiritual intimidation (*o*).

Mr. Justice Keogh, in the *Galway (County)* case, (*p*), said: "General bribery will invalidate an election, even though it be not directly traceable to the candidate; I say that general treating will invalidate an election, even though it be not directly traceable to the candidate; and I say above all things, that general intimidation and undue influence, whether it is lay or ecclesiastical, whether it is the ecclesiastic of our persuasion or the ecclesiastic of another, whether it is the Protestant Episcoplian minister, or the Presbyterian minister, or the Roman Catholic priest, or the minister of any other of those innumerable sects which I believe are to be found existing over the face of the world, will upset every election at which it is practised."

(*l*) *Staleybridge*, 1 O'M. & H. 72; *Salford*, *Ib.* 140; *North Durham*, 2 O'M. & H. 186; *Cheltenham*, 1 O'M. & H. 64; *Stafford*, Judgments, 295; *Nottingham*, 1 O'M. & H. 246; *Dudley*, 2 O'M. & H. 121.

(*m*) *Cheltenham*. *Nottingham*, *Stafford*, above; though as to where intimidation is substantially on the side of the defeated candidate, see, per Grove, J., in *Dudley*, 2 O'M. & H. 121, in which, as well as in the *North Durham* case, the respondents though unseated, were not disqualified from running again, and being re-elected, on the ground that the elections were void, owing to general intimidation, and rioting, in which neither the candidates themselves, nor their agents, took part.

(*n*) Per Burton, J. A., in *North Ontario*, 1 H. E. C. 339.

(*o*) *Charlevoix*, 1 Sup. Ct., per Ritchie, C. J., p. 229.

(*p*) 2 O'M. & H. 56; see also *Soulanges case*, (Sup. Ct.,) 21 U. C. L. J. (N. S.) 50.

PERSONATION AND VOTING BY PROHIBITED PERSONS AND SUBORNATION THEREOF.

Personation is thus defined by section 74 of The Dominion Elections Act 1874 *(q)*.

" A person shall for all purposes of the laws relating to Parliamentary elections be deemed to be guilty of the offence of personation, who, at an election of a member of the House of Commons, applies for a ballot paper in the name of some other person, whether such name be that of a person living or dead, or of a fictitious person, or who having voted once at any such election applies at the same election for a ballot paper in his own name." Offence defined.

Subornation of personation is thus defined by section 97 of the same Act *(r)*.

" Every candidate who corruptly (s) by himself or by or with any other person on his behalf compels or induces or endeavours to induce any person to personate any voter, or to take any false oath in any matter wherein an oath is required under this Act shall be guilty of a misdemeanor, and shall in addition to any other punishment to which he may be liable for such offence, be liable to forfeit the sum of two hundred dollars to any person suing for the same." Compelling or inducing personation.

Personation or the inducing any one to commit personation, or any wilful offence against the latter of the sections above quoted are by section 98 made corrupt practices; and sections 75 and 76 are also to the same effect, the latter providing for the avoidance of the election and disqualification of the candidate or " other person " during the Parliament for which the election is Corrupt Practices.

(q) Sec. 90 of cap. Na. of Acts as devised by Commissioners.

(r) Sec. 91 of cap. Na. of new revised Acts.

(s) The offence of aiding, etc., without the word " corruptly " being used is, by a subsection to s. 74 made punishable by a fine of $200, and imprisonment for a term not exceeding two years.

held and during the *then next Parliament,* the ordinary term of disqualification under other sections being seven years (*t*).

Under Ontario law.

The definitions in section 155 of the Ontario Election Act (*u*) and subsection 2 of section 2 of the Ontario Election Law Amendment Act, 1884, are practically the same as the above; and by section 2, subsection 1 of the last mentioned Act it is declared that "any person who aids or abets, counsels or procures, the commission of the offence of personation shall be deemed guilty of corrupt practice."

Aiding and abetting.

Voting by prohibited persons, and inducing such to vote, prohibited by Ontario Act.

By section 4 of the Ontario Act last mentioned: "Any person who votes or induces or procures any person to vote at any election, knowing that such person has no right to vote at such election, shall be guilty of a corrupt practice, and shall be liable to a penalty of one hundred dollars" (*v*).

Where one of two persons of the same name only is entitled to vote and the other one is urged to vote by an agent who thinks him the one entitled to vote, such agent has been held not a party to the offence of personation (*w*).

In England the payment of money to induce a person to personate a voter was held to amount to bribery (*x*), and Mr. Justice Willes expressed the opinion that inducing personation by others would be sufficient fraud at common law to avoid the election (*y*).

(*t*) See chapter on "Penalties under Dominion Laws," *post.* The word "corruptly" used in section 97 is not found in sections 75 or 76.

(*u*) Rev. Stats. Ont., cap. 10.

(*v*) See further, chapter on Penalties under Ontario Laws, *post;* sec. 5 provides for such votes being struck off the candidates, by whom or whose agent they have been procured, without examination of the ballots. See sec. 11, subs. (b) Dom. Fran. Act, and note, *ante;* see also *W. Peterboro'*, 1 H. E. C. 274.

(*w*) *Gloucester*, 2 O'M. & H. 62; *Ib.* p. 64.

(*x*) *Lisburn*, W. & B. 225.

(*y*) *Coventry*, 1 O'M. & H. 105.

Where a person's name is wrongly entered on the list, though he is entitled to the vote, and he votes under the name given in the list, it is not a case of personation, but merely a misnomer, and the vote is good (z). Misnomer.

HIRING AND PAYING FOR CONVEYANCE OF VOTERS.

Section 96 of the Dominion Elections Act 1874 (a) is as follows:

"And whereas doubts may arise as to whether the hiring of teams and vehicles to convey voters to and from the polls, and the paying of railway fares and other expenses of voters, be or be not according to law, it is declared and enacted, that the hiring or promising to pay or paying for any horse, team, carriage, cab or other vehicle, by any candidate, or by any person on his behalf, to convey any voter or voters to or from the poll, or to or from the neighbourhood thereof, at any election, or the payment by any candidate, or by any person on his behalf, of the travelling and other expenses of any voter, in going to or returning from any election are and shall be unlawful acts; and the person so offending shall forfeit the sum of one hundred dollars to any person who shall sue for the same; and any voter hiring any horse, cab, cart, waggon, sleigh, carriage or other conveyance for any candidate, or for any agent of a candidate, for the purpose of conveying any voter or voters to or from the polling place or places, shall, *ipso facto*, be disqualified from voting at such election, and for every such offence shall forfeit the sum of one hundred dollars to any person suing for the same." Offence defined

Section 154 of The Election Act of Ontario (b) is almost identical in terms. and by both Dominion and Ontario Acts (c) the offence is made a corrupt practice. Ontario. Corrupt Practice.

(z) *Oldham*, 1 O'M. & H. 152.

(a) See cap. Na. s. 89 of Stats. as revised by Commissioners.

(b) Rev. Stats. Ont. cap. 10.

(c) 37 Vic. c. 9, (Dom.) and Rev. Stats. c. 11, s. 2, subs. 6, (Ont.)

Payment after Election.

The payment to a voter of his horse hire or to a person for conveying a voter to the poll, by an agent, *after the election*, and without any previous hiring or promise to pay, has been held not sufficient to avoid the election, owing to the authority of the agent having ceased with the election, and before the time of payment (*d*), but, it is conceived, the evidence required to establish a previous understanding would not require to be very strong and the knowledge and consent of the candidate would, in any event, render it a corrupt practice.

A corrupt practice if conveyance hired, whether voters come or not.

It is within the prohibition of the section if a conveyance be hired to bring in a voter or voters, living at a long distance from the poll, at a time previous to polling day, and *whether the voters came or not*, providing the hiring of the conveyance for such a purpose is proved.

Ignorantia legis.

"Wilful."

Ignorance of the law in this regard, on the part of an agent will not avail to save the election, the offence being made a corrupt practice by section 98, the word "wilful" in that section having been interpreted as *intentional* and the offence being complete if the party intended to hire the conveyance for the purpose of bringing the voter to the poll, though ignorant of the effect of the Act (*e*).

Hiring railway train.

The hiring of a railway train by a candidate or agent comes within the section and avoids the election (*f*).

Free passes.

It has been held by the Supreme Court in the *Berthier* case, (*g*), that the taking unconditionally and gratuitously of a voter to the poll by a railway company or an individual, whatever his occupation may be, or giving a voter a free pass, or a ticket supplied gratuitously by the com-

(*d*) *Brockville*, 1 H. E. C. 139; *Halton*, *Ib.* 736.

(*e*) *Selkirk*, 4 Sup. Ct. 494; see *Halton*, I H. E. C. 736. Under the New Brunswick Provincial Act it has been held, that giving money to provide conveyances to bring voters to the poll, is bribery within the Act, as being "a provision in order to procure the electors to vote," *Hebert* v. *Hannington*, 6 All. 530.

(*f*) *North Simcoe*, 1 H. E. C. 50.

(*g*) 9 Sup. Ct. 102.

pany to the candidate or agent over a railway, or by boat or other conveyance, if unaccompanied by any conditions or stipulations that shall affect the voter's action in reference to the vote to be given, is not prohibited by the section; but that if the ticket, although given unconditionally to a voter by an agent of the candidate, has been paid for, then such a practice is unlawful under section 96, and, by virtue of section 98, a corrupt practice, and would avoid the election.

Given unconditionally not prohibited.

If paid for, a corrupt practice

Sir W. J. Ritchie, C. J., says, (*h*) referring to the first branch of the above decision:

Ritchie, C. J.

"If it is against public policy, as I may think it is, that railway companies or others, having control of public conveyances, should be permitted to do this, its prohibition not being provided for by the statute, it is a *casus omissus*, which can only be remedied by Parliament. The courts cannot declare any act illegal and corrupt, though one candidate may be thereby much benefited, to the injury of the other, which has not been made so by the law."

Mr. Justice Strong says (*i*):

Strong, J.

"For the sake of distinctness, and in order that there may be no misapprehension of the grounds on which this opinion is founded, I think it right to add, though it may involve repetition, that had the tickets been purchased by *Lamarche*, and either paid for or agreed to be paid for, I should have considered the case as coming within the 96th section, which prohibits the payment of travelling expenses; and had the tickets been given to the voters upon the express condition or stipulation that they were to vote for the respondent, or had they promised so to vote, I should have thought the case within the

(*h*) *Berthier*, 9 Sup. Ct. at p. 119.

(*i*) *Ib.* at p. 128.

principle of the actual decision in *Cooper* v. *Slade* (*j*) and so a corrupt act, avoiding the election under section 92."

Ontario. The Ontario Court of Appeal came to a similar decision in the *East Northumberland* case (*k*) under the Provincial Act.

BETTING AND SUPPLYING MONEY TO BET UNDER ONTARIO LAW.

By section 3 of "The Election Law Amendment Act 1884" of Ontario (*l*):

(1) Any candidate who, before or during the election makes a bet or wager, or takes a share or interest in, or in any manner becomes a party to, any bet or wager, upon the result of the election in the electoral district, or in any part thereof, or on any event or contingency relating to the election, shall be guilty of corrupt practice.

(2) Any candidate or other person who provides money to be used by another in betting or wagering upon the result of an election to the Legislative Assembly, or on any event or contingency relating to the election, shall be guilty of corrupt practices.

(3) Any person who for the purpose of influencing an election makes a bet or wager on the result thereof, in the electoral district or any part thereof, or on any event or contingency relating thereto, shall be guilty of corrupt practice.

By section 47 the Act shall be read as part of the *Election Act* and of the *Controverted Elections Act*, (Ontario).

(*j*) 27 L. J. N. S. 449.

(*k*) *East Northumberland, Provincial El. case*, 2 Ont. El. cases.

(*l*) See *ante*, Bribery, p. 256.

RELIEVING SECTIONS IN ONTARIO ACTS.

There are two important sections in the Election Act of Ontario (*m*) peculiar to that Act, which require notice. They are sections 159 and 162 (*mm*). Both have proved to be very embarrassing sections for the Courts to construe and apply.

Rev. Stats. Ont. cap. 10, ss. 159 and 162.

Section 158 provides for the avoidance of the election for any corrupt practice committed by the successful candidate or by his agent whether with or without his consent. Section 159 has been enacted by way of exception, and is as follows :

Sec. 159.

"To prevent the expense and trouble of new elections when unnecessary and useless ; in case of a corrupt act or acts being committed by an agent without the knowledge and consent of the candidate, if the corrupt act or acts was or were of such a trifling nature, or was or were of such trifling extent, that the result cannot have been affected, or be reasonably supposed to have been affected, by such act or acts, either alone or in connection with other illegal practices at the election, such corrupt act or acts shall not avoid the election."

Where result of election not affected by corrupt and illegal acts.

The proportion of votes proved to have been corrupted, to the respondent's majority, is not taken as the sole guide under this section in determining whether the election should be set aside or not. Other "illegal practices," if any are shewn, must be considered in this connection (*n*), as well as the probabilities generally as to the result having been affected. In the *West Hastings* case (*o*), the majority of the respondent was 337, but it appeared in evidence that two agents of the respondent had bribed

Proportion of votes corrupted not the sole criterion.

(*m*) Rev. Stats. Ont., c. 10.

(*mm*) For amendments, see *post*.

(*n*) *Lincoln* (2), 1 H. E. C. 489 ; *Welland* case 1883, 2 Ont. El. cases, (not yet reported).

(*o*) 1 H. E. C. 539.

between forty and fifty voters; that in close proximity to the polls spirituous liquor was sold and given at two taverns during polling hours, and that one of such agents took part in furnishing such liquor, and that such agent had previous to the election furnished drink or other entertainment to a meeting of electors held for the purpose of promoting the election. It was held that the election was void, and Chief Justice Moss further laid down the rule that, *prima facie*, corrupt practices avoid an election, and that the onus of proof that they are not sufficient to affect the result rests upon the respondent.

Onus of proof on respondent to shew that result not affected

In the *West Simcoe* (*p*) case, Mr. Justice Patterson said: "The trifling nature or the trifling extent of the corrupt acts must in some way be shown. In most cases their nature and extent appear from the evidence by which their commission is proved, and nothing further on that head is required. Nothing of that sort appears in this case. We know that the whole majority of the successful candidate was only 35. We know that during the whole of the polling day, one of the safeguards against corruption proved by the Legislature was disregarded. We know but little of what actually went on at that tavern that day, and for the purpose of the statute, actual corruption need not be proven, but the little we do know embraces the Kenny affair, in which the resources of the tavern were clearly used by Harber on behalf of the respondent. The object and purpose of section 159 do not require anything in the shape of an attempt to estimate the number of votes which can be shown or surmised to have been affected by the corrupt act in question, and to balance this against the actual majority. We must keep in mind the careful language of the section which confines its effect to cases where the acts are trifling in their nature or trifling in their extent. No doubt this word *trifling* must be construed in such

Trifling nature and extent of corrupt acts must be shown.

(*p*) *West Simcoe* case 1883, 2 Ont. El. cases, (not yet reported).

case with some reference to the majority, particularly when considering the extent of the corrupt acts, but the Court is not called upon to enter into a *quasi* scrutiny for the purpose of this section. We feel it impossible to say that the keeping open of a tavern for the purpose of selling and giving liquor during the hours of polling, and the selling and giving during these hours, which we have to find as a fact—acts which the law stigmatizes as corrupt practices—were acts trifling in their nature, or trifling in their extent. It may be equally impossible to say that they affected the result, but that is not the form of the question. We have to say that the result cannot have been affected or cannot be reasonably supposed to have been affected by them. We are unable to say this, and therefore to hold that section 159 does not apply to save the election, but that it must be declared void" (*q*).

Keeping open tavern not a trifling act.

An important decision was arrived at by the Court of Appeal in the *East Simcoe* case (*r*) under this section, by which it was decided that the character and position in regard to the election of the agent guilty of the acts claimed to be trifling in nature and extent, and not the acts alone, should be regarded by the Court in forming a judgment under section 159. In that case the respondent's majority was 21 in a total vote of 2800 or 2900. The two learned judges (*s*) who tried the case certified that an agent of the respondent bribed two voters by paying them $4 and $5 respectively, and was guilty of a further corrupt practice in hiring a team to convey voters to the poll, and that two tavern keepers did during polling hours give liquor to certain voters, one of such tavern keepers being held not to be an agent, while as to the other's agency the judges differed. The judges further differed as to the effect of a certain irregularity as to the

E. Simcoe case.

Character and position of the agent to be considered.

(*q*) It had been held that the tavern-keeper was an agent of the respondent.

(*r*) *East Simcoe* Election, 1883; 2 Ont. El. cases, (not yet reported.)

(*s*) Chancellor Boyd and Chief Justice Cameron.

hour of holding the nomination of candidates ; and they differed as to whether section 159 should apply, the chancellor holding that it should and that the election should not be set aside, and Chief Justice Cameron holding that it should not, and that consequently the election should be declared void. The case came before the Court of Appeal, and on the argument before that Court the question of the irregularity on nomination day was dropped, remedial legislation having, in the meantime, been passed. The agent whose acts were complained of was, according to the evidence, the most active agent and manager for the respondent in the largest town in the riding, if not in the whole riding. It was urged that this latter fact should be regarded by the Court in deciding whether section 159 should apply. The majority of the Court *(t)* decided that they must look at the character and position of the party committing the acts, as well as the acts themselves. Patterson, J. A., says: "I think we may properly test the nature of an act, whether corrupt or lawful, by considering the circumstances under which and the person by whom it is committed. I ventured an illustration of this idea in my judgment in the *Welland* case which I may here repeat. Let us suppose the charge made and proved to be that A, an agent, bribed B, a voter, by the payment of one dollar, and let us suppose that A is shown to have had with him a large sum of money under circumstances which raise a strong and not unreasonable suspicion that his object was to use it in purchasing votes, one circumstance being the payment of the dollar to B, but the rest of the money not being traced on the one hand or accounted for on the other. While the extent of this corrupt act, being measured by its influence on the one voter, might be trifling, *its nature* as one overt act of what appeared or might reasonably be assumed to be an arranged system of operations could not

---

(*t*) Hagerty, C. J., Patterson and Osler, J. J. A. ; Burton, J. A. dissenting.

properly be said to be trifling." Osler, J., says: "The position which the briber occupies with relation to the candidate and the conduct of the campaign appears to me, with great respect for those who hold the opposite view, to be a matter of the first importance in gauging the nature or extent of the corrupt act . . . . . What comparison can there be between a deliberate bribe of $1 or $5 given by the chief promoter or manager of the election to a needy voter and his day's wage given by an employer, technically perhaps an agent, to his hired man? It will be said that each is an isolated case and represents only one bribed vote. But that is not so. The latter is comparatively venial, but the former soon becomes notice to every man who is willing to sell his vote, that money may be obtained for it. Bribery cannot justly be described as trifling in its nature, which proclaims to the corruptible portion of the electorate that the managers of the election are willing to traffic in corruption."

Section 161 of the Election Act of Ontario provides that where any corrupt practice has been committed, by or with the actual knowledge or consent of any candidate *(u)*, in addition to his election being void, he shall be disqualified for eight years. Section 162, which follows, provides: **Sec. 161.** **Disqualification of candidate.**

"If it appears to the Court or the Judges *(v)* trying an election petition, that an act constituting in law a corrupt practice was committed by a candidate or with his knowledge and consent, but without any corrupt intent, and in an ignorance which was involuntary and excusable, and that the evidence showed the candidate to have **Candidate may be relieved from penalties and disabilities under certain circumstances.**

(*u*) "And that the next section does not apply then"; see 47 Vic. c. 4, s. 28 and 47 V. c. 2, s. 18.

(*v*) "Or one of them"; see 47 V. c. 4, s. 29 and 48 V. c. 2, s. 18.

honestly desired and in good faith endeavored as far as he could to have the election conducted according to law, the candidate shall not be subject to the penalties and disabilities which he would but for this section incur under the preceding section."

Muskoka case. In the *Muskoka* case (*w*) Mr. Justice Patterson divided the requirements of this section into four parts, as follows :—

If no corrupt intent. Firstly, the act which constitues in law a corrupt practice must have been committed or consented to, without any corrupt intent.

If act committ'd in involuntary and excusable ignorance. Secondly, it must have been committed, or consented to, in an ignorance which was involuntary and excusable.

If candidate honestly desir'd a pure Election. Thirdly, the evidence must show that the candidate honestly desired to have the election conducted according to law.

If candidate endeavoured to have Election legally conducted. Fourthly, the evidence must also show that the candidate in good faith endeavored as far as he could to have the election conducted according to law.

The summing up of the learned judge of the facts in the light of these requirements of the section, was as follows :—"We find that the act of the respondent, in furnishing drink at his expense to a meeting of electors assembled at Commanda Creek, for the purpose of promoting the election, which constitutes in law a corrupt practice, while it appears to have been committed in ignorance that it was a violation of the Statute, does not appear to have been committed in an ignorance which was involuntary and excusable. We are disposed to believe that the respondent was desirous, and that he

(*w*) *Muskoka Election 1883*, 2 Ont. El. cases, (not yet reported).

endeavored to avoid personally committing illegal or corrupt practices, and even to avoid actual knowledge of their commission by others acting in his support ; but we are not satisfied that he was ignorant that such practices were likely to be committed by persons acting on his behalf in the conduct of the election ; and finding that corrupt practices did prevail—and as there is reason to believe did extensively prevail at the election, and amongst those who supported the respondent—we are unable to say that the evidence shows the respondent to have honestly desired and in good faith endeavored, as far as he could, to have the election conducted according to law. We feel ourselves, therefore, compelled to come to the conclusion that the respondent is not relieved by the one hundred and sixty-second section of the statute from the penalties and disabilities incurred under the preceding section." The decision of the *rota* judges was subsequently affirmed on appeal by the Court of Appeal.

In the *South Renfrew* (1st provincial) case, the *rota* judges who tried the case differed as to whether the section applied to relieve the respondent from a charge of corrupt practices proven, or not. They, however, held the election void, and the respondent being again elected, a second petition was filed against him on the ground that he had not been relieved from the disqualification by the certificate of both the former judges, or by certain legislation (held not to be retrospective) which had in the meantime been passed (*x*), and the Court found in favor of the petitioner. The disqualification was, however, removed by 48 Vic., cap. 2, s. 19. Section 18 of the same Act is declaratory of the provisions of the 161st and 162nd *S. Renfrew case*

(*x*) The Election Law Amendment Act 1884, s. 48.

sections of the Election Act and must now be read in connection therewith. It is as follows :—

48 Vic. c. 2, s. 18.

Construction of R. S. O. c. 10, ss. 161 and 162 declared.

"Sections 161 and 162 of *The Election Act* (chapter 10 "of the Revised Statutes) were intended to be construed "and shall hereafter be construed both as respects Acts "heretofore done, and Acts which may hereafter be done "as if the said sections had at the time of the passing "thereof been expressed as the same were amended by "the 28th and 29th sections (*y*) of *The Election Law* "*Amendment Act, 1884*; and it is hereby declared and "enacted, that, by the true intention of the said sections, "and the 38th section of *The Controverted Elections Act* "the practices mentioned in the 161st section aforesaid "and therein called corrupt practice, was and is such "practice only as should be committed with corrupt in-"tent, and involved moral culpability, and as should be "so found by the joint decision of the judges trying the "petition against the candidate (in this act called the "Trial Judges) or by the Court of Appeal; and the prac-"tices so mentioned in the said 161st section did not and "does not include any practice not found by such joint "decision or by the Court of Appeal, to be of the char-"acter aforesaid; and the said practices did not and does "not include a practice committed (as provided by the "162nd section) 'without any corrupt intent, and in an "'ignorance which was involuntary and excusable, and "'where the evidence shewed the candidate to have hon-"'estly desired and in good faith endeavored as far as he "'could to have the election conducted according to law,' "and did not and does not include a practice which is "designated in the 164th section (*z*) of the said *Election*

(*y*) See notes (*u*) and (*v*), *ante* p. 287.

(*z*) The 164th section provides for the punishment of persons found guilty of corrupt practices, other than the candidate.

" *Act* as 'a merely technical breach of law and a practice "'not being an intentional violation of the law, and not' "'involving moral culpability'; and the declarations and "enactments of this section are for all purposes to be con-" strued and to have effect from the time of the passing " of the said Revised Statutes, as if the same had been " expressed therein according to the hereby declared in-" tention of the said enactments."

This section is somewhat involved, but the effect of it would seem to be that disqualification cannot be held to attach to a candidate under the 161st section of the Election Act except in respect of a corrupt practice committed with *corrupt intent* and involving *moral culpability* either by the candidate or by his agent, "with his actual knowledge or consent" (*a*) and then only when it is found to be of that character by the joint decision of the Trial Judges. For instance, the respondent in the *Muskoka* case, above referred to, could not, under this section, be held to be disqualified, according to the judgment of the Trial Judges, for they held that there was no corrupt intent in the act for which he was disqualified. Unfortunately for him, this section did not become law in time to rescue him from the effect of the judgment, though the enactment is declared to be retrospective. The 162nd section of the Election Act would now seem to be useless, as if a corrupt intent be proved either on the part of the candidate or of his agent, by or with his actual knowledge or consent, (assuming "knowledge" and "consent" to be synonymous terms) it would be idle to contend that the act was committed "without any corrupt intent and in an ignorance," etc.

Effect.

No disqualification of candidate unless corrupt intent be shewn,

And found by joint decision of trial judges.

(*a*) See Rev. Stats. Ont. c. 10, s 161.

CHAPTER II.

AGENCY.

Who is an Agent

AN AGENT is a person authorized by the candidate to act on his behalf in affairs connected with the election, and the candidate, as regards his seat, is as liable for acts committed by his agent, as if he himself had been personally concerned therein; although the agent may not only have exceeded the authority committed to him, but have acted in opposition to the express command of the candidate (*b*).

The liability of a candidate for the acts of others is, it will be seen, much wider than that of an ordinary principal for the acts of his agents. The reasons which led to this were stated by Blackburn, J. (*c*), as follows :—" The rule of Parliamentary election law, that a candidate is responsible for the corrupt act of his agent, though he himself not only did not intend it or authorize it, but *bona fide* did his best to hinder it, is a rule that must at all times fall with great hardship upon particular persons. But I may mention the consideration which, no doubt, led the common law, as I may call it, of Parliament to establish it. Corruption, as we all know, in practice and in fact, is seldom or never done by the hand of the can-

(*b*) Leigh and LeMarchant's law of Elections (4th Ed.) p. 72.

(*c*) *Taunton*, 1 O'M. & H. 184.

didate. The two modes in which it was found in practice that corruption was carried on were these: persons were put forward to do all the work of canvassing and conducting an election, and these persons acted corruptly; but the candidate purposely kept himself out of the knowledge of anything about the matter, so that he might have the full benefit of their services; and were it not for this rule which has been established he would not suffer for their misdeeds. That is one of the great reasons. Another great reason would be that no doubt people were put forward as to whom the candidate was carefully kept from knowing they were spending any money, or doing anything with the notion, according to the loose morality that prevailed in election matters, that when the time for petitioning was past, those persons might come to him and say, I did spend that £1,000 for you upon the election; of course I did not tell you about it or say a word about it at the time, but now you are bound in honor to repay me that £1,000 of which you had the benefit, and which, in point of fact, the candidates did feel themselves bound in honor to pay. This, therefore, was another reason for the parliamentary law declaring that the candidate should be responsible for the act of his agent" (*d*).

Grove, J., in the *Wakefield case* (*e*), after referring to the ordinary law of principal and agent, says: "But if that construction of agency were put upon acts done at elections, it would be almost impossible to prevent corruption. Accordingly a wider scope has been given to the term agency in election matters, and a candidate is

(*d*) See also *Cornwall*, 1 H. E. C. 547; *North Ontario*, *Ib.* 304; *W. Toronto*, *Ib.* 97; *N. Ontario*, *Ib.* 785.

(*e*) 2 O'M. & H. 102.

responsible generally, you may say, for the deeds of those who, to his knowledge, for the purpose of promoting his election canvass and do such other acts as may tend to promote his election, provided that the candidate or his authorized agents have reasonable knowledge that these persons are so acting with that object. I think it well that I should say in this respect that here it is almost impossible for any judge to lay down such exact definitions and limits as shall meet every particular case; and it is extremely important that the public should know that, because, were it otherwise—were I, for instance, on the present occasion to pretend to lay down an exact definition of what constituted agency at one election—possibly in some other case that particular definition might be evaded, although what came substantially to the same thing might have taken place. Happily, there is sufficient elasticity in the law to prevent that being the case; and here, again, those who think that they can evade the law by just creeping out of the words which learned judges use, or even which tribunals use, upon a matter of this sort, which is partly law and partly fact, will generally find that they are very much mistaken. It is, therefore, well that it should be understood that it rests with the judge not misapplying or straining the law, but applying the principles of the law to changed states of facts, to form his opinion as to whether there has or has not been what constitutes agency in these election matters. It is well that the public should know that they cannot evade this difficulty by merely getting, as they suppose, out of the technical meaning of certain words and phrases."

Law analagous to that of master and servant. The law as to Parliamentary agency is rather analagous to that of master and servant than to that of ordinary principal and agent; *i. e.*, the candidate is responsible for the acts of his servant done in the course of his employment, whether lawful or not, notwithstanding a prohibition may have been given to him by his master *(f)*.

The idea that a candidate can have no agents until after nomination day is so common an error that it is well to observe here that there is no stated time when the candidate's liability begins, other than the commencement of his candidature. The close of the election terminates the agency. A candidate is not liable for any acts committed by his agent after the election is over, unless he be personally privy to them *(g)*.

When agency commences.

When agency terminates.

A corrupt act, however, done after the election, may be material as throwing light on what took place before the election *(h)*.

A candidate will be held responsible for the acts of sub-agents appointed by an agent, even though the candidate does not know, or is not brought into personal contact with the sub-agent *(i)*. When a candidate puts money into the hands of his agent, and exercises no supervision over the way in which the agent is spending that money, but accredits and trusts him and leaves him the power of spending the money, although he may have given directions that none of the money should be improperly spent, there is such an agency established that the candidate is liable to the fullest extent, not only for what that agent may do, but also for what all those whom that agent em-

(*f*) *Wigan*, Judgments 205; 1 O'M. & H. 191; *Westbury*, 1 O'M. & H. 54; also per Martin, B., *Norwich*, 1 O'M. & H. 10; and *Boston*, 2 O'M. & H. 165.

(*g*) *Bodmin*, 1 O'M & H. 118; *Salford*, 1 O'M. & H. 138; *Norfolk*, (N. Div.), 1 O'M. & H. 243; *Longford*, 2 O'M. & H. 11, 12; *Limerick*, 1 O'M. & H. 261; *King's Lynn*, *Ib.* 208; *Brockville*, 1 H. E. C. 139.

(*h*) *Southampton*, 1 O'M. & H. 222; see *N. Ontario*, 2 Ont. El. cases, 1.

(*i*) *Bewdley*, 1 O'M. & H. 19; *Barnstaple*, 2 O'M. & H. 105-6; *Charlevoix*, 5 Sup. Ct. 133; *Welland*, 1 H. E. C. 187.

ploys may do (*j*). No limit can be placed to the number of the parties through whom the sub-agency may extend (*k*).

The agency may, however, be limited by the scope of the agent's authority or of his delegated authority, as the case may be. "No proposition in election law is better established than that an agent, who is not a general agent, but an agent with powers expressly limited, cannot bind the candidate by anything done beyond the scope of his authority" (*l*). Employing a person to canvass a particular voter or voters will not necessarily constitute him a general agent so as to make the candidate responsible for anything else he might do (*m*). So also asking a master to go round and canvass his workmen would not be an authority to canvass "beyond the scope of the workmen in his employ," and with respect to anything done by him as to voters other than these workmen, there would be no agency (*n*); and members of a committee appointed to look after the voters of a particular ward, but having no authority from the candidate to canvass generally have been held not to have rendered the candidate liable for acts committed in another ward (*o*).

Joint agency by coalition of candidates.

It has been held in England that where candidates "coalesce," that is, make common cause, choosing to stand or fall together, the agents of one are the agents of the other, so that each candidate becomes responsible for the

---

(*j*) *S. Grey*, I H. E. C. 52.

(*k*) *Niagara*, 1 H. E. C. 568.

(*l*) Per Strong, J., in *Berthier*, 9 Sup. Ct 130. The agent in this case was a public speaker, and for his acts beyond those performed in that character, the respondent was held not responsible.

(*m*) *Hereford*, judgments, 111; 1 O'M. & H. 195; *Bodmin*, 1 O'M. & H. 120.

(*n*) *Westbury*, 1 O'M. & H. 47; *N. Norfolk*, 1 O'M. & H. 237.

(*o*) *London*, (Ont.), 1 H. E. C. 214.

acts of the agent of the other candidate with whom he has coalesced, and if a corrupt act is brought home to the one, both are unable to hold their seats (*p*). But acts committed before the coalition will not affect the other candidate unless he was aware of such acts, though where he has such knowledge he will be taken to have adopted the acts (*q*). Where the respective agents for two candidates jointly attended to the registration, but during the election did not act in concert, it was held that there was not sufficient joint action to constitute mutual agency (*r*).

WHAT CONSTITUTES AGENCY.

No answer to a warning from the candidate to an over zealous supporter as to the consequences of some questionable act, is more common than this—"I'm no agent of yours!" Yet in nine cases out of ten, the courts would hold that agency existed. It is well therefore to deal briefly with the question of what constitutes agency.

No precise rules can be given which will answer as tests in every case as to whether agency is established or not. Agency in election matters is a result of law to be drawn from the facts in the case and from the acts of individuals (*s*). "The law of agency in election matters is not a hard and fast law, capable of precise definition; it is a shifting, elastic law, capable of being moulded from time to time to meet the shrewd and astute inven-

(*p*) *Norfolk, (N. Div.)*, judgments, 269; 1 O'M. & H. 240; *Norwich*, 2 O'M. & H. 39.

(*q*) *Malcolm* v. *Perry*, (*Boston, 2nd case*,) 10 L. R. C. P. 168.

(*r*) *Tamworth*, 1 O'M. & H. 83.

(*s*) *Sligo*, judgments. 145; *E. Peterboro'*, 1 H. E. C. 245.

tions of those who in such matters seek to get rid of the consequences of their acts" (*t*).

Agent need not be paid.

It is by no means necessary that it should be shown that person employed in order to be an agent for the purpose of getting votes is paid in the slightest degree, or is in the nature of being a paid person (*u*).

Agency inferred from agency at previous Election.

The agency of a particular person may be inferred from his having acted as agent at an election a short time previously (*v*).

Candidate's wife.

A candidate's wife, if she interferes in the election, is *ipso facto* his agent (*w*).

Any trifling act may be evidence of agency, and an aggregate of such acts may together constitute agency, even though no one of them, apart from the others, might be conclusive. Among the most common of these are, (1) being a member of the convention which nominates the candidate; (2), being a member of an association or committee promoting the election; (3), canvassing alone or with others apart from the candidate; (4), canvassing in company with the candidate; (5), attending meetings and speaking on behalf of the candidate; (6), bringing up voters to the poll.

Being a Member of the Nominating Convention.

Extracts from the judgments of Gwynne J., in three Ontario cases will serve to illustrate the principles which guide the courts in determining whether a delegate to a convention be an agent or not. In the first case he says (*x*): "Now although the respondent was put forward by

(*t*) *N. Ontario*, per Armour, J., H. E. C. 789.

(*u*) *Bewdley*, 1 O'M. & H. 17.

(*v*) *Waterford*, 2 O'M. & H. 2.

(*w*) *Hastings*, judgments, 235.

(*x*) *Welland*, 1 H. E. C. p. 192.

the Reform Association as the candidate of the party, and although he accepted the nomination, and although a candidate put forward by a political Association may so deal with the members of the Association, and may so place himself in their hands with the view of availing himself of the benefits of their organization, and of the influence of the individual members of the Association, as to make them his agents, for whose acts he should be responsible; still it appears to me that it would be going altogether too far to hold that every delegate to a convention assembled for the purpose merely of selecting a candidate, although he never had any intercourse directly or indirectly with the candidate, and although he does not appear to have acted in any instance or canvassed on his behalf, unless in the sole particular case which is charged and relied upon in avoiding the election, is an agent of the candidate, so as to make him responsible for the act complained of. If it could be so held, it would make a delegate opposed to the nomination of the candidate selected by the majority, able to defeat his election by a single case of bribery committed for the express purpose of invalidating the election. In short, in such case the acceptance of the nomination by the candidate selected by the majority would have the effect of constituting every member of the convention, whether a supporter or opposed to the nomination, of the candidate selected; his agent, for whose acts the candidate would be responsible. Such a result would be repugnant to the plainest principles of justice." In another case (y) the same learned judge says: "That a candidate may so avail himself of the services of a political association in canvassing for him and promoting his election,

(y) *N. Grey*, 1 H. E. C. 364.

as to make them his agents, for whose acts he shall be responsible, there cannot, I think, be any doubt; but nothing could be more repugnant to common sense and justice than to hold that because a political association puts forward or supports a particular candidate, therefore every member of that association becomes *ipso facto* his agent." In still another case (z), in which agency was held to be established, he said, "The evidence establishes, beyond all doubt in my mind, that it is part of the constitution and organization of the Reform Association in this riding (whose candidate the respondent was) that the delegates to the convention, consisting of ten persons from each township and five from each village municipality, should so long as they might remain in office—that is, until displaced by other delegates—act in promoting the election of the candidate adopted by the convention, in all respects and in the same manner as persons appointed agents by candidates are in the habit of doing for that purpose; that the candidate looked for, expected and demanded such their assistance and agency to carry his election, and that in consequence thereof, and because of the perfection of the organization as a canvassing and general agency to conduct the election, the candidate chosen by the convention appointed no agent of his own, but used those provided by the organization. The evidence also establishes that the respondent was for six years himself a delegate—that he was well aware of the nature of the organization—that as a delegate he canvassed and acted for other candidates in the promotion of their election, and that he expected and demanded like services from all the delegates, to be rendered to him upon his candi-

(z) *East Northumberland*, 1 H. E. C. 388.

dature; and that to the perfection of that system as an electioneering agency the respondent owes his election. The evidence in like manner establishes that C. R. was a delegate—that he was a supporter of the respondent in the convention and voted for his candidature—that although perhaps not very active at first, he worked for the respondent to promote his election in canvassing for him, arranging for the bringing up of voters, and otherwise as is customary with nominated agents; and that the respondent, as the nominee of the convention, expected and claimed to be entitled to such his support and assistance. Under these circumstances, I must hold that C. R. was a person for whose acts the respondent is responsible." Chief Justice Cameron in a late case (*a*) said: "I entertain a very strong opinion that where a candidate is brought into the field by a recognized association or organization of a political party, the members of such association must be regarded, if nothing takes place to shew a repudiation by themselves or the candidate of their agency, as the latter's agents if they assume to act in his interest, and it would not be in the public interest to allow a candidate to avail himself of the result of their services without also assuming the responsibility of their acts, in so far as his seat may be affected thereby. Otherwise, while in fact relying upon the assistance of the organization, the candidate might escape the consequences of corrupt acts committed by its members by refraining from directly recognizing the individuals of the organization as his agents. It cannot be said that injustice can thereby be done to any interest concerned, though it may render necessary a new election. The opponent of the candidate who has had the

(*a*) *Lennox*, 2 Ont. El. cases, p. 61.

benefit of such agency will not be prejudiced by a new election. The candidate has no right, if he owes his election to the exertions, corrupt and otherwise, of the association, to complain that he is compelled to assume the consequences of those exertions of all kinds, as well injurious as beneficial, and the association certainly has no right to enjoy a triumph acquired through the corrupt agency of any of its members, while the general public are deeply interested in having elections conducted in a manner absolutely free from the taint of any kind of corrupt practice" (b).

Being a member of an Association or Committee promoting the Election.

"If the meeting assembles and has the sanction of the candidate, this is sufficient to render the candidate liable for its acts and those of agents appointed by it" (c). Where the number of those present at a meeting is very large, that is a reason why all present should not be considered as being appointed agents (d).

Volunteer associations or committees working for a candidate without his sanction, express or implied, will not necessarily be held to be his agents (e). Nor will everyone who attends a committee meeting, without its

(b) See *West Simcoe Prov. El. 1883*; 19 C. L. J. N. S. 370, not yet fully reported, but to be reported in 2 Ont. El. cases, where a member of a nominating convention, addressed by the candidate, who intimated that he expected his friends to work for him, was held an agent; see also, *North Ontario*, 1 H. E. C. 304, and *South Ontario*, 1 H. E. C. 420.

(c) Per Spragge, C., in *Cornwall*, 1 H. E. C. 550, *N. Wentworth*, *Ib.* 343; *N. Ontario*, 1 H. E. C. 304; *Northumberland*, *Ib.* 577; *N. Ontario*, *Ib.* 785; *S. Ontario*, 1 H. E. C. at p. 437.

(d) *Cornwall*, 1 H. E. C. 550; see *Westminster*, 1 O'M. & H. 92; *Windsor*, 2 O'M. & H. 89; *Dublin*, 1 O'M. & H. 272.

(e) *Westminster*, 1 O'M. & H. 92; *Staleybridge*, 1 O'M. & H. 70; *Wigan*, *Ib.* 188; *S. Norfolk*, 1 H. E. C. 660.

appearing how he got there or what he was to do, necessarily be held to be an agent for whose corrupt act the candidate is responsible (*f*).

Canvassing alone or with others, apart from the Candidate.

Canvassing may be either by asking a man to vote for the candidate for whom you are canvassing or by begging him not to go to the poll, but to remain neutral and not vote for the adversary (*g*). It has been laid down that a candidate is responsible generally for the deeds of those who, to his knowledge, for the purpose of promoting his election, canvass and do such other acts as may tend to promote his election, provided persons are so acting with that object (*h*). Yet there must be some sanction, express or implied, for the canvassing either by the candidate or his authorized agents (*i*). Where a canvassing book was handed to a supporter of a candidate by one to whom the candidate had delivered a number of such books to be put into good hands by the person to whom the candidate intrusted them, and the supporter canvassed voters and was guilty of a corrupt practice, he was held to be a sub-agent for whose corrupt act the candidate was responsible (*j*).

Canvassing in company with the Candidate.

This kind of canvassing, as well as canvassing apart

(*f*) *Windsor*, 2 O'M. & H. 88; *Durham*, 2 O'M. & H. 134; *N. Grey*, 1 H. E. C. 362.

(*g*) *Westbury*, 1 O'M. & H. 56.

(*h*) *Wakefield*, 2 O'M. & H. 102; *N. Ontario*, 1 H. E. C. 785; *Cornwall*, (3) 1 H. E. C. 803; *Hebert* v. *Hannington*, 6 All. (N. Br.) 530.

(*i*) *S. Norfolk*, 1 H. E. C. 660.

(*j*) *Welland* (2), 1 H. E. C. 187; *N. Ontario*, 1 H. E. C. 304.

from the candidate, does not necessarily constitute the canvasser an agent (*k*); but canvassing in company with the candidate is very strong evidence of agency (*l*). One C. accompanied the respondent when going to a public meeting and canvassed at some houses. On the journey, the respondent cautioned C. not to treat, nor do anything to compromise him and avoid the election. The respondent's election agent paid for C's. meals at the place where the meeting was held. It was held that the evidence shewed that the respondent had availed himself of C's. services, and was therefore responsible for his acts (*m*).

Attending meetings and speaking on behalf of the Candidate.

This, too, affords evidence of agency, though it is not necessarily conclusive. Where the Reeve of a township, who had been politically in accord with the ministerial candidate, but took strong ground against the government, whose candidate the respondent opposed, for having separated his township from the riding, exerted himself strongly in favour of the respondent, attended meetings where the respondent was and spoke in his favour, attended one meeting at the respondent's invitation, and at another stated (though not in the respondent's hearing) that he was acting there on the respondent's behalf, and was once in the respondent's committee room and signed and circulated a circular issued by the respondent's friends—it was held that there was no intention on his or the respondent's part to confer or

(*k*) *Shrewsbury*, 2 O'M. & H. 36; see also *Stroud*, 3 O'M. & H. 11 and *Durham*, 2 O'M. & H. 136; *S. Norfolk*, 1 H. E. C. 660.

(*l*) *Cornwall*, 1 H. E. C. 547.

(*m*) *East Peterboro'*, 1 H. E. C. 245.

accept authority, and therefore the agency was not proved. Mr. Justice Gwynne in this case (*n*) said: "What the nature and extent of the agency is, may be established by direct positive evidence, or may be inferred from the acts and conduct of the parties; but all inference is excluded, if the evidence ignores any intention upon the part of the parties either to confer or accept authority, and at the same time shows with reasonable certainty that acts, which in certain events might be sufficient to warrant the drawing an inference of an authorized agency having been created, are attributable to or explicable by other influences affecting the mind and conduct of the party alleged to be an agent in the performance of the acts relied upon as establishing the agency. In such case there is no agency, and the party assumed to be a principal cannot be affected by the acts of the other."

Bringing up Voter's to the Poll.

This, too, affords evidence of agency, though not of itself very strong.

What does Not constitute Agency.

Certain things have been held not, *per se*, sufficient to constitute agency—such as; (1) being employed as a mere card messenger (*o*); (2) being messenger of a volunteer committee (*p*); (3) being canvasser for an independent association (*q*); (4) being employed as "objector general" at the revision of the voters' lists (*r*).

Where a person, not being the candidate's agent, had made illegal payments, and the candidate not knowing

(*n*) *N. Grey*, 1 H. E. C. p. 366.

(*o*) *Windsor*, 1 O'M. & H. 3.

(*p*) *Staleybridge*, *Ib.* 72.

(*q*) *Westminster*, *Ib.* 91.

(*r*) *Wigan*, judgments 205; 1 O'M. & H. 191; *Halton*, 1 H. E. C. 736.

for what the payments had been made, repaid him, it was held, in an English case, no such satisfaction as to make the person his agent (*s*).

Treacherous agent.

If an agent, though acting for a candidate for the purposes of the election, can be shewn to have sold himself to, or to have been in treaty with the other side, the candidate will not be responsible for his corrupt acts (*t*.) It would require actual proof of authority to commit the illegal acts to make the candidate responsible (*u*). And the same rule applies where the agent is shewn to have acted treacherously out of spite or feeling against the candidate whom he ostensibly supported (*v*).

(*s*) *Tamworth*, 1 O'M. & H. 81.

(*t*) Per evidence of Willes, J., before select committee on Parliamentary and Municipal Elections, 441.

(*u*) Per Blackburn, J., *Stafford*, 1 O'M. & H. 230.

(*v*) *Lennox*, 2 Ont. El. cases, 41

CHAPTER III.

PENALTIES UNDER DOMINION LAWS.

PENALTIES ON CANDIDATE.

Penalties on candidate for corrupt practices committed by him or by his consent.

IF it is proved before any Court, judge, or other tribunal for the trial of Election Petitions, that any corrupt practice (*a*) has been committed by or with the actual knowledge and consent (*b*) of any candidate at an election, or if he be convicted before any competent court of the misdemeanor of bribery or undue influence, he shall be held guilty of corrupt practices, and

His election shall be void.

He shall be incapable of being elected to and of sitting in the House of Commons during the seven years after the date of his being so proved or found guilty.

He shall be incapable of voting at any election of a member of the House of Commons during the seven years after the date of his being so proved or found guilty.

He shall be incapable of holding an office in the nomination of the Crown, or of the Governor

(*a*) As to what are "corrupt practices," see previous chapter on "Corrupt Practices."

(*b*) As to "actual knowledge and consent," see *ante* chapter on *Corrupt Practices—Relieving Sections*, etc.; *N. Wentworth*, H. E. C. 343; *N. Grey*, H. E. C. 362.

(*General*) in Canada during the seven years after the date of his being so proved or found guilty (*c*), 37 Vic. cap. 9 s. 102.

Personation or subornation thereof. By sec. 76 of 37 Vic. cap. 9, if on the trial of any election petition questioning the election or return for any electoral district, any candidate or other person is found by the report of the judge, by himself or his agents with his actual knowledge and consent to have been guilty of personation or by himself or his agents to have aided, abetted, counselled or procured the commission at such election of that offence by any person,

The election shall be declared void.

The candidate *or such other person* shall be incapable of being elected to or sitting in the House of Commons during the parliament for which the election is held and during the then next parliament (*d*).

Employment of disqualified person as canvasser or agent. If, on the trial of any election petition, any candidate is proved to have personally engaged at the election to which such petition relates, as a canvasser or agent (*e*)

(*c*) See new Consolidated and Revised Statutes, C. *Na.* s. 97.

(*d*) This seems to conflict with sec. 102 above referred to, as personation is declared by sec. 75 to be a "corrupt practice," and subornation of personation by sec. 98. (See sec. 98 of new Consolidated Act).

By sec. 97, every candidate who corruptly by himself, or by or with any other person on his behalf, compels or induces, or endeavours to induce any person to personate any voter, or to take any false oath in any matter wherein an oath is required under the Act, shall be guilty of a misdemeanor, and shall in addition to any other punishment to which he may be liable for such offence, be liable to forfeit the sum of $200 to any person suing for the same.

(*e*) It has been held sufficient to bring the case within this sec., if the agent be appointed with the candidate's knowledge and consent, and that a personal interview with him is not necessary—*N. Norfolk*, 1 O'M. & H. 238 ; *Norwich*, 2 O'M. & H. 40. It has been held in England also that the agent must not be merely one who might be employed to such an extent as might make the candidate responsible for corrupt practices committed by him, but he must be employed in the way of managing at least a portion of the election, though he may not be a paid agent. *N. Norfolk*, 1 O'M. & H. 239.

in relation to the election, any person, knowing such person has, within eight years previous to such engagement, been found guilty of any corrupt practice, by any competent legal tribunal, or by the report of any judge or other tribunal for the trial of election petitions,

The election of such candidate shall be void.

37 Vic. cap. 9, s. 103.

Corrupt practice committed by candidate or by agent without knowledge or consent of candidate.

If it is found by the report of any Court, judge or other tribunal for the trial of election petitions, that any corrupt practice has been committed by any candidate at an election, or by his agent, whether with or without the actual knowledge and consent of such candidate,

The election of such candidate shall be void.

37 Vic. cap. 9, s. 101.

Votes of persons bribed, treated, unduly influenced or employed at election to be struck off.

Where a candidate on the trial of an election petition *claiming the seat for any person*, is proved to have been guilty, by himself or by any person on his behalf, of bribery, treating or undue influence in respect of any person who voted at such election, or where any person retained or employed for reward by or on behalf of such candidate for all or any of the purposes of such election, as agent, clerk, messenger or in any other employment, is proved on such trial to have voted at such election,

There shall be struck off from the votes given to such candidate one vote for every person who voted and is proved to have been so bribed (*f*), treated or unduly influenced, or so retained or employed for reward (*g*), 37 Vic. c. 9, s. 73, and, under sec. 94, a vote shall be struck off (*h*) for

(*f*) It has been held under a similar section of the English Act that a guilty intent in the voter bribed must be proved, *Malcolm* v. *Parry*, L. R. 9 C. P. 610; 43 L. J. C. P. 331.

(*g*) As to persons retained or employed, see Dominion Franchise Act, s. 11, subs. b. and note *ante*.

(*h*) By sec. 96, any voter hiring any horse or conveyance for any candidate or his agent, for the purpose of conveying any voters to or from the poll shall, *ipso facto*, be disqualified from voting; but, although the offence is a corrupt practice and avoids the

every person who is proved to have been corruptly treated, even apparently where the petition does not claim the seat.

Treating.

Under the same sec. (94) the candidate guilty of treating as defined by that section shall forfeit the sum of $200 to any person who shall sue for the same, with full costs of suit, in addition to any other penalty to which he may be liable therefor under any other provision of the Act.

Candidate subject to civil and criminal penalties.

The candidate is also subject to the civil and criminal penalties hereinafter referred to, to the same extent as other persons.

PENALTIES ON PERSONS OTHER THAN CANDIDATE.

Corrupt Practices. Disqualification, etc.

Any person other than a candidate, found guilty of any corrupt practice in any proceeding in which, after notice of the charge, he has had an opportunity of being heard *(hh)*,

Shall, during the eight years next after the time at which he is so found guilty, be incapable of being elected to, and of sitting in the House of Commons—

Shall, during the same eight years, be incapable of voting at any election of a member of the House of Commons—

Shall, during the same eight years, be incapable of holding any office in the nomination of the Crown or of the Governor *(General)* in Canada. 37 Vic. c. 9, s. 104. (See new Consolidated Act, s. 99).

---

election (see *Selkirk case*, 4 Sup. Ct. 494), whether his vote or those of other disqualified persons whose names appear on the voters' list can be struck off on the trial of a petition is questionable. See secs. 11, 39 and 58 of the Franchise Act, 48 Vic. c. 40, and notes thereunder *ante*.

(hh) For procedure to procure conviction for corrupt practices, see 39 Vic. c. 9.

In case on the trial of an election petition, it is determined that the election is void by reason of any act of an agent committed without the knowledge and consent of the candidate and that costs shall be awarded to the petitioner in the premises, the agent may be condemned to pay such costs. 38 Vic. c. 10, s. 4.

Personation and subornation thereof.

Corrupt practices include personation and subornation thereof (*i*), but by sec. 76 of 37 Vic. c. 9, a candidate *or other person* found, by himself or his agents with his actual knowledge and consent, to be guilty of these offences is made incapable of being elected to or sitting in the House of Commons *during the continuance of the Parliament for which the election is held and during the then next Parliament*, which may be a longer period than eight years—as well as being subjected to the other penalties imposed by sec. 74, which are a fine of $200 and imprisonment for a term not exceeding six months.

Fine and imprisonment.

Bribery and undue influence a misdemeanor.

By the "Dominion Elections Act 1874," any person committing the offence of bribery, including the receiving or agreeing to receive a bribe, or undue influence as defined by the Act, is declared guilty of a misdemeanor, and shall also be liable to forfeit the sum of $200 to any person who shall sue for the same together with full costs of suit—37 Vic. c. 9, ss. 92, 93, 95 and 109, and imprisonment for any term less than 2 years in default of payment is imposed by sec. 109 (*j*).

Pecuniary penalty.

(*i*) 37 Vic. c. 9, ss. 75 and 98.

(*j*) Sec. 109, see as to constitutionality of this section, *Doyle* v. *Bell* 32, U. C. C. P. 632—11 Ont. Ap. R 326. See as to cumulative penalties, *Joyal* v. *Safford*, 25 L. C. Jur. 166, s. c., also *Milnes* v. *Bale*, 10 L. R. C. P. 591. An informer must sue either in person or by attorney, and therefore an infant suing by next friend cannot maintain an action for a penalty under the Election Act, *Garrett* v. *Roberts*, 10 Ont. Ap. R. 650. See as to delay in prosecuting suit for penalty, *Miles* v. *Roe*, 10 Ont. Pr. R. 218.

Giving refreshments.

The giving or causing to be given to any voter on the nomination day or day of polling on account of such voter having voted or being about to vote, any meat, drink or refreshment or any money or ticket to enable such voter to procure refreshment, shall be deemed an unlawful act, and the person so offending shall forfeit the sum of $10 for each offence to any person suing for the same, with full costs of suit--37 Vic. c. 9, ss. 94 and 109; and imprisonment for any term less than 2 years in default of payment (*k*).

Pecuniary penalty.

Hiring conveyances, etc.

The hiring or promising to pay, or paying for any horse, train, carriage, cab or other vehicle, by any candidate or by any person on his behalf, to convey any voter or voters to or from the poll, or to or from the neighborhood thereof, at any election, or the payment by any candidate or by any person on his behalf, of the travelling and other expenses of any voter, in going to or returning from any election are unlawful acts; and the person so offending shall forfeit the sum of $100 to any person who shall sue for the same; and any voter hiring any horse, cab, cart, etc., for any candidate or for any agent of a candidate, for the purpose of conveying any voter or voters to or from the polling place or places, shall, *ipso facto*, be disqualified from voting, and for every such offence shall forfeit the sum of $100 to any person suing for the same, and imprisonment for any term less than 2 years in default of payment. 37 Vic. c. 9, ss. 96 and 109 (*l*).

Pecuniary penalties.

(*k*) In an action for a penalty under the Quebec Provincial Act, which contains a provision similar to the above, it was held sufficient to allege and prove the giving of drink or other refreshment by a candidate to an Elector during the election, without alleging or proving the existence of any wrong motive whatever, *Philibert* v. *Lacerte*, 3 Q. L. R. 152—S. C. R. 1877—but see cases noted under *Treating*, *ante*.

(*l*) Hiring a railway train comes within section 96, *N. Simcoe*, 1 H. E. C. 50. The offence is a "corrupt practice," *Selkirk* 4 Sup. Ct. 494. The form of action for these pecuniary penalties is by action of debt or information, 37 Vic., c. 9, s. 109; (see also judgment of Wilson, C. J., in *Doyle* v. *Bell*, 32 U. C. C. P. 632; 11 Ont. Ap. R. 326, *ante* p. 311, note (j); *Raymond* v. *Valin*, 6 Q. L R. 146, Q. B. 1880; *Robillard* v. *Lecavalier*, 7 R. L. 662, s. c. 1877, *Tarte* v. *Cimon*, 3 L. N. 195, Q. B. 1880.

In case on the trial of an election petition, it is determined that any person has been guilty of a corrupt practice within the meaning of the Dominion Controverted Elections Act, 1874 or in case there is in the opinion of the judge sufficient evidence available that any person has been guilty of such corrupt practice to warrant his being put on his trial, the judge shall order that he be summoned to appear at a time and place to be fixed in the summons in order to be tried for such offence; and in case of a conviction of a corrupt practice,

Conviction for corrupt practices under 39 Vic. c. 9.

The offender shall be sentenced to imprisonment in the common gaol for a term not exceeding 3 months, with or without hard labour; and to a fine not exceeding $200, and to pay the costs of the prosecution, and if the fine and costs be not paid before the expiration of such term, then to imprisonment for such further time as they shall remain unpaid, not exceeding 3 months. 39 Vic. cap 9, s. 14.

Imprisonment, fine, costs.

No spirituous or fermented liquors or strong drinks shall be sold or given at any hotel, tavern or shop or other place *(ll)* within the limits of any polling district, during the whole of the polling day at any election for the House of Commons *(m)*,

Selling or giving liquors in taverns, etc.

Under a penalty of $100 for every offence; and the offender shall be subject to imprisonment, not exceeding six months, at the discretion of the judge or Court, in default of payment of such fine. 37 Vic. c. 9, s. 91.

No candidate shall at any election, nor shall any other person either provide or furnish drink or other refreshment at the expense of such candidate, to any elector during such election, or pay for, procure or engage to

Entertainment of electors.

(ll) See *ante*, Chapter I, *Treating*.

(m) This is made a corrupt practice under the Ontario Act, though confined to the keeper of the hotel, etc., see *ante* "Corrupt Practices."

pay for any such drink or other refreshment. The offender shall be deemed guilty of a misdemeanor punishable by a fine not exceeding $100, or imprisonment not exceeding 3 months, or both. 37 Vic. c. 9, ss. 87 and 90.

Strangers and others bearing arms.

Any person, other than the Returning officer or his Deputy or the Poll Clerk or Constables, who has not a stated residence in the polling district for at least six months before the day of such election, coming into such polling district during any part of the day, upon which the poll is to remain open, armed with offensive weapons of any kind; or *any person whosoever* who, being in such polling district, shall arm himself with any such offensive weapons, and being thus armed, approach within the distance of one mile of the poll, unless called upon by lawful authority, shall be deemed guilty of a misdemeanor punishable by fine not exceeding $100, or imprisonment not exceeding 3 months, or both. 37 Vic. c. 9, ss. 86 and 90

Party ensigns and favours.

Any candidate or other person furnishing any ensign, standard or set of colours, or other flag or any ribbon, label or like favour with intent that the same be carried or used or worn in the electoral district on the day of election or within 8 days before such day or during the continuance of such election or the polling, as a party flag or badge; and any person carrying such ensign, etc., as a party flag or badge within the electoral district within the aforesaid times, shall be guilty of a misdemeanor punishable by fine not exceeding $100, or imprisonment not exceeding 3 months, or both. 37 Vic. c. 9, ss. 88 and 90.

Battery.

Every person convicted of a battery, committed during any day whereon any election or any poll for any election, is begun, holden or proceeded with, within the distance of two miles of the place where such election is begun, etc., shall be deemed guilty of an aggravated assault and shall be punished accordingly. 37 Vic. c. 9, sec. 85.

Forging or destroying ballot paper.

Any person (1) Forging or counterfeiting or fraudulently altering, defacing or fraudulently destroying any ballot paper or the initials of the Deputy-Returning officer signed theron ;

Supplying ballot paper without authority.

(2) Without authority supplying any ballot paper to any person ;

Stuffing ballot box.

(3) Fraudulently putting into any ballot box any paper other than the ballot paper, which he is authorized by law to put in ;

Taking ballot out of polling place.

(4) Fraudulently taking out of the polling place any ballot paper ;

Destroying or interfering with ballot box.

(5) Without due authority destroying, taking, opening or otherwise interfering with any ballot box or packet of ballot papers then in use for the purposes of the election ;

Attempting such offences.

Or attempting to commit any of such offences—

Penalty—

Shall be guilty of misdemeanor punishable,

On Returning officer and other officers ;

(1) If he be a Returning officer, Deputy-Returning officer or other officer engaged at the election, by a fine not exceeding $1,000, or by imprisonment for any term less than two years, with or without hard labor, in default of payment.

On other persons.

(2) If any other person, by a fine not exceeding $500, or by imprisonment not exceeding six months, with or without hard labour, in default of payment. 37 Vic. c. 9, s. 68.

Elector taking ballot paper out of booth.

No elector shall be allowed to take out of polling station his ballot paper ; and by doing so he incurs a penalty not exceeding $200.

Neglect or refusal to furnish lists to Returning officer.

Every officer who shall omit or refuse to furnish voters' lists, copies or extracts therefrom within a reasonable time to the Returning officer requiring the same, shall incur a penalty of not less than $200, and not exceeding $2,000 (*n*). 37 Vic. c. 9, s. 29.

(*n*) See *Marcotte* v. *Paquin*, 5 Q. L. R., 168 ; S. C. 1879.

Officers or ag'nts at poll communicating information.

Any officer, clerk or agent in attendance at a polling place, communicating before the poll is closed to any person any information as to whether any person on the voters' list has or has not applied for a ballot paper or voted at that polling place;

Officers, agents and others interfering with voter.

Any officer, clerk, agent or other person whomsoever interfering or attempting to interfere with a voter when marking his vote, or otherwise attempting to obtain at the polling place information as to the candidate for whom any voter at such polling place is about to vote or has voted;

Officers, agents or others communicating information at any time.

Any officer, clerk, agent or other person communicating at any time to any person any information obtained at a polling place as to the candidate for whom any voter at such polling place is about to vote or has voted;

Officers, clerks or agents present at counting of votes communicating information.

Every officer, clerk or agent in attendance at the counting of the votes, attempting to ascertain at such counting, or communicating any information obtained at such counting, as to the candidate for whom any vote is given in any particular ballot paper;

Inducing voter to display ballot.

Any person directly or indirectly, inducing any voter to display his ballot paper after he has marked the same, so as to make known to any person the name of the candidate for or against whom he has so marked his vote—

Penalty.

Incurs a fine not exceeding $200, or imprisonment for any term not exceeding 6 months, with or without hard labour, in default of payment.

Maintaining secresy.

The officers and agents present must maintain and aid in maintaining the secrecy of the proceeding under a like penalty (*o*). 37 Vic. c. 9, s. 72.

(*o*) An admission by a defendant that he disclosed such information has been held sufficient to support a conviction without shewing that the voter in fact voted at all. *Reg.* v. *Unkles*, 8 Ir. Rep. C. L. 50. To incur a penalty for "communicating information," it is not enough merely to put it in the power of another to acquire the information; it is necessary to show that the intelligence actually reached the mind

If any person unlawfully, either by violence or stealth takes from any Deputy-Returning officer or Poll Clerk, or from any other person having the lawful custody thereof, or from its lawful place of deposit for the time being, or unlawfully or maliciously destroys, injures or obliterates, or causes to be wilfully or maliciously destroyed, injured or obliterated, or makes or causes to be made any erasure, addition of names, or interlineation of names, into or upon, or aids, counsels or assists in so doing, in, to or upon any list of voters or writ of election, or any return to a writ of election, or any report, certificate or affidavit or any document or paper made, prepared or drawn out according to or for the purpose of meeting the requirements of "The Dominion Elections Act 1874," or any of them, every such offender shall be guilty of felony, and shall be liable to

Stealing or tampering with poll book, returns, etc.

Felony.

Imprisonment in the Penitentiary for any term not exceeding 7 years, nor less than 2 years,

Penalties.

Or to be imprisoned in any other gaol or place of confinement for a period not less than 2 years, with or without hard labour. 37 Vic. c. 9, s. 107.

Every officer and clerk guilty of any wilful misfeasance or any wilful act or omission in contravention of the above Act, shall forfeit to any person aggrieved by such misfeasance, act or omission, a penal sum not exceeding $500, in addition to the amount of all actual

Misfeasance or omission by officers.

Penalty.

of the person to whom the communication is made. It has been held that no one but the Deputy-Returning Officer was authorized, under the Ontario Act (which is similar to the Dominion Elections Act in regard to marking the ballots of those incapacitated from voting), to mark a voter's ballot, or to interfere with or question a voter as to his vote; and the Deputy-Returning Officer permitting the agent of a candidate to become acquainted with the name of the candidate for whom the voter desired to vote, violated the duty imposed on him to conceal from *all* persons the mode of voting, and to maintain the secresy of the proceedings, *Halton (Ont.) Russell et al.* v. *Barber*, 1 H. E. C. 283; see also *Hickson et al.* v. *Abbott*, 25 L. C. J. 289. *Stannanaught* v. *Hazeltine*, 4 C. P. D. 191.

damages thereby occasioned to such person (*p*). 37 Vic. c. 9, s. 70.

(*p*) It has been held under the corresponding sec. in the Ontario Act in an action against a Returning Officer for not delaying his return after receiving notice from the County Judge of a recount, that where such notice had not come to the knowledge of defendant the default was not "wilful," *Hays* v. *Armstrong*, 7 Ont. R. 621. It was also held in the same case by the judge at the trial that the plaintiff, the defeated candidate, was a "person aggrieved" within the section. See further as to "wilful" and "person aggrieved," *Atkins* v. *Ptolemy*, 5 Ont. R. 366. It has been held in England that an action will lie against the presiding officer at a polling station by a party who has lost an election through votes given for him being thrown away for want of the official mark, even though no malice is alleged, and if the duty of delivering papers marked with the official mark be delegated by the presiding officer to a clerk, the action will lie against the latter and not against the presiding officer, the clerk not being appointed by him, but by the Returning officer, the reverse however, being the case under our Act. *Pickering* v. *James*, 8. L R. C. P. 489; By sec. 80 of the Dominion Elections Act, no election shall be declared invalid by reason of a non-compliance with the rules contained in the Act as to the taking of the poll or the counting of the votes, or by reason of any want of qualification in the persons signing the nomination paper, or of any mistake in the use of the forms contained in the schedules, if it appears to the Court that the election was conducted in accordance with the principles laid down in the Act, and the result of the election was not affected. Under this it was held by V. C. Blake, (*Monck*, 1 H. E. C. 725), that the neglect of a Deputy-Returning Officer to initial the ballot papers would not avoid the election, and this decision was commented on and approved of by the Supreme Court in the *Queen's County*, P. E. Island case (7 Sup. Ct. 247), in which a similar neglect was held to come within the saving clause of the Act. The Supreme Court in the *Bothwell case* (8 Sup. Ct. 676), arrived at a similar decision. In that case the Deputy-Returning officer, at the request of one of the agents, who thought the ballot papers were being improperly marked, initialed and numbered about twelve ballot papers, but judging he was wrong at the close of the poll, he in good faith and with an anxious desire to do his duty, and in such a way as not to allow any person to see the front of the ballot paper, and with the assent of the agents of both parties, took the ballots out of the box and obliterated the marks he had put upon them. The ballots were held good, and the irregularities were declared to be within sec. 80. In all these cases, it is to be observed, there was no doubt as to the identity of the ballots with those supplied by the Deputy-Returning officers, and that the secrecy of the votes had been maintained. See also *White et al.* v. *Mackenzie*, 20 L. C. J. 22 S. C. 1875; *Bernatchez* v. *Fortin*, 9 Q. L. R. 81. It was held by Armour, J., in the *E. Hastings* case (1 H. E. C., 764), that where numbers were placed on the ballots corresponding with the numbers attached to names of voters on the voters' list, the Deputy-Returning officers had acted contrary to law, that the ballots must be rejected and the result having been thereby changed, a new election must be held. See also *Montreal Centre Election*, 1 L. N. 496, S. C. 1878.

Any Returning officer, Deputy-Returning officer, Election Clerk or Poll Clerk, who refuses or neglects to perform any of the obligations or formalities required by the Act, shall for each such refusal or neglect forfeit the sum of Two hundred dollars to any person suing for the same (*q*). 37 Vic. c. 9, s. 108. **Neglect of duty by Returning officer, etc.**

If any Returning officer wilfully delays, neglects or refuses duly to return any person elected, such person may, *in case it has been determined on the hearing of an election petition respecting the election*, that such person was entitled to have been returned, sue the Returning officer and recover $500, together with all damages he has sustained and full costs of suit; provided the action be commenced within one year after the commission of the act on which it is grounded, or within six months after the conclusion of the trial of the election petition. 37 Vic. c. 9, s. 106 (*qq*). **Returning officer not returning candidate.** **Penalty.** **Limitation.**

No payment (except in respect of the personal expenses of a candidate) and no advance, loan or deposit, shall be made by or on behalf of any candidate at any election, before or during or after such election, otherwise than through the duly appointed agent of the candidate; any person making any such payment, advance, loan or deposit otherwise than through such agent or agents shall be guilty of a misdemeanor (*r*). 37 Vic. c. 9, s. 121. **Payment of election expenses otherwise than through agent.** **Misdemeanor.**

All persons who have any bills, claims or charges upon a candidate for or in respect of the election must send **Bills to be sent in within one**

(*q*) Under a corresponding section of the Ontario Act it was held that a Deputy-Returning officer who refused the tendered votes of those who had sufficiently shewn their right to vote came within the penalty of the section, *Walton* v. *Apjohn*, 5 Ont. R. 65.

(*qq*) It has been held under the New Brunswick Provincial Act that an action would not lie against a Sheriff for a false return to a writ of election without proof of actual malice, *Stiles* v. *Gilbert*, 4 All. 421.

(*r*) As to what are lawful expenses, see proviso to sec. 92, also *N. Ontario*, 4 Sup. Court, 430 *ante*. As to what are "personal expenses," see sec. 125.

month, or right to recover barred. them in within one month after the day of the election to the agent, or their right to recover will be barred; Provisoes. with a proviso in the event of the death of the person claiming the bill, his legal representative may send it in within a month of his obtaining probate or letters of administration, or becoming otherwise able to act; and also that the bills may be sent to the candidate in case of death or legal incapacity of the agent. The agent is not to pay any bill, charge or claim without the authority of the candidate as well as the approval of the agent. 37 Vic. c. 9, s. 122.

Default in delivering statement of the election expenses. Any agent or candidate making default in delivering to the Returning officer a detailed statement of all election expenses within two months after the election (or in cases where by reason of the death of the creditor no bill has been sent in within such two months, then within one month after such bill has been sent in) shall Penalty. incur a penalty not exceeding $20 for every day's default; and any agent or candidate who wilfully Penalty for false statement. furnishes to the Returning officer any untrue statement shall be guilty of a misdemeanor. 37 Vic. c. 9, s. 123 (*rr*).

Who may not act as agents. No Returning officer or Deputy-Returning officer for any Electoral District nor any partner or clerk of either of them shall act as agent for any candidate in the management or conduct of his election for such Electoral District. If any such person so acts he shall be guilty of a misdemeanor. 37 Vic. c. 9, s. 124.

Proceedings to collect penalties. All penalties and forfeitures (other than fines in cases of misdemeanors) imposed by the Dominion Election Act 1874, shall be recoverable, with full costs of suit, by any person who will sue for the same by action of

---

(*rr*) The personal expenses of the candidate should be included in the statement to be furnished under this section to the returning officer, *per* Taschereau, J., in *Bellechasse case*, 5 Sup. Ct. 91. As to effect upon election of agents not keeping accounts or vouchers or destroying same, see *S. Grey* (Ont). 1 H. E. C. 52; 8 C. L. J., 17; (*E. Toronto, Ont.*) 1 H. E. C., 70; 8 C. L. J. 113.

debt or information, in any of Her Majesty's Courts in the Province in which the cause of action arose, having competent jurisdiction; and in default of payment of the amount which the offender is condemned to pay, within the period fixed by the Court, the offender shall be imprisoned in the common gaol of the place, for any term less than two years, unless such fine and costs be sooner paid (s). 37 Vic. c. 9, s. 109.

Limitation of prosecutions and actions.

Every prosecution for misdemeanor under the Dominion Elections Act 1874, and every action, suit or proceeding for any pecuniary penalty given by the Act to the person suing for the same, shall be commenced within one year after the act committed, and not afterwards (unless the same be prevented by the withdrawal or absconding of the defendant out of the jurisdiction of the Court) and being commenced shall be proceeded with and carried on without wilful delay. 37 Vic. c. 9, s. 110.

Power of Court or Judge trying election petition to impose certain penalties.

Whenever it shall appear to the Court or judge trying an election petition, that any officer, elector, or other person, has contravened any of the provisions of the Dominion Elections Act, 1874—for which contravention he might be liable to a fine or penalty (other than fines and penalties imposed for any offences amounting to a misdemeanor or felony), such Court or judge may order that such officer, elector or other person, be summoned to appear before such Court or judge, at the place, day and hour fixed in such summons for hearing the charge. In default of appearance he shall be condemned on the evidence already adduced on the trial to pay such fine or penalty, and in default of payment to the imprisonment imposed in the particular case. If he do appear the Court or judge, after hearing such party and such

(s) See *Doyle* v. *Bell*, 32 U. C. C. P. 632. The person suing must give security for costs to the extent of $50 before commencing proceedings, 46 Vic. c. 4. See also *Raymond* v. *Valin*, 6 Q. L. R. 146, Q. B. 1880. *Robillard* v. *Lecavalier*, 7 R. L., 662, S. C. 1877, *Tarte* v. *Cimon*, 3. L. N. 195, Q. B., 1880.

evidence as may be adduced, shall give judgment—all fines under the section quoted shall belong to Her Majesty; and no fine shall be imposed thereunder if it shall appear to the judge or Court that the party has already been sued for the same offence, nor shall any such fine be imposed for any offence proved only by the evidence or admission of the party committing it. 37 Vic. c. 9, s. 117.

Double prosecutions forbidden.

Perjury.

Every person taking any oath or affirmation under the Dominion Elections Act 1874, who wilfully swears or affirms falsely, shall be deemed guilty of perjury.

Removal of disqualification procured by perjury.

If at any time after any person has become disqualified for corrupt practices, the witnesses or any of them, on whose testimony such person shall have so become disqualified, are, upon the prosecution of such person, convicted of perjury in respect of such testimony, it shall be lawful for such person to move the Court before which such conviction shall take place, to order, and such Court shall, upon being satisfied that such disqualification was procured by reason of such perjury, order that such disqualification shall thenceforth cease and determine; and the same shall cease and determine accordingly. 37 Vic. c. 9, s. 108.

CHAPTER IV.

PENALTIES UNDER ONTARIO PROVINCIAL LAWS.

*Penalties on Candidate.**

WHEN it is found by the report of the judges upon an election petition that any corrupt practice (*a*) has been committed, by or with the actual knowledge or consent (*b*) of any candidate (*c*) at an election,

Penalties on candidate for corrupt practices committed by him o with his consent.

* With regard to the avoidance of a prior election for the same district, a subsequent election is to be deemed a new election, except as to the personal acts of the candidates and the acts of agents done with the knowledge and consent of the candidates; Rev. Stats. c. 10, s. 166. See *Cornwall* (2), 1 H. E. C. 647.

(*a*) As to what are corrupt practices, see previous chapter on that subject.

(*b*) The words used in s. 102 of the Dom. Election Act are knowledge *and* consent. See Penalties under Dominion laws, *ante;* also "Relieving sections in Ontario Acts," *ante.*

(*c*) By sec. 43 of The Election Law Amendment Act 1884, the expression "candidate" means, unless the context otherwise requires, "any person elected at such election to serve in the Legislative Assembly, and any person who is nominated as a candidate at such election, or is declared by himself or by others to be a candidate, on or after the day of the issue of the writ for such election, or after the dissolution or vacancy in consequence of which such writ has been issued; provided that where a person has been nominated as a candidate, or declared to be a candidate by others, then, (*a*) If he was so nominated or declared without his consent, nothing in this Act shall be construed to impose any liability on such person, unless he has afterwards given his assent to such nomination or declaration or has been elected; and (*b*) If he was so nominated or declared, either without his consent or in his absence and he takes no part in the election, he may, if he thinks fit, make the declaration respecting election expenses contained in the second schedule to this Act. [*Note*—

His election shall be void—Rev. Stats. Ont. c. 10, s. 158.

He shall be incapable of being elected to and of sitting in the Legislative Assembly during the eight (*d*) years next after the date of his being so found guilty.

He shall be incapable of being entered in any voters' list and of voting at any election, during the same eight years.

He shall be incapable of holding any office at the nomination of the Crown or of the Lieutenant Governor, in Ontario, or any municipal office, during the same eight years (*e*). Rev. Stats. Ont. cap. 10, s. 161.

Employment of disqualified person as canvasser or agent.

If on the trial of any election petition, any candidate is proved to have personally engaged at the election to which such petition relates, as a canvasser or agent (*f*) in relation to the election, any person, knowing that such person has, within eight years previous to such engagement, been found guilty of any corrupt practice by any competent legal tribunal, or by the report of the Judges upon an election petition,

---

The second schedule referred to contains no such declaration], and the election agent shall, so far as circumstances admit comply with the provisions of this Act, with respect to expenses [*Note*—No such provisions appear in the Act quoted] incurred on account of or in respect of the conduct or management of the election in like manner as if the candidate had been nominated or declared with his consent."

(*d*) The term under the Dominion Law is *seven* years; see Penalties under Dominion Laws, *ante*.

(*e*) The disqualification does not attach without the concurrent judgment of the two trial judges. See *ante* p. 290, and 48 Vic. (Ont.) c. 2, s. 18; nor where either of such judges find that the corrupt practice was committed "without any corrupt intent and in ignorance which was involuntary and excusable, etc."

(*f*) See Penalties under Dom. Laws, note (*e*).

The election of such candidate shall be void. Rev. Stats. c. 10 s. 165.

Where it is found upon the report of a judge upon an election petition that any corrupt practice has been committed by any candidate at an election or by his agent, whether with or without the actual knowledge and (*g*) consent of such candidate, the election of such candidate, if he has been elected, shall except in the cases mentioned in section one hundred and fifty nine (*h*)—be void. Rev. Stats. c. 10, s. 158.

Corrupt practice committed by candidate or by agent with or without his consent.

In case a candidate or the agent of a candidate is proved to have committed any corrupt practice with respect to a voter, there shall on a scrutiny (*i*) be struck off from the number of votes given for such candidate one vote for every person in regard to whom such corrupt practice is proved to have been committed, and without any examination of the ballot paper or other evidence to ascertain how such voter in fact voted. 47 Vic. (Ont.) c. 4, s. 5.

Votes of persons in regard to whom corrupt practices are proved, struck off.

The candidate is also subject to the pecuniary penalties hereinafter referred to, to the same extent as other persons.

Penalties on persons other than candidate.

Any person other than a candidate, found guilty of any corrupt practice in any proceeding in which, after notice of the charge, he has had an opportunity of being heard (*j*),

Corrupt practices.

(*g*) See note *b*, *ante*.

(*h*) Sec. 159, provides for the election not being avoided where the corrupt acts are "trifling" in nature or extent, and the result was not affected. See *ante* "Relieving Sections in Ontario Acts."

(*i*) A scrutiny is entered upon only when the seat is claimed for the unsuccessful candidate.

(*j*) Sec. 175 of the Ont. Elections Act, as amended by 47 Vic. (Ont.) c. 4, s. 31, provides for the procedure in cases where the guilty persons are not parties to the petition.

Disqualification, etc.

Shall, during the eight years next after the time at which he is so found guilty, be incapable of being elected to and of sitting in the Legislative Assembly;

Shall during the same eight years, be incapable of being registered as a voter and of voting at any election;

Shall during the same eight years be incapable of holding any office in the nomination of the Crown or of the Lieutenant-Governor in Ontario, or any municipal office (*k*). Rev. Stats. cap. 10, s. 164.

Person bribed.

If on the trial of any election petition, it is proved that any elector voting at the election was bribed, besides being guilty of a corrupt practice,

He shall be disqualified from voting at the next general election. Rev. Stats. c. 10, s. 163.

Corrupt practice by elector.

If on the trial of any election petition, it is proved that any corrupt practice has been committed by any elector voting at the election,

His vote shall be null and void. Rev. Stats. c. 10, s. 163.

Bribery.

Every person found guilty (*l*) of bribery (whether he be a briber or a person bribed), in addition to being guilty of a corrupt practice,

Shall incur a penalty of $200 (*m*). Rev. Stats. c. 10, ss. 149 and 150.

(*k*) By subsection to this sec. (164), no person other than a candidate shall be subject to the disabilities above set forth "(1) by reason of a merely technical breach of the law; (2) by reason of any act not being an intentional violation of the law, and not involving moral culpability or affecting the result of the election."

(*l*) As to procedure, see 47 Vic. c. 4, s. 31.

(*m*) The penalties for several offences by the same person would seem to be cumulative. The bribery sections are the same as in the Dominion Act, and under that

Every person furnishing drink or other entertainment, at his expense, to any meeting of electors assembled to promote the election, except at his or her usual place of residence, in addition to being guilty of a corrupt practice, **Treating at meetings.**

Shall incur a penalty of $100. Rev. Stats. c. 10, s. 151.

Every person guilty of corrupt treating, shall incur a penalty of $200, with full costs of suit to any person who sues for the same in addition to any other penalty to which he may be liable. Rev. Stats. c. 10, s. 152. **Corrupt treating.**

Any person giving or causing to be given to any voter on nomination day or day of polling, "on account of such voter being about to vote or having voted" (*n*) any meat, drink or refreshment, or any money or ticket to enable such voter to procure refreshment, **Giving meat, drink, etc., on nomination or polling day.**

Shall forfeit to any person suing for the same, the sum of $10 for each offence, with full costs of suit. Rev. Stats. c. 10, s. 153.

Any candidate or other person hiring or promising to pay or paying for any horse, team, carriage, cab or other vehicle (*o*), on behalf of a candidate, to convey voters to or near or from the poll, or the neighbourhood thereof, or paying, on the same behalf, the travelling and other expenses of any voter, besides being guilty of a corrupt practice, **Hiring conveyances, etc.**

---

the penalties have been held in Quebec cumulative, *Joyal* v. *Safford*, 25 L. C. J. 166. See also *Milnes* v. *Bale*, 10 L. R. C. P. 591. The question was brought before the Court of Appeal in the *Lennox* case, but was not decided. See as to infant suing, *Parrett* v. *Roberts*, 10 Ont. App. R. 650, and as to delay in prosecuting, *Miles* v. *Roe*, 10 Ont. Pr. R. 218.

(*n*) The giving must in some way be connected with "such voter being about to vote or having voted," *per* Richards C. J. in *Jacques Cartier*, 2 Supreme Court, 242. See *ante*, "Treating."

(*o*) Hiring a railway train comes within the section, *N. Simcoe*, 1 H. E. C. 50. It matters not when the hiring took place or whether the voter comes or not, *Selkirk*, 4 Sup. Ct. 494. See *ante*, "Corrupt Practices."

Shall incur a penalty of $100. Rev. Stats. c. 10, s. 154.

Any elector who hires any horse, cab, cart, waggon, sleigh, carriage or other conveyance, for the above purpose,

Shall *ipso facto* be disqualified from voting at such election;

Shall for every such offence incur a penalty of $100. Rev. Stats. c. 10, s. 154.

Undue influence.

Every person who commits the offence of undue influence, as defined by the Election Act, in addition to being guilty of a corrupt practice,

Shall incur a penalty of $200. Rev. Stats. c. 10, s. 155.

Personation.

Any person who knowingly personates and falsely assumes to vote in the name of another person whose name appears on the proper list of voters, whether such other person be then living or dead, or if the name of the said other person be the name of a fictitious person, in addition to being guilty of a corrupt practice,

Shall incur a penalty of $200. Rev. Stats. c. 10, s. 156.

Inducing prohibited persons to vote.

Any person who votes or induces or procures any person to vote at any election, knowing that such person has no right to vote at such election, shall be guilty of a corrupt practice, and

Shall be liable to a penalty of $100. 47 Vic. (Ont.) c. 4, s. 4.

Voting without qualification.

Any person wilfully voting, without having, at the time of his so voting, all the qualifications required by law for entitling him so to vote, for so doing,

Shall incur a penalty of $200; and

His vote shall be null and void, and the burden of proof of having all the said qualifications shall be upon him. Rev. Stats. c. 10, s. 168.

Any person who votes more than once at the same election, for so doing **Voting more than once.**

Shall incur a penalty of $200.

Every vote he gives subsequently to his first shall be null and void. Rev. Stats. c. 10, ss. 86 and 169.

Every keeper of an hotel, tavern, shop, or other place of the same description within a polling subdivision, selling or giving spirituous or fermented liquor or strong drink to any person during the polling day therein or any part thereof, besides being guilty of a corrupt practice, if the offence be committed during polling hours (*p*), **Hotel keepers, etc., selling or giving liquor on polling day.**

Shall incur a penalty of $100 for every offence;

Shall be subject to imprisonment not exceeding six months at the discretion of the judge or Court, in default of payment of such fine. Rev. Stats. c. 10, s. 157.

If, at any time after any person has become disqualified by virtue of the Election Act, the witnesses or any of them on whose testimony such person has so become disqualified, are, upon the prosecution of such person, convicted of perjury, in respect of such testimony, it shall be lawful for such person to move the Court of Appeal to order, and the Court shall, upon being satisfied that such disqualification was procured by reason of perjury, order that such disqualification shall therefore cease and determine, and the same shall cease and determine accordingly. Rev. Stats. c. 10, s. 167. **Removal of disqualification on proof that disqualification was procured by perjury.**

(*p*) See *ante*, Corrupt Practices "selling or giving liquor on polling day under Ontario Law."

No statutory penalty for corrupt practice, where the party charged has first prosecuted a party jointly liable.

No pecuniary penalty or forfeiture imposed by any Act of the Legislature of Ontario, shall be recoverable for any act of bribery or corrupt practice at an election, in case it appears that the person charged and another person or persons were together guilty of the act charged either as giver and receiver, or as accomplices or otherwise, and that the person charged has previously *bona fide* prosecuted such other person or persons or any of them for the said act; but this provision shall not apply in case the judge, before whom the person claiming the benefit thereof is charged, certifies that it clearly appears to him that the person so charged took the first step towards the commission of the offence charged, and that such person was in fact the principal offender. Rev. Stats. c. 10, s. 173.

Proviso.

Disturbing the peace.

Any person disturbing the peace and good order of an election may, under an order signed by a Returning officer or Deputy Returning officer, be imprisoned for any period not later than the final closing of the election or of the poll respectively; which order all persons shall obey under a penalty of $20 for any refusal or neglect so to do. Rev. Stats. c. 10, s. 138. Such arrest shall not exempt the person from any other pains or penalties to which he has become liable—s. 139.

Refusal to deliver up weapons.

Every person refusing upon demand by a Returning officer or Deputy-Returning officer during any part of a day upon which an election or poll is held, to deliver up any offensive weapon with which he may be armed, shall incur a penalty of $20. Rev. Stats. c. 10, s. 140.

Battery.

Every person convicted of a battery committed during any part of such days, within the distance of two miles of the place where the election or poll is held, shall incur a penalty of $50. Rev. Stats. c. 10, s. 141.

Every person, other than the Returning officer, or his deputy or constables, who has not a stated residence in the township, union of townships, ward or subdivision, for at least six months next before the day of election, and who shall come during any part of the day of polling into such township, etc., armed with offensive weapons; or who, being in such township, etc., shall arm himself, during any part of such day, with offensive weapons and thus armed approach within two miles of the polling place, unless called upon to do so, shall incur a penalty of $100. Rev. Stats. c. 10, ss. 142 and 145.

With certain exceptions, no stranger to come armed into any township, etc., while poll open.

Nor armed person to approach within two miles of poll.

Any candidate or other person supplying any flag or set of colours, ribbon, label or like favour to any person, with intent that the same shall be used on the day of election, or within eight days before such day, as a party flag or badge; and any person carrying or using such flag, etc., as a party flag, or badge, on the day of election or polling, or within eight days before such day, shall incur a penalty of $100. Rev. Stats. c. 10, ss. 143, 144 and 145.

Party ensigns or colours not to be supplied or used.

Any person (*a*) fraudulently defacing or destroying any ballot paper, (*b*) without authority supplying any ballot paper to any person, (*c*) fraudulently putting into any ballot box any paper other than the ballot paper which he is authorized by law to put in, (*d*) fraudulently taking out of the polling place any ballot paper, (*e*) without due authority destroying, taking, opening, or otherwise interfering with any ballot box or packet of ballot papers then in use for the purposes of the election; or attempting to commit any of such offences, shall be liable,

Tampering with ballot papers or boxes.

If he is a Returning officer, to imprisonment for any term not exceeding two years, with or without hard labour:—

If he is any other person, to imprisonment for any term not exceeding six months, with or without hard labour. Rev. Stats. c. 10, s. 178.

Any person unlawfully or maliciously destroying, injuring or obliterating any writ of election, return, voters' list, certificate or affidavit or any other document or paper made in accordance with the requirements of the Election Act, or causing or aiding, abetting, counselling or procuring the commission of such offence,

Shall incur a penalty of $2000. Rev. Stats. c. 10, sec. 179.

Every officer, clerk, agent or other person

(1) Communicating before the poll is closed to any person any information as to the number on the voters' list of any person who has or who has not applied for a ballot paper or voted ;

(2) Interfering with or attempting to interfere with a voter when marking his vote, or otherwise attempting to obtain at the polling place information as to the candidate for whom any voter at such polling place is about to vote or has voted ;

(3) Communicating at any time to any person any information obtained at a polling place as to the candidate for whom any voter at such polling place is about to vote or has voted, or as to the number on the back of the ballot paper given to any voter at the polling place, or upon the counterfeit which was attached to such ballot paper, or as to the number prefixed to the name of such voter in the voters' list ;

(4) Attempting to ascertain at the counting of the ballots the number on the back of any ballot

paper, or communicating any information obtained at such counting as to the candidate for whom any vote is given in any particular ballot paper;

(5) Directly or indirectly inducing any voter to display his ballot paper after he has marked the same, so as to make known to any person how he voted (*q*),

Shall be liable on summary conviction before any Stipendary Magistrate, Police Magistrate or two Justices of the Peace to imprisonment for any term not exceeding six months, with or without hard labour. Rev. Stats. c. 10, s. 146.

The officers and agents present must maintain and aid in maintaining the secrecy of the proceedings under a like penalty in case of default. *Ib.*

Voter carrying ballot paper out of polling place.

Any person who has received a ballot paper or tendered ballot paper and leaves the polling place without first delivering the same to the Deputy-Returning officer, thereby forfeits his right to vote. Rev. Stats. cap. 10, s. 99.

Disqualified persons voting.

If any public officer or person mentioned in section 4 of the Election Act (*r*) votes at any election,

He shall thereby forfeit the sum of $2,000;

His vote shall be null and void. Rev. Stats. c. 10, s. 4.

Unqualified Returning officer acting

Any person other than a Sheriff or Registrar, who, unless he is an elector of the Electoral District at the time of his appointment, or has continually resided therein during at least twelve months immediately preceding his appointment, being appointed Returning

(*q*) See *ante*, "Penalties under Dominion Law."

(*r*) See "Ontario Provincial Franchise," *ante*.

officer, acts as such, incurs a penalty of $200. Rev. Stats. c. 10, s. 22.

Persons excluded from being Returning officers, etc., acting.

If any member of the Executive Council, member of the Parliament of the Dominion of Canada or of the Legislative Assembly of Ontario, Minister, Priest or Ecclesiastic, Judge of a Court having general jurisdiction throughout Ontario, or having local jurisdiction throughout any County or other territorial division, person who has served in the Legislature of the Province as member, in the session immediately preceding the election, or in the then present session, is appointed to act and acts as Returning officer, Deputy-Returning officer, Election Clerk or Poll Clerk, he shall incur a penalty of $200. Rev. Stats. c. 10, s. 23.

Penalty for refusal to act as Returning officer.

Every Sheriff or Registrar or other person having the requisite qualifications for acting as Returning officer, who refuses to perform the duty, after having received the Writ of Election, incurs a penalty of $200, unless he claims, by letter to the Clerk of the Crown in Chancery, forwarded within two days after receipt of the Writ, exemption as being a physician or surgeon, miller, postmaster, person sixty years of age or upwards, or a person who has served previously as Returning officer, and if being such a person he be not a Sheriff, Registrar, Town Clerk or Assessor. Rev. Stats. c. 10, ss. 24 and 25.

Refusal or neglect to post up proclamation.

Any Returning officer refusing or neglecting to cause the necessary proclamation of election to be posted up, shall incur a penalty of $200. Rev. Stats. cap. 10 s. 37.

Failure to furnish ballot boxes.

If the Returning officer fails to furnish ballot boxes, he incurs a penalty of $100 in respect of every ballot box he has failed to furnish. s. 41.

Failure to take oath, etc.

If he refuses or neglects to take and subscribe the prescribed oath of office or to annex it with the certificate of his having taken it, to his return, he incurs a penalty of $40, and any Justice of the Peace for the County or District in which the Returning officer resides and before whom he has taken the oath, who fails to deliver to him the certificate, incurs a like penalty. Rev. Stats. cap. 10, s. 42.

Any person appointed as Election Clerk, who refuses to accept the office, or to take the oath or perform the duties, incurs a penalty of $40. s. 45. Refusing to act as Election Clerk.

When an elector present at the nomination, a candidate in person or his agent, demands a poll and the Returning officer neglects or refuses to grant the same, Refusal of a Returning officer to grant a poll.

The election shall be *ipso facto* void.

The Returning officer shall incur a penalty of $1,000. Rev. Stats. cap. 10, s. 50.

Any person appointed Deputy-Returning officer who refuses to accept the office, or to take the oath or perform the duties thereof, incurs a penalty of $100. Rev. Stats. c. 10, s. 61. Refusing to act, etc., as Deputy-Returning officer.

Any person appointed Poll Clerk, who refuses to accept the office or to take the oath or perform the duties, incurs a penalty of $40. Rev. Stats. c. 10, s. 81. Refusing to act as Poll Clerk.

No person who has refused to take the oath or affirmation of qualification required by law, when requested so to do, shall receive a ballot paper or be admitted to vote. If his vote is taken and received it is null and void; and the Deputy-Returning officer shall incur a penalty of $200. Rev. Stats. c. 10, s. 90. Voter who has refused the oath.

A Deputy-Returning officer having reason to know that fraud or violence is being practised, by which undue votes are tendered, or that any voter is not qualified, or has already voted and offers to vote again, or tenders his Failure of D. R. O. to swear voters in certain cases.

vote under a false name or designation, or personates or represents himself falsely as being on the list of voters, such Deputy-Returning officer, under a penalty of $200, shall administer the oath authorized by law, whether required to do so or not by any party. Rev. Stats. c. 10, s. 93.

Refusal of D. R. O. or Poll Clerk to attend and be sworn as to lost voters' list.

A Deputy-Returning officer or Poll Clerk, who, in case any voters' list is stolen, lost or destroyed or otherwise placed beyond the reach of the Deputy-Returning officer, omits to attend personally on the Returning officer or to be sworn or affirmed by the Returning officer in order to be examined as to such loss,

Incurs a penalty of $200; and may be committed by the Returning officer to the common gaol of the County or District, until thence discharged by an order of the Legislative Assembly. Rev. Stats. c. 10, s. 123.

Returning officer may be sued for neglecting to return any person duly elected.

If any Returning officer wilfully delays, neglects or refuses duly to return any person who ought to be returned, such person may, in case it has been so determined on the hearing of an election petition, sue the Returning officer, and shall recover double the damages he has sustained by reason thereof, together with full costs of suit, provided such action be commenced within one year after the commission of the act on which it is grounded, or within six months after the conclusion of the trial relating to such election. Rev. Stats. c. 10, s. 129.

Returning officers, etc., falsifying list, etc.

If any Returning officer, Deputy-Returning officer, or any other person whose duty it is to deliver copies or have the custody of any certified list of voters, wilfully makes any alteration, omission or insertion, or in any way wilfully falsifies any such certified list or copy, every such person shall incur a penalty of $2,000. Rev. Stats. c. 10, s. 177.

Any Deputy-Returning officer or Poll Clerk who refuses or neglects to perform any of the obligations or formalities required of him by this act, shall, for each such refusal or neglect incur a penalty of $200. Rev. Stats. c. 10, s. 180.

Neglect of D. R. O. or Poll Clerk

Every officer or clerk who is guilty of any wilful misfeasance or any wilful act or omission in contravention of this Act, shall, in addition to any other penalty or liability to which he may be subject, forfeit to any person aggrieved by such misfeasance, act or omission, a penal sum of $400. Rev. Stats. c. 10, s. 181.

Misfeasance of officers

Where there is no voters' list, in case a Deputy-Returning officer rejects the vote of a person entitled to vote, if his rejecting the vote was in good faith and from believing, and having reasonable grounds for believing, that such person was not entitled to vote, such Deputy-Returning officer shall not be subject to any penalty (*s*). 47 Vic. (Ont). c. 4, s. 20.

D. R. O. rejecting vote in good faith, where there is no voters' list.

No person disqualified and incompetent to vote, under section 4 of the Election Act (*t*) shall act as agent for any candidate under penalty of $2,000. Rev. Stats. c. 10, s. 192.

Disqualified person acting as agent.

An agent, who has received a certificate entitling him to vote at a polling place other than the one at which he would otherwise be entitled to vote, and who votes without having first taken an oath of qualification, incurs a penalty of $400. 46 Vic. c. 2, s. 4, subsection (5).

Agent voting on certificate without having taken oath.

(*s*) See *Walton* v. *Apjohn*, 5 Ont. R. 65, in consequence of which case the section was passed.

(*t*) See *ante*, "Ontario Provincial Franchise."

Returning officer giving certificate to more than two agents of same candidate.

A Returning officer giving to more than two agents of the same candidate at any one polling place a certificate under section 87 of the Election Act, entitling them to vote at such polling place, instead of their regular polling place, incurs a penalty of $400. 46 Vic. c. 2, s. 4, subs. (5).

Procedure, etc.

All penalties imposed by the Election Act are recoverable with full costs, by any person who will sue by action of debt or information ; and in default of payment, imprisonment until the debt and costs are paid is prescribed. Rev. Stats. c. 10, s. 182. Procedure by summons in case of charges of corrupt practices against persons not parties to an election petition is provided for by 47 Vic. c. 4, s. 31.

Payment of Election expenses, etc.

Provisions similar to those in the Dominion Act relative to the payment of the candidate's election expenses and the delivery of detailed statements to the Returning officer for publication (*u*) are contained in the Ontario Act (*v*), the only material difference being the omission to declare the violation of the provisions a misdemeanor, as in the Dominion Statutes, and the amount of the penalty for default in delivery of the statement, which is placed at $25 per day.

(*u*) See *ante*, "Penalties under Dominion Laws" and notes.

(*v*) Rev. Stats. Ont. c. 10, secs. 183 to 186 inclusive ; as to what "personal expenses" of Candidate includes, see 42 Vic. (Ont.) c. 4. s. 19.

CHAPTER V.

CONDUCT OF THE ELECTION.

An election, speaking generally, will be void at Common Law if it be so irregularly conducted as to prevent it in the opinion of the judge from being a true election (*a*). Thus, where, owing to a mistake of the Returning officer, several polling places were closed during the whole of the polling day, and others during a considerable part of it, and a large number of electors were in consequence unable to vote, the election was declared void at Common Law (*b*). The Common Law of England relating to Parliamentary elections is in force in this country (*c*).

When election void at Common Law for irregularity.

Common Law in force here.

By section 13 of the Dominion Elections Act in cases where, from unforeseen delays, accident or otherwise, the proclamation could not be posted up so as to leave the required eight days' delay between the posting up of the proclamation and the nomination day appointed, or in case of death of any candidate after his being nominated, the Returning officer may fix another day for the nomination of candidates, which day shall be the nearest day

Unforeseen delays, etc., in posting up proclamation, or death of candidate.

New day to be fixed for nomination.

(*a*) *Hackney*, 2 O'M. and H. 77; *Woodward* v. *Sarsons*, 10 L. R. C. P. 733.

(*b*) *Hackney* 2 O'M. & H. 77.

(*c*) *Cornwall (Dom.) Election*, *Bergin* v. *Macdonald*, 1 H. E. C. 547.

possible after allowing the requisite number of days between the posting up of the proclamation and the nomination day.

Ontario Act.

Under the Ontario Act this provision is extended also to cases "where, from unforeseen delays, accidents or otherwise, the Returning officer is unable to open the election within the prescribed hours on the day he fixed for that purpose" (*d*). This amendment arose out of the circumstances of the *East Simcoe* case, in which case the Returning officer was delayed by a snow storm from reaching the place of nomination within the prescribed hours, but the nominations were received after his arrival, no objections being then raised, and the election proceeded, a poll being demanded. The learned judges who tried the case differed as to the effect of this irregularity, Chancellor Boyd considering that it did not avoid the election, and Chief Justice Cameron taking the opposite view (*e*). The case went to the Court of Appeal, but the election was declared void by that Court on other grounds. The amendment in the Provincial Act, however, provides for such cases of Provincial elections in the future.

Nomination not held at time appointed.

Non-compliance with rules, etc., not to invalidate elect'n, in certain cases.

Section 80 of the Dominion Elections Act provides that no election shall be declared invalid by reason of a non-compliance with the rules contained in the Act as to the taking of the poll or the counting of the votes, or by reason of any want of qualification in the persons sign-

(*d*) 47 Vic. c. 4, s. 37.

(*e*) Considered judgments were delivered by both judges, though not yet reported, in which the English authorities are reviewed.

Seven days' notice of the election instead of eight has been held by Canadian Parliamentary Committees in the *Cornwall case*, Pat. El. Prec. 103, *Stormont case*, *Ib*. 107, and *Norfolk case*, *Ib*. 79, not to be fatal where the result was not affected. See also *Limerick* P. & K. 365, and *Athlone*, B. & Arn. 126.

ing a nomination paper received by the Returning officer, or of any mistake in the use of the forms contained in the schedules to the Act, if it appears to the tribunal having cognizance of the question that the election was conducted in accordance with the principles laid down in the Act, and that such non-compliance or mistake *did not affect the result of the election.*

The Ontario Election Act contains a similar provision (*f*), while by section 48 of the Ontario Election Law Amendment Act 1884. it is declared "that it has been and is, the policy of the election law, and the intention and meaning of the several statutes in that behalf, that no election was or is void for any irregularity on the part of the Returning officer, unless it appears to the tribunal having cognizance of the question that the irregularity affected the result of the election." This, it is presumed, was intended to provide for a concurrent judgment by the two judges, who under the Ontario law, try election cases, before the election could be set aside for such irregularity. **Ontario Act.**

The provisions in both Dominion and Ontario Acts are very similar to those contained in section 13 of the Imperial Ballot Act 1872. **English Ballot Act.**

In the Hackney case (*g*) the borough, containing about 41,000 electors, was divided for purposes of the election into 19 polling places: two of these, where about 3,000 electors were entitled then and there only to vote, were by a mistake of the Returning officer closed throughout the polling day; and three other polling **Polls not closed by mistake, etc.**

(*f*) Rev. Stats. cap. 9, s. 197, which includes "a failure to hold a poll at any place appointed for holding a poll" among the mistakes which the section is designed to meet. See also 47 Vic. c. 4, s. 32.

(*g*) *Hackney*, 2 O'M. & H. 77. *Drogheda*, 2 O'M. & H. 202.

places, where about 4,000 electors were to vote, were closed during part of the day. Grove, J., declared the election void, both at common law and under the statute on the ground that the electors had no fair opportunity of recording their votes: It was contended that the petitioner must satisfy the Court that the majority of votes would have been the other way, if the five polling places had not been closed; but the judge said he could not enter into an examination as to how the electors would have voted. "I am very strongly inclined to think," he further said, "that the expression, 'the result of the election,' does not in this act necessarily mean the result as to another candidate having been elected at the poll The result may be of various kinds. . . . . . It will also be observed that the words used in the section are not 'did not alter the result of the election,' but, 'did not affect the result of the election.' Does not the word 'affect' mean substantially 'bear upon the result?'" Lord Coleridge in another case (*h*) said: "We think, though there was an election in the sense of their having been a selection by the will of the constituency, that the question must in like manner be, whether the departure from the prescribed method of election is so great that the tribunal is satisfied, as matter of fact, that the election was not an election under the existing law. It is not enough to say that great mistakes were made in carrying out the election under those laws; it is necessary to be able to say that, either wilfully or erroneously, the election was not carried out under those laws, but under some other method."

Meaning of words "affect the result."

Slight irregularity will not vitiate election.

Slight irregularity in the conduct of the election will not render it void, if it be shewn to have been conducted

(*h*) *Woodward* v. *Sarsons*, 10 L. R. C. P. 733, *Warrington*, 1 O'M. & H. 44.

substantially in accordance with the provisions of the Act.

In the *East Simcoe case* (*i*), one poll was not opened until between half past one and two in the afternoon of the polling day, but it appeared there was ample time from two to five to poll all the votes at that subdivision, and that all who desired to vote could have done so, and did in fact vote thereat with three or four exceptions,—three of them arriving too late. At another poll, through a blunder of the officials the supply of ballot papers ran out, and in consequence, and while waiting for instructions, the poll was closed for about half an hour. Both the Chancellor and Cameron, C. J., held that these irregularities did not *per se* affect the result and were cured by the section of the Act already alluded to (*j*), although the respondent's majority was but 21 out of a total vote polled of 2,800 or 2,900 (*k*). *E. Simcoe case.*

In cases of confusion in a polling station, the presiding officer is justified in having the room cleared and order restored before proceeding with the poll (*l*). **Returning officer may clear polling booth to restore order.**

Where at some of the polling stations two rooms were used for the purposes of voting, between which was no internal communication, but to pass from one to the other a small landing had to be crossed; each voter having received his ballot in one room crossed to the other where he filled it up, recrossed to the first room, and delivered it. A policeman was stationed on the **Improper arrangements at polling place.**

(*i*) Not yet reported—to be reported in 2 Ont. El. Cases.

(*j*) Rev. Stats. Ont. c. 10, s. 197, amended by 47 V. c. 4, s. 32.

(*k*) See also *Drogheda*, 2 O'M. & H. 201. But see *Gribbin* v. *Kirker* 7 Ir. Rep. C. L. 30, where election held void on the ground of votes received after 4 o'clock though the doors were closed at that time and no votes taken, except those already inside.

(*l*) *Worcester* 3 O'M. & H. 188.

landing to prevent any communication between the voters and other persons. The election was held good (*m*).

Irregularities as to assigning voters their districts.

In the *Greenock* case (*n*) where irregularities had been committed in dividing the borough into polling districts and assigning to voters their proper booths, the election was held void.

Infringement of rules as to secrecy by agents.

Where the respondent's personation agent at each polling place was furnished with a register of the voters to which tickets were attached opposite the name of each voter, and as soon as a voter had voted the agent tore off a ticket and put it in his pocket, and afterwards gave it to some person outside the polling station, by which means persons outside knew, while the poll was going on, who had voted and who had not voted; it was contended that this proceeding was a wilful and deliberate violation of the provisions of the Act, and that in consequence the election ought to be declared void; but the Court refused to declare the election void for these acts of agents and election managers, who were however liable to punishment under the Act (*o*).

Neglect of D. R. O. to initial ballots.

The neglect of a Deputy-Returning officer to initial the ballots will not avoid the election, such neglect coming within the saving clause of the Act (*p*).

Improp'r marks by D. R. O.

Where a Deputy-Returning officer, at the request of one of the agents, who thought the ballot papers were being improperly marked, initialed and numbered about twelve ballot papers, but finding he was wrong at the close of the poll, he, in good faith and with an anxious

(*m*) Drogheda, 2 O'M. & H. 201.

(*n*) 1 O'M. & H. 249.

(*o*) *Bolton case*, 2 O'M. & H. 138.

(*p*) *Monck*, 1 H. E. C. 725; *Queen's Coy. case*, 7 Sup. Ct. 247.

desire to do his duty, and in such a way as not to allow any person to see the front of the ballot paper, and with the assent of the agents of both parties, took the ballots out of the box and obliterated the marks he had put upon them, the ballots were held good and the irregularities within section 80 of the Dominion Act (*q*).

Where the presiding officer wrapped up the voting papers of illiterate voters each in the corresponding declaration of inability to read and placed them in the ballot box, so that it would have been possible for the voters to be identified at the counting of the votes, though this was not in fact done; it did not vitiate the election (*r*).

Numbers plac'd on ballots.

Where, however, numbers were placed on the ballots corresponding with the numbers attached to names of voters on the voters' list, thereby rendering it possible to identify the voters with the ballots, it was held that such ballots must be rejected, and the result being to place the respondent in the minority, the election was declared void (*s*). Though, if the voters were not in fact identified, nor such ballots sufficient in number to change the result the case might be different. Though the votes would be void, the election would not necessarily be avoided (*t*). Neither the votes nor the election would now be, in case the numbers or marks were made by the Deputy-Returning officer, avoided under the Ontario Provincial Law (*tt*).

Result not changed.

Wrong voters' list used.

The election will not necessarily be set aside because a

(*q*) *Bothwell case*, 8 Sup. Ct. 676.

(*r*) *Woodward* v. *Sarsons*, 10 L. R. C. P. 733. 748. See *Montreal Centre*, 1 L. N. 496.

(*s*) *E. Hastings*, 1 H. E. C. 764; *Bothwell*, 8 Sup. Ct. 676; see *ante*, Penalties under Dom. Laws—note *p*.

(*t*) *Woodward* v. *Sarsons*—*supra*.

(*tt*) 42 Vic. c. 4. s. 18—See *Russel* (2) 1. H. E. C. 519.

wrong voters' list has been used. Richards, C. J., in the *Monck* case (*u*) said, "I am now considering this point, assuming that the last list sent in is irregular, and not the one which the statute requires. I think the party desirous of setting aside the election must go much further, and shew that some voter who by that list was entitled to vote had tendered his vote, and that it was rejected, and that there are a sufficient number of such votes to affect the result of the election. Taking an extreme view in favour of the petitioner, he would be bound to shew that there were persons whose names were on the proper list, and who were entitled to vote, but did not vote at the election, and that there were a sufficient number of such voters to affect the result, supposing they had all voted for the petitioner."

Where, however, 35 persons whose names were on the list used, but not on the list which should have been used, voted for the respondent, and these being struck off, the respondent was left in a minority of 19, the other candidate for whom the seat was claimed was declared elected (*v*).

Nomination paper. The nomination paper of B., one of the candidates at an election, was signed by twenty-five persons, and had the affidavit of the attesting witness duly sworn to as required by the statute. The Election Clerk found that one of the twenty-five persons was not entered on the voters' lists, and thereupon the Returning officer and Election Clerk compared the names on the nomination paper with the certified voters' lists in his possession, and on finding that only twenty-four of the persons who had so signed were duly qualified electors, he rejected

(*u*) 32 U. C. Q. B. 153. A majority of those votes appearing on the list used, but not upon the list which should have been used, were polled for the *petitioner's side.*

(*v*) *Prince Edward Election (2) Ont.* 1 H. E. C. 160.

B's. nomination paper, and returned the respondent. It was held that he should have received the nomination paper; and that if the election had gone on, the defect in the nomination paper would not, according to the 80th section of the Dominion Elections Act, have affected the result of the election. Wilson, J., however, in giving judgment said: "I am of opinion the Returning officer is both a ministerial and a judicial officer. He has not now, as formerly, to hold an inquisition into the capacity or qualification of a candidate or voter; but I feel assured if a person appeared and was nominated, and such candidate were a woman or a mere child, that the Returning officer could decline to receive such nomination, and in like manner he can decline to receive the nomination of a Chief Justice or the Speaker of the Senate. I think also he may refuse a nomination paper signed by less than twenty-five electors, because the Act requires that the nomination shall be by twenty-five. I am disposed to think, too, he can reject a paper signed by twenty-five, if it were declared by the candidate that the paper was a sham; that the names were those of persons who were not electors at all, and never had been; or that half the names were forgeries; and if there were good reasons for the Returning officer to believe that statement, and he did believe it. . . . . I think, however, with much hesitation, that the defect in this case, which I have no doubt exists, was one to which the Returning officer should not have yielded" (*w*). No nomination paper is required under the Ontario Act.

Returning officer both a ministerial and a judicial officer.

It has been held that an omission by a candidate to appoint an agent for election expenses on the day of election will not render his nomination bad (*x*).

Omission to appoint financial agent.

(*w*) *South Renfrew* (2), 1. H. E. C. 705.

(*x*) *Mayo* 2 O'M. & H. 191.

Nomination paper, acceptance, and deposit essential under Dominion Act.

A nomination paper, duly signed, and accompanied by the consent in writing of the person nominated (unless he be absent from the Province, when such absence shall be stated in nomination paper), and a deposit of $200 must, however, be handed to the Returning officer before the close of the time allowed for nomination, to render the nomination valid under the Dominion law *(y)*.

A Returning officer is justified in refusing to count the votes contained in an unsigned statement from a Deputy-Returning officer, to which the affidavit prescribed by the Act is not annexed *(z)*.

(*y*) 37 Vic. c. 9, s. 19; 45 Vic. c. 3, s. 8.

(*z*) *Bothwell*, 8 Sup. Ct. judgment of Galt, J., p. 686.

CHAPTER VI.

BALLOT PAPERS.

As the question as to which ballots should be counted and which rejected at the close of the poll, as well as on a recount, is a most important one; both to the election officers and to candidates and their agents, a summary of the decisions arrived at by the Courts, upon the subject, will be here given. The effect of mistakes by Deputy-Returning officers in omitting to initial the ballot papers or in numbering them has been already considered (*a*). The effect of mistakes or ignorance on the part of voters remains to be considered. In former times there were considerable differences between the Dominion and Ontario laws regarding ballots, but the laws of the Dominion and Province have now so far been assimilated (*b*), that the decisions may be considered as applicable to elections under either law.

Mistakes of Deputy-Retur'g officers.

Ontario laws.

Sir W. J. Ritchie, Chief Justice of the Supreme Court, in the *Bothwell case* (*c*) says, "After a good deal of con-

Rule laid down by Supreme Court as to bal-

(*a*) See "Penalties under Dominion-Laws" note (*p*) page 318 *ante*, also "Conduct of the Election," *ante*.

(*b*) Sec. 41 Vic. (Dom). c. 6, s. 6; Rev. Stats. Ont. c. 10, s. 97, amended by 42 Vic. (Ont.) c. 4, s. 13.

(*c*) 8 Sup. Ct. at p. 696. The rule laid down by the Chief Justice was concurred in by a majority of the Court, viz: Fournier, Henry and Gwynne JJ.

lot marks.

sideration, I find it impossible to lay down a hard and fast rule by which it can be determined whether a mark is a good or a bad cross. I think that whenever the mark evidences an attempt or intention to make a cross, though the cross may be in some respects imperfect, it should be counted, unless from the peculiarity of the mark made, it can be reasonably inferred that there was not an honest design simply to make a cross, but there was also an intention so to mark the paper that it could be identified, in which case the ballot should, in my opinion, be rejected. But, if the mark made indicates no design of complying with the law, but, on the contrary, a clear intent not to mark with a cross as the law directs, as for instance, by making a straight line or a round O, then such non-compliance with the law, in my opinion, renders the ballot null; the irresistible presumption from such a plain and wilful departure from the terms of the Statute being that it was so marked for a sinister purpose" (*d*). In pursuance of the principle thus adopted, his lordship held to be

Valid Ballots.

Ballots, when good.

1.—A ballot marked with an inverted V.

2.—A ballot marked with more than one cross for the same candidate.

In the *Queen's County case* (*e*) ballots containing names of four candidates were held valid in the following cases:

3.—Ballots containing two crosses, one on the line above the first name and one on the line above the

(*d*) The Court declined to follow *Woodward* v. *Sarsons*, L. R. 10 C. P. 733 upon this point.

(*e*) 7 Sup. Ct. 247.

second name, valid for the two first named candidates.

4.—Ballots containing two crosses, one on the line above the first name, and one on the line dividing the second and third compartments, valid for the first named candidate.

5.—Ballots containing properly made crosses in two of the compartments of the ballot paper, with a slight lead pencil stroke in another compartment.

6.—Ballots marked in the proper compartments thus, Y.

In the *North Victoria case* (*f*) the following were held valid:

7.—Ballots with a cross to the right just after the candidate's name, but in the same column, and not in the column on the right hand side of the name, (anywhere within the division where candidate's name is, is now sufficient) (*g*).

8.—Ballots with an ill-formed cross, or with small lines at the ends of the cross, or with a line across the centre or one of the limbs of the cross, or with a curved line like the blades of an anchor.

In the *Monck case (h)* the following were held sufficient:

9.—An irregular mark in the figure of a cross, so long as it does not lose the form of a cross.

10.—A cross not in the proper compartment of the ballot paper, but still to the right of the candidate's name (*i*).

(*f*) 1 H. E. C. 671.

(*g*) See 41 Vic. (Dom.) c. 6, s. 6; and 42 Vic. (Ont.) c. 4, s. 13.

(*h*) 1 H. E. C. 725.

(*i*) The form of the ballot paper has been changed, and a cross anywhere within the division containing the candidate's name is now sufficient. See 41 Vic. (Dom.) c. 6; s. 6; 42 V. (Ont.) c. 4, s. 13.

11.—A cross with a line before it.

12.—A cross rightly placed, with two additional crosses, one across the other candidate's name, and the other to the left.

13.—A cross in the right place on the back of the ballot paper (this however is overruled in *Queen's County case* (*j*) and was not followed in the *South Wentworth, Ontario, case* (*k*).

14.—A double cross or two crosses.

15.—Ballot paper inadvertently torn.

16.—Inadvertent marks in addition to the cross.

17.—Cross made with pen and ink instead of pencil (*l*).

A voter who had inadvertently torn his ballot in two, and, whose ballot was rejected on the counting of votes was allowed his vote in an Ontario case (*m*), the evidence proving that no trick was intended for the purpose of shewing how he intended to vote.

The following have been held to be

Invalid Ballots.

When bad. 1.—Ballots marked with a straight line (*n*).

2.—Ballots marked with an O (*o*).

3.—Ballots marked with a cross in the right place on the back, instead of on the printed side (*p*).

4.—Ballots marked with an *x* instead of a cross (*q*).

(*j*) 7 Sup. Ct. 247.

(*k*) *South Wentworth*, 1 H. E. C. 531.

(*l*) The Deputy-Returning officer having supplied the pen and ink instead of pencil.

(*m*) *S. Wentworth*, 1 H. E. C. 531.

(*n*) *Bothwell*, 8 Sup. Ct. 676. *S. Wentworth*, 1 H. E. C. 531, *Monck Ib.* 725; *N. Victoria*, *Ib.* 671.

(*o*) *Bothwell*, 8 Sup. Ct. 676.

(*p*) *Queen's Coy.* 7 Sup. Ct. 247; *S. Wentworth*, 1 H. E. C. 531. See also *Berwick upon-Tweed*, 3 O'M. & H. 182.

(*q*) *Queen's Coy.*, *Supra.*

5.—Ballots with the candidate's name written thereon in addition to the cross (r).

6.—Ballots with marks in addition to the cross, by which the voter might be identified, although not put there by the voter in order that he might be identified (s).

7.—Ballots marked with a number of lines (t).

8.—Ballots with a cross for each candidate (u).

9.—Ballots marked with the initials of the voter or some mark, known as being one used by him (v).

10.—Two single strokes not crossing (w).

English authorities.

The English and Scotch Courts came to different conclusions from the above in several instances, in the *Wigtown cases* (x) and in *Woodward* v. *Sarsons* (y). The learned judges in the Canadian Courts have however justified their departure from the rules laid down in these decisions by pointing out that the English Act is merely directory in some respects in which our Acts are mandatory (z).

(r) *N. Victoria*, 1 H. E. C. 671.

(s) *Ibid.*

(t) *Ib.*

(u) *Ib.*

(v) *Monck*, 1 H. E. C. 725.

(w) *Ibid.*

(x) 2 O'M. & H. 217 and 233.

(y) 10 L. R. C. P. 733.

(z) Per *Gwynne, J.*, in *Bothwel'*, 8 Sup. Ct. p. 718; Moss, C. J., in *S. Wentworth*, 1 H. E. C. at p. 535. Leigh & LeMarchant's Law of Elections, 4 Ed. p. 181.

CHAPTER VII.

PERSONS WHO MAY NOT BE ELECTED NOR SIT AND VOTE.

Common Law disqualifications.

In the absence of statutory enactments, the common political law governs in England and her dependencies (*a*). Under it the following are incapable of executing the trust of members:

Minors (*b*).

Women (*c*).

Lunatics and idiots (*d*).

Traitors (*e*).

Felons (*f*).

(*a*) Bourinot's Parliamentary Proc. p. 112, note 4.

(*b*) In the opinion of Coke, infants were disqualified at Common law. In *Trenchard's case* (2 Hatsell 9; 10 Comm. J. 508), however, an admitted minor was declared duly elected; but in *Lawson's case* (18 Comm. J. 672), a member's petition was withdrawn on account of minority. Minors were sometimes connived at in Parliament, as in the case of Charles James Fox, who sat and spoke before he became of age. See Lely & Foulkes Par. El. Acts, 347.

(*c*) 1 Seldon's Works, 1083; Lely & Foulkes Parly. El. Acts, 347.

(*d*) 4 Inst. 48; 1 Bl. Com. 175; Todd's Parl. Law, 81; Bourinot's Parly. Pro. p. 122, note 4; Lely & Foulkes Parl. El. Acts, 348. A member sane, when returned, has his seat vacated if he become insane, *Grampound* D'Ewes, 126; but the lunacy must be incurable, *Alcock's case*, 66 Com. J. 226; 2 Hatsell, 35 *n*: *Crooks' case*, Ont. Leg. J., Vol. 17, App. No. 1.

(*e*) Todd's Parl. Law, 81.

(*f*) *Ibid.*

Outlaws in criminal prosecutions (*g*).

Infamous persons (*h*).

Returning officers (*hh*).

The above is not an exhaustive list (*i*).

Some of those hereafter mentioned as disqualified by statutory enactment would very possibly be also disqualified by common law.

By section 39 of the British North America Act (1867), a senator shall not be capable of being elected to or of sitting or voting as a member of the House of Commons. Senators.

By 35 Vic. c. 15, and 36 Vic. cap. 2 (Dominion Stats.), members of the legislative council or assembly of any province now, or hereafter to be included within the Dominion are incapable of being elected to or of sitting and voting in the House of Commons. A member of the House of Commons who accepts a seat in a provincial legislature must vacate his seat in the former body; and any person violating these Acts is liable to a penalty of $2,000 for every day he sits and votes. Members of Provincial Legislatures.

By statutes of the several provinces, no senator or member of the House of Commons can sit in the legislative councils or assemblies of the provinces; with this single exception that a senator may sit in the legislative council of Quebec (*j*). Members of House of Commons disqualified from sitting in Provincial Legislatures. Exception.

A member of a provincial legislature desiring to become a candidate for the House of Commons may, Member of a Legislature may resign and be

(*g*) Todd's Parl. Law, 81.

(*h*) *Ibid* 83.

(*hh*) *Ib.*

(*i*) Ministers of all professions were rendered ineligible in Canada by Imp. Act 31 Geo. III, c. 31, s. 21, see Todd's Parl. Law, 83; but see Imp. Act 3 & 4 Vic. (Union Act) c. 35. Avowed infidels would also appear to be disqualified according to Todd.

(*j*) Bourinot's Parl. Pro. p. 125.

elected to the Commons, and *vice versa*. however, resign his seat in the provincial house; but he should be careful to see that his resignation is regularly made (*k*). So also, a member of the House of Commons may resign his seat by giving, in his place in the House, notice of his intention to resign; or by a declaration of such intention in writing under his hand and seal made before two witnesses. If during a recess, and there be no speaker, or the member be himself speaker, he may address and cause to be delivered such declaration to any two members of the House; but no member shall tender his resignation while his election is lawfully contested, or until after the expiration of the time during which it may by law be contested on other grounds than corruption or bribery (*l*).

Manner of resigning.

Holder of office of emolument under the Cr'wn

No person accepting or holding any office, commission or employment, permanent or temporary in the service of the Government of Canada, at the nomination of the Crown, or at the nomination of any of the officers of the Government of Canada, to which any salary, fee, wages, allowance, emolument or profit of any kind is attached, is eligible as a member of the House of Commons, nor shall sit or vote therein (*m*).

(*k*) Two notable cases arising out of informalities in resignations came before the House, one in the session of 1874, and the other in the session of 1883. In the first case the member was speaker of the Legislative Assembly of Prince Edward Island, and resigned his seat by letter addressed to the Lieutenant-Governor of the Island, before becoming a candidate for the House of Commons, to which he was elected and returned. The Committee on Privileges sustained his election. An Act of indemnity was however passed. In the other case the returning officer made a "double return" and the House itself decided the question against the candidate who had failed to formally resign his seat in the Legislature before the election, and in favour of the candidate who received the next highest number of votes at the election. Both cases came from Prince Edward Island. See Bourinot's Parl. Pro. pp. 125—6—7—8; Can. Com. J. (1874) 50, 51, 55; 37 Vic. c. 11; Hansard p. 16; and Can. Com. J. (1883) 1.

(*l*) 41 Vic. c. 5. ss. 12 & 13.

(*m*) *Ib.* s. 1.

Every Sheriff, Registrar of Deeds, Clerk of the Peace, and County Crown Attorney in any of the provinces, is likewise ineligible (*n*). Sheriffs, Registrars, Clerks of Peace & County Attorneys.

Ministers of the Crown are not, however, disqualified by virtue of their office, provided they be elected while holding office (*o*). Ministers of Crown not disqualified.

A Minister may resign one portfolio and accept another within one month of such resignation, without thereby vacating his seat, unless the Administration of which he was a member shall have resigned and a new Administration shall have been formed, and shall have occupied the said offices (*oo*). A minister may exchange one portfolio for another without vacating his seat

No person whosoever, directly or indirectly, alone or with any other, by himself or by the interposition of any trustee or third party, holding or enjoying, undertaking or executing any contract or agreement, express or implied, with or for the Government of Canada on behalf of the Crown, or with or for any of the offices of the Government of Canada, for which any public money of Canada is to be paid, shall be eligible as a member of the House of Commons (*p*); nor shall he sit or vote in the Contract'rs with the Governm'nt

(*n*) 41 Vic. c. 5, s. 1.

(*o*) *Ib.*

(*oo*) *Ib.*

(*p*) Where nothing remains to be done under the contract, but the payment of the consideration by the Government Department, the section does not apply. A contract was entered into in June, 1868, for the supply of goods for the public service of India. The contract was completely executed by the contractors by the delivery and acceptance of the goods by the 23rd October, 1868; but the contractors did not receive payment from the India office until the 18th January, 1869. In the interval, viz: on the 18th Nov., 1868, one of the contractors was elected a member of the House of Commons; it was held that, assuming the contract to be within 22 Geo. 3, c. 45, s. 1 (which corresponds substantially with the Canadian statute), it did not avoid the election, *Royse* v. *Birley*, 4 L. R. C. P. 296. A firm, in which a member of the House of Commons in England was a partner, sold and delivered goods for the service of a lunatic asylum which had been appropriated to criminal lunatics under the royal sign manual, pursuant to 23 & 24 Vic. c. 75, in ignorance that they were

said House (*q*). If any such person or any person disqualified by holding an office of emolument or being a Sheriff, Registrar, Clerk of the Peace or County Attorney, as before mentioned, be nevertheless returned as a member, his election and return shall be null and void (*r*).

If any member of the House of Commons accepts any office or commission or is concerned or interested in any contract, agreement, service or work which would, as above stated, render him incapable of being elected, or knowingly sells any goods, wares or merchandize to, or performs any service for the Government or for any of the officers of the Government of Canada, for which any public money of Canada is paid or to be paid, whether the contract or sale be expressed or implied, and whether the transaction be single or continuous, his seat is thereby vacated; and the member so disqualified by office or contract, whether the disqualification arise

Penalty.

before or after his election, incurs a penalty of $200 for every day he sits or votes. The disqualification attaches though the transaction be begun and concluded during a recess of Parliament (*s*).

---

dealing with a Government Institution; this was held not to amount to a disqualification under 22 Geo. 3, c. 45, s. 1; Leigh & LeM's. Law of Elections, 4th Ed. p. 269. Where a firm in which a candidate was a partner sent a tender to the Government Stationery Department, which tender was accepted and the goods supplied by the firm accordingly; it was held a disqualification, although arrangements had been completed for a dissolution of partnership and the deed was actually signed three days after the declaration of the poll. (Committees' Reports, Vol. VII, March 15, 1869). A speaker of the Canadian House of Commons was editor and proprietor of a newspaper, and had received money in payment for printing and stationery furnished "per agreement" to the Post Office Department. The committee on privileges reported his election void, reversing a former precedent of 1864, Can. Com. J. (1877) 357, App. No. 8. See also Bourinot's Parl. Pro. 131-2-3.

(*q*) 41 Vic. (Dom). c. 5, sec. 2.

(*r*) *Ib.* s. 3.

(*s*) *Ib.* ss. 4, 5 & 6.

It is also provided (*t*) that "in every contract, agreement, or commission to be made, entered into or accepted by any person with the Government of Canada, or any of the departments or officers of the Government of Canada, there shall be inserted an express condition, that no member of the House of Commons shall be admitted to any share or part of such contract, agreement or commission, or to any benefit to arise therefrom"; and a penalty of $2,000 and full costs of suit attaches to every offence against this provision.

Government contracts to contain a clause that no member shall become interested therein.

Penalty.

This statute does not disqualify a member of the House of Commons who is a shareholder in any incorporated company having a contract with the Government of Canada, except companies undertaking contracts for the building of public works, and any company incorporated for the construction of the Canadian Pacific Railway (*u*).

Shareholder in incorporated company not disqualified.

Exceptions.

Nor does the Act disqualify any person on whom the completion of a contract devolves by descent or limitation, or by marriage or as devisee, legatee, executor or administrator, until twelve months after the same has so devolved; nor any contractor for the loan of money to the Government under the authority of Parliament, after public competition, or respecting the purchase or payment of the public stock or debentures of Canada, on terms common to all persons; nor any officer of the militia, or militia man, not receiving any salary or emolument out of the public money of Canada, except only his daily pay when called out for drill or on active service, or allowances, or sums paid for enrolment (*v*).

Nor persons on whom contracts devolve,

Nor lenders of money to Government,

Nor militia officers or men.

(*t*) 41 Vic. (Dom). c. 5. s. 8.

(*u*) *Ib.* s. 7.

(*v*) *Ib.* s. 9.

Revising offic'rs disqualified.

A revising officer is disqualified from being a candidate in any electoral district, for which or any part of which he has been such revising officer during the time he holds office and for two years thereafter (*w*).

Corrupt Practices.

The disqualifications for Corrupt Practices at elections, etc., have been already pointed out in the chapter on "Penalties under Dominion Laws."

A member cannot serve for more than one constituency.

A member of Parliament already returned for one constituency is ineligible for any other until his first seat is vacated (*x*). In case a member is returned for two constituencies he must make his election for which of the places he will serve by formally resigning his seat in the other when the House is in session (*y*).

Aliens not qualified.

Aliens are not eligible unless naturalized under an Act of the Parliament of Great Britain or of the United Kingdom of Great Britain and Ireland, or of the Legislature of one of the confederated Provinces (*z*).

No property qualification required.

No qualification in real estate is now required of any candidate for a seat in the House of Commons of Canada (*a*).

No Senator or Privy Councill'r eligible as a member of Ont. Leg. Assembly.

No Senator, and no Privy Councillor of the Dominion of Canada who is a member of the House of Commons, shall be eligible as a member of the Legislative Assembly of Ontario, nor shall sit or vote in the same (*b*).

Members of House of Commons ineligible.

If any member of the Legislative Assembly sits and votes as a member of the House of Commons, his election to the Assembly thereby becomes void (*c*).

(*w*) Electoral Franchise Act. (48 Vic.) s. 12, *ante*.

(*x*) May Parl. Pro. p. 32.

(*y*) Bourinot's Parl. Pro. p. 139.

(*z*) 37 Vic. (Dom). c. 9, s. 20.

(*a*) *Ibid*.

(*b*) Rev. Stats. Ont. c. 12, s. 5.

(*c*) *Ib*. s. 6.

Persons holding offices of emolument at the nomination of the Crown ineligible.

No person accepting or holding any office, commission or employment either in the service of the Dominion of Canada, or in the service of the Government of Ontario, at the nomination of the Crown or of the Lieutenant-Governor, to which any salary, or any fee, allowance or emolument in lieu of any salary from the Crown or from the Province is attached ; or accepting or holding any office, commission or employment of profit at the nomination of the Crown, or of the Government, or of any head of a Department in the Government of Ontario, whether such profit is or is not payable out of the public funds; shall be eligible as a member of the Legislative Assembly, or shall sit or vote in the same during the time he holds such office, commission or employment (*d*).

Exceptions—Members of Executive Council; officers in Army, Navy and Militia and Militiamen; J. P's., Notaries and Coroners.

Members of the Executive Council, officers of Her Majesty's Army or Navy, officers of the Militia and Militiamen (other than officers on the Militia Staff receiving permanent salaries), Justices of the Peace, Notaries and Coroners are, however, not ineligible, unless otherwise disqualified (*e*).

Public contractors ineligible.

No person whosoever holding or enjoying, undertaking or executing, directly or indirectly, alone or with any other, by himself or by the interposition of any trustee or third party, any contract or agreement with Her Majesty, or with any public officer or department, with respect to the public service of Ontario, or under which any public money of Ontario is to be paid for any service or work, matter or thing, shall be eligible as a member of the Legislative Assembly, nor shall he sit or vote in the same (*f*).

(*d*) Rev. Stats. Ont. c. 12, s. 7. But this does not apply to any person who was on 2nd March, 1872, a member of the Assembly, and who, at the time of his election held such an office, etc., s. 7, subs. 2.

(*e*) Rev. Stats. Ont. c. 12, s. 7 and 42 Vic. (Ont.) c. 2, s. 7.

(*f*) Rev. Stats. Ont. c. 12, s. 8.

The Provincial Act 42 Vic. cap. 2, contains the following provisions:

Sureties of Sheriffs, etc., not ineligible as members of the Legislative Assembly.

"8. A person shall not be incapable of being elected a member of the Legislative Assembly by reason of his being a surety for a sheriff, registrar, county attorney, clerk or bailiff of a division court, or other public officer, or by reason of his being a surety or contractor for the payment of the maintenance of a patient of a public asylum for the insane, unless such person is otherwise disqualified.

"(2) But any person who is elected a member of the Legislative Assembly, being at the time of his election such surety as aforesaid, shall, before he sits or votes in the Legislative Assembly, take and complete such action as may be requisite to relieve him from any thereafter accruing liability in respect of his suretyship, and no person who is liable as such surety in respect of any accruing matter shall sit or vote in the Legislative Assembly. (See R. S. O. cap. 3, sec. 14, and similar provisions in other Acts).

Preceding section not a declaration of disqualification.

"9. The provisions of the preceding section shall not be regarded as a legislative declaration that the person in said section described, or any of them, come within the disqualification of the said section *(ff)*."

Election of disqualified person void.

If any person disqualified or declared incapable of being elected a member of the Legislative Assembly, be nevertheless elected and returned as a member, his election and return shall be void (*g*).

Member becoming member of Ex'cutive Council vacates his seat, but may

A member of the Assembly on becoming a member of the Executive Council, vacates his seat, but he may be re-elected, if not otherwise disqualified. A member of

(*ff*) See Leigh & LeM's. Law of Elections, 4 Ed. p. 269.

(*g*) Rev. Stats. Ont. c. 12, s. 9.

the Executive Council may, however, resign one portfolio and within one month of such resignation accept another portfolio, without vacating his seat, unless the Administration of which such person was a member has resigned, and a new administration occupies the said offices (*h*). be re-elected, and may exch'ge portfolio.

Pecuniary penalty on disqualified person sitting and voting.

If any person, declared ineligible by the Provincial Act, sits and votes, he incurs a penalty of $2,000 for every day on which he so sits and votes (*i*).

Members precluded from acting as Election officers

Members of the Assembly are precluded from acting as Returning officers, Deputy-Returning officers, Election Clerks or Poll Clerks, under a penalty of $200 (*j*).

Common Law disqualificat'ns.

The common law disqualifications before mentioned apply to members of the Legislative Assembly (*k*).

No qualification in real estate is required of any candidate for a seat in the Assembly (*l*).

Corrupt Practices.

The disqualifications for Corrupt Practices are already dealt with in the Chapter on "Penalties under Ontario Laws" (*m*).

(*h*) Rev. Stats. Ont. c. 12, s. 10.

(*i*) *Ibid* s. 11, and see same section as to proceedings for recovery of penalty.

(*j*) Rev. Stats. c. 10, s. 23.

(*k*) See case of Mr. Crooks, Ont. Leg. J., Vol. 17, App. No. 1.

(*l*) Rev. Stats. Ont. c. 10, s. 3.

(*m*) As to formalities requisite for resignation of a seat in the Legislative Assembly, see Rev. Stats. Ont. c. 12, s. 14.

APPENDIX.

MISCELLANEOUS FORMS.

(1)

Form of application by person desiring to be put on Preliminary List of Voters under Dominion Franchise Act. (See Resolutions of Ontario Revising Officers *ante* p. 88) (*a*).

APPLICATION TO BE PUT ON LIST.

I, of the of in the County of hereby apply to be put on the Voters' List for the House of Commons for the Municipality of in the Electoral Riding of , at the preliminary revision of said Voters' List.

(Signature)

To His Hon.

Revising Officer, for

(2)

Form of Declaration in support of application to be put on preliminary list under *Dominion Franchise Act*. (See Resolutions of Ontario Rev. Officers *ante* p. 88).

IN THE MATTER OF THE ELECTORAL FRANCHISE ACT.

PROVINCE OF ONTARIO,
County of
To WIT: } I, of

in the County of , do solemnly declare: 1. That I *am* a British subject of the full age of twenty one years, and am not by the said Act or by any law of the Dominion of Canada disqualified or prevented from voting. 2 That I am entitled to be a Voter as *(here state nature of qualification, also residence and P. O. address)*, and that by reason of such qualification I am entitled to be placed on the List of Voters, under the Electoral Franchise Act for the year commencing 1st of January, 188 , for the Electoral District of . And I make this solemn declaration, conscientiously believing the same to be true, and by virtue of the Act passed in the thirty-seventh year of Her Majesty's reign, intituled "An Act for the suppression of voluntary and extra-judicial oaths."

Declared before me at the
of in the County of
this day of
in the year of our Lord 188 . }

A Justice of the Peace, etc., (*or a Notary Public*).

(*a*) The form of Notice of Complaint or application to be given for the preliminary or final version by a person objecting to, or desiring to add names, will be found in the Schedule of Forms to the Act, *ante* p. 84 (Form E).

(3)

Form of application by person on behalf of other persons desiring to have their names placed on preliminary list under the Dominion Franchise Act. (See Resolutions of Ont. Revising Officers *ante* p. 88).

APPLICATION TO HAVE NAMES PUT ON LIST.

I, of the of in the County of hereby apply on behalf of the persons named in the schedule to the annexed declaration to have their names put on the Voters' List for the House of Commons for the Municipality of in the Electoral District of at the preliminary revision of said Voters' List.

(Signature)

To His Hon.

Revising Officer for

---

(4)

Form of Declaration to be made by a person on behalf of one or more Electors, desiring to have their names put on the preliminary list under the Dominion Franchise Act. See *Resolutions* of Ont. Revising Officers *ante* p. 88.

IN THE MATTER OF THE ELECTORAL FRANCHISE ACT.

PROVINCE OF ONTARIO,
County of
TO WIT: } I, of

in the County of , do solemnly declare:

1st. That I know the parties whose names are set forth in the first column in the schedule on back of this form, and know that they are all of the full age of twenty-one years and British subjects, and that none of them are by the said Act or by any law of the Dominion of Canada disqualified or prevented from voting.

2nd. I have reason to believe, and do believe, that all the persons whose names are set forth in the first column of the said schedule are entitled to vote at elections for the House of Commons in the Electoral District of

3rd. That column No. 2 sets forth their place of residence; No. 3, their P.O. address; No. 4, nature of qualification; No. 5, municipality where qualification is situated; No. 6, the description of qualifying property; No. 7, the nature of title; No. 8, the name of parent, if qualified as son of farmer or other owner of real property, and name of Landlord if qualification is as tenant. And I have a personal knowledge of the matters herein deposed to, and I know the said particulars to be true; and I make this solemn declaration, conscientiously believing the same to be true, and by virtue of the Act passed in the thirty-seventh year of Her Majesty's reign, intituled, "An Act for the suppression of voluntary and extra-judicial oaths."

Declared before me at the
of in the County of
this
day of in the year of our
Lord, 188 } ______________

____

____

A Justice of the Peace etc., *or* (*a Notary Public*).

FORM OF SCHEDULE.

NAME IN FULL (SURNAME FIRST).	RESIDENCE.	P. O. ADDRESS.	Nature of Qualification.	Municipality or Place where Qualification is situate, if Real Estate.	Concession, Street and No. of Lot or other particular description of Qualifying Property.	Nature of Title to Qualifying Property.	Name of Parent if the Voter is Qualified as a Son of a Farmer or other owner of Real Property; also nature of Parent's Title to the Real Property.	Name of Landlord if Voter is Qualified as Tenant, and nature of Landlord's Title.

Dated 188 .

(5)

Form of affirmation by wage-earner desiring to have his name entered on the Assessment Roll pursuant to the Assessment Amendment Act 1885 (Ontario) s. 5, subs. (2).

"I, *A. B.*, being a wage-earner within the meaning of *The Assessment Act* and any Act amending the same, do sincerely and truly affirm and declare, that I am of the full age of twenty-one years; that I am a subject of Her Majesty by birth or naturalization; that I am actually resident and domiciled in this city of (*or* town, village, *or* township *as the case may be*) at (*giving the locality of his residence or the name of the street and the number (if any) of such residence, or such other reasonable description as will easily permit of its being verified and ascertained*); that my post office address is ; and that during the twelve months next preceding this day of in the year (*the date to be filled in here is that of the day, month, and year upon which this affirmation is made and signed*) I have derived and earned wages and income from my trade, (occupation, calling), office or profession, of not less than two hundred and fifty dollars."

Witness, A. B.

X. Y., of (*add residence and occupation*).

And in case of a wage-earner claiming or entitled to be entered in the assessment roll of a Township, there shall be added to the last words of the foregoing affirmation these further words:

"Including and estimating as part of said two hundred and fifty dollars, the fair value of board and lodgings given to or received, or had by me as or in lieu of wages during said twelve months."

(6)

Form of Nomination Paper, consent and oath of attestation under The Dominion Elections Act, 1874, (schedules F. and G).

We, the undersigned Electors of the Electoral District of . hereby nominate (*names, residence and additions or descriptions of person or persons nominated*) as a candidate at the election now about to be held of a member to represent the said Electoral District in the House of Commons of Canada.

Witness our hands at in the said Electoral District this day of 18 .

Signed, by the said electors, in presence of of (*additions*) } *Signatures of 25 Electors with residence and additions.*

Signature of Witness or Witnesses and additions.

I, the said , nominated in the foregoing Nomination Paper, hereby consent to such nomination.

Witness my hand at , this day of 188 .

Signed by the said nominee, in presence of of (*additions*) } *Signature of Nominee, with residence and additions.*

Signature of Witness and additions.

Oath of attestation of Nomination Paper to be made by the person or one or more of the persons producing the paper to the Returning officer, (Dom. Election Act, 1874, s. 21.)

I, A. B., of , (*additions*) solemnly swear, (*or if he be one of the persons permitted by law to affirm in civil cases*, solemnly affirm) that I know, (*mentioning the names of the signers known to him*), and that they are duly qualified as Electors of the Electoral District of , to vote at an election of a member to serve in the House of Commons of Canada, and that they respectively signed the foregoing (*or* within) nomination paper in my presence; and further (*if the case be so*), that I know the said , thereby nominated as a candidate, and that he signed his consent to the nomination in my presence.

Sworn (*or* affirmed) before me at , this , day of 18 . } (*Signature*), A. B.

C. B.,

Justice of the Peace.

(*This form may be varied according to circumstances, the intention of the Act being complied with, and the assent of the candidate may be sworn to by a separate elector, if the facts require it to be so*).

---

(7)

Form of appointment of agent to represent a candidate at the poll.

I, one of the candidates at the election of a member of the House of Commons (*or* of the Legislative Assembly of the Province of Ontario) for the Electoral District of , do hereby nominate and appoint (*name, residence and addition of agent*) to represent me at the polling station of Polling District number in the Township (*or as the case may be*) of during the hours appointed for polling, and at the counting of the votes thereat.

Witness, (*Signature*)

(*Signature of Witness.*)

(8)

Form of appointment of Financial Agent to be handed to Returning Officer on or before the Nomination day.

I, , one of the candidates at the election of a member of the House of Commons (*or*, the Legislative Assembly of the Province of Ontario,) now about to be held for the Electoral District of do hereby declare that I have appointed as the agent through whom all payments (except in respect of my personal expenses) on my behalf at the said election are to be made; and to whom all bills, charges and claims upon me are to be sent within one month after the day of the declaration of the election; and that the address of my said agent is at (*Address of Agent*).

Dated this, etc.

To
Returning Officer at the
said election. } (*Signature of Candidate.*)

RESOLUTIONS OF QUEBEC REVISING OFFICERS.

Extract from Proceedings of Quebec Revising Officers' meeting, held at Quebec, January 14th, 1886.

Procédant ensuite à l'examen du dit Acte, l'assemblée est d'opinion :

1. Que quand ils ne sont pas autrement qualifiés, les Curés doivent être inscrits comme *usufruitiers*, et les instituteurs, les sacristains et les gardiens de gares de chemin de fer, comme *occupants*.

2. Que dans les districts organisés, aucun nom ne doit être entré sur la liste préliminaire, s'il ne se trouve pas sur les derniers rôles de cotisation ou d'évaluation ou sur les dernières listes électorales revisées, à moins qu'application ait été faite par écrit par la personne, qui veut faire entrer son nom sur la liste, ou par quelqu'un pour elle, énonçant les raisons qui lui donnent le droit de faire inscrire son nom sur la liste préliminaire, et que la dite application ait été remise au Reviseur.

3. Que le Reviseur, en recevant l'application dont il est parlé ci dessus, ne doit la prendre en considération, que quand elle sera appuyée d'une déclaration solennelle et de pièces ou preuves par lui jugées satisfaisantes.

4. Que le Reviseur doit entrer sur la liste les noms de toutes personnes ayant le cens électoral quand même, lors de la confection de la liste, elles seraient déqualifiées pour voter *(a)*.

5. Qu'en vertu de la section 16, il sera affiché un exemplaire et il devra être adressé par la poste, deux exemplaires de la liste électorale à chacun des officiers nommés dans la dite section, que copie de cette interprétation soit communiquée à l'Hon. Secrétaire d'Etat pour avoir l'opinion des officiers en loi ; et que cette interprétation sera la règle de conduite des Reviseurs, si le Secrétaire d'Etat ne leur communique des instructions contraires..

6. Que pour la Revision préliminaire, le Reviseur ne doit siéger qu'à un seul endroit dans la division électorale pour laquelle il est nommé.

7. Que pour la revision finale, il n'est pas nécessaire que la Reviseur siège dans chaque arrondissement de votation ; mais seulement dans chaque municipalité.

(a) See p. 41, note (y) *ante*.

INDEX.

PAGE

M

N

PAGE

S

V

W

www.ingramcontent.com/pod-product-compliance
Lightning Source LLC
Chambersburg PA
CBHW032306280326
41932CB00009B/713

* 9 7 8 3 3 3 7 1 8 9 5 2 5 *